SUSTAINABLE BROWNFIELD DEVELOPMENT

While industrial and chemical innovations have contributed extensively to human advancement, the darker part of their legacy has been the hundreds of thousands of polluted sites left behind. Governments at all levels have rallied to support the remediation and reuse of these land resources and put many of the nation's brownfields back into productive use. This book presents two dozen brownfield projects in the United States that have incorporated sustainability, highlighting project features, best management practices, and lessons from the field regarding the underlying policies and practices that enabled these projects to be completed or, in some cases, stalled, altered or abandoned.

The case studies represent an array of brownfield projects that aimed to go beyond conventional practice and include a range and variety of end uses (e.g., corner gas stations, industrial, office, residential, brightfields, green space, mixed-use, and transit-oriented developments). The cases investigate site histories, planning and development and examine sustainability characteristics to understand how projects overcame the barriers to brownfield reuse and the implementation of sustainability features and derive a series of lessons learned, including innovative policies, programs, and/or funding mechanisms that helped make these projects work.

Sustainable Brownfield Development will be of interest to developers, planners, consultants and community representatives interested in environmental policy, urban planning, community development, ecological restoration, economic development, and parks planning by providing direction and inspiration for those eager to erase the blight of the past and build a more sustainable future.

Christopher De Sousa is a Professor of Urban and Regional Planning at Ryerson University and was previously at the University of Wisconsin-Milwaukee. His research focuses on brownfields redevelopment in the United States and Canada. De Sousa is past President of the Canadian Brownfields Network, a Steering Committee Member of the US Agency for Toxic Substances and Disease Registry Brownfields/Land Reuse Health Initiative, and on the Management Committee of Ryerson's Center for Urban Research and Land Development.

SUSTAINABLE BROWNFIELD DEVELOPMENT

Building a Sustainable Future on Sites of our Polluting Past

Christopher De Sousa

NEW YORK AND LONDON

First published 2021
by Routledge
605 Third Avenue, New York, NY 10158

and by Routledge
2 Park Square, Milton Park, Abingdon, Oxon, OX14 4RN

Routledge is an imprint of the Taylor & Francis Group, an informa business

© 2021 Taylor & Francis

The right of Christopher De Sousa to be identified as author of this work has been asserted by him in accordance with sections 77 and 78 of the Copyright, Designs and Patents Act 1988.

All rights reserved. No part of this book may be reprinted or reproduced or utilised in any form or by any electronic, mechanical, or other means, now known or hereafter invented, including photocopying and recording, or in any information storage or retrieval system, without permission in writing from the publishers.

Trademark notice: Product or corporate names may be trademarks or registered trademarks, and are used only for identification and explanation without intent to infringe.

Library of Congress Cataloging-in-Publication Data
A catalog record for this title has been requested

ISBN: 9780367359461 (hbk)
ISBN: 9780367359454 (pbk)
ISBN: 9780429342783 (ebk)

Typeset in Interstate
by Apex CoVantage, LLC

This book is dedicated to the many coordinators, community members, practitioners, government officials, developers, and stakeholders involved in envisioning and moving forward the sustainable brownfield projects. Your hard work and resilience are an inspiration to those pursuing brownfield developments and a more sustainable future. The book is also dedicated to the community of brownfield researchers, both scholarly and professional, in the United States and globally, who work to understand and overcome brownfield challenges and help communities turn derelict spaces into productive and beloved places. The commitment, resilience, and sincere intentions of all those mentioned above gave me the strength to pull this manuscript together with the hope that it can add to the pursuit of a more sustainable future.

CONTENTS

List of Figures ix
List of Tables x
Acknowledgments xi

1 Brownfields Background 1

    Introduction 1
    Brownfields 101 2
    Outcomes and Expectations 14
    References 14

2 Sustainability and Brownfields 16

    Introduction 16
    Sustainable Development 16
    References 29

3 Industrial and Commercial Redevelopment 33

    The Chicago Center for Green Technology (CCGT) 33
    Milwaukee's Menomonee River Valley 41
    References 57

4 Office Redevelopment 60

    Montgomery Park, Baltimore, Maryland 60
    Heifer International, Little Rock, Arkansas 70
    References 82

5 Residential Redevelopment 85

    Artspace Commons, Salt Lake City, Utah 85
    Anvil Mountain, Silverton, Colorado 93
    References 99

6 Green and Community Space Redevelopment 101

    Moran Plant, Burlington, Vermont 101

Elmhurst Park, New York City — 110
Freshkills Park, New York City — 115
James & Maria Luisa Haynes Recreation Center at Chacon Creek, Laredo, Texas — 125
Allen-Morrison Pilot, Lynchburg, Virginia — 130
References — 134

7 Corner Gas Station Brownfields — 138

June Key Delta Community Center, Portland, Oregon — 138
Tabor Commons, Portland, Oregon — 149
Green Avenue, Greenville, South Carolina — 157
References — 163

8 Main Streets, Neighborhoods, and Towns — 165

Focus: HOPE, Detroit, Michigan — 165
Samoa Town/Humboldt County, California — 170
Jackson Square Redevelopment Initiative, Boston, Massachusetts — 175
Commercial Street Historic District, Springfield, Missouri — 183
References — 187

9 Mixed-Use Complete Communities — 190

Atlantic Station, Atlanta, Georgia — 190
South Waterfront, Portland, Oregon — 201
Langdale and Riverdale Mills, City of Valley, Alabama — 214
The Waterfront, Allentown, Pennsylvania — 219
References — 223

10 Brightfields — 227

Brockton Brightfield, Brockton, Massachusetts — 227
Holmes Road/Sunnyside Landfill, Houston, Texas — 232
References — 238

11 Project Characteristics and Lessons Learned — 240

Reference — 253

Index — 255

LIST OF FIGURES

3.1	Chicago Center for Green Technology, Illinois, 2009	37
3.2	Milwaukee Road Shops during demolition, Wisconsin	51
3.3	Menomonee Valley Industrial Center and Community Park, Milwaukee, Wisconsin, 2010	51
4.1	Montgomery Park, Baltimore, Maryland, 2010	61
4.2	Heifer International Center (right) and Heifer Village (left) taken from the Clinton Library, Little Rock, Arkansas, 2010	77
5.1	Artspace Commons, Salt Lake City, Utah, 2011	91
5.2	Rose Walsh Smelter site, Anvil Mountain, Colorado	94
6.1	Moran Plant, Burlington, Vermont, 2009	102
6.2	Moran FRAME, Burlington, Vermont	108
6.3	Elmhurst Park playground, Queens, New York, 2011	113
6.4	Freshkills Park, Staten Island, New York	117
6.5	James & Maria Luisa Haynes Recreation Center at Chacon Creek, Laredo, Texas	125
6.6	Allen-Morrison, Schenkel Farm, and Lynchburg City Stadium, Virginia	131
7.1	ARCO Gas Station, Portland, Oregon, 2010	139
7.2	June Key Delta Community Center, Portland, Oregon, 2016	142
7.3	Café au Play, Portland, Oregon, 2010	152
7.4	Green Avenue Memorial Park, Greenville, South Carolina, 2019	162
8.1	HOPE Community Park, Detroit, Michigan, 2016	168
8.2	Samoa, California	172
8.3	Preliminary Site Plan and Building Map, Jackson Square, Boston, Massachusetts, 2006	177
8.4	Jackson Commons and Urban Edge, Boston, Massachusetts	179
8.5	233E (left) and 299E Commercial Street, Springfield, Missouri	185
9.1	Atlantic Station atop the parking deck, Atlanta, Georgia, 2010	193
9.2	South Waterfront, Portland, Oregon, 2010	206
9.3	Langdale Mill, Valley, Alabama	215
9.4	The Waterfront site, Allentown, Pennsylvania	220
10.1	Brockton Brightfield, Massachusetts	230
10.2	Holmes Road/Sunnyside Landfill, Houston, Texas	233

LIST OF TABLES

2.1	Sustainable Brownfield Development Case Studies	28
3.1	Timeline – Chicago Center for Green Technology	42
3.2	Timeline – Milwaukee's Menomonee Valley	56
4.1	Timeline – Montgomery Park, Baltimore, Maryland	70
4.2	Timeline – Heifer International, Little Rock, Arkansas	81
5.1	Timeline – Artspace Commons, Salt Lake City, Utah	92
5.2	Timeline – Anvil Mountain, Silverton, Colorado	98
6.1	Timeline – Moran Center, Burlington, Vermont	109
6.2	Timeline – Elmhurst Park, Queens, New York	123
6.3	Timeline – Freshkills Park, New York	124
6.4	Timeline – James & Maria Luisa Haynes Recreation Center at Chacon Creek, Laredo, Texas	130
6.5	Timeline – Allen-Morrison Pilot, Lynchburg, Virginia	134
7.1	Timeline – June Key Delta Community Center, Portland, Oregon	144
7.2	Timeline – Tabor Commons, Portland, Oregon	155
7.3	Timeline – Green Avenue, Greenville, South Carolina	162
8.1	Timeline – Focus: HOPE, Detroit, Michigan	170
8.2	Timeline – Samoa Town/Humboldt County, California	174
8.3	Timeline – Jackson Square, Boston, Massachusetts	182
8.4	Timeline – Commercial Street Historic District, Springfield, Missouri	186
9.1	Timeline – Atlantic Station, Atlanta, Georgia	201
9.2	Timeline – South Waterfront, Portland, Oregon	213
9.3	Timeline – Langdale and Riverdale Mills, City of Valley, Alabama	219
9.4	Timeline – The Waterfront, Allentown, Pennsylvania	223
10.1	Timeline – Brockton Brightfields, Massachusetts	232
10.2	Timeline – Holmes Road/Sunnyside Landfill, Houston, Texas	237

ACKNOWLEDGMENTS

I am indebted to numerous individuals and organizations for their inspiration, support, guidance, input, funding, and research for this book. First and foremost, I would like to thank the community, public, non-profit, and private-sector stakeholders involved in the projects described in this book who have inspired me with their vision and perseverance and graciously shared their time, knowledge, and data with me over the years. I also want to express my gratitude to the other members of the Sustainable Brownfields Consortium based at the University of Illinois at Chicago for putting together the original research proposal and for their support and guidance throughout the project, including researchers and technical advisors from UIC (Susan Kaplan, Serap Erdal, Thomas Theis, Thomas Brecheisen), the University of Illinois at Urbana-Champaign (John Braden, Marylyn O'Hara), Resources for the Future (Joshua Linn), and Kandiyo (Michal Krause).

I want to sincerely thank the students from the University of Wisconsin-Milwaukee and Ryerson University who have helped me with this project over the years. I am especially indebted to my research assistants for their help with gathering information and preparing earlier drafts of several case studies: at UWM Jason Tilidetzke (Menomonee Valley Benchmarking Initiative, plus photography with Greg Latsch), Chengbin Deng, Kevin Duffy, Laura Lynn Roedl, Elizabeth Durkin, Leyla Sanati, and Matthew Armbrust, and at Ryerson Nikolas Kohek, Evan Turunen, Marta Brocki, Taranjeet Grewal, Karla Alag, Reanne Ridsdale, Isabel Lima, David Godin (Montgomery Park), Michael Testaguzza (Artspace Commons, Heifer International), Lily-Ann D'Souza (Holmes Landfill, Green Avenue Greenville, Langdale, Atlantic Station, South Waterfront), Michael Hayek (Langdale, Anvil Mountain, Montgomery Park), Thierry Spiess (Brockton Brightfield). The students in my Planning for Sustainability and Brownfield courses back in 2008 and 2009 who helped me scope out BMP case studies also deserve a thank you, including Dan Adams, Gabrielle Apostoli, Kyle Beining, Zachary Bentzler, Kevin Duffy, Colin Fleming, Sam Friesen, Alexandra Gould, Christopher Guzek, Phin Hanson, Scott Hennings, Jeff Hintz, Christopher Marx, Scott McComb, Ashley Moncado, Joe Peterangelo, Sean Ryan, Brian Schweigl, Tim Streitz, Andy Tillman, and John Vogt.

This project would not have been possible without the gracious support of funders and supporters. I want to thank the US EPA for supporting this research with a Brownfields Training, Research, and Technical Assistance Grant (#TR-83418401-0). I am also thankful to

Ryerson University and Dr Usha George, former Dean of the Faculty of Community Services, for providing me with a Dean's Research Grant and an Undergraduate Research Opportunity Research Assistant to update the case studies and complete the project. Most of all, I would like to thank my family, particularly my partner Sonya, children, and parents, for all of their support, encouragement, and patience.

1 Brownfields Background

Introduction

The tragedy at Love Canal raised national awareness and concern about the impact that pollution was having on our health and the natural environment. Warnings from scientists like Rachel Carson in her seminal book *Silent Spring* suddenly seemed to be playing out, as families and children wondered if the chemicals that lurked beneath their homes, schools, and neighborhoods were making them sick. A combination of media attention and intense community activism led President Jimmy Carter to announce a federal health emergency on August 7, 1978; the first time emergency funds were granted for a non-natural disaster. Congress also passed the Comprehensive Environmental Response, Compensation, and Liability Act (CERCLA) in 1980. Better known as Superfund, it put a tax on chemical and petroleum industries and allowed the federal government to respond directly to releases or threatened releases of hazardous substances that might endanger public health and the environment.

While the response was too slow for some, the uncertainty was too much for others. As scientists and regulators worked to understand the science of contamination better, the number of known and potentially contaminated sites across the country kept piling up into the hundreds of thousands as deindustrialization fed the inventory. Purchasers and developers seemed content to secure a cleaner and greener future in America's suburbs, leaving tainted sites to idle and rust.

Mayors of the proud American cities that built the country grew impatient, however, and pushed for reform. In response, the federal government in the early 1990s began to shift from being enforcement-driven regulators of risk post-Love Canal to facilitators of remediation, reuse, and redevelopment. Most potentially contaminated sites were re-labeled as brownfields, and policies, programs, and procedures were developed and tested to get people and markets to change their perception of these sites from liabilities to opportunities and help the phoenix rise from the ashes. Cleaning and reusing land, removing blight, and getting the urban real estate market back on track was also seen as the more responsible and sustainable thing to do compared with the rampant auto-dependent sprawl gobbling up the countryside. But some were not satisfied with building the same-old conventional projects on brownfields. Instead of sustainability by default, they felt that brownfield projects should be sustainable by design, incorporating best-practices in environmental, social, and economic sustainability to give rise to a smarter and more resilient phoenix.

This book tells the stories of two dozen brownfield projects throughout the United States that sought to raise the bar and lay the foundation for sustainable brownfield development. It highlights project features, Best Management Practices (BMPs), and lessons from the field regarding the underlying policies, practices, and people that enabled many projects to succeed and, in some cases, be stalled, altered or abandoned. Ten of these case studies are considered early and trendsetting BMPs in the brownfields arena. The others are pilot projects that were allocated funding by the US Environmental Protection Agency (US EPA) in their early stages to incorporate sustainability as part of a Sustainable Brownfields Pilot program launched in 2008. The book is based on research funded by the US EPA from 2009 to 2013, along with updates carried out between 2017 to the present. The added time made it possible to track the progress of both the pilots and the BMPs, allowing for a longer-term retrospective to see if the seeds planted at the pilots took hold and to assess the impact of these sustainable projects on the community and development sector.

The primary aim of the book is to present an array of detailed case studies of brownfield projects that aspired to go beyond conventional and become "sustainable," as well as to draw insights from the whole sample of cases. The research was conducted via structured interviews with project coordinators, while BMPs also involved interviews with multiple stakeholders, including developers, planners, consultants, and community representatives. The in-depth case studies examine site histories, sustainability characteristics and describe how projects overcame the barriers to both brownfield reuse and the implementation of sustainability features. Lessons learned regarding what helped make these projects work, as well as project impacts, are also discussed.

The book is divided into 11 chapters. The first chapter introduces the reader to the brownfield issue, including the definition, scope of the problem, the evolution of policy, planning, and management in the US, and an overview of the development process from site assessment to development. The second chapter reviews policy and practitioner efforts, as well as scholarly literature, linking brownfields and sustainability in the US and abroad. The aim is to provide the reader with a sense of the historical evolution of this effort, including research on both the sustainability impacts of brownfields redevelopment and efforts to make brownfields redevelopment more sustainable.

In Chapters 3 to 10, case studies are organized by end-use (i.e., corner gas stations, industrial, office, residential, brightfields, community and green space, mixed-use, and transit-oriented developments). Each case study is examined in-depth (i.e., site history, project vision, project characteristics, and development) and includes a discussion of benefits, barriers, lessons learned, and a timeline. The final chapter synthesizes lessons learned from the whole sample of case studies and discusses ways to advance sustainable brownfield development in the US and abroad.

Brownfields 101

Definition and Scope

Efforts to manage contaminated sites in the United States have evolved considerably since Love Canal spurred policy-makers into action in the late 1970s. Given the serious concern regarding the impact of chemicals on human health and the environment, initial management efforts aimed to identify and repair sites with known contamination problems, as well as those suspected of being contaminated based on their prior use. The first step that regulators had to take, therefore, was to understand better the risks posed by contaminants, identify the sources of contamination, and figure out how to manage them.

A contaminant is defined broadly as any physical, chemical, biological, or radiological substance found in our air, water, or soil. While we can handle small amounts of some contaminants, they may pose a risk if we are exposed to them at certain levels for too long. A critical scientific step, therefore, was to gain a better understanding of which contaminants were harmful and at what level of exposure. This proved to be a formidable task given the sheer quantity and variety of chemicals produced since the late 19th century to make the products that support our daily lives, ranging from pesticides for agriculture to petrochemicals for transportation. Today, detailed lists have been generated with toxicity information for hundreds of contaminants of concern.

While knowledge of contaminants is vital, even more important for assessing and managing risk is knowing how we come into contact with them, often referred to as exposure pathways. People can be exposed to a wide range of contaminants through ingestion of polluted soil (directly or even indirectly through food produced on contaminated properties), inhalation of airborne particulates from soil or abandoned chemicals, and direct skin contact with contaminated soil, water, or airborne particles. Knowledge of both contaminants and exposure allows for the assessment of risk to human health, including cancer and non-cancer hazards such as respiratory, neurological, reproductive effects. While risk varies for every property and land-use scenario (and can be calculated accordingly), screening tables posted by environmental agencies allow risk assessors to determine whether the level of contamination found at a site warrants further investigation or cleanup based on certain "generic" assumptions of how the land is going to be used (e.g., homes or parks versus industrial and commercial properties). The US EPA also provides guidance on assessing ecological risks to plants and animals in the environment that may be affected by exposure to one or more environmental stressors, including chemicals, land-use change, disease, invasive species, and climate change.

Better knowledge of risk and exposure allowed for the identification of "known" contaminated sites, which by definition have soil, groundwater, or surface water with contaminant levels exceeding those considered safe by regulators. The distinction is often made between known contaminated sites that have undergone testing and potentially contaminated sites suspected of being polluted based on their former use (i.e., waste disposal, manufacturing, military, petroleum-based activities, former dry cleaners, etc.). The term *brownfields* became widely adopted in the early 1990s to address the negative connotations associated with the label *potentially contaminated*, even though the definition remained similar (Bartsch, 1996). That is, abandoned, idled, or under-used industrial and commercial facilities where expansion or redevelopment is complicated by real or perceived environmental contamination. In their seminal work, Noonan and Vidich (1992, p. 248) provide a table listing different types of properties and their probability of being contaminated based on their former land use. For instance, vacant rural land and residential property have a low likelihood of contamination (20 percent). In comparison, uses such as former coal-gas plants (99 percent), metal-plating plants (90 percent), landfills (90 percent), vehicle-maintenance facilities (82 percent), gas stations (88 percent), dry cleaners (74 percent), and urban vacant/abandoned land (85 percent) have a much higher probability of contamination.

In terms of the number of brownfields in the United States, there is no national inventory that allows for accurate accounting. The US EPA (n.d.a) estimates that there are more than 450,000 brownfields across the country, while other estimates put the number at 500,000 to 600,000 or more (Simons, 1998a, 1998b). The most severe sites containing hazardous materials deemed to pose the highest risk to human health and the environment are put on a National Priorities List (NPL) upon completion of a Hazard Ranking System (HRS) screening. As of August 2020, there were 1,335 active NPL sites, according to the US EPA, along with another 51 proposed NPL sites (424 have been deleted). The EPA also maintained information on hazardous-waste site assessment and remediation from 1983 onward via the Comprehensive Environmental Response, Compensation, and Liability Information System (CERCLIS), but this has recently been replaced by the Superfund Enterprise Management System (SEMS).

Many state and city governments also maintain brownfield inventories, although there is no standardized approach for identifying the sites to be included or the information maintained. Information on potentially hazardous sites is typically drawn from an array of data sources related to waste management and storage, spills, and existing industrial facilities that manage hazardous materials. States also maintain inventories of brownfield projects that have gone through their cleanup programs. These typically contain information related to site ownership, location, assessment, remediation, institutional controls, and other land-use limitations or conditions put in place following cleanup.

One of the most widely referenced sources of information regarding the number of urban brownfields in the country is the brownfields surveys administered to local governments by the US Conference of Mayors since the mid-1990s. In 2008, for example, 188 of the responding cities estimated that they had more than 24,896 brownfields with an average site size of approximately 14 acres (US Conference of Mayors, 2008, p. 9). One hundred and seventy-six cities had an estimated 83,949 acres of idle or abandoned land, and 150 of those also estimated that 3,282 sites were 'mothballed', meaning the current owner had no intention of redeveloping or selling due to environmental impact concerns.

Motivating Factors: Why Brownfields?

While the fear associated with health and environmental risk sparked federal and state government efforts to manage contamination, it also stunted investment in potentially contaminated property throughout much of the 1980s. This contributed to public welfare issues tied to blight that are of particular concern to local governments, such as poor aesthetics, nuisance, odors, and declining property values. As such, municipal goals associated with brownfields redevelopment prioritize neighborhood revitalization, increasing the city's tax base and job creation, followed by environmental protection (US Conference of Mayors, 2010, p. 10). Also, public-sector officials at all levels of government emphasize blight elimination, liability reduction, environmental justice, business retention, reuse of existing infrastructure, enhanced property values, improved health, and the catalytic effect that brownfield projects often trigger.

The decision by the private sector to invest in brownfield development is typically motivated by economic factors, such as landowners divesting liability risks/costs and developers taking advantage of reduced brownfields property prices in up-and-coming property markets to maximize their return on investment. Interviews conducted with private-sector stakeholders in Milwaukee, WI, and Chicago, IL, indicate that the factors attracting them to brownfields for housing development, for example, also relate to location and surrounding amenities (De Sousa, 2008, p. 215). Developers and landowners are also motivated by environmental issues that can affect their bottom line, such as the need to conform to environmental regulations and to protect the health and safety of those utilizing their projects and residing in surrounding communities.

More and more, community development organizations and non-profits are interested in working on brownfields in communities with weaker real estate markets. Community-based non-profits typically seek to rebuild low-income neighborhoods for the benefit of local residents and tend to be more concerned with the social implications of development projects and how such projects contribute to affordable housing, neighborhood stabilization, and improving quality of life (Dewar & Deitrick 2004, p. 159). These organizations are flexible and can play multiple roles in brownfields redevelopment, including education, outreach, facilitation, and advocacy.

Overall, stakeholders have become increasingly involved in brownfields to achieve a much broader set of environmental, social, and economic outcomes, which one could argue might be better served by building sustainably instead of conventionally.

Overcoming the Barriers to Brownfields Redevelopment

Despite the many desirable environmental, economic, and social goals associated with the cleanup and reuse of brownfields, redevelopment has been hampered by a series of risks and challenges that impose real costs and risks to all interested parties. All levels of government in the US have spent decades working to overcome these barriers, the most critical of which include regulation and uncertainty regarding who is liable for addressing contamination, the process governing the assessment and remediation of sites, access to funding and financing to undertake cleanup and redevelopment, and spurring reuse in areas with weak demand for real estate. What follows aims to provide readers with a sense of the evolution of policy efforts to overcome these barriers thus far.

The Evolving Regulatory Landscape

Concern over hazardous materials and the disposal of toxic waste began to grow in the 1950s and 1960s as more and more scientific research, including Rachel Carson's *Silent Spring*, sounded alarms about chemicals used in agriculture and for other purposes. The US EPA, which was formed in December 1970, allowed the federal government to play a leading role in hazardous waste management and to work with state governments and other stakeholders to gather more information regarding the chemistry, transport, and disposal of hazardous material. The Resource Conservation and Recovery Act (RCRA) enacted in 1976 established federal authority for controls over hazardous and other waste from generation to disposal (cradle to grave). Congress also passed the Toxic Substances Control

Act (TSCA) in that same year to provide the EPA with the authority to protect public health and the environment through controls on toxic chemicals that pose an unreasonable risk of injury (US EPA, n.d.b).

Well-publicized disasters, including Love Canal and a fire at a sizeable chemical-waste treatment facility in Bridgeport, New Jersey that left six dead and 35 in hospital in 1977, intensified public awareness and led to CERCLA (Superfund) passed by Congress in 1980 (Public Law 96-510, HR 7020, SEC 104(a)(1)). Superfund gave the EPA and other federal agencies the regulatory authority to respond to a release, or threat of a release, of a hazardous substance or "any pollutant or contaminant which may present an immediate and substantial danger to public health or welfare." The legislation enabled the federal government to recover the costs of cleanup actions from responsible parties or to clean up sites at their own expense. The EPA also published a numerically based Hazard Ranking System in 1981 for evaluating environmental hazards at sites and used the system to generate the first National Priorities List identifying 406 sites as the nation's top priorities for cleanup under Superfund. In 1986, the Superfund Amendments and Reauthorization Act (SARA) was passed by Congress to strengthen CERCLA's enforcement provisions, encourage voluntary settlements instead of litigation, stress the importance of permanent remedies and innovative treatment technologies, increase state involvement in the Superfund program, increase the focus on human health problems posed by hazardous waste sites, and encourage greater citizen participation in cleanup (US EPA, n.d.b).

Beginning in the early 1990s, the reaction against the enforcement-oriented Superfund apparatus intensified on the part of local governments and the private sector, both of which felt that it "put a chill" on investing in potentially contaminated land rather than facilitating it. An international study conducted by The Business Roundtable (1993, p. 1) compared the approaches of various countries to contamination issues and concluded that "no other country has adopted a program that is as cumbersome, inefficient, slow and costly as the US Superfund program." One of the main concerns with Superfund was that its "strict" and "joint and several" liability provisions made investors leery of becoming involved in any property suspected of possessing contamination. "Strict liability" allows for the assessment of liability for damages without requiring proof of negligence (i.e., responsible parties are financially liable even if the release of contaminants was legal at the time). Under "joint and several liability," parties who contribute to a site's pollution are each liable as if they alone polluted the site; therefore, the government can recover all costs from any party regardless of its degree of involvement in causing the problem. This meant that property owners responsible for contaminating a site would be held liable for the cost of cleanup and that any *new* property owner or bank would be considered just as culpable as the actual offenders. While this compels landowners and potential purchasers to act responsibly and to practice due diligence before investing in a property, it also minimized interest in redeveloping such sites and encouraged lawsuits aimed at deciding who should pay for site cleanup.

Within the US EPA, a task force was set up in 1991 to perform a '30-Day Study' on Superfund improvements, which proposed initiatives for accelerating the rate of cleanups and improving how the risks at hazardous waste sites are evaluated (US EPA, n.d.b). This led to the more streamlined Superfund Accelerated Cleanup Model (SACM) in 1992 and a focus on construction completion as a metric to track accomplishments at Superfund sites. The EPA and many state and local governments also started to address these inefficiencies more aggressively, leading to a focus on redevelopment and on ways to harness and facilitate the market's ability to resolve the issue. Both policy and the general discourse began to shift from public health and liability under the banner of "contaminated land management" to economic development and urban revitalization associated with "brownfields redevelopment."

In 1993, the EPA launched the Brownfields Initiative to redevelop abandoned, idle, or underused industrial and commercial sites where expansion or redevelopment is complicated by real or perceived environmental contamination. This led to the introduction of the Brownfields Action Agenda in 1995 to ignite interest in brownfields redevelopment. This agenda had four main components: (1) it provided seed funds for pilot programs to test redevelopment models and to facilitate stakeholder cooperation; (2) it clarified the liability of prospective purchasers, lenders, property owners, and others regarding their association with a site; (3) it fostered partnerships among the different levels of government and community representatives aimed at developing strategies for promoting public participation and community involvement in decision making; and (4) it incorporated job development and training opportunities into brownfields efforts. The agenda also put into place the administrative structures for linking brownfields redevelopment with other relevant socioeconomic issues at the local level, while allowing the EPA to reform and use CERCLA to focus solely on managing highest-risk contaminated properties. With interest and momentum building, the EPA launched the Brownfields National Partnership in 1997 to link the efforts of more than 25 organizations and federal agencies and to make over 100 commitments of $300 million in federal investment to facilitate the cleanup and redevelopment of over 5,000 brownfields throughout the country (US EPA, n.d.b).

By June 2000, all 50 states had participated in the federal government's brownfields program. Individual states throughout the country devised voluntary cleanup/response programs (VCP/VRP) to loosen the rigid structures that both federal and state Superfund-style legislation had imposed (Meyer & Lyons, 2000). The newer programs offered more flexible cleanup options and afforded the private sector more leeway to work on its own terms on marketable projects. At the same time, they provided technical assistance, financial support, and protection from liability. Nationwide, the federal brownfield initiatives and the voluntary cleanup approach culminated in the 2002 passage of the federal Small Business Liability Relief and Brownfields Revitalization Act (Public Law 107-118; HR 2869), which codified much of the EPA's progressive practices, policies, and guidance. The Act expanded the EPA's Brownfields Program, boosted funding for assessment and cleanup, enhanced roles for state and tribal voluntary response programs, and provided landowners who met certain statutory criteria protection from Superfund liability (i.e., they qualify as bona fide prospective purchasers, contiguous property owners, or innocent landowners).

Under state voluntary cleanup programs, cleanup of a site is voluntary unless it is deemed hazardous to public health and safety. The EPA remains involved in the development and operation of state programs, negotiating their content with state governments, signing Memoranda of Agreement or Memoranda of Understanding with states to endorse many of them, and setting out criteria to evaluate them. If a brownfield cleanup is carried out properly via the state's program, it provides a Certificate of Completion and No Further Action and/or Covenants Not to Sue Certificate to help prevent future liability litigation. A vital element of the Brownfields Act was the creation of the federal enforcement bar, which ensures that when a site goes through a state review program, the state becomes the primary regulator. This means that the federal government cannot use Superfund enforcement authority on that brownfield site. Consequently, state agencies started to play a more active role in technical assistance and review through their voluntary cleanup programs; usually reviewing and approving work plans and remedial objectives put forward by the responsible party at the beginning of the remediation process and then reviewing its cleanup work for adequacy at the end. Although many states have powers to "reopen" a cleanup, an early study by Simons, Pendergrass, and Winson-Geideman (2003, p. 265) found through a systematic inventory of VCP administrators in the United States that the incidence of reopeners was relatively low (between 0.1 and 0.2 percent).

The shift in the government's role from regulator to facilitator has allowed brownfields policy to evolve and maintain broad political support. The Brownfields Utilization, Investment, and Local Development (BUILD) Act (2017-2018) amends the brownfields provisions of CERCLA and reauthorizes EPA's Brownfields Program to 2022. The Act has made changes that affect brownfield grants (e.g., adjusting ranking criteria, increasing funding, providing additional offerings, supporting administrative costs, expanding eligibility), ownership and liability provisions, and state and tribal Response Programs. It continues to be redevelopment-focused but also supports more environmentally oriented and socially diverse outcomes by adjusting ranking criteria to assist green components (e.g., renewable energy, waterfront reuse) and by providing more grant support and liability protection to government entities and non-profits redeveloping less marketable areas (e.g., small communities, indigenous communities, rural areas, and disadvantaged areas).

Site Assessment and Cleanup Basics

The most important issue from a health and environmental protection standpoint has been devising procedures and techniques to ensure that soil, groundwater, and other media are properly assessed for contamination risks and, if necessary, that any risks are properly addressed before the site is reused. The initial scientific task, therefore, was to determine the risks posed by different contaminants based on likely exposure to them. This led to the creation of screening tables based on certain "generic" exposure assumptions based on the use of land that reveals whether levels of contamination warrant further investigation or cleanup, or whether no further research or action is required.

To conduct the proper due diligence, those interested in acquiring, remediating, and/or redeveloping a brownfield typically embark on the course of action put forward by the American Society for Testing and Materials (ASTM), which outlines "all appropriate inquiries" that must be carried out by "bona fide prospective purchasers, contiguous property owners or innocent landowners" who are purchasing potentially contaminated properties and intend to claim a limitation on CERCLA liability in conjunction with the property purchase." The first step is a Phase I Environmental Site Assessment (ESA), generally conducted by an environmental professional, that involves a review of historical records to determine ownership of a site and to identify chemical processes that were occurring at the site. It also typically includes a site visit to view existing conditions and evaluate any hazardous past activity, interviews with past and present occupants and owners, assessment of risks posed by the neighboring property, and a review of public records (plans, aerial photographs, maps, title records, etc.). It does not include any sampling.

If such an assessment identifies concerns, then a Phase II ESA, also guided by ASTM standards, is required. This is an intrusive investigation wherein original samples of soil, groundwater, and building materials are collected to identify whether contaminant levels exceed those considered safe according to approved screening tables. A Phase III ESA includes the comprehensive characterization, evaluation, and management of contaminated materials from a site, including their potential removal and legal disposal. A Phase III ESA usually involves the assessment of alternative cleanup methods, costs and procedures for performing the cleanup, and any follow-up monitoring of residual contaminants. It is also at this stage where the party responsible for the site must determine whether it will be remediated to levels considered safe for generic alternative land uses (e.g., residential, industrial) or whether a risk-based corrective action approach will be applied wherein soil and groundwater are remediated or managed to levels of tolerance and risk exposure considered safe for a specific development project to be conducted at a particular site.

As for the remediation of contaminated property, the most common way to categorize available technologies is based on whether contaminated soil and/or groundwater is treated in place (in-situ technologies) or removed from the ground for treatment (ex-situ technologies). A common, and typically least costly, ex-situ remediation method is 'dig-and-dump,' wherein contaminated soil is excavated from the site and placed in a suitable landfill facility. Other standard ex-situ treatment options include:

- bioremediation – microbial digestion of specific organic chemicals;
- vapor extraction – chemicals removed via aeration;
- thermal desorption – temperatures raised to volatilize compounds from the soil for vapor extraction;
- soil washing – contaminants washed from fine soils;
- solidification-stabilization technologies – specially formulated additive is applied to the soil to generate a low-hazard, low-leaching material, usually for onsite reuse;
- pump and treat – pumping contaminated groundwater from wells and managing it in an above-ground water-treatment plant.

In-situ techniques are somewhat similar in their basic technological approach (biological, vapor, thermal, solidification, chemical), but are utilized without removing the soil or groundwater from the site. These approaches usually target a greater area and depth, but they take more time to carry out. Another popular in-situ method is phytoremediation, which uses trees and plants (such as willow) to extract heavy metals and other contaminants from the ground over time. States are becoming more amenable to in-situ management strategies involving engineering and institutional controls that reduce remediation costs and make brownfield redevelopment projects more efficient and economically viable. These strategies allow more contamination to remain onsite, as long as an engineered barrier or a legal/institutional agreement is in place to limit access or actions that will expose users to a health risk. Soil contaminants, for example, can be fenced in or paved over, and permeable reactive materials can be placed in the subsurface to degrade or absorb dissolved contaminants as the groundwater passes through them. Institutional controls limiting access or site use may also be combined with monitored, natural attenuation to allow biological processes to absorb, dilute, or biodegrade contaminants without human intervention, as long as exposure is limited. Closures with residual contamination typically include legal requirements on the property owner to maintain certain safeguards concerning handling excavated contaminated soil, managing a cap, or accessing groundwater from the site.

Development, Funding, and Financing

In addition to improving certainty over regulatory and cleanup matters, significant attention has been devoted to managing the additional costs typically associated with the brownfield remediation and redevelopment process. The shift to facilitating remediation as part of a redevelopment required environmental regulators to become less focused on landowners and litigation, and more focused on the property development activities of developers and local governments. A recent publication by the US EPA (2019) provides a succinct description of three archetypal brownfield scenarios and the stages of the redevelopment process that those involved must understand:

1. Private-Led Brownfields Redevelopment: Most often occurs when a property is located in a healthy market wherein the developer can generate a profitable project with an acceptable return on their investment. The developer is responsible for the redevelopment process, which includes typical planning, construction, and marketing activities, as well as environmental site assessment (which may require public investment) and cleanup to meet regulatory requirements. A developer usually needs private financing through debt or equity to complete the project.
2. Public-Led Brownfields Redevelopment: Public development most often occurs when there is little private-sector interest in a property because of a weak market and/or limited development potential of a site. In this scenario, a municipality takes responsibility for the entire assessment and cleanup process, typically taking ownership of the property (via purchase, foreclosure, or eminent domain), conducting site assessment and cleanup activities, and either preparing it for construction activity (shovel ready) and selling it to a developer, or developing it for public use (e.g., park, school, or municipal building).
3. Public-Private Partnership Brownfields Redevelopment: Occurs when there is an agreement between at least one public-sector entity and one private-sector organization to combine resources and efforts to accomplish a project, whereby the public entity typically provides some initial funding for site assessment and infrastructure and a private-sector developer funds and manages the pre-development and construction process.

Allowing the market to function with minimal public intervention is typically considered optimal for both the public and private sectors. But this is not always the case for brownfields given their additional costs and risks, as well as the fact that many sites are located in weaker market areas that cannot sustain more costly development.

The EPA publication goes on to describe the three stages in the brownfield redevelopment process typically undertaken by developers, including pre-development, development, and management. It starts the pre-development phase with the developer assessing the feasibility of a project, but it is essential to take one step further back to consider the developer's broader consideration of the local real estate market in which the property sits. Various factors are often taken into account at this stage, and the increasing availability of digital property and land use information can allow for comprehensive and strategic screening of a community to identify parcels of infill opportunity. An initial screening of opportunities in an area can involve a review of sale and rental values, information regarding proximity to the downtown core, roads and transit, parcel size, zoning, permitted density and height, existing land utilization (with a preference for more easily acquired unbuilt sites such as parking lots, vacant sites, underutilized buildings, followed by actively used properties), walkability, nearby amenities (e.g., schools, open space, fire/police stations, cultural space), land assembly, the complexity of property ownership (multiple vs single, public vs private), historical designation, and availability of government support. Interestingly, previous work conducted on residential brownfields redevelopment in Milwaukee (De Sousa, 2008) found that early projects built in that city were considered a great niche market for a handful of experienced developers with a deep understanding of the local market and sites that they claimed "scared away the competition."

Once a developer has identified a site, they begin to engage in the pre-development phase, which involves further research into project viability and feasibility. They will conduct their due diligence by performing property and environmental assessments, researching land and building titles, and communicating with key stakeholders. They will also carry out various analyses of the physical and regulatory development potential of the property, assess the market, and estimate feasibility via a "back of the envelope" calculation. If there are no fatal flaws, the developer will move forward by generating an in-depth financial pro forma and negotiating their contract terms to purchase the site. These negotiations are a method of risk management and address critical issues, such as liability, financial risk, environmental covenants, institutional controls, and regulatory assurances. These negotiations lead to an agreement to purchase the property from the seller (i.e., a letter of intent or Purchase and Sale Agreement).

The purpose of the pro forma is to provide a concise description of projected cost, income, and profitability of a project from its inception to its final sale or leasing. The pro forma calculations carried out consider only the returns generated in the first (stable) year of the hypothetical scenarios. A discounted cash flow analysis is used to calculate development costs accrued throughout the development process, from date of land purchase to the moment when the developments are sold or leased. Important is obtaining accurate data related to typical project costs (e.g., building costs, development fees, architectural fees, general administration fees, etc.), revenues, and timelines, as well as any additional cost, revenue, and time implications associated with brownfield projects (e.g., demolition, site assessment, and remediation activities and approvals, legal and consulting expenses, financing and contingency fees, insurance, the potential impact of brownfield action on sale values, etc.). The pro forma will be used throughout the redevelopment process to guide site design, cleanup, and construction in a manner that minimizes cost and maximizes profit.

The developer then begins the preparation of a redevelopment plan, which generally includes: a community engagement plan to build public and regulatory support for the project; a visual site plan used to communicate with stakeholders, regulatory officials, economic development leaders, and the real estate market; a redevelopment implementation strategy for obtaining regulatory approvals, community support, and implementing the redevelopment plan; and a resource roadmap identifying public incentives that may be available to help finance the development or infrastructure improvements (US EPA, 2019). The developer will also identify sources of funds to pay for the assessment, remediation, purchase, and redevelopment activities.

The development phase of the project includes permitting, environmental cleanup, construction, financing, and marketing activities that culminate with the completion of the project and a formal opening. The developer has acquired financing at this point, which may involve private equity (investment funds or high-net-worth individuals), along with construction financing from banks, grants, and public sources and permanent financing from mortgages, Tax Increment Financing schemes, tax credits, or other sources. As such, they are particularly sensitive to cost and time overruns caused by delayed approvals and any unexpected cleanup and development costs required to complete the project. The project is also marketed to potential buyers or tenants, which may be more challenging in weak market areas or if buyers have concerns about the history of the site and whether risks have been managed appropriately. A brownfield project may be considered successfully redeveloped after construction is complete, ownership and leasing transactions are finalized, and the property is occupied and operating as its planned reuse (US EPA, 2019).

In the final management phase, the developer decides whether to hold the property for the long-term and assume responsibility for operation and maintenance or sell the property to another entity that will take over long-term responsibility for operations and maintenance. If the developer chooses to sell the property, they must ensure that ongoing maintenance required under the remedial action plan, and any institutional controls, are transferred to the new buyer.

If a market works as it should and a high demand exists for a particular parcel or product, then the landowner is expected to reduce the cost of that parcel to cover the additional cost associated with managing brownfield issues. Interviews conducted with residential developers operating in several North American cities reveal that when a market is strong, many felt that the government should just "get out of the way" and let the market operate. Many developers have also been able to profit by negotiating significant discounts on a potentially contaminated property based on estimated cleanup costs, and then minimizing those costs through the use of innovative technologies or the integration of novel site design and cleanup approaches. In many cases, however, the value of land in a particular location and the profit generated from reuse is simply not enough to cover brownfields-related costs *and* entice private capital. This is where government agencies, economic development officials, and other stakeholders come in with an array of financial tools to make brownfield projects work. Indeed, research by Paull (2008, p. 6) for the Northeast-Midwest Institute estimates that most brownfield projects (between 55 and 80 percent) involve some form of public subsidy. The primary goal, however, is to use tools that incur the least public expense to achieve the highest returns in terms of employment and rateables (i.e., property that generates tax income for local governments).

In the 2010 US Conference of Mayors' report, cities identified the most valuable tools for redeveloping brownfield sites as follows: (1) EPA site assessment funding, (2) private-sector investment, (3) EPA cleanup funds and state programs, (4) redevelopment funds, (5) local incentives, and (6) insurance. To assist with economic feasibility, state and local governments typically offer incentives that the US EPA (2007, p. 4) has grouped into three broad categories: offsets to brownfields financing needs, tax incentives, and direct financing.

Offsets refer to financially indirect measures, such as technical assistance, process facilitation, and project support. Popular among developers is the creation of a one-stop-shop for government assistance that allows representatives from multiple local and state agencies who oversee different aspects of the development process to work in a coordinated manner to reduce procedural headaches and costly time delays. Some local governments have also compiled brownfield inventories/portfolios with the location of potential opportunity sites and the tools available to support their redevelopment. Local government can also add market value to areas where brownfields are clustered by rewriting neighborhood plans, rezoning parcels to more profitable uses, increasing heights and densities, and targeting their capital spending to improve infrastructure.

Government tax incentives have been used historically to steer investment capital to weaker market areas and to promote specific types of economic development. Tax incentive programs (e.g., credits, abatements, or forgiveness) can improve a brownfield project's viability by allowing funds to be applied to brownfield redevelopment expenses. Federal and state governments can offer tax incentives to retain or attract businesses to particular areas of need, as well as to construct low-income housing. The New Markets Tax Credit (NMTC) program, established in 2000 as part of the Community Renewal Tax Relief Act of 2000, has been used to spur revitalization efforts on brownfields by providing tax credit incentives to investors for equity investments in certified Community Development Entities that invest in low-income communities. The Opportunity Zone incentive is a relatively new and promising tool established by Congress in the Tax Cuts and Jobs Act of 2017 that seeks to encourage long-term investments in high-poverty census tracts. Simply put, those investing their capital gains in a Qualified Opportunity Fund that invests in these zones will receive a break on paying federal capital gains tax in the short term (15% in 2019) and will pay no capital gains taxes on their opportunity zone investment if they hold it for at least a decade. This is significant for brownfields located in qualified zones because it includes investments made in land and structures redeveloped to improve safety and comply with environmental standards.

Direct financing of brownfields-related costs through grants, loans, and other means (e.g., revolving, low-interest, forgivable loans, tax increment financing, ESA grants) has a direct impact on the developer's pro forma. These funds can be used to cover front-end costs associated with site assessment, or for remediation, demolition, and other site-preparation activities needed to ready the property for construction. In addition to helping finance specific components of a project, these tools and other public insurance products can be used to increase the lender's comfort by limiting the risk of potential losses or defaults.

Outcomes and Expectations

Moving from an enforcement-driven to a more facilitation-oriented approach has borne significant fruit in terms of brownfields remediation and revitalization. A look at the EPA's own brownfields website highlights the accomplishments of its Brownfields Program and that of state and tribal partners in terms of thousands of properties enrolled, assessed, remediated, and made ready for reuse, as well as the billions of dollars of investment and hundreds of thousands of jobs created. While the EPA and government entities face continuing pressure to address barriers to brownfield investment and to generate taxes and employment, there is a growing demand for redevelopment to realize broader community goals related to protecting environmental health and safety, combating sprawl, revitalizing neighborhoods, improving quality of life, and promoting sustainability. The EPA's website does note the benefits of redeveloping brownfields instead of greenfields, such as reducing vehicle miles traveled and associated emissions, stormwater runoff, crime, and increasing surrounding property values and related tax revenues for local government. But most of these benefits are derived from conventional redevelopment. This book focuses on projects that have opted, purposefully, to infuse sustainability into their redevelopment plan with and without the assistance of the US EPA. The next chapter examines what it means to be a sustainable brownfield project and preliminary efforts taken to get us there.

References

Bartsch, C. (1996). Paying for our industrial past. *Commentary* (Winter), 14–24.
De Sousa, C. (2008). *Brownfields redevelopment and the quest for sustainability.* Elsevier Science/Emerald Group Publishing.
Dewar, M., & Deitrick, S. (2004). The role of community development corporations in brownfield redevelopment. In R. Greenstein and Y. Sungu-Eryilmaz (Eds.), *Recycling the city: The use and reuse of urban land* (pp. 159–174). Lincoln Institute of Land Policy.
Meyer, P. B., & Lyons, T. S. (2000). Lessons from private sector brownfield redevelopers: Planning public support for urban regeneration. *Journal of the American Planning Association, 66*(1), 46–57.
Noonan, F., & Vidich, C. A. (1992). Decision analysis for utilizing hazardous waste site assessments in real estate acquisition. *Risk Analysis, 12*(2), 245–251.
Paull, E. (2008). *The environmental and economic impacts of brownfields redevelopment.* Northeast-Midwest Institute.
Simons, R. A. (1998a). How many urban brownfields are out there? An economic base contraction analysis of 31 US Cities. *Public Works Management & Policy, 2*(3), 267–273.
Simons, R. A. (1998b). *Turning brownfields into greenbacks: Developing and financing environmentally contaminated urban real estate.* Urban Land Institute.
Simons, R. A., Pendergrass, J., & Winson-Geideman, K. (2003). Quantifying long-term environmental regulatory risk for brownfields: Are reopeners really an issue? *Journal of Environmental Planning and Management, 46*(2), 257–269.
The Business Roundtable. (1993). *The business roundtable comparison of superfund with programs in other countries.* The Business Roundtable.

US Conference of Mayors. (2008). *Recycling America's land: A national report on brownfields redevelopment* (Volume VII). US Conference of Mayors.
US Conference of Mayors. (2010). *Recycling America's land: A national report on brownfields redevelopment (1993-2010)* (Volume IX). US Conference of Mayors.
US EPA. (2007). *Financing brownfields: State program highlights* (Report EPA 560-F-07-252). US EPA Office of Solid Waste and Emergency Response, prepared by ICF International.
US EPA. (2019). *Anatomy of brownfields redevelopment* (Report EPA 560-F-19-012). US EPA Office of Brownfields and Land Revitalization.
US EPA. (n.d.a). What is a brownfield? *Overview of EPA's brownfields program.* www.epa.gov/brownfields
US EPA. (n.d.b). Superfund history. *Superfund.* www.epa.gov/superfund

2 Sustainability and Brownfields

Introduction

The overarching objectives associated with the management of contaminated lands and brownfields have expanded considerably since the late 1970s, shifting from an initial focus on managing health and environmental risk to developing and implementing mechanisms for stimulating real estate, economic development, and return on private investment. As our ability to manage risks and costs has advanced and the perception of these sites has improved, stakeholders are hoping to use brownfields to achieve a broader range of environmental, social, and economic goals as specified under the rubric of sustainability. These sustainability objectives are not new, however, but have always been core to the government's environmental mission and have underpinned efforts to address the brownfields problem. This chapter provides a brief background on sustainable development and then examines the US EPA's efforts to advance sustainability through brownfields. The scholarly literature that links brownfields and sustainability in the United States and abroad is also discussed. The chapter ends with a brief description of the research approach taken to identify the case studies and the methods employed to gather information.

Sustainable Development

Since its introduction in the mid-1980s, sustainable development has become a widely embraced model for integrating environmental needs with economic and social ones in human development. The World Commission on Environment and Development's (1987, p. 3) characterization of sustainable development as "development that meets the needs of the present without compromising the ability of future generations to meet their own needs" has become a sacred mantra among environmentalists and other urbanists. The crux of the approach is to be found in the concept that sustainable development can be attained without compromising the environment, suggesting ways in which a balance and interconnectedness can be maintained among the environmental, social, and economic requirements of human societies (Haughton and Hunter, 1994). In effect, sustainable development seeks to coordinate the protection of natural systems with a guarantee of fundamental social rights (from health care to cultural expression) and with the provision of an economic system that will provide opportunities for all while having a limited impact on the natural and social spheres. It also works at multiple scales, as evidenced by the range of indicators devised to track progress toward sustainability at global, national, regional, neighborhood, and site-specific levels.

The model most widely used to depict sustainable development is the UN's three pillars, popularly portrayed by three overlapping circles representing economic, social, and environmental resources with sustainability being achieved in the middle when all three are taken into consideration. While there has been no shortage of debate regarding the model and the objectives and activities within each circle, the figure has come to represent the relationship between these interdependent and interconnected spheres and the need to be mindful of them in development.

The UN (United Nations General Assembly, 2015) recently put forward a more comprehensive list of 17 Sustainable Development Goals intended to address global challenges with targets set for 2030, including: no poverty; zero hunger; good health and well-being; quality education; gender equality; clean water and sanitation; affordable and clean energy; decent work and economic growth; industry, innovation and infrastructure; reduced inequality; sustainable cities and communities; responsible consumption and production; climate action; life below water; life on land; peace and justice; strong institutions; and partnerships to achieve the goal.

Goal 11 seeks to make cities and communities inclusive, safe, resilient, and sustainable, given that it is at the urban scale where the environmental, social, and economic dimensions of development often conflict and vie for prominence (Campbell, 1996, 2016). Indeed, while cities today only occupy about 2% of the planet's land area, they are responsible for producing 70% of the global economy, consuming over 60% of global energy, and generating 70% of global greenhouse gas emissions and waste (United Nations General Assembly, 2016). The international community started to focus extensively on urbanization and urban settlement at the first Habitat conference back in 1976, which led to the concept of sustainability being advanced by the UN over a decade later. Numerous international conferences have taken place every few years since, including the most recent Habitat 3 conference in 2016. At that conference, international stakeholders noted that even though the planet has entered an unprecedented era of increasing urbanization, cities should be seen as a source of solutions to the challenges that our world is facing rather than their cause. And, if well-planned and well-managed, urbanization can be a powerful tool for sustainable development.

The principles and recommendations outlined within the *New Urban Agenda* report generated by the Habitat 3 conference continue to emphasize the proper management of the city's urban form and the smart reuse of its built environment (i.e., its land, buildings, and infrastructure) as a necessary step towards achieving sustainable development. To counteract the negative consequences associated with urban sprawl, those seeking to attain sustainability have advocated for more compact urban form with higher residential densities, enhanced employment opportunities, greater access to public transportation, and mixed land use activities. Such goals are to be achieved by encouraging infill redevelopment in older and already built-up areas, whether through the intensification of existing land-use activities or the rebuilding of vacant or under-utilized sites. Of the numerous "transformative commitments" for sustainable urban development put forward in the *New Urban Agenda* (United Nations General Assembly, 2016), the three most applicable for those involved in brownfields redevelopment include:

> 51. We commit ourselves to promoting the development of urban spatial frameworks, including urban planning and design instruments that support sustainable management and use of natural resources and land, appropriate compactness and density, polycentrism and mixed uses, through infill or planned urban extension strategies, as applicable, to trigger economies of scale and agglomeration, strengthen food system planning and enhance resource efficiency, urban resilience and environmental sustainability.
>
> 52. We encourage spatial development strategies that take into account, as appropriate, the need to guide urban extension, prioritizing urban renewal by planning for the provision of accessible and well-connected infrastructure and services, sustainable population densities and compact design and integration of new neighbourhoods into the urban fabric, preventing urban sprawl and marginalization.
>
> 97. We will promote planned urban extensions and infill, prioritizing renewal, regeneration and retrofitting of urban areas, as appropriate, including the upgrading of slums and informal settlements, providing high-quality buildings and public spaces, promoting integrated and participatory approaches involving all relevant stakeholders and inhabitants and avoiding spatial and socioeconomic segregation and gentrification, while preserving cultural heritage and preventing and containing urban sprawl.

Brownfields and Sustainable Development and the US EPA

The National Environmental Policy Act of 1969 (42 USC 4331(a)) committed the US to sustainability even before the concept was popularized, declaring it a national policy "to create and maintain conditions under which humans and nature can exist in productive harmony, that permit fulfilling the social, economic and other requirements of present and future generations." In the years since NEPA was enacted, the US EPA has looked to advance sustainability through policy, as well as through the greening of its own operations by incorporating sustainability principles into its decision-making procedures and tracking progress through the use of sustainability indicators. Although some studies have been critical of government efforts to advance sustainability, a 2009 publication by the Environmental Law Institute identifies six areas where considerable progress has occurred, including brownfields redevelopment (Dernbach, 2009). The author of the chapter on brownfields for that volume maintains, however, that not all brownfields redevelopment is consistent with smart growth and sustainability principles because sites are often developed on a parcel-by-parcel basis outside of a broader sustainability plan (Eisen, 2009, p. 57). Eisen suggests that for these programs "to achieve sustainability, states should increase the use of area-wide brownfields initiatives, develop measures to assess progress toward sustainability, promote 'green building' practices in site reuse, and develop 'second generation' policies to improve performance of state voluntary programs."

While sustainability has always been important to the EPA's brownfield efforts, policies and programs to address the problem seem to have evolved incrementally towards it as the agency tackles the risk and economic issues perceived to be the most pressing. As far back as 1982, there was growing concern about the social consequences of contaminated lands as protests over a landfill in Warren County, North Carolina, raised new concerns about the unequal distribution of environmental threats in disadvantaged and minority communities. This ultimately fostered the onset of the environmental justice movement and led to the creation of an Environmental Justice Task Force in the EPA's Office of Solid Waste and Emergency Response in 1994 to address broader social concerns.

The 1993 Brownfields Initiative, 1995 Brownfields Action Agenda, and 1997 Brownfields National Partnership represent a significant effort by government in general, and by an environmental agency in particular, to acknowledge, understand, and figure out ways to align brownfield cleanup and reuse objectives in the environmental sphere of sustainability with real estate and economic development goals in the economic one. The shift in the culture of the agency from the regulator to the facilitator is significant and commendable. As an environmental agency, however, the EPA continued to look for ways to make real estate and economic development more sustainable via their brownfields initiatives. In 1998 and 1999, it published two comprehensive reports on the *Characteristics of Sustainable Brownfield Projects* and a *Sustainable Brownfields Model Framework*. These responded to the (US EPA 1998, p. i): "short-term 'use-it-and-leave-it' approaches to development and to help communities make advances toward sustainability by re-using these brownfield assets, and developing processes that help prevent the creation of more brownfields over the coming decades."

The first study used a review of the literature, an examination of early brownfield pilot activities, and interviews with brownfield informants to isolate critical elements associated with sustainable brownfields redevelopment. Summarized below, these elements and their characteristics begin to tie specific criteria or processes that apply to brownfield redevelopment and can be manipulated at the project level to influence the project and community sustainability.

- Community Profiling
  - develop environmental baseline inventory (important landscape features and ecological assets);
  - define the composition, character, needs of the community;
  - preserve natural, cultural, historic resources and develop self-reliance;
  - determine the economic basis of the community, investment climate, and develop labor force.
- Comprehensive Community Planning
  - develop private-public partnership;
  - incorporate community concerns into the decision-making processes;
  - integrate the regional ecosystem(s) perspective;

- include "Best Practices" for sustainability (e.g., carrying capacity, urban growth, minimize automobile use, economic self-sufficiency, stakeholder consensus, equalize benefits).
- Organizational Focus and Structure
    - emphasize need for strong community and public leadership;
    - include all project stakeholders and concerned or interested citizens;
    - centralize local government coordination, point-of-contact, and authority;
    - integrate all public and private resources.
- Site Identification and Characterization
    - determine which party is best to initiate and perform the site characterization;
    - obtain accurate ecological information (site assessment and delineation);
    - assess the redevelopment potential of the site (use, infrastructure, economic conditions);
    - illustrate the basis of prioritizing the site over other candidate sites.
- Risk Management and Restoration
    - identify and clarify the barriers to effective risk management (owners, developers, community);
    - address the community concerns (risk communication);
    - address the project participant concerns (participation, liability, perceptions);
    - identify the tools for Risk Management (project management and government roles).
- Legal/Regulatory Issues
    - CERCLA (regulatory requirements);
    - RCRA, Clean Air Act, Clean Water Act, Toxic Substances Control Act, etc.
- Site Marketing and Redevelopment
    - promote program factors (community expectations, ownership, development);
    - promote ecological factors (eco-industrial development, parks, and landscape);
    - promote socioeconomic factors (property and use rights);
    - site marketing (community assets, markets, feasibility).
- Technology Applications
    - energy technology (conservation, renewables);
    - environmental technology (pollution prevention, waste minimization, site remediation, ecological monitoring);
    - transportation technology (alternative fuels and vehicles, intelligent transportation);
    - telecom/information technology (GIS);
    - public safety technology.
- Project Funding/Finance
    - redevelopment processes requiring funding (assessment, remediation, planning, outreach, development);
    - public sources of funds, primarily for the initial stages of the project;
    - private sources of funds (owners, responsible parties, prospective purchasers, investors, banks).

- Environmental Justice
  - early, adequate and meaningful community involvement in decision-making;
  - stakeholders who are committed to effecting a change for the better;
  - equal access to all information relating to the redevelopment;
  - willingness to negotiate to achieve a win-win situation;
  - environmental equity, equitable costs and equitable benefits for all.

The second study provides a model framework to assist and guide communities, municipalities, and other government organizations in planning and implementing sustainable brownfields redevelopment. It was also intended to be used by the EPA to guide the assessment of their pilot projects and develop further tools to advance sustainable approaches. Simply put, the model framework seeks to infuse the broader parameters, elements, and characteristics associated with sustainable brownfields redevelopment into the planning and development process already being performed at brownfield sites (i.e., project initiation, planning, evaluation, staging, implementation, and synthesis). This is important to ensure that the pursuit of sustainability does not decrease the chance of project success by placing a burden on a brownfield redevelopment project not required for conventional projects (US EPA, 1998, p. 29). The study advances Eisen's recommendations related to the integration of community-wide planning, the use of innovative technologies, and the advancement of sustainability metrics. The study also recommends that the US EPA support and analyze additional sustainable brownfields redevelopment case studies, including privately funded ones, over the long term to assess the contribution that sustainable elements and characteristics are having on current and future generations.

The US EPA continued to advance sustainable brownfields redevelopment after that via numerous initiatives, including conferences, awards programs, partnerships, project funding, publications, and research funding. Since 2003, the EPA and the International City Managers' Association have jointly organized the National Brownfields Training Conference, which attracts several thousand attendees, including local government leaders, developers, end-users of redeveloped brownfields sites, community members, and investors. Sustainability issues related to green design, community development, and environmental justice have always been prominent at this conference.

The US EPA has also created and supported the delivery of numerous award programs aimed at celebrating brownfield projects, people, and other related activities that go beyond the conventional and embrace broader sustainability approaches. In 2000, for instance, it handed out the first Citizen's Excellence in Community Involvement Award aimed at recognizing individuals or community groups that are making a significant contribution to a Superfund cleanup. It also launched the Environmental Justice Achievement Awards program in 2008, recognizing partnerships that address local environmental justice concerns and result in positive environmental and human health benefits in communities. Other awards in support of best practice brownfield projects have included the National Award for Smart Growth Achievement (2002 to 2015) and the Phoenix Awards created in 1997 to recognize outstanding achievement and innovation relating to environmental and community issues.

The US EPA has increasingly engaged with and promoted government and non-profit partners advancing sustainable brownfields reuse. A guide published by the EPA in 2006 outlines numerous resources and organizations supporting sustainable reuse, including programs run by federal agencies (e.g., Department of Energy, Housing and Urban Development, Department of Treasury), national private and non-profit organizations (e.g., US Green Building Council, Groundwork USA, National Association of Homebuilders, Natural Resources Defense Council, etc.), and a sample of noteworthy regional, state and local programs (e.g., Build Green Colorado, Sustainable Oregon, etc.). One particularly noteworthy relationship with the Congress for New Urbanism resulted in the development of a Smart Scorecard for Development Projects in 2002 to help decision-makers, municipal planners and staff, neighborhood organizations, and developers determine whether projects were fulfilling sustainability goals (Fleissig and Jacobsen, 2002). Another was support for the American Society of Landscape Architects to develop the Sustainable Sites Initiative Guidelines for Performance Benchmarks outlining how to design sites to maximize ecological benefits and minimize deleterious consequences. The EPA also engaged in numerous international brownfield partnerships aimed at sharing best practices, with the oldest and perhaps most productive being with Germany that has resulted in an array of sustainable brownfield redevelopment tools.

The EPA has also tried to advance sustainable brownfield redevelopment via its funding and pilot programs. Although pilot programs have been around since the onset of the brownfield program in the mid-1990s, and have supported conventional projects that have contributed to sustainability by default (US EPA, 1998), some pilot programs have intended to support projects that deliberately incorporate sustainability and smart growth principles. In 2007 the EPA announced the first Environmentally Responsible and Redevelopment Reuse (ER3) Project agreement to remediate and sustainably redevelop the Daly West Mine Superfund Site in Empire Canyon, a historic ore mining and processing area in Park City, Utah. In 2008 the Brownfield Sustainability Pilots program was initiated by the EPA's Office of Brownfields and Land Revitalization (OBLR) to seed sustainable brownfields revitalization at 16 pilot locations that are examined in detail in this book. In 2009 the EPA along with the Departments of Housing and Urban Development (HUD) and Transportation (DOT) formed the Partnership for Sustainable Communities to coordinate investments and align policies to support community efforts. In 2010, the OBLR also helped launch the Environmental Workforce Development and Job Training program within the EPA to help increase job training opportunities beyond the traditional scope of hazardous waste assessment and cleanup.

The US EPA, along with government and non-government partners, has also published several reports on sustainable brownfields development and related topics. Several describe progress made by programs and partnerships that they have funded, including the Brownfield Sustainability Pilots (2009a) and the Partnership for Sustainable Communities programs (2012a, 2014a). While the former provides more of a description of each pilot, the 2014 publication summarizes some significant policy changes and collaborations that ensued from the partnership, as well as contributions made by the programs five years after their initiation. Key internal changes made by the EPA, for instance, fell into three categories, including increasing flexibility in federal programs and removing barriers to investment,

Sustainability and Brownfields 23

leveraging federal and local know-how to engage communities and share knowledge and tools, and delivering a broader range of socioeconomic and environmental benefits through public investments. Other notable reports examine specific topics for improving the sustainability of brownfield and contaminated land projects, such as incorporating ecological revitalization (2009b), green remediation techniques (2008), sustainable materials management (2013a), urban agriculture (2011b), green infrastructure (2013b), environmental justice (1996, 2016a), renewable energy (2012b), community action (2019), and climate mitigation, adaptation, and resilience (2016b). The EPA has also published land revitalization case studies of completed and ongoing land revitalization technical assistance projects to highlight successful approaches and lessons learned (2011a, 2014b). One report entitled *Creating Equitable, Healthy, and Sustainable Communities* (2013c) identifies strategies that bring together smart growth, environmental justice, and equitable development principles for community-based organizations, local and regional decision-makers, developers, and others to use to build healthy, sustainable, and inclusive communities in low-income, minority, tribal, and overburdened communities.

Brownfields and Sustainability in the Scholarly Literature

The scholarly and professional literature on brownfields redevelopment has expanded considerably in geographic scope and focus over the last four decades. Indeed, a recent analysis of over 600 academic papers published on the topic from 1995 to 2017 by Lin et al. (2019) identifies 17 clusters of research that they place into six categories: (1) sustainable brownfield reuse; (2) brownfield soils; (3) brownfield actors; (4) decision-making; (5) brownfield reuse impacts; and (6) brownfield reuse evaluation and prioritization. Scholarly literature on sustainable brownfield reuse has typically fallen into two categories: (1) studies that examine economic, social, and environmental outcomes of brownfield projects and programs; and (2) studies that examine policy and planning efforts aimed at remediating and redeveloping brownfields in a more sustainable manner. The aim here is to provide a brief overview of some fundamental studies in this area; it does not purport to be an exhaustive review.

Tracking the performance of brownfield programs through economic indicators like the value of redeveloped projects, taxes, employment, and surrounding property values has been a critical focus of research given the need to justify public support for private investment in brownfield remediation and redevelopment (Kotval-K, 2016). Lange and McNeil (2004), Winson-Geideman et al. (2004), and Hula and Bromley-Trujillo (2010) assess how programs have performed concerning various economic measures and explain why tracking such information is necessary to those responsible for managing brownfields. Periodic updates of state voluntary response programs published by the EPA have been particularly informative, listing the thousands of sites involved in state voluntary cleanup programs. Several scholarly studies have examined the type of redevelopment taking place in state voluntary programs in particular cities. For example, in an examination of 116 Baltimore properties in Maryland's program from 1997 to the end of 2006, Guignet and Alberini (2010) found that the program led to the identification and assessment of 1,175 acres of contaminated land that tended to be located in areas zoned as industrial, and away from residential neighborhoods. Another study by Alberini (2007) in Colorado found residential development to be most prominent. An economic consideration that has been the subject of increasing study is the impact of brownfield redevelopment on surrounding property value. Examining a sample of 48 projects funded by the US EPA's Brownfields Program, Haninger et al. (2017) find, for example, surrounding property value increases of 5.0% to 11.5% on average, reaching as high as 15.2%. Sullivan takes the surrounding property value findings generated by Hanninger et al. (2017) and calculates the concomitant increase in the residential tax base to be between $29 million and $97 million (in 2014 USD) for a single tax year.

The most significant environmental consideration associated with brownfields, often measured alongside economic outcomes, has been the area of brownfield land assessed, remediated, redeveloped, and put back into productive use (Hersh, 2017). One of the most highly cited studies is by Deason et al. (2001), who found that 1 acre (0.405 ha) of brownfield land could accommodate the same development as 4.5 acres (1.8 ha) of suburban greenfield land. The literature produced on brownfield indicators has focused on the impact of redevelopment on an array of environmental issues ranging from urban microclimate (Koch et al., 2018) to transport (Amekudzi et al., 2003) and commuting impact (Nagengast et al., 2011). The conversion of brownfields into parks and green space in the US has also received some attention in the environmental literature, with studies by De Sousa (2004), Siikamäki and Wernstedt (2008), and Schilling and Logan (2008) reviewing the opportunity, conceptualization, design, planning, and implementation of various types of urban recreation and park space projects on brownfields and vacant land. Many studies have also examined the potential of brownfields for enhancing both urban and nonurban ecological systems. Burger et al. (2004) focus on properties owned by the US Department of Energy, Levi and Kocher (2006) examine the potential of brownfields as nature preserves along the California coastline, Mathey et al. (2015) assess the potential of green urban brownfields to provide a broad array of ecosystem services, and Carroll (2016) examines urban agriculture. Another emerging topic in the environmental and economic realm is research on efforts to locate renewable energy facilities (solar, wind, landfill gas, or biomass) on brownfields (Jensen, 2010; National Association of Local Government Environmental Professionals, 2012; Ribeiro, 2007; Tansel et al., 2013).

Issues of social and environmental justice first emerged when studies like the one produced by the United Church of Christ in 1987 and Bullard in 1990 found that brownfields and other environmental hazards in the US concentrate in communities of color and other low-income areas. Several studies have critically examined whether brownfield programs are addressing environmental justice, as well as broader social justice goals, with NEJAC (1996) and Solitare and Greenberg (2002) focusing on federal efforts, Harton (2008) on a state program, and McCarthy (2009) and Bryson (2012) on local initiatives. Solitare and Greenberg's (2002) evaluation of the US EPA's Brownfields Assessment Pilot Program found that the agency is working toward justice by disproportionately awarding grants to the most economically distressed cities. Essoka (2010) and Maantay and Maroko (2018) question, however, whether brownfield redevelopment, including for green space, is contributing to gentrification and displacement in minority neighborhoods. Harclerode, et al. (2015) and Cappuyns (2016) examine ways to support the integration of social factors and indicators into brownfields decision-making processes to support revitalization without gentrification. Public health researchers are increasingly engaged in efforts to address inequality and enhance broader community health through improved brownfields redevelopment and land reuse models (Berman et al., 2019).

Some research has examined brownfields and sustainability more holistically. These include a handful of books on the subject, studies examining sustainability indicators or frameworks used to infuse sustainability into projects or track redevelopment outcomes, and critical examinations of policy and planning efforts aimed at sustainable brownfields development. Books by Greenstein and Sungu-Eryilmaz (2004), De Sousa (2008), Sarni (2009), and Hollander et al. (2010) review the issue of brownfields and sustainability and provide brief examples of best practices. The work by Sarni (2009), for instance, offers a professional account of best practices, case studies, and innovative ideas on how to increase brownfield property values through sustainable remediation and green building techniques. Heberle et al. (2017) chronicle the development, evolution, and legacy of HUD's Sustainable Communities Initiative, which served as the hub for interagency collaboration initiated via the Partnership for Sustainable Communities program with the US EPA and Department of Transportation. It praises the effort for coordinating and aligning interagency leadership and staff, widely distributing grants to an array of sustainability-oriented initiatives, and investing substantially in capacity-building interventions, but also highlights the need for future research to uncover the "ripple effects" of the sustainability initiative over time. Some studies propose or employ a broader array of sustainability indicators to track redevelopment outcomes (De Sousa, 2002; Doick et al., 2009; ICMA, 2002; Nagengast et al., 2011; Pediaditi et al., 2006; Wedding & Crawford-Brown, 2007). Work by Ridsdale and Noble (2016) and Bartke and Schwarze (2015) provides an exciting overview of the increasing number of sustainable evaluation and assessment tools available to help incorporate sustainability concepts and methods into brownfields remediation and redevelopment. The latter finds that, in addition to there being no perfect tools, the user requirements of decision-makers must take precedence over those designing the tools for the tools to be meaningful and useful in practice. Thornton et al. (2007) examine incentives used in Europe to promote sustainable brownfields regeneration versus conventional reuse, finding that they are only partially effective in facilitating and delivering sustainability via reuse of soil/construction waste, maintenance of heritage buildings, land use/urban design and citizen participation processes.

The evolution of brownfields regeneration policy in Europe and the UK has also moved to align brownfields redevelopment with the sustainable development policy agenda. According to Adams and Watkins (2002), linking sustainable development to broader quality-of-life objectives in land use has several implications: (1) the presumption that sustainable development can improve environmental quality and human welfare at the same time, which is in contrast to the doom-laden environmental discourse of the past; (2) the contradictions at the local level between economic development and environmental protection; and (3) the gross oversimplification that brownfield development is necessarily always sustainable and greenfield development is unsustainable. The authors go on to discuss the difference between strong definitions of sustainability, which call for more rigorous environmental protection via an ecosystem approach, versus weaker definitions, which allow more flexibility for linking various economic, social, and environmental interests. Dixon (2007,

p. 2381) notes that since 1997 the UK government has used brownfield recycling to underpin urban regeneration and firmly linked it with sustainability. This has been enshrined in English national policy and underwritten in planning policy guidance in which brownfield housing targets by the late 1990s required half of all new homes to be built on reused sites (raised to 60% by 2008).

Dixon (2007) develops a conceptual framework for understanding the evolving policy agenda associated with brownfield regeneration and the role of the private development industry. He first describes the popular POST model wherein the process of redeveloping brownfields encompasses: a "policy push" aimed at getting redevelopment to achieve key sustainability benefits (i.e., urban regeneration, environmental improvement, greenfield protection); "development frictions" caused by the costs, risks, and regulatory obstacles affecting remediation and redevelopment; and an "opportunity pull" seeking the realization of benefits to all stakeholders in creating sustainable urban communities (i.e., developer profit, attractive locales for residents and employees). Dixon then expands this conceptual framework by integrating it with the triple bottom line concept of sustainability to understand better how developers engage with sustainability at the local level to achieve a broader array of economic, social, and environmental goals. In a review of several development cases, he found that while developers seem to be adapting to POST's brownfield dynamic, they are struggling to come to terms with sustainability in all spheres, and despite some success, there is continued skepticism over the sustainability agenda and the ability to approach it in an integrated way via brownfield regeneration projects.

The idea of bringing together the challenge of remediation with brownfield reuse in sustainable development also spread into national policy in Europe in the late 1990s. Initiatives and expert networks sought to develop strategies for sustainable brownfield development and remediation, such as the RESCUE sustainability assessment tool, SMART-e internet platform, and ASTM Standard Guide for Brownfields Redevelopment. However, Bleicher and Gross (2010) argue that the quality of these approaches and documents has been uneven, with some deep on theory and light on practice (RESCUE), and others treating sustainability primarily as an eye-catching label (ASTM) or in need of more precise grounding on the principles of sustainability (SMART-e). They put forward a decision-support tool to overcome these issues.

The tracking of brownfields policy and practice has come under particular scrutiny in the US ever since the traditional top-down contaminated lands policy under CERCLA was effectively replaced by the more results-oriented bottom-up Brownfields Action Agenda. The EPA and other researchers, including groups such as the Northeast-Midwest Institute and the Institute for Responsible Management, monitored the results of early pilot programs to determine what was working and what was not. One concern that emerged among researchers and government officials was that the policies being implemented and the outcomes examined were becoming too narrow in scope, focusing only on economic development impacts and ignoring sustainable development and other community goals altogether. A review by the US EPA's Office of Program Evaluation in 2002 found, ironically, that its own brownfields performance measures were designed only to take into account development and economic outcomes, failing to contribute to its role in protecting human health and safeguarding the environment (US EPA, 2002). In response was a growing call for governments to devise ways of tracking and assessing socioeconomic and environmental consequences of brownfield policies (CUED, 2000; Dair and Williams, 2001; De Sousa 2005; Simons and El Jaouhari, 2001; US Conference of Mayors, 2000; US EPA, 1998, 1999). Many relevant benchmarks for tracking the sustainability of brownfields redevelopment have been put forward since by a variety of government and non-government sources in the United States, although the application of these broader tracking approaches post-development has proven to be challenging.

Many comprehensive indicator-based approaches to checklist the application of sustainability and urban regeneration to buildings, projects, and district-wide developments have also emerged over the last decade, the most popular of which has been the Leadership in Energy and Environmental Design (LEED) rating system introduced in the late 1990s by the US Green Building Council. LEED is a green rating program for designing, constructing, and certifying buildings. It is divided into five categories related to location, water conservation, energy, materials, and indoor environmental quality, plus an innovation and design category. Each category contains a specific number of credits, and each credit carries one or more possible points. Brownfield redevelopment has typically been allocated points within the Sustainable Sites category. A project that earns enough points can become "LEED Certified," and then work its way up the ladder to Silver, Gold, and Platinum as it incorporates more green features. While less than ten percent of first-generation LEED projects in the US were allocated points for brownfields redevelopment, this has increased over time, particularly for LEED-ND (neighborhood development) projects that seek to help create better, more sustainable, well-connected neighborhoods.

Methodological Considerations

While research for this project initially sought to add to the professional and scholarly literature in a scientific way, it was the moving and inspiring stories of those trying to realize a more sustainable future for their communities that fueled my desire to follow their progress over time and to tell their stories in detail. The case studies emerged from a multi-disciplinary and multi-university research collaboration that commenced in late 2008 with funding from the US EPA. The Sustainable Brownfields Consortium, as our group came to be called, involved the University of Illinois at Chicago (where it was based), University of Illinois at Urbana-Champaign, Resources for the Future, Kandiyo, Hellmuth + Bicknese Architects, the University of Wisconsin-Milwaukee (where I was initially based), and Ryerson University (where I moved in 2011). The sub-project I was responsible for involved the identification of best management practices (BMPs) in the sustainable redevelopment of brownfields to draw lessons regarding the underlying policies and practices that enabled these projects to be built.

Ten sustainably redeveloped brownfield BMPs that were constructed or virtually completed by 2010 were examined via a comprehensive case study approach. These projects were identified via a review of the literature and from discussions with brownfield coordinators from the ten different EPA regions with consideration also given to project end use (residential, industrial, commercial, green space), location, size, and sustainability focus (i.e., green building and design, restoration, equitable development, public health). In-depth case study research was carried out from 2009 and 2013 to investigate site histories, examine sustainability features, understand how projects overcame the barriers to brownfield reuse and the implementation of sustainability features, and to derive a series of lessons learned regarding innovative policies, programs, and/or funding mechanisms that helped make these projects work. The research was based on structured interviews with an array of stakeholders involved in each case (at least 4–6 per case), including developers, planners, consultants, and community representatives. As this research proposal was being developed, the US EPA initiated the Sustainable Brownfields Pilots program in July 2008 that provided 16 projects with $25,000 to $50,000 in technical assistance funding to integrate sustainability and brownfields redevelopment. From a research perspective, this provided an opportunity to examine projects from their early stages. Case study research for the Pilots was less intensive due to budgetary considerations and involved telephone interviews with one or two contacts from each. While the original intention was to write a brief web profile for each pilot, I became fascinated with watching them grow. It should be noted that research was not conducted for two of the 16 pilots. The project in Oklahoma did not move forward when it was found that the building could not support a green roof, and the one in Cleveland wasn't a development project but involved writing a report on re-using residential building material (see Table 2.1 listing all case studies examined).

Table 2.1 Sustainable Brownfield Development Case Studies

Chapter	End/Land Use	Case Study
3	Industrial and Commercial	• Chicago Center for Green Technology, Chicago IL (BMP) • Menomonee Valley, Milwaukee WI (BMP)
4	Office	• Montgomery Park, Baltimore MD (BMP) • Heifer International, Little Rock AR (BMP)
5	Residential	• Artspace Commons, Salt Lake City UT (BMP) • Anvil Mountain, Silverton CO (Pilot)
6	Community and Green Spaces	• Moran Plant, Burlington VT (Pilot) • Elmhurst Park, New York NY (BMP) • Freshkills Park, New York NY (BMP) • Haynes Recreation Center, Loaredo TX (Pilot) • Allen Morrison, Lynchburg VA (Pilot)
7	Corner Gas Stations	• June Key Delta House, Portland OR (Pilot) • Tabor Commons, Portland OR (Pilot) • Green Avenue, Greenville, SC (Pilot)
8	Mainstreets, Neighborhoods, and Towns	• Focus Hope, Detroit MI (Pilot) • Samoa Peninsula, Humboldt County, CA (Pilot) • Jackson Square, Boston MA (Pilot) • Commercial Street District, Springfield MO (Pilot)
9	Mixed-Use and TODs	• Atlantic Station, Atlanta GA (BMP) • South Waterfront, Portland OR (BMP) • Langdale and Riverdale Mills, Valley AL (Pilot) • The Waterfront, Allentown PA (Pilot)
10	Brightfields	• Brockton Brightfield, Brockton MA (BMP) • Holmes Road/Sunnyside Landfill, Houston Solar, Houston TX (Pilot)

Case studies for some of the projects were posted on the Sustainable Brownfields Consortium website hosted by the University of Illinois–Chicago in 2013/14, but the initial desire to write up all of the case studies into a book was dashed by a decade of School Director responsibilities. Fortunately, updates for all BMPs and Pilots were conducted in 2016 and 2017 with support from Ryerson University, in addition to those made in 2019 and 2020 while preparing the book. The longer timeline was advantageous because it made it possible to observe how the BMPs and Pilots developed and evolved and to assess their long-term impacts on the communities and organizations involved.

Table 2.1 lists all of the case studies examined in the book and notes whether they are BMPs or Pilots. As I typically note in my methods section, it is obvious that no single analysis can presume to be exhaustive and all-encompassing given the size and complexity of brownfields policy-making and the enormous amount of activity it has generated. Suffice it to say that the objective here is to inform sustainable brownfield development practice and to explain general patterns that can be used as frameworks for future research and development efforts in this domain.

References

Adams, D., & Watkins, C. (2002). *Greenfields, brownfields and housing development*. Blackwell Science.

Alberini, A. (2007). Determinants and effects on property values of participation in voluntary cleanup programs: The case of Colorado. *Contemporary Economic Policy*, 25(3), 415–432.

Amekudzi, A., McNeil, S., & Koutsopoulos, H. N. (2003). Assessing extrajurisdictional and areawide impacts of clustered brownfield developments. *Journal of Urban Planning and Development*, 129(1), 27–44.

Bartke, S., & Schwarze, R. (2015). No perfect tools: Trade-offs of sustainability principles and user requirements in designing support tools for land-use decisions between greenfields and brownfields. *Journal of Environmental Management*, 153, 11–24.

Berman, L., Ballogg, M., & Erdal, S. (2019). A 5-step land reuse and redevelopment model: Resources to spur local initiatives. *Journal of Environmental Health*, 81(6), 36.

Bleicher, A., & Gross, M. (2010). Sustainability assessment and the revitalization of contaminated sites: Operationalizing sustainable development for local problems. *International Journal of Sustainable Development & World Ecology*, 17(1), 57–66.

Bryson, J. (2012). Brownfields gentrification: Redevelopment planning and environmental justice in Spokane, Washington. *Environmental Justice*, 5(1), 26–31.

Bullard, R. (1990). *Dumping in Dixie: Race, class and environmental quality*. Westview.

Burger, J., Carletta, M. A., Lowrie, K., Miller, K. T., & Greenberg, M. (2004). Assessing ecological resources for remediation and future land uses on contaminated lands. *Environmental Management*, 34(1), 1–10.

Campbell, S. D. (1996). Green cities, growing cities, just cities? Urban planning and the contradictions of sustainable development. *Journal of the American Planning Association*, 62(3), 296–312.

Campbell, S. D. (2016). The planner's triangle revisited: Sustainability and the evolution of a planning ideal that can't stand still. *Journal of the American Planning Association*, 82(4), 388–397.

Cappuyns, V. (2016). Inclusion of social indicators in decision support tools for the selection of sustainable site remediation options. *Journal of Environmental Management*, 184, 45–56.

Carroll, A. (2016). Brownfields as sites for urban farms. In C. Cogger, S. Brown, K. McIvor, & E. Snyder (Eds.), *Sowing seeds in the city* (pp. 339–349). Springer.

CUED. (2000). *Brownfields redevelopment: Performance evaluation*. Council for Urban Economic Development.

Dair, C. and Williams, K. (2001). Sustainable brownfield re-use: Who should be involved, and what should they be doing? *Town and Country Planning*, 70(6), 180–182.

De Sousa, C. A. (2002). Measuring the public costs and benefits of brownfield versus greenfield development in the Greater Toronto area. *Environment and Planning B: Planning and Design*, 29(2), 251–280.

De Sousa, C. A. (2004). The greening of brownfields in American cities. *Journal of Environmental Planning and Management, 47*(4), 579–600.

De Sousa, C. (2005). Policy performance and brownfield redevelopment in Milwaukee, Wisconsin. *The Professional Geographer, 57*(2), 312–327.

De Sousa, C. A. (2008). *Brownfields redevelopment and the quest for sustainability*. Emerald Group Publishing.

Deason, J., Sherk, G. W., & Carroll, G. A. (2001). *Public policies and private decisions affecting the redevelopment of brownfields: An analysis of critical factors, relative weights and areal differentials*. Environmental and Energy Management Program, The George Washington University.

Dernbach, J. C. (2009). *Agenda for a sustainable America*. Environmental Law Institute.

Dixon, T. (2007). The property development industry and sustainable urban brownfield regeneration in England: An analysis of case studies in Thames Gateway and Greater Manchester. *Urban Studies, 44*(12), 2379–2400.

Doick, K. J., Sellers, G., Castan-Broto, V., & Silverthorne, T. (2009). Understanding success in the context of brownfield greening projects: The requirement for outcome evaluation in urban greenspace success assessment. *Urban Forestry & Urban Greening, 8*(3), 163–178.

Eisen, J. B. (2009). Brownfields development: From individual sites to smart growth. In J. C. Dernbach (Ed.), *Agenda for a sustainable America* (pp. 57–70). Environmental Law Institute.

Essoka, J. D. (2010). The gentrifying effects of brownfields redevelopment. *Western Journal of Black Studies, 34*(3), 299.

Fleissig, W., & Jacobsen, V. (2002). *Smart scorecard for development projects*. In Collaboration with the Congress for New Urbanism and the US Environmental Protection Agency.

Greenstein, R., & Sungu-Eryilmaz, Y. (Eds.). (2004). *Recycling the city: The use and re-use of urban land*. Lincoln Institute of Land Policy.

Guignet, D., & Alberini, A. (2010). Voluntary cleanup programs and redevelopment potential: Lessons from Baltimore, Maryland. *Cityscape*, 7–36.

Haninger, K., Ma, L., & Timmins, C. (2017). The value of brownfield remediation. *Journal of the Association of Environmental and Resource Economists, 4*(1), 197–241.

Harclerode, M., Ridsdale, D. R., Darmendrail, D., Bardos, P., Alexandrescu, F., Nathanail, P., Pizzol, L. & Rizzo, E. (2015). Integrating the social dimension in remediation decision-making: State of the practice and way forward. *Remediation Journal, 26*(1), 11–42.

Harton, O. N. (2008). Indiana's brownfields initiatives: A vehicle for pursing environmental justice or just blowing smoke? *Indiana Law Review, 41*, 215.

Heberle, L., McReynolds, B., Sizemore, S., & Schilling, J. (2017). HUD's sustainable communities initiative: An emerging model of place-based federal policy and collaborative capacity building. *Cityscape: A Journal of Policy Development and Research, 19*(3), 9–37.

Hersh, B. (Ed.). (2017). *Urban redevelopment: A North American reader*. Routledge.

Hollander, J., Kirkwood, N., & Gold, J. (2010). *Principles of brownfield regeneration: Cleanup, design, and re-use of derelict land*. Island Press.

Haughton, G. & Hunter, C. (1994). *Sustainable cities*. Jessica Kingsley Publishers.

Hula, R. C., & Bromley-Trujillo, R. (2010). Cleaning up the mess: Redevelopment of urban brownfields. *Economic Development Quarterly, 24*(3), 276–287.

International City/County Management Association. (2002). *Measuring success in brownfields redevelopment programs*. International City/County Management Association.

Jensen, B. B. (2010). *Brownfields to green energy: Redeveloping contaminated lands with large-scale renewable energy facilities* [Doctoral dissertation]. Massachusetts Institute of Technology.

Koch, F., Bilke, L., Helbig, C., & Schlink, U. (2018). Compact or cool? The impact of brownfield redevelopment on inner-city micro climate. *Sustainable Cities and Society, 38*, 31–41.

Kotval-K, Z. (2016). Brownfield redevelopment: Why public investments can pay off. *Economic Development Quarterly, 30*(3), 275–282.

Lange, D., & McNeil, S. (2004). Clean it and they will come? Defining successful brownfield development. *Journal of Urban Planning and Development, 130*(2), 101–108.

Levi, D., & Kocher, S. (2006). The use of coastal brownfields as nature preserves. *Environment and Behavior, 38*(6), 802–819.

Lin, H., Zhu, Y., Ahmad, N., & Han, Q. (2019). A scientometric analysis and visualization of global research on brownfields. *Environmental Science and Pollution Research, 26*(17), 17666–17684.

Maantay, J. A., & Maroko, A. R. (2018). Brownfields to greenfields: Environmental justice versus environmental gentrification. *International Journal of Environmental Research and Public Health, 15*(10), 2233.

Mathey, J., Rößler, S., Banse, J., Lehmann, I., & Bräuer, A. (2015). Brownfields as an element of green infrastructure for implementing ecosystem services into urban areas. *Journal of Urban Planning and Development, 141*(3), A4015001.

McCarthy, L. (2009). Off the mark? Efficiency in targeting the most marketable sites rather than equity in public assistance for brownfield redevelopment. *Economic Development Quarterly, 23*(3), 211-228.

Nagengast, A., Hendrickson, C., & Lange, D. (2011). Commuting from US brownfield and greenfield residential development neighborhoods. *Journal of Urban Planning and Development, 137*(3), 298-304.

National Association of Local Government Environmental Professionals (2012). *Cultivating green energy on brownfields: A nuts and bolts primer for local governments*. National Association of Local Government Environmental Professionals.

National Environmental Justice Advisory Council (NEJAC) (1996). *Environmental justice, urban revitalization, and brownfields: The search for authentic signs of hope* (US EPA Report 500-R-96-002). NEJAC.

Pediaditi, K., Wehrmeyer, W., Burningham, K., Brebbia, C. A., Brebbia, A., & Mander, U. (2006). Evaluating brownfield redevelopment projects: A review of existing sustainability indicator tools and their adoption by the UK development industry. In C. A. Brebbia (Ed.), *Brownfield sites III: Prevention, assessment, rehabilitation and development of brownfield sites* (Vol. 94) (pp. 51-60). Wit Press.

Ribeiro, L. (2007). Waste to watts: A "brightfield" installation has the potential to bring renewed life to a brownfield site. *Refocus, 8*(2), 46-49.

Ridsdale, D. R., & Noble, B. F. (2016). Assessing sustainable remediation frameworks using sustainability principles. *Journal of Environmental Management, 184*, 36-44.

Sarni, W. (2009). *Greening brownfields: Remediation through sustainable development*. McGraw-Hill Professional.

Schilling, J., & Logan, J. (2008). Greening the rust belt: A green infrastructure model for right sizing America's shrinking cities. *Journal of the American Planning Association, 74*(4), 451-466.

Siikamäki, J., & Wernstedt, K. (2008). Turning brownfields into greenspaces: Examining incentives and barriers to revitalization. *Journal of Health Politics, Policy and Law, 33*(3), 559-593.

Simons, R., & El Jaouhari, A. E. (2001). Local government intervention in the brownfields arena. *Commentary* (Fall), 12-18.

Solitare, L., & Greenberg, M. (2002). Is the US Environmental Protection Agency brownfields assessment pilot program environmentally just? *Environmental Health Perspectives, 110*(suppl 2), 249-257.

Tansel, B., Varala, P. K., & Londono, V. (2013). Solar energy harvesting at closed landfills: Energy yield and wind loads on solar panels on top and side slopes. *Sustainable Cities and Society, 8*, 42-47.

Thornton, G., Franz, M., Edwards, D., Pahlen, G., & Nathanail, P. (2007). The challenge of sustainability: Incentives for brownfield regeneration in Europe. *Environmental Science & Policy, 10*(2), 116-134.

United Church of Christ (1987). *Toxic waste and race in the United States: A national report on the racial and socio-economic characteristics of communities with hazardous waste sites*. United Church of Christ.

United Nations General Assembly (2015). *Transforming our world: The 2030 agenda for sustainable development* (United Nations A/RES/70/1). UN.

United Nations General Assembly. (2016). *New urban agenda: Quito declaration on sustainable cities and human settlements for all* (United Nations A/RES/71/56). UN.

US Conference on Mayors (2000). *Recycling America's land: A national report on brownfields redevelopment* (Volume III). US Conference on Mayors.

US EPA (1996). *Environmental justice, urban revitalization, and brownfields: The search for authentic signs of hope* (EPA 500-R-96-002). National Environmental Justice Advisory Council Waste and Facility Siting Subcommittee.

US EPA (1998). *Characteristics of sustainable brownfields projects* (EPA500-R-98-001). Office of Solid Waste and Emergency Response.

US EPA (1999). *Sustainable brownfields model framework* (EPA500-R-99-001). Office of Solid Waste and Emergency Response.

US EPA (2002). *Observations on EPA's Plans for Implementing Brownfields Performance Measures* (2002-M-00016). Office of Inspector General, Final Memorandum Report.

US EPA (2006). *Sustainable re-use of brownfields: Resources for communities* (EPA560-F-06-247). Office of Solid Waste and Emergency Response.

US EPA (2008). *Green remediation: Incorporating sustainable environmental practices into remediation of contaminated sites* (EPA 542-R-08-002). Office of Solid Waste and Emergency Response.

US EPA (2009a). *Building a sustainable future: A report on the Environmental Protection Agency's Brownfield's Sustainability Pilots* (EPA-560-F-09-500). Office of Brownfields and Land Revitalization.

US EPA (2009b). *Ecological revitalization: Turning contaminated properties into community assets.* (EPA-542-R-08-003). Office of Solid Waste and Emergency Response.

US EPA (2011a). *Land revitalization success stories* (EPA 560-K-11-001). Office of Solid Waste and Emergency Response.

US EPA (2011b). *Brownfields and urban agriculture: Interim guidelines for safe gardening practices.* (EPA 560/S-11/001). Region 5 Superfund Division

US EPA (2012a). *Partnership for sustainable communities: Three years of helping communities achieve their visions for growth and prosperity* (EPA 231-R-12-001). Office of Sustainable Communities

US EPA (2012b). *Handbook on siting renewable energy projects while addressing environmental issues.* Office of Solid Waste and Emergency Response, RE-Powering America's Land Initiative.

US EPA (2013a). *Sustainable materials management in site cleanup* (EPA 542-F-13-001). Office of Solid Waste and Emergency Response.

US EPA (2013b). *Implementing stormwater infiltration practices at vacant parcels and brownfield sites* (EPA 905-F-13-001). Office of Solid Waste and Emergency Response, Office of Water.

US EPA (2013c). *Creating equitable, healthy, and sustainable communities: Strategies for advancing smart growth, environmental justice, and equitable development* (US EPA 231-K-10-005). Office of Sustainable Communities.

US EPA (2014a) *Partnership for sustainable communities: Five years of learning from communities and coordinating federal investments* (EPA 231-R-14-004). Office of Sustainable Communities.

US EPA (2014b). *Land revitalization success stories 2014* (EPA 560-F-14-208). Office of Solid Waste and Emergency Response.

US EPA (2016a). *National Environmental Justice Advisory Council 20-year retrospective report (1994-2014)* (EPA-300-R-16-002). Office of Environmental Justice

US EPA (2016b). *Climate smart brownfields* (EPA 560-F-16-005). Office of Solid Waste and Emergency Response.

US EPA (2019). *Community actions that drive brownfields redevelopment* (EPA 560-R-19-002). Office of Brownfields and Land Revitalization.

Wedding, G. C., & Crawford-Brown, D. (2007). Measuring site-level success in brownfield redevelopments: A focus on sustainability and green building. *Journal of Environmental Management, 85*(2), 483–495.

Winson-Geideman, K., Simons, R. A., & Pendergrass, J. (2004). Tracking remediation and redevelopment trends of brownfield clean-up programmes: The Cook County experience. *Journal of Environmental Planning and Management, 47*(3), 393–405.

World Commission on Environment and Development. (1987). *Our common future*. Oxford University Press.

3 Industrial and Commercial Redevelopment

While many involved in the management of brownfields spend much of their time figuring out ways to wipe away the rust left behind from our industrial past, a few have taken the opportunity to envision an industrial future that is green and sustainable. The two award-winning case studies examined in this chapter – the Chicago Center for Green Technology and Milwaukee's Menomonee Valley – laid a foundation and set a high bar for their respective cities and the brownfields industry. The journeys these projects have taken from inception to today offer lessons for cities seeking to revitalize and rebrand their employment areas in a way that supports economic development and counteracts the chronic unemployment and related social and environmental inequities caused by industrial decline.

The Chicago Center for Green Technology (CCGT)

Despite the emphasis on new and modern buildings equipped with the latest technology to point the way to a greener urban future, lessons on developing more sustainably are often best told through a project that has successfully reclaimed, renovated, and reused the embodied energy of an older building. The CCGT was redeveloped by the city to become an enduring model of adaptive reuse and sustainable best practice on brownfields; taking a nondescript 1950s-era building on a 17-acre parcel piled with illegally dumped debris and turning it into the first brownfield, renovated structure, and municipal building in the US to receive a Platinum LEED rating. The CCGT was also used by the city to educate the development community about brownfields and sustainable technologies when it opened its doors in 2002. Although the educational programs ended in 2014 due to budget cuts, this trendsetting building still hosts tenants with progressive green and equity-oriented missions and has spawned a new green district.

Site History

The CCGT is in the Kinzie Industrial Corridor within the East Garfield Park neighborhood. The corridor is of particular significance to Chicago's economy, hosting the highest number of firms of any of the city's designated industrial areas (Camiros et al., 1998). It has been the focus of a publicly led redevelopment project since 1996 to preserve and revitalize the area's industrial character after it started experiencing disinvestment and decline. In combination with other publicly led economic development initiatives, such as the Chicago Brownfields Initiative and HUD's Empowerment Zone designation, the redevelopment project aimed to facilitate the transition of the corridor through new investment in manufacturing activities.

The corridor's industrial character was influenced by the construction of the city's first railroad, the Galena and Chicago Union Railroad, parallel to Kinzie Street in 1851 (Camiros et al., 1998). The property of the original CCGT building at 445 N. Sacramento Boulevard was developed in 1952 west of the industrial corridor's rail yards. The Sacramento Crushing Company was using the 17-acre property to recycle construction and demolition debris (US EPA, 2005a). In 1995, however, the city of Chicago's Department of Environment (DOE) discovered that the company had violated the conditions of its recycling permit (US EPA, 2005a). Staff at the DOE maintained that Sacramento Crushing had been accepting "more material than it could process, including lower-quality material" for which there is no market (Henderson, 2002). Unable to process the oversupply of waste material, the company began to store the debris onsite, leading to the creation of an unregulated landfill (US EPA, 2005a). By the time the Illinois EPA cited Sacramento Crushing for illegally developing and operating a solid-waste storage and treatment facility, the 17-acre property was covered in 600,000 cubic yards of construction waste and debris (US EPA, 2005a). The accumulated waste was dumped into 70-foot-high piles, some of which sank 15 feet into the ground (US EPA, 2005a). The property was commonly referred to as an "environmental mess" by city officials and media reports at the time (Henderson, 2002).

The Sacramento Crushing Company filed for bankruptcy in 1996. The Chicago Department of Environment (DOE) intervened in the court proceedings, however, and convinced the trial judge that the company had mismanaged itself as opposed to being affected by fluctuating market conditions (Henderson, 2002). The DOE acquired the property after it had been in receivership status for one year, while the Sacramento Crushing Company's bank tried unsuccessfully to have the site cleaned up (Henderson, 2002).

The DOE assumed responsibility for cleaning up the site when it acquired ownership rights to the property in 1996. Before any environmental site assessments could be performed, clearing the site of construction and demolition debris took 18 months and cost $9 million (city of Chicago, 2003a; US Green Building Council, 2008). The DOE was able to offset the cleanup costs with financial assistance from several sources obtained through the Chicago Brownfields Initiative, including funds from HUD and the EPA (city of Chicago, 2003a; US EPA, 2005a). The DOE also sold salvageable waste material to other recycling facilities and city departments for use as inputs in their infrastructure projects. The foundation of the parking garage at Millennium Park, for instance, was built by the Chicago Department of Transportation using recycled material from the debris at the CCGT property. Meanwhile, the two-story 28,000 square foot building on the property was deconstructed to its basic structure (Henderson, 2002; US EPA, 2005a).

An attempt was made to sell the property in 1999 after it was appraised for $800,000 (Henderson, 2002). Any potential buyers would have had to compensate the city for the remediation and cleanup costs. In the end, the city had a "vacant lot and a derelict building that nobody wanted" (Henderson, 2002). However, what was once seen as a mess of waste material eventually inspired an innovative model for energy efficiency and sustainable community development.

Project Vision

As with many redevelopment initiatives, the project vision for the brownfield property evolved to address the economic and social needs of the surrounding community. While the Chicago DOE initially thought the building could be developed for private commercial use, a confluence of factors contributed to the final project vision as a mixed-use industrial and commercial facility with green public education and programming services.

Initially, three organizations with different priorities had approached the DOE in search of office space or developable land. Greencorps Chicago, a DOE program that provides green industry job training and assistance to community members, had outgrown its leased space (Henderson, 2002). Spire Solar Chicago, a firm specializing in the manufacture and installation of photovoltaic systems, wished to relocate to a brownfield (Henderson, 2002). Lastly, the environment committee of the Chicago chapter of the American Institute of Architects (AIA) expressed interest in designing a green building; but was frustrated in its search to find a willing client (Henderson, 2002).

A formal vision for the CCGT began to develop through strategic planning exercises in the DOE and an analysis of existing multi-function environmental education centers. With funding from a settlement between the city and the Commonwealth Edison Company earmarked for "renewable energy and energy conservation projects," Chicago's environmental commissioner at the time, William Abolt, resolved to combine the needs of the three organizations through the development of the vacant brownfield. Through a public-private partnership, the city would contribute $5 million toward the redevelopment of the building with technical guidance led by a design team of environmentally conscious architects from the AIA's Chicago chapter. The building would provide Spire Solar Chicago with manufacturing and commercial space for its operations, offer Greencorps Chicago space for its programming while adding a satellite office for DOE field employees (Henderson, 2002). In effect, synthesizing the needs of the three organizations gave rise to an innovative solution with benefits that would extend to the surrounding industrial corridor and the city of Chicago.

The project vision put forward by Abolt would also fulfill the objectives of a broader, citywide urban revitalization strategy known as the Chicago Brownfields Initiative to recycle underutilized properties. The purpose of the initiative was to promote "industrial and economic redevelopment, job creation, and tax revenues while addressing environmental problems" on underutilized properties in industrial areas (city of Chicago, 2003a; Higgins, 2008). In Abolt's vision, the CCGT redevelopment had the potential to attract private investment to the Kinzie Industrial Corridor if it proved to be successful.

In addition to being an example of brownfield remediation and redevelopment, the retrofitted CCGT building would also serve as a model of sustainable design to encourage and promote the adoption of energy-efficient and renewable technologies in future new and rehab projects. This vision complemented other sustainability initiatives led by Mayor Richard Daley, such as the construction of a green roof on Chicago's City Hall, an energy-conservation code for new and renovated buildings, and subsidizing photovoltaic solar panels on public building roofs (Henderson, 2002).

Project Characteristics and Development

By 1999 the property had been acquired by the city, cleared of debris, and prepared for redevelopment. Also agreed upon was a project vision incorporating energy efficiency and sustainable design. A design team of environmentally conscious professionals led by the Chicago-based architectural firm Farr Associates was subsequently assembled (Henderson, 2002). The team opted to design and build the CCGT according to the US Green Building Council's (USGBC) LEED Green Building Rating System (US Green Building Council, 2008). When the USGBC introduced its LEED Version 1.0 Rating System in 1999, the design team agreed to target the highest rating possible, Platinum certification (US Green Building Council, 2008).

The decision to aim for LEED certification, according to Douglas Farr, principal of Farr Associates, was that it set a comprehensive performance standard for green building (Henderson, 2002). The CCGT aimed to accrue 36 points to attain LEED Platinum certification, although it surpassed the requirement by two points (US Green Building Council, 2008). Through a collaborative design charrette, the team of architects, landscape architects, engineers, and sustainability professionals chose strategies that addressed site planning, energy consumption, building materials, indoor environmental quality, and water efficiency (US Green Building Council, 2008). Examples from each strategy are summarized here and reflect the integrated character of the redevelopment.

Project Characteristics

A combination of design strategies was used in the site planning of the project to offset the urban heat island effect. The high albedo (light-colored) material used in the construction of the parking lot, for instance, reflects solar energy rather than absorbing it. When combined with the site's extensive tree canopy and landscaping, these green design strategies keep the parking and pedestrian areas cool during the summer months. The redevelopment also scored a LEED point for reusing existing infrastructure and minimizing the ecological footprint of the project, and another for its proximity to public transit.

The CCGT building was designed to maximize energy efficiency and to use 40% less energy than a code-compliant building of the same size (US Green Building Council, 2008). The combination of renewable energy technologies with energy conservation strategies addresses the supply and demand of energy to achieve energy performance goals. On the supply side, solar panels located on the roof, the south side of the building, and adjacent to the parking lot aimed to supply nearly 25% of the CCGT's electricity (see Figure 3.1) (city of Chicago, 2003b). A geothermal system uses the relatively consistent ground temperature to heat and cool the building. On the demand side, low-emission windows and doors reflect solar radiation during the summer and absorb it in the winter, decreasing heating and cooling costs throughout the year. A smart lighting system regulates indoor lighting based on the amount

Industrial and Commercial Redevelopment 37

of natural sunlight in a room. Fluorescent light bulbs throughout the building also minimize energy consumption when electric light is needed (city of Chicago, 2003a). These energy efficiency strategies were estimated to contribute to annual energy savings of $29,000 (US Green Building Council, 2008).

Figure 3.1 Chicago Center for Green Technology, Illinois, 2009

Building materials were carefully considered in the development of the CCGT to limit the amount of waste incurred through construction and to minimize indoor air pollution. The design team was able to limit the environmental cost of construction by utilizing 100% of the original building's structural shell, sourcing materials with recycled content wherever possible, and purchasing from local suppliers. For instance, 36% of all the building materials had recycled content, and over 50% of the building materials (excluding mechanical and plumbing systems) were manufactured or assembled within 300 miles of the construction site (US Green Building Council, 2008). Moreover, 84% of the waste produced through construction was diverted from the landfill (US Green Building Council, 2008). Also, non-toxic building materials were used to minimize indoor air pollution, effectively limiting the emission of volatile organic compounds (VOCs) (US Green Building Council, 2008). The building is equipped with a displacement ventilation system that feeds fresh air near the floor and removes stale air at the ceiling level, providing occupants with high-quality clean air (city of Chicago, 2003b).

A variety of green strategies were employed to address water conservation and stormwater management concerns on the 17-acre property. The water efficiency strategies act as an integrated system, first by absorbing rainwater, and then by filtering runoff, to reduce the impact of the building on broader ecological functions. A 2,500 square foot green roof absorbs rainfall and cools the building during the summer months (city of Chicago, 2003a; Chicago Department of Environment, 2009). Four cisterns collect and store up to 12,000 gallons of excess rainwater that drains from the roof to irrigate plants (city of Chicago, 2003a). Bioswales funnel rainwater from the parking lot to a reconstructed wetland, while also filtering pollutants (city of Chicago, 2003a). Three different examples of permeable paving on the site illustrate how rainwater can percolate into the ground rather than going into the municipal sewer system. A retention pond functions as a reservoir for rainwater not collected or absorbed by the other onsite water conservation strategies, and also serves as a habitat for wildlife. These water efficiency strategies effectively address stormwater management onsite by reducing the amount of rainwater runoff entering the sewer system by 50% (city of Chicago, 2003b).

In addition to being a model of energy efficiency and sustainable design, the CCGT also contributes to Chicago's economic and social development through its collaborative relationship with Greencorps Chicago, a career development and community gardening program created by the DOE in 1994. The program links environmental stewardship and restoration activities with job training and public engagement to create natural spaces that are "safe, healthy, and sustainable" (Greencorps, 2009a). On the career development side, Greencorps Chicago offers Chicago-area residents a nine-month paid position in the DOE's Green Industry job training program. Recruits participate in field and classroom instruction in landscaping and horticulture, environmental health and safety, electronics recycling, and weatherization (Greencorps, 2009b). Historically, the program partnered with social service agencies to provide work experience and employment opportunities to underemployed and unemployed individuals, including ex-offenders (Greencorps, 2009b). Ninety percent of the program recruits are ex-offenders searching for opportunities to upgrade their skills and employment prospects to achieve self-sufficiency (city of Chicago, 2009). On the community gardening side, the program provides free plants and technical assistance to facilitate the creation of community gardens throughout the city. Community groups must complete a certification process to participate in the program, as well as workshops covering topics such as garden design, installation and maintenance, and community group organization (Greencorps, 2009a). Technical assistance is provided by DOE staff as well as trainees in the career development program. This approach engages residents in the city's delivery of environmental services while simultaneously educating them about the benefits of ecological restoration and sustainability.

The native gardens and landscaping on the CCGT property offered onsite demonstration and learning opportunities for both components of the Greencorps Chicago program. In turn, recruits of the job training program maintain CCGT's gardens, reducing the operating costs of the Center. The collaborative relationship between the CCGT and Greencorps Chicago contributes to community development through job training, capacity building, and community greening initiatives.

The CCGT offered guided and self-guided tours of the building and grounds. The Center also offered a variety of free educational programs for both professionals and the general public related to architecture, building and construction management, do-it-yourself greening, engineering, green business, interior design, and landscape design. Before ceasing operations in 2014, between 15,000 and 30,000 visitors accessed the CCGT each year for educational programming, job training, tours, and green building resources (K. Worthington, personal communication, 2014).

Project Development

The city of Chicago introduced the Chicago Brownfields Initiative (CBI) in 1993 to provide leadership in brownfield remediation and development. The CBI outlined a process to return brownfield sites to productive use by "acquiring, cleaning, and coordinating" brownfield redevelopment (Higgins, 2008). The transformation of the original site into the CCGT evolved based on the approach established through the CBI. Under the CBI, properties were evaluated for accessibility and control, and estimates obtained for cleanup costs and developmental value. The city acquired properties through a negotiated purchase price, lien foreclosure, or tax reactivation, and then added them to its investment portfolio. Environmental cleanup strategies and cost estimates were determined. Then properties were enrolled in the Illinois EPA's voluntary Site Remediation Program to obtain a "No Further Remediation" (NFR) letter upon successful completion and then marketed for development (city of Chicago, 2003a).

The CCGT property enrolled in the state program in December of 1999. The site was divided into two separate parcels for regulatory approvals; one 3.5-acre parcel consisting of the CCGT building and its immediate surroundings and the other 13 acres to the east of the building. The site also required the removal of an underground storage tank. Phase II ESAs at the two sites uncovered contaminants typical of former industrial properties at levels slightly above those considered safe for future industrial use (e.g., arsenic, benzo(a)pyrene, dibenzo(a,h) anthracene). Various engineered barriers (e.g., clean soil, concrete, building foundation, parking lots) were employed in different parts of the small site to cap the problem areas. The Illinois EPA issued an NFR Letter for the smaller property in January 2003, noting that the measures effectively minimized the risk of exposure for an industrial/commercial land use. The other site received its NFR letter in November 2007, using engineered barriers, along with institutional controls that prohibit the installation of potable water supply wells and require a worker safety plan for any future excavation and construction.

Project Financing

The total cost to clean and redevelop the brownfield property and vacant building came to $14.4 million (US Green Building Council, 2008). Management of the construction and demolition waste that was illegally stored onsite cost the DOE $9 million ($6 million to dispose of unrecyclable debris and $3 million to crush and process salvageable waste material for reuse). Loans and incentives from the HUD, the EPA, and General Obligation Bonds consolidated through the CBI financed cleanup and remediation. The remaining $5.4 million for the construction and renovation of the building and property came from a settlement between the city and the Commonwealth Edison Company (US Green Building Council, 2008).

The CCGT completed construction in 2002. It was subsequently certified LEED Platinum in 2003. As planned, the building is a mixed-used commercial and manufacturing facility that also serves as a model of energy efficiency and sustainable design. The CCGT's tenants originally included Spire Solar and Greencorps Chicago, as well as a satellite office for DOE field employees. WRD Environmental, a landscape architecture firm, established its headquarters at the CCGT when Spire Solar relocated its operations elsewhere in Chicago. WRD Environmental has since partnered with the DOE to further develop the Greencorps program (US EPA, 2005a). NeighborSpace, a non-profit organization committed to the acquisition and protection of community public space, also began operating from the CCGT in 2011.

Benefits, Barriers, and Lessons Learned

While the CCGT is renowned as a model of energy efficiency and technology, the success attributed to its design and redevelopment benefitted from a broader vision for economic, environmental, and social sustainability. Through this integrated approach, the CCGT became an incubator for urban revitalization in one of Chicago's most economically distressed industrial corridors (see project timeline, Table 3.1).

In the early 1990s, Chicago's economy was affected by de-industrialization synonymous with rustbelt decline. The city recognized that public intervention was necessary to remediate and redevelop brownfields. This is particularly true of Mayor Richard Daley, who commented that "if the city doesn't take responsibility for brownfield sites like this, no one else will" (Henderson, 2002). Chicago adopted an integrated approach to employment-oriented development and introduced strategies that considered the environmental and economic conditions of the affected industrial areas – the CBI and the Kinzie Industrial Conservation Area Redevelopment Project, an economic policy to stimulate development through Tax Increment Financing. As such, the transformation of the brownfield to the CCGT was possible because of Chicago's strategy of linking environmental restoration with industrial real estate development to create jobs and generate tax revenue (US EPA, 2005a). Accordingly, several factors contributed to the development of the CCGT as a model, such as public leadership, funding, and support from senior levels of government, changing attitudes, and perhaps most importantly, timing. Each factor was a necessary condition but would have been insufficient on its own.

Through this strategic approach, the CCGT has contributed to the revitalization of the distressed Kinzie corridor by demonstrating the benefits of constructing energy-efficient and sustainably designed buildings. The CCGT also contributed to employee retention in the Kinzie corridor by retaining 450 jobs from a neighboring company that was planning to leave the city and employment growth through the creation of 38 new jobs. Moreover, by providing opportunities for job training through Greencorps Chicago, the CCGT has the potential to create additional employment opportunities (US EPA, 2005b).

CCGT has also sparked the creation of a small "green" cluster of landscape-oriented businesses next to the site. Christy Webber Landscapes is a full-service landscape company that works throughout Chicago. Their LEED Platinum headquarters building, known as Rancho Verde,

Industrial and Commercial Redevelopment   41

has won numerous awards for its innovative, environmentally sensitive approach to the redevelopment of a brownfield site. Charles J. Fiore Nursery and Landscape Supply sell premium grade plant materials, stone, and landscape products to the building industry and home gardeners.

The successful implementation of green design principles in the development of the CCGT provided the city with the momentum to expand its application in future projects. This was accomplished through changes to building codes, site planning, and zoning requirements to address stormwater management and the urban heat island effect on a site-by-site basis.

Limited financial resources were the main barrier to the development of the CCGT. While there was no shortage of ideas to increase energy efficiency or restore ecological functions, it was impossible to implement them all according to interviewees. Trade-offs were necessary to prevent the project from going over budget and to adhere to other principles of sustainability so that "one kind of environmental virtue had to be weighed against another, and any virtue had to be weighed against the cost of obtaining it" (Henderson, 2002). For instance, extensive landscaping was added to the project at a premium cost but considered vital because it contributed to the creation of a stormwater best management practice. Acquiring the right technical expertise to build, monitor, and maintain the facility was also considered a challenge because many of the renewable energy technologies were new at the time.

The CCGT evolved to offer public education programming due to overwhelming interest from the community. While this came as a bit of a surprise, it was later acknowledged that community consultation during the design and development phase would have avoided this oversight (United States Conference of Mayors, 2010). Doug Farr of the design team commented that the addition of classrooms, or the flexibility to add them through an adaptable design, would have also been considered. Linkages to the community have fortunately become more established through the Center's educational activities and collaborative relationship with Greencorps Chicago. While the benefits of providing public tours, workshops, and green building resources were initially felt to outweigh the costs, an ongoing barrier to offering these services was the need to sustain funding for staffing and service delivery. Some of these barriers were addressed through partnerships with building tenants and creative thinking from city staff and volunteers. Still, unfortunately, the educational component of the CCGT was shut down in 2014 after struggling with funding following the retirement of its vital supporter, former Mayor Richard M. Daley, in 2011.

Milwaukee's Menomonee River Valley[1]

Site History

The Menomonee River Valley project is a successful attempt to revitalize the industrial heart of the city of Milwaukee – rebuilding the industrial district while incorporating sustainability, remediation, and reintegration into the local community. The Valley has always played a pivotal role in the economic life of the city. It spans almost half a mile north to south and three miles east to west, with an area of over 1,200 acres. Flowing through it is the Menomonee River, whose abundant natural resources once sustained Native American populations. The Valley's accessibility to railways, Lake Michigan, and local river systems made it a prime location for industrial activity in the 1800s. In 1869, a group of business leaders supported by

42 Industrial and Commercial Redevelopment

Table 3.1 Timeline – Chicago Center for Green Technology

Year	Description
1952	Construction of the original building at 445 N. Sacramento Blvd, Chicago, Illinois
1995	Chicago DOE discovers "environmental mess" at 445 N. Sacramento Blvd site
1995–1996	The Chicago DOE takes legal action against the Sacramento Crushing Company for violating the conditions of its permit to recycle construction debris
1996	The Sacramento Crushing Company files for bankruptcy
1997	The Chicago DOE acquires ownership of the property
1997–1998	The site is cleared of 600,000 tons of waste and debris at a cost of $9 million
1999–2001	The Chicago Department of Environment collaborates with the US Department of Energy's Brightfields program and a design team led by Farr Associates to experiment with the design of an energy efficient building
2002	The CCGT opens to the public
2003	The CCGT is certified LEED Platinum by the US GBC
2003	The Comprehensive NFR letter is issued by the Illinois EPA after the city of Chicago fulfilled the Site Remediation Program requirements for brownfield remediation
2003	Chicago Building Congress Merit Award; American Institute of Architects Top Ten Green Building Award; US EPA Phoenix Award
2011	NeighborSpace moves into CCGT
2014	Chicago Center for Green Technology ceases operations, but tenants remain

local authorities planned a network of canals and slips in the Valley that were surrounded by parcels of land for industrial use (Gurda, 1999). The project took a decade to complete and required vast quantities of material to fill in the marsh, including dredge spoil, gravel, and municipal and industrial wastes. Larger industrial complexes, including tanneries, breweries, stockyards, and railroad shops, dotted the Valley by the late 1800s (Gurda, 2003). The transformation of the Valley from a natural system to an industrialized one is the feature that has most epitomized Milwaukee's evolution and, unfortunately, highlights the unsustainable model of past industrialization efforts.

By the end of the 19th century, dense residential communities spread along the Valley's bluffs. Industry prospered well into the 1920s, and only the Great Depression could curtail its growth, which quickly picked up again during World War II. The industrial engine began to decelerate, however, in the decades following the war. Highway construction made it possible for people to live further away from their workplace and for manufacturers to use roads instead of rail and water to transport goods. Although the opening of Milwaukee County Stadium in 1953 and the Valley Power Plant in 1969 did breathe some life into the district, it suffered the same fate as many industrial areas in the rustbelt. It witnessed employment drop from over 50,000 jobs in the 1920s to approximately 20,000 jobs in the mid-1970s to barely 7,095 jobs by 1997 (city of Milwaukee, 1975; White et al., 1988). With its economic decline, a host of problems emerged in the Valley and its surrounding neighborhoods, including unemployment, a reduced tax base, and pollution.

Project Vision

The vision for a revitalized Menomonee Valley evolved in a coordinated manner, with many studies and collaborative initiatives employed to address historical perceptions and discern future directions. While the city made a few efforts to revitalize the Valley in the late 1970s (i.e., rebuilding several roads, clearing blight, acquiring land, and locating a handful of city facilities in the area), more attention was devoted to its renewal when Mayor John Norquist took office in 1988 (Gurda, 2003). Given that several longstanding manufacturers continued to operate in the Valley, there also emerged a new desire for amenities to reconnect it with the surrounding community. Amenities contemplated, planned, or added in the early 1990s included Marquette University's Valley Fields athletic complex, the Potawatomi Bingo and Casino, a new stadium for the Milwaukee Brewers, and the Hank Aaron State Greenway Trail. These projects, along with the rapid conversion of warehouse and industrial property into residential lofts and retail shops in the Historic Third Ward just east of the Valley, made it necessary for the city and affected stakeholders to decide on the future of this industrial district. Fortunately, Milwaukee's Department of City Development, local businesses, and critical stakeholders in the surrounding community did come to a general agreement that the area needed to be revitalized to provide "family-supporting" jobs.

The city of Milwaukee prepared a plan for the Valley entitled *Market Study, Engineering, and Land Use Plan for the Menomonee Valley* (city of Milwaukee, 1998) in 1998 that was a vital step in the evolution of the project's vision. A critical component of this plan was a preliminary analysis of the status of the Valley as it related to stakeholder desires, real estate market conditions, engineering infrastructure, and environmental pollution. Public outreach and stakeholder participation efforts, including workshops, interviews, and surveys, revealed that many wished to see industry remain and expand in the Valley. Manufacturers were concerned, however, about whether the haphazard mixing of entertainment and other uses would affect the long-term viability of heavy manufacturing. Market research revealed the importance of existing manufacturing employment in the area. It also highlighted the attributes for manufacturers offered by the Valley, such as its central location, access to freeways, proximity to downtown, and access to labor. The successful office conversion of a large tannery complex in the eastern end of the Valley also pointed to the potential for growth in that sector, raising the possibility that office uses might act as a buffer against escalating residential and retail encroachment from the east. While the plan found additional recreational space was not required to serve residents, there was support for passive green space to enhance the image of the district and to serve as functional infrastructure for flood control, biking and walking. Research and public outreach also revealed that there was little appetite for retail activity in the Valley, given that it would compete with struggling retail in surrounding neighborhoods and emerging retail in the Historic Third Ward.

An engineering analysis prepared for the city's plan revealed access to rail and water was an asset, but access and circulation for vehicles, transit, and pedestrians needed significant improvement. As for environmental conditions, very little comprehensive information about soil and groundwater contamination could be pulled together for the plan, but what did exist pointed to a high likelihood of brownfield issues resulting from over a century of heavy manufacturing and landfilling.

In all, the plan recommended the Valley be upgraded and revitalized to retain and strengthen existing industries, attract new industries in the west and center, promote "compatible" mixed-use development (mainly in the eastern end), and maintain and protect adjacent neighborhoods and business areas. Based on preliminary research and consultation, the plan recommended several action items to move the project forward (city of Milwaukee, 1998):

- a public/private partnership should be formed to implement the Land Use Plan;
- the city of Milwaukee zoning ordinance should be amended to facilitate the implementation of the Land Use Plan;
- environmental and soil analyses should be undertaken at all sites suitable for redevelopment in the priority areas;
- financing for environmental remediation and site improvements should be made available;
- a Partnership and other official representatives of the city should take the leadership role in promoting redevelopment within the Valley;
- land uses that degrade the environment or impede redevelopment should be eliminated;
- roadway reconstruction projects to support redevelopment in the Valley should be undertaken; and
- the appearance of the Menomonee Valley should be enhanced through the creation of green space and other visual amenities.

Although the city produced the plan in consultation with many stakeholders, its first action item was to formalize the emerging public-private partnership by establishing the Menomonee Valley Partners (MVP) in November 1999. Supported initially with funds from a US EPA Brownfields Redevelopment Pilot Grant ($200,000) received by the city in 1998, the MVP became a 501(c)(3) non-profit organization that would facilitate business, neighborhood, and public partners in efforts to revitalize the Valley. MVP hired its first staff member in 2000 and continues to operate. The MVP is advised by a board of directors with 20 stakeholders committed to and affected by the Valley's future. Stakeholders are required to work together to develop and implement action agenda items in a manner that respects the interests of the other partners. At the same time, the individual members indirectly commit to ensuring that their own activities contribute to moving the vision of the partnership forward.

It is important to note that while the MVP was a new entity, members of the MVP board represented longstanding and respected businesses, non-profits, and civic organizations that had been operating in the local community well before the 1990s. This structure also helped formalize the role of stakeholders in the partnership, balance power among participants, and enhance the credibility of individual members. Other key stakeholder groups that played pivotal roles in developing and implementing the Valley vision include public partners (the city of Milwaukee's Department of City Development and Department of Public Works, the Wisconsin Department of Natural Resources, and the Wisconsin Department of Transportation), business partners (Menomonee Valley Business Improvement District BID#26, established in 1999), and the Sixteenth Street Community Health Center, a local non-profit operating in the neighborhood south of the Valley since the late 1960s which led the charge for a vision that incorporated sustainability principles.

Incorporating sustainability into the visioning process was considered an essential matter to stakeholders. In 1999, the EPA awarded a $250,000 grant to the Sixteenth Street

Community Health Center through its Sustainable Development Challenge Grant program to look into ways of incorporating sustainability into the Valley's redevelopment. Sixteenth Street and PDI, a private consulting group then under the management of a professor from UW-Milwaukee's School of Architecture and Urban Planning, organized a two-day charrette in which design professionals, non-profits, government agencies, local universities, students, and community members were charged with the task of raising the bar on redevelopment and restoration activities for Milwaukee's Menomonee River Valley. The goal was to forge a strategy that could attract high-quality investors and family-supporting jobs to the Valley, restore property value to the tax rolls, and re-establish a sense of pride in the community while reducing environmental impacts.

Seven Keys for Sustainability were put forward to guide the charrette and link it to the city's Land Use Plan and the infrastructure activities planned for the Valley. These included: (1) transportation and circulation, access, and linkage, responsive to infrastructure plans; (2) mixed-use and density; (3) bundling utilities in a single corridor; (4) cost-effective environmental remediation and engineered solutions based on site conditions and uses; (5) green building; (6) open space and habitat restoration; and (7) utilizing the river as an amenity. The charrette resulted in the production of a comprehensive report entitled *Vision for Smart Growth* outlining ideas for the eastern, central, and western portions of the Valley (Sixteenth Street Community Health Center, 2000). The exciting plans and designs addressed each of the Keys for Sustainability. They provided an inspiring description of "what could be," which brought further attention to the Valley's assets and potential. The report also confirmed that a broader sustainably oriented approach was both viable and attractive.

Project Characteristics and Development

The account of the Valley's redevelopment is described below in a spatial manner, focusing first on Valley-wide considerations, then sub-regions (west, east, south), followed by a description of some specific projects. It should be noted that many of these initiatives occurred simultaneously (see Table 3.2). In terms of Valley-wide considerations, those involved in the redevelopment knew early on that it was necessary to address two primary issues, the negative stigma associated with what had become Wisconsin's most notorious brownfield and the Valley's poor accessibility. To provide information on environmental and soil conditions, the MVP, city of Milwaukee, Wisconsin Department of Natural Resources (DNR), EPA, and the US Geologic Survey conducted soil and groundwater investigations. Of particular concern were initial indications that groundwater flow might be moving between parcels, which meant contamination could be spreading, and the cleanup of one property might not improve groundwater conditions adequately (Dunning et al., 2004). The city of Milwaukee used funds from an EPA Brownfields Redevelopment Pilot Grant to also conduct an ESA using an "area-wide" approach. The study was divided into two parts: a physical characterization of the groundwater (location, flow, etc.) and chemical sampling to assess area-wide contamination. Modeling for the physical characterization revealed the two significant receptors for shallow groundwater were Milwaukee's Deep Tunnel System and Lake Michigan. Fortunately, the travel time to these receptors was very slow, allowing many dissolved contaminants to naturally attenuate.

To complete the physical characterization and begin chemical sampling, the city of Milwaukee received an additional $150,000 from the EPA. Sampling revealed that groundwater impacts higher than background or DNR regulatory standards were not present on a Valley-wide basis, and groundwater quality at any point in the Valley was reflective of its relative location. Thus, sites with no soil contamination were unlikely to find groundwater contamination. Furthermore, subsurface conditions were found to be conducive to biodegradation, making natural attenuation a viable remedial option for groundwater contamination related to specific properties. Overall, the study concluded that there was a minimal risk from existing groundwater contamination, which alleviated many area-wide concerns. While individual properties may have had site-specific concerns, therefore, their respective landowners and purchasers could manage them individually without fear of re-contamination by adjacent parcels (Dunning et al., 2004).

As for sub-regional considerations, several significant projects were initiated in the early 1990s to improve access and mobility within the Valley, including the Hank Aaron State Trail, Miller Park, the Sixth Street Viaduct, and Canal Street. While the individual projects are each important, more significant was the fact that the group of projects brought the attention and resources of various stakeholders and government agencies to the Valley. In 1991, the Wisconsin State Legislature directed the DNR to study the feasibility of establishing a Henry Aaron State Park on the Menomonee River adjacent to the demolished old Milwaukee County Stadium (Wisconsin Department of Natural Resources, 1996). More comprehensive planning for a greenway trail to connect the Valley from west to east started in 1992, with the DNR taking the lead in planning, constructing, and managing the trail. Other partners included the city of Milwaukee (involved primarily in raising funds, releasing land, and maintaining the trail), various federal agencies (financial support), local community groups and neighborhood associations (e.g., Friends of the Hank Aaron State Trail have helped to raise awareness and funds), and private landowners (e.g., Miller Park Stadium Corporation and The Sigma Group, an engineering firm located in the Valley, donated easements for the trail and helped to finance development and re-naturalization activities). The state trail, Wisconsin's first in an urban area, officially opened in 2000 on the Valley's west side and was connected to Sixth Street in the Valley's east end by 2007.

Construction of Miller Park for the Milwaukee Brewers also commenced in late 1996 and was completed in 2001. As part of the project, 260 acres immediately surrounding the stadium were improved through the expenditure of $72 million in government funds, with $36 million from the state of Wisconsin, $18 million from Milwaukee County, and $18 million from the city of Milwaukee (Munsey & Suppes, 2007). Much of this went to improving accessibility to the stadium and the west end of the Valley through freeway relocation, new entrances and exits, and new roads and walkways. Numerous amenities and landscaping features were added around the stadium that complemented the Hank Aaron Trail and provided Brewer fans with a glimpse of what a revitalized Valley could look like.

On the opposite end of the Valley, long-term discussions about replacing the almost 100-year-old Sixth Street Viaduct were beginning to bear fruit. The city and state signed an agreement in 1991, affirming the city as the lead agency responsible for the design and construction of the viaduct. Construction costs of $50 million were to be shared between the state (75%), County (12.5%), and city (12.5%) (Lovely, 2001). Despite several delays, construction commenced in 2000, and what could have been a standalone bridge project was now touted as a "Gateway to the Menomonee Valley." The sleek, sail-like cable-stayed bridge took 15 months to construct and slopes down 900 feet (274 meters) from the north end of the Valley to bring vehicles and people down into the Valley floor at Canal Street, then slopes back up to meet the south end.

With significant new access points on the west and east ends, the next major infrastructure project was the reconstruction of Canal Street to connect the two. The city and state began to reconstruct Canal Street from the Sixth Street Viaduct west to 25th Street east beginning in 2004. That project included pavement reconstruction, new traffic signals, a railroad spur, a multi-use trail, and a roundabout at 25th Street. In the summer of 2004, the governor of Wisconsin and Milwaukee's Mayor announced a package to use $5 million in federal transportation funds and $3 million in city funds to extend Canal Street from 25th Street west to Miller Park. The project was completed in 2006 at an estimated cost of over $40 million, with approximately $2.5 million for demolition and site remediation.

Attention was also given to pedestrian and bicycle mobility in the Valley, with improvements to stairwells descending into it from several overpasses and construction of the Valley Passage, which opened on November 8, 2010. The Valley Passage, consisting of a bridge, railroad underpass, and trail, re-established a historical connection from the Valley to Milwaukee's dense southside neighborhoods. It was constructed through a partnership between the Wisconsin Department of Transportation, Wisconsin Department of Natural Resources, the city of Milwaukee, Menomonee Valley Partners, and the Urban Ecology Center (Menomonee Valley Partners, 2011). The DOT led the design and construction of the Valley Passage and Trail extension, while it and the other partners acquired land and secured funding from the federal government (which covered more than 80% of costs) and other sources (e.g., DNR's Knowles-Nelson Stewardship Program). The city of Milwaukee maintains the trail lighting, bridge, and retaining walls.

To ensure new construction in the Valley met sustainability-oriented objectives, the Sixteenth Street Community Health Center, MVP, and the city initiated consultation in 2002 to develop guidelines for green building and family-sustaining wages. The Menomonee Valley Sustainable Design Guidelines provide guidance and lessons learned from other projects to help simplify sustainable design, enhance building performance, improve aesthetic quality, and expedite local and state permitting and approvals processes (Menomonee Valley Partners, 2006). The first iteration of the guidelines was completed in 2004, in line with the US Green Building Council's LEED rating system, and touches on the following issues:

- site design – site analysis & planning, stormwater management, natural landscaping, parking & transportation, exterior site lighting;
- building design & energy use – building design, energy efficiency, daylighting & internal lighting, alternative energy, building commissioning;
- materials & resources – exterior & interior materials, water conservation;
- construction & demolition – waste & recycling, erosion & dust control, pre-occupancy controls for indoor air quality;
- indoor environmental quality – indoor air quality, acoustic quality;

- operations & maintenance – operations manual & monitoring, facility maintenance, maintenance and stewardship of site and landscape elements (Menomonee Valley Partners, 2006).

According to the MVP, by 2011, 12 companies had incorporated green building elements into their projects, and it hit a milestone soon after of one million square feet of facilities built using the Menomonee Valley Sustainable Design Guidelines. The guidelines were updated in 2017 by the MVP (2017b), and all new developments in the Menomonee Valley must comply with them. To support their implementation, MVP also provides a *Guidelines Evaluation Form* to help track a development's compliance and a *Menomonee Valley Native Species List* with the trees, shrubs, forbs, and grasses native to the Valley.

In 2002, MVP also convened a workgroup of business and community representatives to establish a family-sustaining living wage target for the Valley. In 2003, MVP recommended that employers moving into the Valley pay a wage of $12 per hour, and in 2005 the recommendation was formally adopted as policy for land sales by the city. This wage was double Wisconsin's minimum wage at the time, which had been raised to $5.70 per hour in 2005 from the previous rate of $5.15 per hour. Employers not offering the Family Sustaining Wage for all employees were asked to prepare a "Sustainable Wage Plan" summarizing the steps they will take to meet the family-sustaining wage in one to three years. Employers were also encouraged to provide health insurance and to recruit a workforce reflective of the city's population via several local non-profit organizations. Given the Menomonee Valley was in a federal Renewal Community, employers could also qualify for significant tax credits ($1,500 per person) if they hired workers who live locally, although this program ended in 2009.

To track progress toward sustainability, the Sixteenth Street Community Health Center collaborated with the University of Wisconsin-Milwaukee on the Menomonee Valley Benchmarking Initiative (MVBI). The core objectives of the MVBI were: (1) to raise awareness in the community regarding the current state of the Menomonee Valley and the progress made towards its revitalization; (2) to create an information clearinghouse on data related to environmental, economic, and social indicators; (3) to promote the principles of sustainability in an urban context by exploring issues and assembling data in a more holistic manner that considers economic, environmental and social concerns; (4) to generate a practical synthesis of the raw data for the benefit of a wide variety of users; and (5) to stimulate research interest in the Valley as a complex laboratory for studying urban environments. In 2001, Indicator Work Group meetings were conducted to identify critical *issues of concern* for the Valley and to select specific *indicators* for investigating those issues. The Economic Work Group identified four key issues and 21 benchmarks, the Social/Community Work Group identified four key issues and 18 benchmarks, and the Environmental Work Group identified four key issues and 12 benchmarks (De Sousa et al., 2009).

Preparing the first MVBI report involved identifying stakeholders willing to supply existing data or gather new data, and then to report the results. While some of the data could be obtained from existing government datasets, a significant amount had to be collected from scratch. For this reason, an essential component of the MVBI process was establishing a protocol for future data collection. The results of the first *State of the Valley* study were published in 2003, with updated and expanded studies published in 2005 and 2013 (the latter funded by the same grant that funded the present research). The reports begin with an introduction to the Valley and the MVBI and include maps of the study areas. Indicator analyses are sorted into three sections (Economy, Environment, and Community), and each section commences with an introductory page that highlights the most relevant results from the section. The analysis of each indicator addresses three fundamental questions: (1) What has been measured? (i.e., benchmark, sources of data, and methodological approach); (2) Why is it important? (i.e., explains the indicator's role in achieving sustainability); and (3) How are we doing? (i.e., describes the performance of each indicator). The analysis of each indicator is summarized on a single page with tables, figures, and maps clarifying the results and providing a snapshot view of performance. Following the indicator analyses, a section entitled Vital Signs presents raw data by Census tract to be used by local community groups for their planning and programming activities (MVBI, 2005, 2013).

As for seminal projects, redevelopment of the 140-acre Milwaukee Railroad Shops property in the western end of the Valley into an industrial center provided the most exciting opportunity for stakeholders to convert sustainable visions, designs, and guidelines into a reality. In 2002, the Sixteenth Street Community Health Center, together with the city and other sponsors, organized a national design competition referred to as *Natural Landscapes for Living Communities* to plan the redevelopment and greening of the property even before the city had acquired it. Once home to a cluster of railroad-related manufacturing plants that started operation in 1879, the property was abandoned in 1985 when the Milwaukee Road went bankrupt. The blighted site later became the subject of Milwaukee's most extensive eminent domain action, and the Redevelopment Authority of the city eventually acquired the land from Chicago-based CMC Heartland Partners for $3.55 million in August of 2003.

The land use, infrastructure, and sustainability visions that had evolved during the planning and design charrette exercises became entrenched as criteria presented to four teams in a design competition (Sixteenth Street Community Health Center, 2002a, 2002b). These included designing an industrial park accommodating at least 1.2 million square feet of development, extending Canal Street, expanding the Hank Aaron State Trail, interconnecting the railroad property to Mitchell Park and neighborhoods to the north and south of the Valley, devising site-specific storm and floodwater management techniques, resolving site-specific environmental and geotechnical issues, landscaping the area, and establishing community connections to the site through open space planning, educational opportunities, and signage.

The winning design, selected in the summer of 2002, was put forward by the team of Wenk Associates, Applied Ecological Services, and the architecture, planning, and engineering firm HNTB. It incorporated the criteria above and integrated natural process and development in a manner that recognizes the Valley as an industrial and transportation hub, while also seeking to regenerate the landscape and reconnect the community (Sixteenth Street Community Health Center, 2002b). The design provided for 70 acres of light industrial development, a mile segment of the Hank Aaron State Trail, and 70 acres of streets, parks, and natural areas along the banks of the Menomonee River. From this design, the city generated the *Menomonee Valley Industrial Center and Community Park Land Use Plan* in 2006 to guide redevelopment.

To make the site shovel ready for redevelopment, the city established a $16 million TIF District in 2004 to pay the cost of site remediation, demolition, filling and grading, stormwater utilities, local roadways, and infrastructure. The site required massive cleanup, demolition, removal, and management of six miles of brick sewers, asbestos, and over a million square feet (93,000 m2) of old building foundations. Also, 700,000 cubic yards of fill were trucked from a nearby interchange project to create an environmental cap to manage risk and raise the site out of the flood plain. The city aggressively raised funds for remediation and redevelopment, winning more than 20 local, state, and federal grants and dozens of private donations totaling $24 million (Misky & Nemke, 2010). The goal of the city was to achieve flexible closure for the site so that future property owners were not required to manage environmental closure of their individual properties. In addition to soil contamination, many new buildings constructed in the Valley also require passive methane/soil gas collection systems that are funded in part by public tax credits and incentives (city of Milwaukee, 2006).

The Menomonee Valley Community Park portion of the Shops site provides an amenity for businesses located in the Valley and green space for residents. Material reuse was a vital component of this development; with building debris used to create landscaped mounds, highway project fill to raise the site, crushed concrete to build stormwater conveyance structures, glass to make pathway railings and beams to build park benches and tables (see Figure 3.2) (Misky & Nemke, 2010). The stormwater portion of the park provides public infrastructure by conveying, storing, and treating stormwater for the parcels in the industrial site, as well as for Canal Street and other internal roads. The shared stormwater facility made it unnecessary for developers to set aside land for their own private detention ponds, saving them money and allowing the city to maximize the build-out of the industrial site (see Figure 3.3). Annual management costs are shared through fees paid by individual business owners in the Industrial Center and the city.

Some of the park space was not economically feasible to develop due to its odd shape, and some portions contain demolition debris converted into vegetated bluffs that are encumbered with environmental use restrictions consistent with the Wisconsin DNR-approved Remedial Action Plan for the area (city of Milwaukee, 2006). Stakeholders worked together to transform a vacant railroad switching yard from the site, known as Airline Yards, into a 24-acre public park. In 2013, the park was opened and named "Three Bridges Park." This project included riverfront paths, community gardens, and new bridges to connect it to adjacent communities. The park is part of the Hank Aaron State Trail and provides an outdoor classroom for the Urban Ecology Center, a non-profit environmental education and stewardship group.

The Menomonee Valley Industrial Center was ready in 2006, had ten businesses by 2016, and sold the last two acres in 2018 to a commercial printing company (splat!dpi) and Badger Railing (for expansion), both to be completed by spring 2019 (Daykin, 2018). The city was ahead of schedule in terms of land sales, despite the 2008/09 economic downturn, and properties sold for slightly more than initially expected for a price similar to suburban greenfield sites (Peterangelo and Henken, 2014). While some of these firms relocated from other parts of Milwaukee (e.g., Badger Railing, Charter Wire), some foreign firms have also moved into the Valley (e.g., Ingeteam and Caleffi). Several new businesses in the Industrial Center used New Market Tax Credit loans through the Milwaukee Economic Development Corporation for their projects. MVP had noted by 2011 that there were around 1,100 jobs in the Industrial

Industrial and Commercial Redevelopment 51

Figure 3.2 Milwaukee Road Shops during demolition, Wisconsin (MVBI, 2013)

Figure 3.3 Menomonee Valley Industrial Center and Community Park, Milwaukee, Wisconsin, 2010

Center, which was on target for its goal of 1,200 jobs (C. Zetts from Menomonee Valley Partners, personal email communication, May 17, 2010). The goal was met in 2011, and by 2018 the Center had more than 1,400 employees (Daykin, 2018). The Tax Increment District also reached its target of $45 million by 2012 (city of Milwaukee, 2015a).

Following the success of the West-End's conceptual design, Wenk and Associates worked with MVP and the city to develop a vision for the central and eastern Valley. Much of the plan dealt with connecting the Valley via Canal Street and the Hank Aaron State Trail, as outlined above. Several other notable developments that occurred in the central Valley include The Sigma Group headquarters in 2003, which raised the bar on sustainable construction, the former Stockyards property, for which the living wage guidelines were initially created, and the iconic Harley Davidson Museum.

The development of a new headquarters building for The Sigma Group, an environmental engineering and services company with extensive involvement in Valley affairs, set a high bar for buildings in the Valley. Sigma addressed a variety of soil, groundwater, methane, and geotechnical challenges in the planning, design, orientation, and construction of its facility. Its site also accommodates public access to the Menomonee River with a walkway that borders the river's edge and links with the Hank Aaron Trail. Both the building and site incorporate numerous green building features, including natural daylighting, stormwater management, beneficial reuse of materials, and a high-efficiency HVAC system. The building materials also complement the neighboring drawbridge and blend in with the industrial look of the Valley. Indeed, Sigma was honored with the 2003 Mayor's Design Award for the project.

Upon completing its headquarters in December 2003, The Sigma Group worked with the Sixteenth Street Community Health Center to evaluate the impact of its project on the Menomonee Valley compared with its previous office space (The Sigma Group, 2004). The study aimed to provide measurable indicators for several dozen short- and long-term sustainability-oriented benchmarks. Variables examined related to environmental impacts (e.g., soil risk, air emissions, stormwater discharge, tree canopy, resource utilization, increase in public river access), economic/business impacts (e.g., real estate value, annual tax revenue, employment, security, aesthetics), and employment/social benefits (e.g., employee commute, employee morale, employee participation in the community). This study provided an example of how developers should consider the broader sustainability implications of their buildings on the Valley.

Another notable project across the street from Sigma is the Canal Street Commerce Center, a light industrial and office building on the former Milwaukee Stockyards property that now houses multiple businesses, including Helios USA, Wisconsin's first solar panel manufacturer. At the eastern gateway to the Valley, Milwaukee's beloved Harley Davidson constructed a museum that, while initially criticized for its low job density, was praised for incorporating the Menomonee Valley Sustainable Design Guidelines, stormwater treatment areas, and public river access.

With the Menomonee Valley Industrial Center full on the Valley's west end, the city's focus continues to shift east to create more industrial and other developable space. The city created a detailed development plan in 2009 for several parcels in the eastern and central Valley and established a $6.4 million TIF District for the 17-acre Reed Street Yards property to support public improvements such as new roads, water, sewer, a riverwalk, an extension of the Hank Aaron State Trail, and dock wall repairs (city of Milwaukee, 2009). The TIF district would also help fund the construction of building foundations and environmental remediation. The MVP also helped create the Menomonee Valley 2.0 Plan adopted by the city council on June 2, 2015. This new plan aims to establish a series of industry clusters in addition to further improving connectivity to the Valley, projecting a further 2 million square feet of industrial space and 1,700 more jobs (city of Milwaukee, 2015b). Several studies and charrettes have engaged the community in the Valley's next chapter, including the 2018 Menomonee Valley Design Charrette hosted by MVP, the city, and UW-Milwaukee that focused on 45 acres on six brownfields.

A second wave of new projects also swept into the Valley in 2018, with most set for completion in 2019. They include a second hotel tower for the Potawatomi Hotel and Casino, the conversion of a former warehouse into office space, a historic building converted into a furniture gallery, and, in true Milwaukee form, several craft breweries. The new furniture gallery is one of 22 historical buildings that are part of the St. Paul Avenue Industrial Historic District, a district targeted by the MVP that is quickly becoming a home décor and design destination for the whole region. MVP and the city continue to work to unlock and fill-in underutilized buildings and industrial spaces throughout the Valley by working with long-time owners to get these sites shovel ready for new development (Daykin, 2018). The city is also working on long-range plans to expand the RiverWalk that runs along the Milwaukee River in the downtown core, into the Menomonee River in the Valley, where the two rivers connect.

The Menomonee Valley has relied on a significant amount of funding from both public and private sources. A comprehensive review by the Public Policy Forum estimates that public sector entities contributed at least $200 million for Valley projects since 1998 ($\approx$ 45% City, 35% Federal, 20% State) (Peterangelo & Henken, 2014, p. 35). This has facilitated at least $828 million in private sector investment, including roughly $536 million from the Forest County Potawatomi, for an overall investment of more than $1 billion and return of four private dollars for every public dollar (n.b., this does not include $400 million for the Miller Park Stadium paid for primarily by a regional sales tax). The largest source of public funding for the Valley has come from six TIF districts established by the city with an authorized expenditure of $47 million, all but one performing as, or better, than expected (Peterangelo & Henken, 2014).

Benefits, Barriers, and Lessons Learned

While efforts to bring employment back to brownfields face underlying challenges from globalization and de-industrialization, Milwaukee continues to press forward in an attempt to reap the benefits that employment-oriented redevelopment brings about. The city and its partners have also raised the bar in terms of creating and implanting a vision for sustainability that not only reuses brownfield property, but incorporates family-supporting wages, sound design, ecological restoration, and linkages to the surrounding community (see timeline, Table 3.2).

One key obstacle to incorporating sustainability elements into the Valley's redevelopment that continues to pose a challenge are the real and perceived costs associated with sustainable design and landscaping. These elements added to initial expenditures, and it was sometimes difficult to convince companies of their long-term benefits. Remediating brownfields was also more complicated when combined with desires for stormwater management. Fortunately, overcoming these obstacles was facilitated by the momentum of redevelopment in the Valley, with the ongoing challenge being the expansion of roads and infrastructure to the other parts of the Valley to keep up with demand. To overcome the obstacles, several interviewees highlighted the need for more funds to encourage sustainable elements and a better understanding among government officials, as well as private businesses and community members, about the benefits of both brownfields redevelopment and sustainability.

In terms of benefits, the primary one for the city has been an increased tax base and employment, as well as indirect benefits associated with multiplier and surrounding property value effects. A key benefit to the city of incorporating sustainable elements into the development of the Valley is that it has already been a "deciding factor" for several companies in choosing the area because it complements their progressive missions. Companies also like the many amenities offered in the Valley that make it a great place to work.

Valley redevelopment has increased confidence in the city's brownfields program and has facilitated its ability to attract funding from upper levels of government. It has also led to more support for tackling more ambitious large-scale brownfield projects in other parts of the city that involve merging reindustrialization and sustainability, such as Century City and the Inner Harbor. Century City, also referred to as the 30th Street Industrial Corridor, lies in one of the city's most economically challenged districts. While attracting businesses and jobs is of the highest priority, attention is also being paid to environmental justice issues, public safety, and stormwater management. Akin to the Valley's design charrette process, city officials, faculty and students from the UW-Milwaukee and other public and private-sector stakeholders have also set out to re-envisage Milwaukee's Inner Harbor and port area. The MVP continues to lead the charge to revitalize other parts of the Valley, such as the retail district on West St. Paul Avenue on the Valley's northern border.

Several key lessons that emerge from the Menomonee Valley redevelopment experience that can be applied to other cities interested in sustainable reindustrialization and economic development include:

- make early efforts to consult and understand the needs of the community and affected stakeholders to better incorporate their ideas into visions and plans;
- involve respected stakeholders and community representatives who were active in the community before the project, will be there throughout the project, and will remain in the community long after it is completed;
- undertake market research and scientific studies to assess the scope of problems, needs, possible solution strategies, and even post-development impacts, as sound science helps demystify barriers and point to practical solutions;
- facilitate and support public-private partnerships like the Menomonee Valley Partners that allow for balanced participation of multiple stakeholders; help enhance buy-in and

Industrial and Commercial Redevelopment 55

faith in the process; and make stakeholders more willing to compromise, be patient, contribute to the process, and continue to invest in the quality of life of the businesses and residents of the region long after the projects are done;
- offer early seed funding, such as the EPA grants used in the Valley, to explore sustainability and to help incorporate it throughout the planning, development, and even post-development assessment;
- ensure that local government, in particular, is willing and capable of playing a central role in visioning, planning, site acquisition, site preparation, project funding, redevelopment, and post-closure activities;
- work tirelessly to pull together funding from all levels of government and other sources to address complex brownfield projects, infrastructure, industrial redevelopment, and sustainability.

MVP's 2017 annual report (MVP, 2017a) highlighted Milwaukee's success in revitalizing the Menomonee Valley, which includes the following:

- 300 acres of brownfields redeveloped;
- 51 new companies have opened in the Valley;
- 30,000+ people visit Three Bridges Park Annually;
- 100,000+ people use Hank Aaron State Trail;
- 1 million sq. ft. of green buildings have been constructed;
- 10 million visitors each year; and
- 5,200+ family-supporting jobs have been created.

2019 marked 20 years since the MVP was formed to help lead the transformation of the district. The 2019 annual report provides a concise timeline of projects that have become a reality and describes what comes next to keep the area thriving. Below are examples of the activities and policies aimed at making the Menomonee Valley a sustainable place to work and play. The list of initiatives continues to expand as the stakeholders and the MVP shift from property redevelopment to enhancing operations and quality of life in the district and surrounding communities.

- Economic
  - land acquisition and assembly;
  - infrastructure, access, and connectivity;
  - financial assistance for cleanup, redevelopment and job creation;
  - Business Improvement District representation;
  - business and employment resources (MVP):
    - business-to-business networking opportunities;
    - events programming;
    - employee services (health and wellness, yoga);
    - public safety resources;
    - transportation options;
    - tours of the Menomonee Valley.
  - Menomonee Valley Development Guidelines.

56 Industrial and Commercial Redevelopment

- Environmental
  - brownfields remediation and land reuse;
  - material recycling;
  - stewardship programs (MVP Stew Crews);
  - Sustainable Design Guidelines;
  - recreation areas and access (Hank Aaron State Trail, Airline Yards, canoeing and kayaking, fishing);
  - Urban Ecology Center branch (a private non-profit environmental education and community center);
  - stormwater management;
  - native planting;
  - landscape and riverbank restoration;
  - Airline Yards.
- Community/Society
  - public art;
  - tours;
  - annual events (Bike to Work Week, 5K Run, etc.);
  - Harley-Davidson Museum;
  - Marquette Valley Fields;
  - Miller Park;
  - Mitchell Park Domes;
  - Potawatomi Bingo Casino and hotel.

From a cleanup perspective, one of the most significant accomplishments made while writing the book was the case closure letter issued by Wisconsin's DNR on May 1, 2020, confirming that cleanup work in the Menomonee Valley Industrial Center was officially complete.

Table 3.2 Timeline – Milwaukee's Menomonee Valley

Year	Description
1896	Valley marsh filled to prepare site for industry
1996–2001	Miller Park construction and opening
1996	Henry Aaron State Park Trail Feasibility Study, Master Plan, and Environmental Assessment
1998	Market Study, Engineering, and Land Use Plan for the Menomonee Valley
1998	City of Milwaukee receives a US EPA Brownfields Redevelopment Pilot Grant for the Valley
1999	Menomonee Valley Business Improvement District (BID #26) formed
	Menomonee Valley Partners established
1999	Sixteenth Street Community Health Center Awarded EPA Sustainable Development Challenge Grant
1999	Menomonee River Valley Design charrette
2000	First four miles of the Hank Aaron State Trail is constructed
2002	National design competition for the Milwaukee Road (Industrial Center) site
2002	Sigma Environmental Services, Inc., Area-wide Groundwater Investigation Report for the Menomonee River Valley Brownfields Demonstration Pilot Project

Year	Description
2002	Sixth Street Viaduct constructed
2003	Menomonee Valley Benchmarking Initiative – first report published
2003	City of Milwaukee acquires former Milwaukee Road Shops property
2004	Sustainable Guidelines Created
2004	Sigma Group Building, the first green building in the Valley, opens
2004	Simulation of Groundwater Flow, Study Surface Water Flow, and a Deep Sewer Tunnel System in the Menomonee Valley, Milwaukee, Wisconsin
2006	Menomonee Valley Industrial Center and Community Park Master Land Use Plan
2006	Opening of Canal Street
2006	Hank Aaron State Trail opens
2006	Harley Davidson Museum breaks ground
2006	Stockyards property breaks ground
2006	Menomonee Valley Industrial Center's first tenant – Palermo's Pizza
2006	Falk Corporation celebrates 150 years in the Valley
2008	Canal Street Commerce Center Completed
	Harley Davidson Museum Opens
2009	Menomonee Valley Redevelopment and Community Park receive the EPA Region 5 Phoenix Award for Excellence in Brownfield Redevelopment
2010	Valley Passage opened
2012	Urban Ecology Center – Menomonee Valley Branch Opens
2013	Three-Bridges Park opens
2014	Potawatomi Hotel Grand Opening
2015	Menomonee Valley 2.0 Plan is adopted by Milwaukee Common Council
2016	Menomonee River Concrete Removal Complete
2018	Menomonee Valley Design Charrette
2018	Last two properties in the Menomonee Valley Industrial Center are under development
2019	The Wisconsin Department of Natural Resources, Milwaukee County, City of Milwaukee, Milwaukee Metropolitan Sewerage District, We Energies and the Environmental Protection Agency announced an agreement to commit funds to cleaning parts of the Milwaukee estuary and area rivers, including the confluence of the Milwaukee, Menomonee, and Kinnickinnic Rivers at the eastern end of the Valley that lead to the estuary that spills into Lake Michigan
2020	Industrial equipment manufacturer Rite-Hite releases renderings of new Milwaukee headquarters for 300 employees in Reed Street Yards at the eastern end of the Valley
2020	Wisconsin's DNR issues a case closure letter confirming completion of cleanup of Menomonee Valley Industrial Center

Note

1 Portions of this section are reproduced from De Sousa, C. (2011). Creating the green industrial district: Transforming Milwaukee's Menomonee Valley from a blighted brownfield into a sustainable place to work and play. In Matthew I. Slavin (Ed.), *Sustainability in America's Cities*. Copyright © 2011 Island Press. Reproduced by permission of Island Press, Washington, DC.

References

Camiros, Ltd., Applied Real Estate Analysis Inc., & Sonoc/Hutter/Lee Ltd. (1998). *Kinzie Industrial Conservation Area tax increment redevelopment plan and project* (Report prepared for the city of Chicago). Camiros, Ltd., Applied Real Estate Analysis Inc., & Sonoc/Hutter/Lee Ltd.

Chicago Department of Environment. (2009). *Stormwater BMP monitoring: A case study of the Chicago Center for Green Technology*. City of Chicago.

City of Chicago. (2003a). *Chicago Brownfields Initiative – Recycling our past, investing in our future*. Report prepared by Department of the Environment and the Department of Planning and Development.

City of Chicago. (2003b). *Chicago Center for Green Technology, self-guided tour*. Brochure prepared by the Department of the Environment and the Chicago Center for Green Technology.

City of Chicago. (2009). *US Conference of Mayors/Wal-Mart foundation green jobs training initiative best practices grants*. Report prepared by the city of Chicago.

City of Milwaukee. (1975). *Menomonee Valley 1975 business needs and attitudes survey* (Report prepared for the City of Milwaukee Department of City Planning). Dun and Bradstreet Inc.

City of Milwaukee. (1998). *Market study, engineering, and land use plan for the Menomonee Valley* (Report prepared for the Department of City Development, City of Milwaukee). Lockwood Greene Consulting, Fluor Daniel Consulting, Trkla, Pettigrew, Allen, and Payne, Inc., and Edwards and Associates.

City of Milwaukee. (2006). *Menomonee Valley Industrial Center and Community Park master land use plan*. Report prepared by the City of Milwaukee, Redevelopment Authority of the City of Milwaukee, Department of City Development.

City of Milwaukee. (2009). *TID 75 – Reed Street Yards, periodic report*. Report prepared by the city of Milwaukee, Department of City Development.

City of Milwaukee. (2015a). *TID 53 – Menomonee Valley Shops Periodic Report*. December 31. City of Milwaukee.

City of Milwaukee. (2015b) *Menomonee Valley 2.0: A Plan for the* Area. Milwaukee Comprehensive Plan, Department of City Development.

De Sousa, C., Gramling, B., & LeMoine, K. (2009). Evaluating progress toward sustainable development in Milwaukee's Menomonee River Valley: Linking brownfields redevelopment with community quality of life. In J. Sirgy, D. Rahtz, & R. Phillips (Eds.), *Community quality-of-life indicators: Best cases III* (pp. 80–100). Springer.

Dunning, C. P., Feinstein, D. T. Hunt, R. J., & Krohelski, J. T. (2004). *Simulation of ground-water flow, surface-water flow, and a deep sewer tunnel system in the Menomonee Valley, Milwaukee, Wisconsin*. US Department of the Interior and the US Geological Survey Scientific Investigations Report 2004-5031 conducted in cooperation with the US EPA, Region 5, and City of Milwaukee.

Daykin, T. (2018). Milwaukee's award-winning Menomonee Valley Industrial Center is ready for its second act. August 31, *Milwaukee Journal Sentinel*.

Greencorps. (2009a). *Greencorps Chicago Green Industry Job Training*. Greencorps.

Greencorps. (2009b). *Program Information*. Greencorps.

Gurda, J. (1999). *The making of Milwaukee*. Milwaukee County Historical Society.

Gurda, J. (2003). *The Menomonee Valley: A historical overview*. Report prepared for the Menomonee Valley Partners.

Henderson, H. (2002). How green can you get? May 2, *Chicago Reader*.

Higgins, J. (2008). Evaluating the Chicago Brownfields Initiative: The effects of city-initiated brownfield redevelopment on surrounding communities. *Northwestern Journal of Law and Social Policy*, 3(2), 240–262.

Lovely, L. (2001). Milwaukee's old sixth street viaduct yields to modern cable-stayed spans. July 2. Construction Equipment Guide – Midwest Edition.

Menomonee Valley Partners. (2006). *Sustainable design guidelines for the Menomonee River Valley*. Report prepared by the Menomonee Valley Partners, City of Milwaukee, and the Sixteenth Street Community Health Center.

Menomonee Valley Partners. (2011). *Valley passage*. Menomonee Valley Partners.

Menomonee Valley Partners. (2017a). *Menomonee Valley Partners annual report, 2017*. Menomonee Valley Partners.

Menomonee Valley Partners. (2017b). *Sustainable design guidelines for the Menomonee River Valley*. Report prepared by the Menomonee Valley Partners, City of Milwaukee Department of City Development.

Misky, D., & Nemke, C. (2010). From blighted to beautiful. *Government Engineering*, May–June, 14–16.

Munsey & Suppes. (2007). Milwaukee Brewers Miller Park. April 23. Ballparks.com.

MVBI. (2005). *2005 state of the Valley: Evaluating change in Milwaukee's Menomonee Valley*. Report Prepared by B. Gramling, Sixteenth Street Community Health Center, Department of Environmental Health and C. De Sousa, University of Wisconsin-Milwaukee, Center for Urban Initiatives and Research.

MVBI. (2013) *Ten years of benchmarking change in the Valley*. Report prepared in collaboration with the

University of Wisconsin-Milwaukee and the Sixteenth Street Community Health Center J. Tilidetzke, C. De Sousa and B. Gramling. https://static1.squarespace.com/static/5b1738a7f8370aa49cd05cf8/t/5bc628e90d9297fb20ed93bd/1539713266618/277-the2013mvbiintroductionpages1to11.pdf

Peterangelo, J. & Henken, R. (2014) *Redevelopment in Milwaukee's Menomonee Valley: What worked and why?* Public Policy Forum.

Sixteenth Street Community Health Center. (2000). *A Vision for smart growth: Sustainable development design charrette, Milwaukee's Menomonee River Valley 1999-2000*. Sixteenth Street Community Health Center, Department of Environmental Health.

Sixteenth Street Community Health Center. (2002a). *Menomonee River Valley national design competition, executive summary*. Competition and report sponsored by the Sixteenth Street Community Health Center, Menomonee Valley Partners Inc., the City of Milwaukee, the Milwaukee Metropolitan Sewerage District, Wisconsin Department of Natural Resources and Milwaukee County.

Sixteenth Street Community Health Center. (2002b). *Menomonee River Valley national design competition*. Sixteenth Street Community Health Center, Department of Environmental Health.

The Sigma Group. (2004). *Locating in Milwaukee's Menomonee River Valley, an impact report*. The Sigma Group and the Sixteenth Street Community Health Center.

US EPA. (2005a). *From brownfield to brightfield in Chicago, IL*. Revitalizing Southeastern Communities, A Brownfields Toolkit. US EPA Region 4.

US EPA. (2005b). *Revitalizing southeastern communities: Chicago, IL demonstrates national brownfields leadership*. Revitalizing Southeastern Communities, A Brownfields Toolkit. US EPA Region 4.

US Green Building Council. (2008). *Chicago Center for Green Building*. US Green Building Council.

United States Conference of Mayors. (2010). *Reclaiming the land, revitalizing communities - Brownfields redevelopment, a compendium of best practices, Volume 4*. United States Conference of Mayors.

White, S., Zipp, J., Paetsch, J., & Reynolds, P. (1988). *The changing Milwaukee industrial structure, 1979-1988*. The Urban Research Center, University of Wisconsin-Milwaukee.

Wisconsin Department of Natural Resources. (1996). *Henry Aaron State Trail, feasibility study master plan and environmental assessment*. Menomonee Valley Greenway Advisory Committee, National Park Service, and Wisconsin Department of Natural Resources.

Interviews

Chicago Center for Green Technology

- Durnbaugh, A. (2009). Deputy Commissioner, Department of Environment, city of Chicago.
- Graham, D. (2009). Department of Environment, city of Chicago.
- Moloney, S. (2009). Project Coordinator, Chicago Center for Green Technology, Department of Environment, city of Chicago.
- Worthington, K. (2009, 2014). Deputy Commissioner, Urban Management and Brownfields Redevelopment, Department of Environment, city of Chicago.

Milwaukee's Menomonee River Valley

- Misky, D. (2011). Assistant Executive Director, Redevelopment Authority of the city of Milwaukee.
- Zetts, C. (2010) Associate Director, Menomonee Valley Partners.

4 Office Redevelopment

While manufacturing reached its highest share of total employment in the US in 1968 and has been undergoing a steady decline ever since, there has fortunately been a concomitant rise in service-based work feeding a growing demand for office space (Chapman and Walker, 1991). The case studies described in this chapter include a landmark adaptive reuse project in Baltimore that turned an abandoned Montgomery Ward warehouse into a green building that set a standard for heritage preservation and is the largest office property in Greater Baltimore. The Heifer International World Headquarters project in Little Rock, Arkansas, helped turn the state's largest cluster of brownfields into a LEED Platinum-certified building where the humanitarian agency can pursue the global mission of alleviating poverty and hunger through sustainable development. As with the cases in the previous chapter, these projects helped advance revitalization in struggling neighborhoods near the central core.

Montgomery Park, Baltimore, Maryland

Montgomery Park Business Center (MPBC) is another trendsetting and award-winning adaptive reuse brownfield project located in Baltimore, Maryland. Project developer Himmelrich Associates, Inc. has demonstrated leadership in its sensitive conversion of the vacant 1.3 million sq. ft., eight-story, nationally listed art deco heritage Catalogue House building into a LEED Gold caliber office building. Remediation of the brownfield occurred under the auspices of Maryland's Department of the Environment, which is also a tenant of the building (see Figure 4.1). The ambitious project utilized a variety of brownfields, heritage retention, and green building tax incentives and financing tools from the city of Baltimore, state of Maryland, and the Federal Government (The Center for Brownfields Initiatives at the University of New Orleans, 2010). While it came to the market during the Great Recession, a steadily growing list of tenants from both the private and public sector have leased over 65% of the building space, and over 1,800 workers are onsite daily (Paull, n.d.a). An estimated 3,500 to 5,000 workers will be onsite when the building is fully leased.

Office Redevelopment 61

Figure 4.1 Montgomery Park, Baltimore, Maryland, 2010

Site History

The MPBC is in the Baltimore-West office submarket approximately 1.5 miles southwest of the Central Business District (CBRE, 2013). The site is adjacent to Washington Boulevard, an essential cross-town arterial road, and close to Interstate 95, Interstate 395, and state highways 295 and 1. The building sits on a 16.5-acre parcel of land that is part of a 27.5-acre site divided by a railway. The property is located in an industrial area and is part of the West Baltimore Empowerment Zone (Paull, n.d.a). Neighboring buildings include a gasoline station, an MTA bus terminal, Carroll Park (recreational park owned by the city), and assorted industrial buildings.

Commercial enterprises have continuously occupied the site since the beginning of the 20th century. Industrial land uses have included brick manufacturing, paint and varnish production, and general manufacturing (Maryland Department of the Environment, 2001). The former Catalog House office building dates back to 1927 when construction finished on a new Mid-Atlantic regional distribution center and headquarters for the Montgomery Ward catalog company (Himmelrich Associates, Inc., 2013). Energetic lobbying by the Baltimore Association of Commerce and local elected officials convinced the Montgomery Ward company that Baltimore was an advantageous location for a new regional headquarters and distribution center (Himmelrich Associates, Inc., 2013). The enormous 1.3 million sq. ft. eight-story structure was built between 1925 and 1927 by Wells Bros. Construction Company and featured 143,000 sq. ft. floors, high ceilings, art deco architectural details, a clean whitewash façade, a large rooftop sign, and extensive surface parking (National Parks Service, 2000).

Understanding the history of land uses on the site was critical to the redevelopment of the MPBC project. According to Sanford Fire Insurance records, a large gas station with six gasoline storage tanks was built on the MPBC property fronting Washington Boulevard before 1950 and demolished in 1968 (Maryland Department of the Environment, 2001). In 1961, the gas station expanded to include a 14-garage bay automobile service facility with a 500-gallon waste oil underground storage tank (Maryland Department of the Environment, 2001). The service station expanded further to include an additional service facility building with two garage bays and hydraulic lifts where both private and Montgomery Ward-owned vehicles were fuelled and serviced (Maryland Department of the Environment, 2001).

Project Vision

MPBC is a premier Class-A office complex with cutting-edge green building attributes. Samuel Himmelrich Jr's vision for the project in 2000 was to save the building from being demolished, retain a nationally significant piece of Baltimore's built heritage, and create a modern office development that would attract tenants, generate profit, and nurture the Baltimore knowledge economy. The project also serves as a model for both the successful redevelopment of a brownfield site and a productive working partnership between the project proponent and several levels of government. From the outset of the renovation and redevelopment process, a consistent goal was to create a high-performance green building that was economically advantageous for its owner and tenants. From this flowed an emphasis on proven, low-maintenance green building features that would reduce operating costs while improving tenant productivity. The project gained access to several funding mechanisms, including grants, due to the inclusion of green building features, the preservation and restoration of a nationally listed historic building, and the site's location within an Empowerment Zone.

Project Characteristics and Development

MPBC incorporates a wide array of green building features working toward LEED Gold accreditation by the US Green Building Council (Himmelrich Associates, Inc., 2013). The green building features target three categories: (1) site features; (2) building features – exterior; and (3) building features – interior. The single most significant green site feature of the project is its reuse of the existing site and structure of the building. Preserving the building and restoring it within heritage conservation guidelines extends the useful life of the original materials and energy inputs and minimizes the new materials, energy, and capital. The pavers near the building entrance were salvaged from the floor of a factory elsewhere in Baltimore, diverting them from the waste stream. Stormwater infiltrates through the "Red" surface parking lot due to the porous "Glassphalt" paving material made of crushed glass recovered from the building's 70,000 original single-pane windows (Maryland Department of the Environment, 2003). Native, drought-tolerant plants that require no irrigation and limited maintenance were also selected for site landscaping. Stormwater is also channeled into bioretention ponds that trap and filter stormwater runoff. A drain field at the bottom of Monroe Street collects rainwater from Monroe Street and the MPBC property. A sand filtration system cleans this non-potable greywater, and it is pumped to an underground 10,000 gallon cistern used for toilet flushing (Maryland Department of the Environment, 2003). Cycling end-of-trip facilities include a secure bike lock-up area and changing room with showers. A local bus stop is located adjacent to the MPBC, and a state grant helped support the initial operation of a morning and evening shuttle bus connecting it to Camden Station with bus and light rail transit services (Maryland Department of the Environment, 2003).

As for the building's exterior, a signature feature of the redevelopment is the creation of 30,000 sq. ft. of green roofs across the complex (Maryland Department of the Environment, 2001). A $92,000 grant from the US EPA helped underwrite the cost of the green roofs (Maryland Department of the Environment, 2001). The purpose of the green roofs is to minimize stormwater runoff, reduce building energy costs by increasing the effective roof insulation, reduce noise transmission from rooftop mechanical equipment to interior workspace, and to improve the visible appeal of the rooftops. The green roof assembly is made of a PVC membrane sitting on the roof, Styrofoam insulation board, two layers of textile fabric to prevent root penetration, and 4 inches of soil with a maximum weight load of 18 pounds per square inch (Maryland Department of the Environment, 2003). The soil mixture is 75-80% inert expanded slate from an abandoned local quarry mixed with 20-25% water-soluble, nutrient-rich organic material comprised of mushroom substrate sourced from a local organic mushroom farm (Maryland Department of the Environment, 2003). They were seeded with hardy, drought-tolerant plants with a density of approximately two plants per square foot, for a total of 61,000 plants (Maryland Department of the Environment, 2003). Upon maturity, the green roofs aim to reduce peak roof temperature to approximately 80 degrees, while a standard bare roof can reach up to 140 degrees (Maryland Department of the Environment, 2003).

The MPBC has 70,000 windows that were all replaced during the redevelopment. The original steel casings were preserved, and the panes of glass were removed and pulverized to create the "Glassphalt" permeable paving surface used in the building's "Red" parking lot. Modern double-paned commercial glazing was installed, and every third set can be opened to allow for cross-ventilation cooling and fresh air. The glazing features several energy-saving attributes: "low-E" coatings that reduce the transmission of heat from the sun to the interior of the building, and invisible argon gas is sealed between the windowpanes to improve the window assembly's insulating properties (Maryland Department of the Environment, 2003). The new windows exceeded Maryland efficiency guidelines while still retaining the minimum 75% daylight transmission qualities stipulated by preservation guidelines (Maryland Department of the Environment, 2003).

The MPBC utilizes an innovative Ice Storage Tank cooling system to reduce energy consumption. The system consists of a rooftop tank that contains filtered greywater, through which runs a sealed coiled pipe containing a water-ethylene glycol mixture (Maryland Department of the Environment, 2003). During the night, when electricity rates are low, a conventional refrigeration unit cools the water-ethylene glycol mixture in the pipe to 17 degrees Fahrenheit. It circulates it through the water in the tank, causing the water to freeze solid (Maryland Department of the Environment, 2003). During the day, when electricity rates are high, the building's HVAC system uses heat exchangers to draw waste heat out of the building's indoor air exhaust vents. The waste heat energy from the air is transferred through a heat exchanger to the water-ethylene glycol mixture and piped through the frozen water block in the rooftop ice storage tanks. As the mixture passes through the ice block, it drops in temperature to approximately 45 degrees Fahrenheit and contributes to the slow melting of the ice block throughout the day. The cooled water-ethylene glycol mixture then passes through a pre-chiller heat exchanger on the building's fresh air intake system, which lowers the temperature of the air before it reaches the air conditioning unit (Maryland Department of the Environment, 2003). The water-ethylene glycol mixture then completes the loop by passing again through the heat exchanger on the indoor air exhaust system.

The Ice Storage Tank system works in concert with an "economizer" automated building control suite that measures the temperature and properties of indoor and outdoor air using a network of sensors. The economizer evaluates how much heating or cooling is required to reach the desired indoor air temperature and factors in the heating and cooling capacity of the exhaust heat recovery units and the Ice Storage Tank system (Maryland Department of the Environment, 2003). The economizer also measures indoor carbon dioxide levels and pumps additional fresh oxygen-rich outdoor air into the building's air handling system to ensure productive and comfortable indoor air quality.

As for the building interior, all lights were also replaced during the renovation. The primary indoor workspaces have high-efficiency, low-mercury fluorescent lights. Ambient light sensors control the number of lights lit in each ballast to deliver a consistently comfortable indoor light level while minimizing electricity consumption (Maryland Department of the Environment, 2003). Ambient light sensors also control the wattage of lights throughout the building to save electricity and maximize productivity. LED exit lights were used throughout the building and require (up to) 87.5% less power than conventional incandescent bulbs (Maryland Department of the Environment, 2003).

The building uses a raised floor system that creates a continuous void space below the load-bearing floor tiles where water and plumbing are run, along with electrical conduit, telecommunications, and networking cables, and air handling vents. This system greatly simplifies the installation and upgrade of utilities and services in the building, allowing for easy maintenance and cleaning access. It facilitates the reorganization of floor plans to suit changing tenant needs or the emergence of new technologies. The raised floor structure used in the renovation was recycled from a building renovation project in New York City.

The carpeting used throughout the MPBC is a square tile system made up of 18" x 18" tiles (Maryland Department of the Environment, 2003). This system allows tiles in high-traffic areas that become worn or damaged to be individually removed and replaced, and simplifies access to the raised floor system. The "Earth Squares" carpet tiles are manufactured by the Milliken Company of Spartanburg, South Carolina, in a process that uses 100% post-consumer waste as feedstock for the creation of new tiles (Maryland Department of the Environment, 2003). To partially meet the needs of the massive facility, 230,000 sq. ft. of carpet was removed during a renovation from a Federal Building in Texas and remanufactured by washing, re-texturing, and re-coloring the original carpet and cutting it into tiles.

In addition to carpeting, Marmoleum and Bamboo flooring are used in the break rooms and reception area, respectively (Maryland Department of the Environment, 2003). Marmoleum is a type of linoleum made from plentiful natural raw materials (Linseed oil, Wood flour, Cork flour, Rosin, natural pigments free of heavy metals, and Jute) (Maryland Department of the Environment, 2003). The bamboo floors use Mao Zhu bamboo, which renews rapidly, sourced from Greenwood Products Company, which guarantees the lowest formaldehyde emissions in the industry and exceeds all US indoor air quality standards (Maryland Department of the Environment, 2003).

All of the toilets in the MPBC use non-potable greywater that is captured from rainfall and the Monroe Street sand-filtered field drain and stored in a 10,000-gallon cistern. The completely waterless urinals in the MPBC men's rooms were the first in Baltimore, and each saves up to 45,000 gallons of water annually (Maryland Department of the Environment, 2003). Significant water savings are also realized through low-flow dual-flush toilets, aerated faucets in all the washrooms and kitchens, and low-flow showerheads in the fitness center (Maryland Department of the Environment, 2003). Recycled content is used throughout the restrooms. The concrete sink tops are recycled, ceramic tiling is sourced from 70% post-consumer sources, and the plastic used in the stall doors is sourced from 100% post-consumer sources (Maryland Department of the Environment, 2003).

Creating a productive work environment is the most critical aspect of designing an office building. The original floor plates of the MPBC are inherently energy-efficient due to the presence of high ceilings and a relatively shallow distance between the outer edge of the building and the interior. At the time of the MPBC's design in the mid-1920s, interior lighting was dim by modern standards, and architects had no choice but to maximize the use of natural light. During the renovation, utilizing the inherent advantages of the original building design was the focus of the interior space planning process, and modern office spaces were created to accentuate high ceilings and access to daylight as crucial competitive advantages of the MPBC over its competitors. The standard office plan recommends the placement of open office spaces on the exterior perimeter of each floor and the location of cubicles and enclosed offices and meeting rooms on the interior (Maryland Department of the Environment, 2003). Window shades have pinholes that allow natural light transmission while also blocking some light to ensure that the summer heat on the south and western sides of the building is not excessive (Maryland Department of the Environment, 2003). All of the interior paint used is free of VOCs, acoustic ceiling tiles are formaldehyde-free and contain 79% recycled content, and efficient elevators use up to 66% less electricity than conventional (Maryland Department of the Environment, 2003).

The workstations that come standard have walls made of a material called Homasote, which is made from 100% post-consumer newsprint and is itself recyclable (Maryland Department of the Environment, 2003). Homasote is free of asbestos and formaldehyde and has excellent sound-dampening properties. Instead of glue, the workstation surfaces are made using an Ultra Violet curing process on the surface sealant that prevents the off-gassing of VOCs (Maryland Department of the Environment, 2003). The work surface is made of recycled wheat board, and the workstation trim is made of ash wood that can be replaced without disassembling the workstation (Maryland Department of the Environment, 2003).

Part of the requirements for achieving LEED Gold was developing and executing a plan for construction waste diversion. Ninety percent of the original plumbing and sprinklers were retained and recommissioned following testing (Maryland Department of the Environment, 2003). Eighty percent of the material removed during the renovation was diverted from the waste stream and recycled onsite, including 3 million pounds of metal, 5,800 cubic yards of wood, 24,840 points of copper, and 8,036 board feet of timber (Maryland Department of the Environment, 2003).

Brownfield Cleanup

A significant part of the project involved the investigation and cleanup of the MPBC site. A variety of contaminants were discovered, including lead paint and asbestos commonly found in buildings of its era, as well as petroleum products and polychlorinated biphenyls (PCBs) frequently associated with automotive service and fuel storage facilities. In February 1992, a cleanup process began to address the contamination risk posed by the numerous underground storage tanks. Two underground storage tanks were removed, including the service station's 500-gallon waste oil tank and a 25,000-gallon heating oil tank, while a 15,000-gallon oil tank located beneath the structure was abandoned in place (Maryland Department of the Environment, 2001). Soil contamination was observed during the excavation of the underground storage tanks, and a total of 194 tons of soil was excavated and transported off-site for disposal (Maryland Department of the Environment, 2001).

In March 1992, soil samples were taken in the vicinity of the two removed oil tanks and the third abandoned-in-place tank, and four monitoring wells were installed to provide long-term sample collection (Maryland Department of the Environment, 2001). In August 1994, based on the findings of the samples and the ongoing monitoring, the Maryland Department of the Environment accepted the Underground Storage Tank Closure Report submitted. In January 1995, the Department issued a Notice of Compliance (Maryland Department of the Environment, 2001).

A more rigorous Phase II Environmental Assessment subsurface investigation was initiated in November 1999 that included a geophysical survey, a soil gas survey (33 sample locations), eight bored soil samples, and six groundwater samples (Maryland Department of the Environment, 2001). The investigation determined there was limited hydrocarbon soil contamination present. Still, groundwater samples found elevated levels of inorganic compounds – nickel, chromium, and lead – at two locations, including from the site of the former gas and service station that also yielded VOCs (Maryland Department of the Environment, 2001).

In March 2000, a prospective purchaser – Carroll Park, LLC, c/o Himmelrich Associates – submitted a Voluntary Cleanup Program (VCP) application for a 'No Further Requirements' determination from the Maryland Department of the Environment. The Maryland Department of the Environment determined that some additional information was required, including further soil and groundwater sampling, investigation of the anomalies that had been identified by the Phase II soil sampling in the vicinity of the floor drain associated with a spray paint booth in the former merchandise service area of the Montgomery Ward facility, and soil excavation to evaluate the presence of a septic tank that was noted on an old property map (Maryland Department of the Environment, 2001). In January 2001, the additional investigations required by the Maryland Department of the Environment were completed. On February 5, 2001, the Department issued a No Further Requirements Determination on the use of the property for commercial or industrial purposes, with the expressed prohibition of groundwater use for any purpose (Maryland Department of the Environment, 2001). In all, Paull (n.d.a) notes that approximately $3 million was spent on the cleanup of lead paint, petroleum, and PCBs.

Project Financing

Securing over $75 million in capital required for the project was a challenge. A variety of grants and loans from the Federal Government, the state of Maryland, and the city of Baltimore were secured by Himmelrich Associates, Inc., along with private equity, a philanthropic contribution, and commercial financing (Paull, n.d.a, n.d.b; Rajab, 2004). These included: Green roof grant from US EPA $92,000; Citibank Construction Loan $29.8 million; the city of Baltimore - HUD Section 108 loan $8 million; Empower Baltimore Management Corp. $4.5 million; Lubert Adler Real Estate Fund $1 million; Maryland Brownfields Revitalization Incentive Program $2 million; reimbursements from Tenants $1.98 million; Maryland State Tax Credit investor equity $13.87 million (Historic Preservation); Federal Tax Credit Investor Equity $13.66 million (Historic Preservation); and general Partner Equity $1 million. The $29.8 million construction loan was secured from Citibank in large part because Himmelrich Associates demonstrated that it had secured numerous government loans and grants.

Benefits, Barriers, and Lessons Learned

The project has created significant economic benefits for the West Side Empowerment Zone of Baltimore, Himmelrich Associates, and tenants (see project timeline Table 4.1). The amount of employment in the West Side Empowerment Zone is expected to increase significantly, with 1,800 workers onsite daily in 2013 and an expectation of 3,500 to 5,000 jobs retained/created once fully leased. The building was 66 percent leased by 2017 to tenants, including the Maryland Lottery Agency, Maryland Department of the Environment, M&T Bank, United Way of Central Maryland, and Urban Teachers (Sieron, 2017). Tenant acquisition for the large building continues despite continuous headwinds in the Baltimore office market caused by: the 2008 recession; the Federal Government budget sequestration in 2013, and the ripple effect this has had on leasing trends of local firms (CBRE, 2013); and now the COVID crisis. The green elements of the building continue to be upgraded and historic elements curated and celebrated, which continues to attract tenants with a social mandate and supportive of sustainability objectives.

The reuse of the existing building, other recycling initiatives, and grants from external agencies meant that the project was relatively inexpensive to build ($83 per-square-foot, which was low in comparison to the cost of new construction). Additionally, various green building systems in the building reduce operating costs for Himmelrich Associates. More economical development and operating costs benefit both Himmelrich Associates and tenants. These savings also make the structure more competitive in the office rental market in Baltimore, and thereby help ensure that the project realizes economic benefits for the West Side Empowerment Zone generally.

That being said, project financing proved to be extremely challenging as the project was not fiscally viable without the use of multiple grants. This was further exasperated by a great deal of uncertainty regarding contamination and the regulatory approvals process, which slowed the sale of the property. In 2013, a glut of new office space coming online in the Baltimore market also depressed rents and lowered net operating income. This highlights the fact that for any project to be fiscally viable, it must carefully consider market conditions.

In terms of economic lessons learned, public grants and loans were needed to secure private financing for the project, especially in the face of financing challenges during the recession; in their absence, the project may not have been able to proceed. Had the project not advanced, the economic benefits to the West Side Empowerment Zone would not have been realized. As such, the project demonstrates the value of these types of incentives in making a project fiscally viable and improving conditions in depressed localities.

Concerning the environment, the project aimed for LEED Gold certification by piloting multiple green building features, some of which (the maintenance-heavy waterless urinals and green roof) have proven to be less successful than hoped. In contrast, others (the Ice Tank System) have been found to work as well or better than predicted. The project demonstrates the feasibility of incorporating multiple green building features into a renovation project. In addition, no new buildings were constructed on the site as part of the redevelopment, saving a significant amount of material relative to new construction.

Soil contamination proved to be a significant barrier as it required substantial remediation at a cost that exceeded $2 million. Also, the payback period of the green building features was difficult to factor into the budget. Lastly, the project remains automobile-dependent, with good connections to several highways and a large amount of surface parking. It should be remembered that the project had made some headway in both these regards by providing improvements to cycling infrastructure and a shuttle service to public transit, as well as a porous, "Red" surface, parking lot.

A critical lesson from the project is that while operating cost savings are quantifiable benefits that support the inclusion of green building features, less measurable attributes like indoor air quality, extensive recycling, and the use of renewable building materials still have value to tenants and workers. There was also some uncertainty about some of the green building features because many had never been used in Baltimore. But by introducing these features into the Baltimore context, their viability/feasibility could be better understood by local developers and contractors in the future. Indeed, the developer of this project should be commended for his willingness to try new products and for his keen and inspirational sense of how the green building features affect the quality and bottom line of the project from both a capital and long-term operating cost perspective.

The surrounding community has also benefited from the redevelopment of the MPBC. It removed contamination and blight and preserved and refurbished a nationally significant building. The project has also brought employment to a declining part of Baltimore and has reinvigorated the local economy. The significant concentration of workers attracted by the redevelopment creates opportunities for new businesses in the vicinity, which could further stimulate the local economy. Public transit shuttle service and cycling infrastructure promotes less automobile dependency and decreases congestion and increases access to the site for people without a car. The municipality also gains increased revenue from property taxes, the potential for further improvement to properties in the area, and reduced water and stormwater demands for the site relative to conventional buildings.

While the combination of incentives and tax credits were instrumental in making the project financially feasible and ultimately delivering jobs and other improvements to the neighborhood, the only significant barrier remaining is the condition of the surrounding community itself. Further incentives and tax credits to surrounding properties may be essential to support new development in the area, which will help the long-term success of the project itself.

The MPBC project also seems to be part of, as well as a catalyst for, a broader trend towards redevelopment and truly exceptional repurposing of existing brownfield and historically significant sites using green technology in the Baltimore area, including:

- Brewers Hill: A mixed retail, light industrial, residential brownfield redevelopment on the site of two former locally significant breweries – the Gunther Brewery and the National Brewery. Several historic buildings have been retained and repurposed. The redevelopment includes 1 million sq. ft. of office, retail, and residential space on 27 acres of land. Several green building features have been built into the reconstruction, including a green roof, a grey stormwater system, and the use of recycled material (Brewers Hill, 2012). Other development in the local neighborhood continues with more retail and residential projects.
- American Can: A retail and office complex that has attracted several information technologies firms, retail stores, and restaurants. The site was a former brownfield and contained a historic metal can manufacturing facility. The existing buildings were retained and repurposed (US EPA, 2013a).
- American Brewery: Located in one of Baltimore's poorest neighborhoods, the former American Brewery building is now the headquarters of Humanim, a social service nonprofit. Humanim repaired the historic building with the help of tax credits and philanthropic dollars (Foster, 2009). Before this, the building was abandoned for nearly 40 years (Humanim Inc., 2013). The building now houses employment programs and clinical support services for area residents and has proved to be a catalyst for other development in the neighborhood (Foster, 2009).
- Tide Point Business Park: Formerly the site of Procter & Gamble soap producing plants, the historic buildings were renovated, and a new building was added to house high tech companies and other business, but was sold to one of its main tenants, Under Armour, in 2011 which has continued to improve the building. The project has improved water quality in the adjacent harbor through increased filtration (W Architecture & Landscape Architecture, 2013).
- Clipper Mill (Whitehall Mill): A mixed-use community with residential, retail, and commercial office space. The site was formerly a large machine manufacturing plant that had to undergo $1.2 million in environmental remediation. All five historic buildings were maintained, and renovations included the addition of green infrastructure elements, including a living-wall, a green roof, and a porous paving system. The site is near a light rail line, and there is a shuttle service to other modes of public transit.
- Union Mill: A historically significant former mill, the site was redeveloped with the original stone building being renovated and expanded. Various green infrastructure elements were included in the redevelopment, and the building is LEED-certified (US EPA, 2013b). The site underwent remediation under the Maryland Voluntary Cleanup Program. Today the site has more than 25,000 sq. ft. of office space for non-profit organizations as well as 56 apartment units at discounted rates for Baltimore area teachers (Seawall Development Company, 2013).

Table 4.1 Timeline – Montgomery Park, Baltimore, Maryland

Year	Description
1985	Montgomery Ward closed the Baltimore distribution site
1992, February	Two underground oil storage tanks were removed (a 500-gallon waste oil tank and a 25,000-gallon heating oil tank) while a third (15,000-gallon oil tank) located beneath the building was abandoned in place. 194 tons of contaminated soil was excavated and transported off-site for appropriate disposal. Additional site sampling begins from the vicinity of the two removed oil tanks and the third abandoned-in-place tank, and monitoring wells were installed
1995	The Maryland Department of the Environment issued a Notice of Compliance for the Underground Storage Tank Closure Report
1999	A Phase II Environmental Assessment was initiated and included: a geophysical survey; a soil gas survey (33 sample locations); eight bored soil samples; and six groundwater samples
2000	Montgomery Ward declares bankruptcy after over 125 years in business, although the Baltimore building had stood vacant for more than a decade and was slated for demolition
2000	Prior to purchasing the property, Carroll Park, LLC, c/o Himmelrich Associates, submitted a Voluntary Cleanup Program (VCP) application 'No Further Requirements' determination from the Maryland Department of the Environment
2000	Development team acquires property and commences interior cleaning and environmental remediation activities
2001, February	The Maryland Department of the Environment issues No Further Requirements Determination on the use of the property for commercial or industrial purposes, with the expressed prohibition of groundwater use for any purpose
2001 to 2003	Lead paint abatement (interior and exterior) and asbestos removal
2002	MPBC opened for business and first tenant, the Maryland Department of the Environment, moves in
2003	Wins Environmental Protection Agency's 2003 Phoenix Award
2016	Major tenant United Way of Central Maryland moves in
2017	Building is two-thirds occupied

Heifer International, Little Rock, Arkansas

An emerging cluster of non-profit organizations is leading a post-industrial urban recovery in Little Rock, Arkansas. Among the NGOs is Heifer International, a humanitarian agency with a mandate to alleviate poverty and hunger through sustainable development. As Arkansas' first LEED Platinum-certified facility, Heifer International's head office offers a case study in sustainable building design that advances brownfield revitalization and demonstrates the transformative benefits of pursuing a sustainable approach. The Heifer International World Headquarters is part of a larger remaking of east Little Rock. Together with the neighboring Clinton Presidential Library, Heifer International is part of a greenbelt along the Arkansas River that aims to provide open green space and a natural wetlands habitat for the citizens of east Little Rock. The two complexes together offer roughly 60 acres of combined green space, most of which had previously been abandoned industrial lands (Wildlife Habitat Council, 2004).

Site History

The Heifer site is located east of the historic downtown core, from which it is separated by Interstate 30. Many industrial uses surrounded it historically that gave way to low-rise residential neighborhoods to the east and northwest. The site was made up of nine different properties used primarily for industrial purposes, and at the time of purchase by Heifer, none had seen active use for some time. There were several one-story warehouse buildings on the land, which was paved (Swindle, 2010). Two of the parcels were known brownfields, including the 5.6-acre Union Pacific Railroad rail yard (vacated in the mid-1990s but used as a rail yard since before 1900), and the 3.97-acre Superior Trucking Company property (used as a freight terminal from the 1940s to 2003) (Devine & Greene, 2005). The remaining industrial properties included the former Harbor, Best Metal, Gray, Central Transport, and Pfeifer Plumbing and Heating properties (Devine & Greene, 2005). Rowland et al. (2008) note that at 21 acres, these were the most significant brownfield recoveries in Arkansas at the time.

The location choice of Heifer was the result of a confluence of several factors, including a great deal of reinvestment in the historic downtown core and south of Heifer (i.e., the Clinton Presidential Center), a sustained period of growth for the non-profit, and underuse in the industrial area. When the site was selected, several positive developments were occurring in the near vicinity. Firstly, the recently developed River Market District in downtown Little Rock raised development interest in the downtown core (Little Rock Downtown Partnership, 2013a), which had previously been struggling (Day, 2010). Development pressure in the Downtown was enhanced by several amenities already available in the area, such as numerous hotels, the Little Rock Convention and Visitor Bureau, the Historic Arkansas Museum, the Arkansas Art Center, and several other exciting spaces and places (Arkansas Business Limited Partnership, 2006). Revitalization drove up office rental rates, which was also a factor in Heifer's decision to move out of several rented downtown office spaces and consolidate 200-plus staff scattered throughout Little Rock in one location (Altes, 2007). Also, it had just been confirmed that the Clinton Presidential Library would be located adjacent to the downtown core, and the Clinton Foundation petitioned Heifer to purchase the adjoining property to help create a sixty-acre greenbelt along the Arkansas River (Luoni, 2008). The location of the library was not by coincidence either; in 1997, then-President Bill Clinton consciously chose a brownfield as the site of the proposed Clinton Presidential Center to spark reinvestment in the languishing Downtown (Luoni, 2008).

Project Vision

Heifer is an organization that strives to promote sustainability and environmental stewardship the world over, so the company understandably chose to incorporate these principles into the location, construction, and use of their new world headquarters. The non-profit's goal since its inception in 1944 has been to combat world hunger and poverty by providing training in environmentally sound agriculture and donating livestock to help needy families become self-reliant in a sustained and sustainable way (Heifer International, n.d.b).

By reusing a vacant brownfield, Heifer incorporated sustainability into the location of its new building. It chose to revitalize an existing portion of the urban built environment and, at the same time, avoid putting further stress on Little Rock's development services, transportation systems, and natural environment. Also, the building's location with drainage into the Arkansas River meant that transforming the site into a giant wetland sponge would reduce the amount of polluted stormwater runoff entering the river (Industrial Economic Incorporated, 2007).

Another of Heifer's key goals was to demonstrate the principles of sustainability in the design of their building. To develop a sustainable building, Heifer created a 15-member Smart Building Committee to ensure the new headquarters would achieve a high LEED rating (Cockram, 2007). This commitment to green building on brownfields helped Heifer secure aid from the US EPA in the form of technical, financial, planning, outreach, and design expertise (US EPA, 2006). The building was initially planned to achieve a silver LEED rating, but as the project evolved, Heifer International began to realize that a LEED platinum rating was possible (Cockram, 2007). The first hope of using 35 percent less energy than a compliant building was increased to a goal of 55 percent, according to project architect Reese Rowland. Heifer was able to push for further energy efficiencies using the rationale that in the future, it would allow funds to go towards poverty and hunger initiatives versus building operations (US Department of Energy, 2011).

To realize these savings, the design team coordinated significantly with the construction team to ensure that the projected efficiencies would become a reality and LEED targets met. Contractors would discuss alternative materials that were efficient and locally available, including many that were being used in the market for the first time (Heifer International, n.d.a). The US Department of Energy notes that numerous changes were also made to the building after the fact to ensure efficiencies were realized (Heifer International, n.d.a).

The last reason why Heifer wanted to produce a sustainable building was to educate visitors about the principles of sustainability and environmental stewardship (Altes, 2007); what Anne Laidlaw of the Arkansas Building Authority called "practicing what they preach" (Laidlaw, 2010). This was also noted by Rowland, who stated that "the goal was to design a sustainable headquarters in Little Rock, Arkansas, that would exemplify Heifer's mission and express their sustainable attributes for educational purposes" (Rowland et al., 2008). To meet the educational goals of the building, Heifer decided to build more than just a headquarters to house its employees; it also planned a welcome pavilion featuring galleries and a shop, an educational center, and a replica "Global Village" (Altes, 2007). There was a tremendous increase in donations towards a capital campaign for construction (international program funds were not used), and, as a result, Heifer decided to purchase two times more land than initially planned to expand the potential for educational exhibits (Heifer International, n.d.a).

The Murphy Keller Education Center was phase two of the development project, which Heifer expected to begin designing five years after the completion of its Headquarters (Libby, 2012). But the green elements of the building, along with interest in Heifer's legacy of successful non-profit work, began attracting 50 to 60 visitors to the Headquarters building per day, which encouraged them to initiate planning for phase two one year after the Headquarters opened (Libby, 2012). The center is used to educate visitors about Heifer's programs, and green building tours outline the various strategies and efficiencies built into the headquarters, educational center, and natural wetlands surrounding those buildings (Heifer International, n.d.c). The education center was expected to see an average of 75,000 visitors per year (Libby, 2012). The Murphy Keller Education Center did not seek LEED certification but is Green Globes Certified (scoring 3 out of 4 Green Globes).

Supplementary plans for the construction of a Global Village, phase three of the project, were also in the works starting in 2011. This part of the development complements the education center by providing a real-life replica of several impoverished communities that was to serve as an aid to teach patrons about solutions to world hunger and poverty (US EPA, 2006).

Project Characteristics and Development

In 1997, Heifer's CEO was approached by President Clinton and encouraged to locate Heifer's building in the area to create a non-profit corridor (Swindle, 2010). Heifer hired a local real estate agent (Rowland et al., 2008) to acquire about 21 acres of contiguous parcels from nine different property owners. Before design and construction could begin, the site needed to be assessed and cleaned up. This site was enrolled in Arkansas' Brownfields Program, giving Heifer access to assistance in the form of a Targeted Brownfield Assessment and federal liability protection from the EPA and ADEQ (Arkansas Department of Environmental Quality, 2009). ADEQ funded and provided technical support for the completion of the comprehensive ESA, which was only available to non-profits and municipalities (Arkansas Department of Environmental Quality, 2009). In March of 2004 ADEQ issued a final Property Development Decision Document (PDDD) that outlined the remedy for the former railroad and Superior Brownfields properties and the action necessary for the property to be declared ready for reuse (Devine & Greene, 2005). A petroleum storage tank investigation was carried out on the Gray and Pfeifer parcels on the site, and in April of 2004, ADEQ approved the final cleanup and closure of the fuel tank areas. Voluntary soil investigation and cleanup activities were conducted on the Central Transport, Gray and Pfeifer portions of the site, and a sitewide groundwater investigation occurred with no constituents of concern found to be above ADEQ cleanup standards (Devine & Greene, 2005). The following actions were taken to meet all the requirements of the PDDD. The top few inches of the soil lightly contaminated with creosote and diesel fuel was removed and used by the city of Little Rock in its landfill to cover each day's deposit of garbage (Rowland et al., 2008). The city took all 4,200 truckloads of Heifer's contaminated gravel, waiving the tipping fee, and used it instead of clean fill to bury trash, providing a benefit for both projects (Beranek, 2010). On the Gray and Pfeifer lands, the abandoned gasoline and diesel fuel tanks were removed and disposed of in a proper manner (Devine & Greene, 2005). Upon completion of all required work, a letter was sent by ADEQ and the EPA to Heifer on January 27, 2005, acknowledging that the site was Ready for Reuse. When this letter was released, the Heifer site officially became the largest reclaimed brownfield in all of Arkansas (Heifer International, n.d.a).

Gerald Cound of Crossroads Green notes that "right off the bat, the ADEQ, the EPA, and Heifer worked together as partners on the project and frequently met" (Cound, 2010). There is little doubt that this relationship was partially responsible for the quick cleanup process and the cooperative methods used to carry this out. It also sets a positive precedent for future brownfield reclamation projects; developers can expect to work with rather than against regulatory bodies in Arkansas to solve brownfield problems.

The design of the Heifer site, from a site plan perspective, is based on the metaphor of ripples in a pond as reflected by the *concentric circles* rippling outward from their center at a public entrance commons (Altes, 2007). The various rings (i.e., a pedestrian ring, the welcome center ring [phase two], the wetland ring, the office building ring, and the vehicular traffic ring) represent Heifer's "passing on the gift" policy, whereby at least one offspring of any livestock they donate must be donated to another individual in the same village (Cockram, 2007). It also represents Heifer's expectation that those they educate go on to teach others in their community, which makes its economic development model sustainable (Cockram, 2007).

Zoning for the site was revised to UU-Urban Use, which according to Bryan Day, Assistant City Manager with the city of Little Rock, was put in place in the mid-1990s along the riverfront. This zoning is form-based and more concerned with whether a project fits into an area, as opposed to its specific use (Day, 2010). Several internal streets had to be closed to redevelop the site and were conveyed to Heifer at no cost, and a new road was also built by the city to service the site (World Avenue) at no cost to Heifer (Rowland et al., 2008). The city also consented to run a new streetcar system near the site and changed local bus routes to provide better access for employees and visitors (Day, 2010). These in-kind services from the city also helped entice Heifer to the area.

As noted by Anne Laidlaw from the Arkansas Building Authority, Heifer did an excellent job linking their site with the Presidential Library via parks, trails, and common elements. She notes that this "has created the synergy between buildings," with people parking at one and walking between the two to visit both green buildings (Laidlaw, 2010).

Heifer incorporated sustainability and greening into every aspect of the project. Concerning building material, Heifer recycled and reused 97 percent of all existing material from the vacant buildings by crushing and reusing the bricks, mortar, pavement, and other rubble as fill for various portions of the redevelopment (Altes, 2007; Wildlife Habitat Council, 2004). The gravel pave system used in the parking lot is mostly (90 percent) made from this product. Not all bricks were crushed, as Heifer employees helped recycle some for sidewalks and a circular portion of the driveway (Industrial Economic Incorporated, 2007). The steel frames of the old buildings were taken to local foundries, recycled, and used in the new construction. In the end, the savings garnered from recycling material paid for the cost of demolishing the buildings (Rowland et al., 2008).

Construction materials were chosen based on their regional availability, which cut down on transportation costs and supported local business. The aluminum and steel were made or recycled at facilities located within a few blocks of the project (Environmental Design and Construction, 2007). Other examples of locally sourced products include Arkansas limestone used on the exterior of the building, Mississippi delta pine used to surface the fourth-floor ceiling, and soybeans and cotton used in the production of the building's insulation, among many others (Heifer International, n.d.a).

The Heifer building uses anywhere from 52 to 55 percent less energy than a standard comparable structure (Cockram, 2007; Environmental Design and Construction, 2007; Rowland et al., 2008). This was achieved through various building features such as optimized daylighting, dimming controls, occupancy sensors, and innovative air circulation methods

(Altes, 2007). Daylighting is complemented by occupancy sensors and supplemented by T5 lamps for artificial light. The semi-circular east-west positioning of the building, combined with its narrow and open floor plan, allows for maximum sunlight to penetrate the structure while offering views of the Arkansas River (Cockram, 2007; Environmental Design and Construction, 2007). Creative shading techniques that employ vertical fins and horizontal sunshades limit unwanted solar heat gain while redirecting daylight into the building's interior (Wildlife Habitat Council, 2004). Even the glass is crafted to reduce thermal transmission, with a high 68 percent visible light transmission to allow daylighting, along with a U-value of .29 and a solar heat gain coefficient of .38 to reduce building heat. Also, light sensors in the building react to the amount of natural sunlight entering at any given moment, and as such artificial light is only used when needed (Heifer International, 2013a). The new Murphy Keller Education Center is also 90 percent daylit and 50 percent ventilated using operable windows (Libby, 2012).

The new headquarters has a raised floor system comprised of steel and concrete that leaves 18 inches of separation beneath the floor (Rowland et al., 2008). This improves ventilation and makes heating and cooling more efficient because of water's superior thermal capabilities and its location on the floor rather than overhead (Heifer International, n.d.a). Two of the building's three staircases float over the wetland features rather than resting inside the building. These glass-wrapped stairs have openings at their base and five stories up, allowing natural convection to pull cold air off the water and cool the space (Heifer International, n.d.a; Altes, 2007).

Compared with a conventional building, the Heifer headquarters uses 65 percent less potable water due to numerous conservation measures. The most significant is a four-story, approximately 30,000-gallon cistern that collects rainwater from the roof and stores it in a water tank located in the middle of the main stairwell, with stairs wrapping around it (Rowland at al., 2008). Water from the cistern is used for toilets and other greywater systems in the building, as well as to water landscaping and to naturally cool the building (Cockram, 2007; Industrial Economic Incorporated, 2007; Environmental Design and Construction, 2007).

One of Heifer's main priorities was to build a natural wetland on the property, but they also needed a relatively large parking lot (337-parking spaces) (US EPA, 2006). To achieve both, they created approximately 30,000 sq. ft. of permeable gravel parking instead of using conventional asphalt. Concrete is used in areas of higher traffic volume (e.g., driveways) because it uses fewer harmful chemicals compared with asphalt. All stormwater that hits the parking lot or concrete driveways is either absorbed through the gravel or directed into bioswales that slow down stormwater runoff and filter out harmful chemicals, with any further overflow ending up in a large retention basin. In total, the wetland and native landscaping itself is 32,670 sq. ft. and can hold over 700,000 gallons of water (Industrial Economic Incorporated, 2007).

The benefits of this system are numerous. Firstly, it dramatically improves water quality in an area where runoff from hard parking lots and roof surfaces is the single most significant contributor of nonpoint source pollution into the river and local watersheds (Luoni, 2008). It is estimated that the innovative wetland system will help avoid 180 lbs of nitrogen and 260 lbs of suspended solids from entering the Arkansas River over ten years (Industrial Economic Incorporated, 2007). Secondly, the parking lot uses two-thirds less water for irrigation than a conventional lot, which saves an estimated $65,343 annually (Industrial Economic Incorporated, 2007). Thirdly, Heifer International did not have to hook up to the city's stormwater management system and provides an example for other new development. Lastly, the system saves Heifer some capital costs, as traditional civil engineering systems used to control stormwater like pipes, curbs, gutters, and catch basins are not needed (Luoni, 2008).

Concerning economic and social elements, the development of the World Headquarters building allowed Heifer to consolidate all their employees into a single office, as well as add new employees (between 2006 and 2008, 70–80 employees came on board) (Swindle, 2010). As noted by Eric Swindle, then Director of Facilities Management for Heifer, the site housed 256 employees in 2010 but can hold 405. A significant number of jobs were brought within walking distance of several low-income neighborhoods, where previously vacant industrial uses existed (Swindle, 2010). Also, these jobs are located in a green building with a healthier environment for employees (Libby, 2012).

Sustainable transportation modes are supported by the site's central location, as well as various actions that were taken by Heifer. The site is located near a major interstate and between the Little Rock Airport and Downtown. The strategic location of the site minimizes travel time for the large number of people that visit the campus for conferences, workshops, and tourism, as well as for its employees. There are also several residential areas located within walking distance. The site is also bisected by a new bike trail connecting North Little Rock to Little Rock and situated near a new light rail line (Swindle, 2010). To supplement this, Heifer influenced a route change to the local bus service to get better service for the site (Laidlaw, 2010; Swindle, 2010). It also subsidizes public transportation costs for its employees, provides onsite bike parking, and made six premium parking spots for carpooling (Industrial Economic Incorporated, 2007).

As mentioned, the $13.5 million, 16,000 sq. ft. Murphy Keller Education Center opened in 2009 to educate the public about sustainable building techniques and poverty and hunger reduction strategies. Generally known as Heifer Village, the mixed-use education center and meeting facility designed by architect Reese Rowland, who also designed the headquarters building, can hold up to 250 people for seminars, conferences, special events, and other celebrations (see Figure 4.2). Eric Swindle noted that Heifer was keen to promote sustainable local agriculture and community gardening in phase three of the redevelopment, the Heifer Urban Farm, which is preceded by an educational garden exhibition in the educational center. Opened in fall 2016, Heifer's Urban Farm is a three-acre, multi-purpose garden that models the work of Heifer farmers in the US and internationally. Visitors can interact with "animal ambassadors," tour greenhouses and low-till organic gardens from which Heifer harvests thousands of pounds of produce for local food banks, and learn about the eco-friendly practices Heifer applies in the field. In the fall of 2018, Heifer and HATponics (a sustainable aquaponics company with roots in humanitarian aid) opened the world's first commercial renewable energy-operated aquaponics facility on the Urban Farm. It aims to feed about 200 people a day when fully operational and uses a system sold by

Figure 4.2 Heifer International Center (right) and Heifer Village (left) taken from the Clinton Library, Little Rock, Arkansas, 2010

HATponics for $150,000 that packs the equivalent of a 2.5-acre farm into a shipping container for delivery around the world (HATponics, 2020).

Project Financing

The total cost of phase one of the project was estimated to range from $17.9 to $19 million, or roughly $189 per square foot, which is the average cost of office space in Little Rock (Altes, 2007; Laidlaw, 2010; US Department of Energy, 2011). As such, the project is not seen as extravagant, even with all its green initiatives, which is vital for an organization supported by individual donors who demand fiscal responsibility. It also shows developers that green technology does not have to be overly expensive. The cost of the building made economic sense for Heifer because it allowed the rent they would be paying in four dispersed locations to be converted into a mortgage payment that would result in cost savings as early as 2010 (Heifer International, 2013a).

Funding for this specific project came in the form of traditional loans obtained by Heifer International, as well as a capital campaign that was so successful it allowed for the building to be larger than initially intended (US Department of Energy, 2011). Financial assistance for soil testing came from the EPA and ADEQ, who wanted the flagship project to help raise awareness of the brownfield potential in Polaski County (Swindle, 2010). Heifer also took advantage of the revolving loan fund provided by the ADEQ to help pay for site remediation (Swindle, 2010). The city was eager to retain Heifer as an employer and kick start regeneration of the east end, and offered several in-kind services and conveying streets at no cost.

The creation of the wetlands and permeable parking lot did add cost to the project beyond what it would have been for a conventional parking lot (Wildlife Habitat Council, 2004). This additional cost was offset to some degree by grant funding from the EPA's Office of Solid Waste and Emergency Response to develop the permeable parking lot (Industrial Economic Incorporated, 2007). The creation of the parking lot contributed to the functioning of the wetland, which, in turn, has realized several cost efficiencies. Heifer also uses two-thirds less water for irrigation of its parking lot landscaping than a conventional lot because of its natural irrigation system and use of local plants (Industrial Economic Incorporated, 2007). It also uses 65 percent less potable water than a conventional building (Rowland et al., 2008), which is why Heifer's water bill is several times lower than average for a building of its size (Swindle, 2010). As for energy efficiency, for any cost that would not be part of a conventional office building, the design team used a payback period of seven to ten years as a baseline to determine its viability (US Department of Energy, 2011). As noted by Altes (2007), the building purchased 43 percent less energy than a standard structure of its size due to the various energy efficiency features, resulting in a $1.10–$1.25 per square foot electric bill versus a standard $2.12 (Swindle, 2010). Savings from using recycled materials also paid for the cost of demolishing the buildings and using locally available materials also cut down on transportation costs.

Benefits, Barriers, and Lessons Learned

Heifer International's headquarters and the campus is an excellent model for sustainable brownfield projects (see timeline Table 4.2). It is an example of an integrative approach to brownfield redevelopment, green design, and urban recovery based on the principles of sustainability. Interviewees noted that it was viewed in the development industry as an "example of how to deal with brownfield challenges . . . and encourages people to look at brownfields as an opportunity". The many awards won by the project make it a role model for future developments and thrust to the forefront the funding and technical assistance opportunities provided by the EPA and ADEQ.

The cooperation, financial and technical assistance of various state- and municipal-level agencies was essential in the Heifer project. The decisive role of the ADEQ, EPA, and the city of Little Rock was crucial in the development of a sustainable building and site. These agencies were dealing, however, with a client who wanted to build a sustainable building and, as such, had very little to do with influencing its green character. To foster more sustainable design on brownfield sites, a few interviewees noted the need to be more vocal in advocating for these types of approaches.

Brownfield redevelopment can be daunting enough for developers without considering the complications which can be added by a green building. To counteract this, agencies such as the ADEQ are advised to put greater focus on educating potential developers by providing technical and financial assistance to brownfield projects. Also, these agencies should begin to make their funding and support contingent on a certain green standard in new brownfield projects, which an interviewee noted was not done in the past. Another potential course of action for these agencies could be to provide tax credits to help finance projects at the front end that will eventually have long term payoffs. It should be remembered, however, that the collaboration and non-confrontational nature of the EPA and ADEQ was considered to be one of the integral aspects of the Heifer process. Therefore, while pushing for green buildings on brownfield sites, agencies must ensure they remain non-confrontational but rather cooperative so that the process of brownfield redevelopment is viewed in a positive light, which will eventually translate into more projects.

It is also important to remember that liability remains a crucial issue with brownfields. The importance of liability and risk management is highlighted by the fact that it was mentioned by several interviewees when discussing barriers to this project from a brownfield perspective. In every case, the main takeaway is that state agencies must continue to help developers manage the potential risk of liability.

The presence of other catalytic projects was also significant in Heifer's decision to locate on a brownfield site. It is no coincidence that the Heifer project took place during a time when much of downtown Little Rock was experiencing regeneration. As noted by the Little Rock Downtown Partnership, "since 1996, approximately $2 billion in investments has come into the Downtown Little Rock area" (Little Rock Downtown Partnership, 2013b). The lesson learned here is that the better the land market is in an area, the more attractive the brownfield redevelopment will be. But unfortunately, many brownfields are not blessed with a prime location immediately adjacent to a downtown core.

Thankfully, regeneration in industrial areas can be kick started from significant investments, as seen with the Presidential Center. As noted by Laidlaw, "once the Presidential Library was decided, it influenced Heifer to build its headquarters and education center." The interviewee went on to say that the Clinton Presidential Center and Heifer "influenced redevelopment of Downtown, these were catalytic projects. The area became an attraction when it was previously dead." It may be essential to consider that the early pioneers (such as the Presidential Center) are, in many cases, needed to kick start regeneration. These projects may need to be further incentivized and not held up to the same green standards as latter entrants. State agencies will have more leverage with latter entrants than early pioneers.

Heifer is also an excellent example of the benefits of green design, which can influence the general public's mindset as well as the actions of both private businesses and public agencies. Rowland notes that the Heifer headquarters has brought public attention to green design (Rowland et al., 2008), which is supported by the fact that 50 to 60 people per day would come to visit the build (Libby, 2012). Heifer embraced and expanded its role as an exemplary green project by building the Murphy Keller Education Center and running a Green Building tour (Heifer International, 2013b). Heifer Village was expected to see an average of 75,000 visitors per year (Libby, 2012). As education about the benefits of these types of buildings increases, so should knowledge about their benefits, and hopefully, the public will begin to expect and demand this type of development.

One barrier in communicating the benefits of green buildings occurred during the attempt to certify the Murphy Keller Education Center. As noted by an interviewee, the education center could not claim a variety of points in the LEED rating system because it shared a range of services with the first building (e.g., electricity, water, heating, and cooling). In essence, Heifer "was penalized for building another building on the site, they were not going to make it to LEED platinum again because of this," and would have received LEED Silver instead. From a public perception point of view, this would not send the right message about the benefits of green design and give the impression that it was not successful. This barrier turned into a positive because it allowed Heifer to showcase an alternative green building rating system (the Green Globes system) and provide developers with alternative ways to showcase the sustainable initiatives in their buildings in a manner that is most beneficial to their project.

This barrier also demonstrates that the LEED rating system is not perfect and needs to continue to add flexibility to its standards over time, something it appears willing to do with new versions. The hope is that LEED will continue to refine itself in a way that makes certification less cumbersome and more accepting of innovative green projects, while at the same time maintaining its credibility.

In addition to bringing public notice to green design, the Heifer headquarters has also demonstrated the various financial efficiencies which the business sector stands to gain by developing a green building. As noted by an interviewee, "Heifer has spared thousands in energy that goes back into their poverty programs. Other companies look at this in terms of their bottom line budgets." Also, the improved "indoor air quality and natural lighting have increased productivity and teamwork," which can further impact a company's bottom line. A few interviewees noted that more companies have "come on board" with green design over the last few years based on energy savings and natural light benefits realized by Heifer. It should be noted that one of the reasons why Heifer has experienced savings in operation costs is because Heifer focused on strategies that have a 5- to 19-year payback period (Cockram, 2007). This can be conceived of as a barrier in some cases as it resulted in particular green initiatives not being implemented, such as the installation of solar cells on the roof or a car charging station in the parking lot. However, this could also be construed as a benefit. By focusing on strategies that have a 5- to 19-year payback period, Heifer has demonstrated to the business community that multiple quick wins can be realized through environmental design. This appears to be the trend in the local business community. Laidlaw noted that many new buildings are staying away from the "flashy" green projects that look too expensive while still achieving similar efficiency results (Laidlaw, 2010).

The Heifer project has not only influenced the business sector, but several interviewees noted that it has significantly changed public agencies. After the Heifer building, the city has created a sustainability group and waives permit fees if residents build energy-efficient homes. The state also started a Sustainable Building Design Program in 2009 to provide cheap loans to state agencies for energy-efficient retrofits to existing state buildings, and intends to ensure that all new state-owned facilities are designed for maximum efficiency (Laidlaw, 2010).

Heifer was able to successfully promote green design from a financial perspective to the business community and public agencies because the company has monitored the innovative systems it has put in place to communicate better their successes (Rowland et al., 2008). Rowland noted that many companies "want to be green but don't want to spend more money and need to be educated about the potential benefits of green design to legitimize increased expenditure" (Rowland et al., 2008). Monitoring has helped Heifer communicate the benefits successfully, while also helping to identify problems as it did in 2010. A recommissioning plan initiated in 2011 to assess what was causing the building's Energy Star Score to drop (from 90 in 2007 to 72 in 2011) led to repairs that quickly improved the rating to 91 at less than a one-year payback (Kuhn, 2014). The Heifer case is also used, therefore, as an example of the value of commissioning and recommissioning services for managing increasingly complex green building systems, which explains why even the US Green Building Council has added commissioning as a prerequisite to LEED certification (Kuhn, 2014).

In addition to demonstrating the various efficiencies which the business sector stands to gain by developing a green building, the Heifer building has also begun to change the mindsets of the multiple parties involved in development. It can sometimes be challenging to be innovative, which can result in pushback from several sources. For example, Heifer itself was tentative about having an open-concept office with glass walls rather than more traditional separated workspaces. During the project, it was also difficult to change the mindset of contractors and the development company as well as educate the city (about water collection). As noted by one interviewee, a key obstacle experienced during the project was not that people were opposed to breaking new ground, but that they just didn't know how certain ideas would work out in reality. Breaking down common perceptions and demonstrating how these projects can work from a functional perspective is considered an essential accomplishment of this project. As the different parties (i.e., developers, contractors, and state agencies) became more educated, and companies understand how spaces can function to produce better results, promoting green development will become easier.

The twin non-profit developments of the Heifer lands and the Clinton Presidential Center are seen as a considerable part of urban revitalization in downtown Little Rock, transforming a previously blighted portion of the city center into two landmark tourist attractions. They have also improved safety in the area by bringing people to newly created public spaces (Cound, 2010), enhanced employment opportunities for nearby low-income neighborhoods (Beranek, 2010; Swindle, 2010), increased the local tax base and surrounding property values, and opened up the door for future redevelopment in the area immediately east of downtown. The decision to co-locate has attracted further non-profits to build new offices in Little Rock, bringing with them more jobs as well as increased property values. Overall, a cumulative effect of the two developments is that it has started to put an end to the historic rich-poor divide that existed along interstate 30 (Day, 2010).

Table 4.2 Timeline – Heifer International, Little Rock, Arkansas

Year	Description
Late 1800s to early 1900s	Development of a rail yard, east of downtown Little Rock on the Arkansas River. Industrial and manufacturing operations cluster around the rail yard
2000	Heifer International decides to establish a campus and consolidate several satellite offices into one facility, with "public space for educational and outreach programs" (Altes, 2007)
2002	The Heifer International project is named a Green Building on Brownfields pilot project by the US EPA, which entails "technical, financial, planning, outreach and design expertise" (Devine & Greene, 2005)
June 2003	Heifer International is awarded an OSWER Innovations grant to design an environmentally friendly parking plaza (Industrial Economic Incorporated, 2007)

(Continued)

Table 4.2 Continued

Year	Description
October 2003	Ground breaking for construction at the site begins as scheduled. The collaborative technical assistance provided by the ADEQ and EPA is instrumental in this (US EPA, 2006)
March 12, 2004	The ADEQ issues the final Property Development Decision Document (PDDD) (Devine & Greene, 2005)
January 27, 2005	The ADEQ and EPA Region 6 together determine that the Heifer International site is Ready for Reuse (Devine & Greene, 2005)
2006	Phase one of the project is complete; the 94,000 square foot Heifer International headquarters.
2006	Within one year of completion the Heifer International headquarters was receiving 50 to 60 visitors a day and as a result planning design and eventually development of phase two, what is today the Murphy Keller Education Center, begun, four years ahead of schedule (Libby, 2012)
2005–2006	Heifer International headquarters receives the following awards: (2005) Sierra Club of Arkansas Conservation Award; (2006) ASID South Central Region Interior Design Award, AIA Arkansas Honor Award, AIA Arkansas Member Honors Award, ASLA Arkansas Honor
August 30, 2007	The US Green Building Council announces that Phase one of the Heifer International Village was awarded a Platinum LEED rating (the first in Arkansas) (Heifer International, 2013a)
2007	Heifer International headquarters receives the following awards: National AIA Committee on the Environment's (COTE) Top Ten Green Projects, American Architecture Award Chicago Athenaeum Museum, American Institute of Steel Construction (AISC) Awards National Winner, EPA 2006 Phoenix award Region 6, Metal Architecture Magazine Design Award, Environmental Design and Construction Excellence in Design Awards – Finalist, AIA Gulf States Region Honor Award
2008	Heifer International Headquarters building was named a National AIA (American Institute of Architects) Institute Honor Award Winner
2009	Construction of the Murphy Keller Education Center is complete (phase two of the Heifer International Village plan) (Libby, 2012)
2013	Heifer's hosts its first annual Feast in the Field event to raise funds for Arkansas farmers
2016	Heifer's Urban Farm (phase three) opens on November 15
2017	Heifer's hosts its first annual Urban Farm Fest where locals visit the site for an evening of food trucks, lawn games, drinks, and music, with proceeds benefiting the Heifer USA program
2018	HATponics and Heifer International open the world's first commercial renewable energy-operated aquaponics farm at the Urban Farm

References

Altes, T. K. (2007). *Heifer International Center; circle of life: A charity dedicated to nourishing families builds a new office as a model of harmony with nature*. January. Green Source, the Magazine of Sustainable Design.

Arkansas Business Limited Partnership. (2006). *Little Rock*. Arkansas Business Publishing Group.

Arkansas Department of Environmental Quality. (2009). *Brownfields toolbox*. State of Arkansas.

Brewers Hill. (2012). *Obrecht commercial real estate*. December 17. Brewershill.net

CBRE. (2013). *Baltimore office market view 1Q2013*. CBRE Global Research and Consulting.

Chapman, K. & Walker, D. (1991). *Industrial location*. Basil Blackwell.

Cockram, M. (2007). Big ripples. April 4, *Architecture Week*, E1.1.

Devine, M. K., Greene, R. E. (2005). *Ready for reuse determination*. Arkansas Department of Environmental Quality.

Environmental Design and Construction. (2007). High-performance building envelopes web exclusive: Heifer International world headquarters. *EDC Magazine*, May 7.

Foster, M. (2009). The American brewery: An east Baltimore comeback. July 17, *Preservation Nation Magazine*.

HATponics. (2020). *Portable farm*. September 24. HATponics Sustainable Agriculture.

Heifer International. (2013a). *Green Building News*. June 18. Heifer International.

Heifer International. (2013b). *Heifer Village*. June 16. Heifer International.

Heifer International. (n.d.a). *Building green on the Arkansas River, building hope around the world*. Heifer International Brochure RP8506000.

Heifer International. (n.d.b). *Heifer education and lifelong learning programs*. Heifer International Brochure RP8708000.

Heifer International. (n.d.c). *Heifer Village*. Heifer International Brochure JN26972.

Himmelrich Associates, Inc. (2013). *History*. January 18. Montgomery Park.com

Humanim Inc. (2013). *American brewery*. December 17. Humanim.

Industrial Economic Incorporated. (2007). *Green parking lot case study*. Heifer International Inc.

Kuhn, T. (2014). *Building recommissioning helps heifer international meet challenges of reliability, efficiency, and sustainability*. September 26. Facilities Management News and Education.

Libby, B. (2012). *Building it forward to extend charity's headquarters*. August 14. Eco Building Pulse, Architect, The American Institute of Architects.

Little Rock Downtown Partnership. (2013a). *Live downtown*. June 16. Downtown Little Rock.com.

Little Rock Downtown Partnership. (2013b). *Invest downtown*. June 16. Downtown Little Rock.com.

Luoni, S. (2008). Speaking of places - Little Rock's emerging non-profit corridor. *Places*, 20(1), 70-75.

Maryland Department of the Environment. (2001). *Montgomery Ward Business Center*. Maryland Department of the Environment.

Maryland Department of the Environment. (2003). *Green building features of Montgomery Park, frequently asked questions*. Maryland Department of the Environment.

National Parks Service. (2000). *Montgomery Ward warehouse and retail store*. September 14. National Register of Historic Places.

Paull, E. (n.d.a.). *Overcoming Risks and Issues in Using HUD 108 to fill in a private development project - Montgomery Park*. Redevelopmenteconomics.com.

Paull, E. (n.d.b). *Baltimore, MD recycles a national landmark into the Montgomery Park Business Center*. Baltimore Development Corporation, Revitalizing Southeaster Communities: A Brownfields Toolkit.

Rajab, K. W. (2004). *Brownfield redevelopment in Baltimore city: A case study of the Can Company and Montgomery Park Business Center* [Unpublished Masters thesis]. Morgan State University.

Rowland, R., Kuhn, T., & Hodoway, J. (2008). Case Study, Heifer International; Passing on the Gift. *High Performing Buildings*, 4-13.

Seawall Development Company. (2013). *About union mill*. December 17. The Union Mill.

Sieron, M. (2017) These are the largest office buildings in the Baltimore area. September 22, *Baltimore Business Journal*, Commercial Real Estate.

The Center for Brownfields Initiatives at the University of New Orleans. (2010). *EPA Region 3 - Montgomery Park Business Center, Baltimore, Maryland*. June 30. University of New Orleans.

US Department of Energy. (2011). *Buildings database; Heifer International Headquarters*. US Department of Energy.

US EPA. (2006). *Heifer International; Little Rock Ark*. US EPA Region 6.

US EPA. (2013a). *Smart growth illustrated, the Can Company, Baltimore, Maryland*. December 17. US EPA Smart Growth.

US EPA. (2013b). *Land revitalization spring '10 newsletter - Maryland's voluntary cleanup program and the union mill property*. September 25. US EPA.

W Architecture & Landscape Architecture. (2013). *Tide point*. December 17. W Architecture & Landscape Architecture.

Wildlife Habitat Council. (2004). *Heifer International new world headquarters case study*. Wildlife Habitat Council.

Interviews

Montgomery Park, Baltimore, Maryland

- Carrol, J. (2010). Maryland Department of Environment.
- Himmelrich, S. (2010). Himmelrich Associates, Inc.
- Mills, S. (2010). Himmelrich Associates Inc.
- Stein, E. (2020) Leasing Director, Himmelrich Associates Inc.
- Suskauer, G. (2010). Director of the Brownfields Initiative/Policy Analyst, Baltimore Development Corporation.
- Vaughn, V. (2010). Associate, Chesapeake Community Advisors Inc., Community Development Consultants.

Heifer International, Little Rock, Arkansas

- Beranek, D. (2010). President, Little Rock, McClelland Consulting Engineers.
- Cound, G. (2010). Crossroads Green – Living Environment Design and Consulting, Little Rock.
- Day, B. (2010). Assistant City Manager, city of Little Rock.
- Laidlaw, A. (2010). Director, Arkansas Building Authority.
- Rhodes, C. Jr. (2010). Chief, Hazardous Waste Division, Arkansas Department of Environmental Quality.
- Rowland, R. (2010). Principal, Polk Stanley, Wilcox Architects.
- Swindle, E. (2010). Director of Facilities Management, Heifer International.

5 Residential Redevelopment

A vibrant and viable community is one in which all types of people wish to live, work, and play at all stages of their lives. As such, housing is perhaps the most critical element in the creation of such a community. This chapter reviews brownfields-to-housing case studies that have sought to raise the bar on green building and sustainability including Artspace Commons, a Best Management Practice example in Salt Lake City, Utah, where a non-profit took a brownfield in a depressed district and used it to create a residential project where residents could literally live, work, and play; and Anvil Mountain in Silverton Colorado, where leaders employed US EPA Pilot funds to plan and build affordable and energy-efficient housing for locals priced out of the expensive market that caters to tourists.

Artspace Commons, Salt Lake City, Utah

Site History

Artspace Commons is put forward as a best practice in brownfields revitalization for its ability to establish an intricate balance between the environmental, economic, and social aspects of sustainability. This mixed-use development, completed in 2010, offers affordable housing and commercial space that addresses the needs of artists and not-for-profit organizations, while also acting as a catalyst for revitalization in an up-and-coming post-industrial district. While projects that address affordability are sometimes built to the lowest common dominator to remain economically viable, Artspace Commons not only addresses the legacy of industrial contamination onsite but has also achieved LEED Gold status through innovative building design. To realize this balance, Artspace financed the Commons through a complicated New Markets Tax Credit (NMTC) partnership, making the project a showcase not only for brownfield revitalization, affordability, and green building design but also for progressive financing.

Artspace Commons is located in Salt Lake City's Granary District, which is bounded by 600 South, West Temple, and I-15. Named for the silos that sprouted up along the historic rail corridor, the Granary District was once a gateway for a robust mix of light and heavy industries, warehouses, and granary silos. As modern freeways were introduced to the area, rail was pushed westward, pulling much of the District's historic manufacturing along with it. The resulting built form is characterized by low-density warehouses and commercial buildings, many of which have stood for over 50 years (Ellin, 2012). Despite a steady decline, the area has retained some light industrial uses (McKellar, 2013). There has been an increase in new housing developments and service-orientated commercial development alongside a burgeoning new creative culture focused on food, art, and music since the mid-2000s (Redevelopment Agency of Salt Lake City, n.d.; Thompson, 2012). This trend has been supported by the relatively inexpensive real estate in the area as well as its proximity to Salt Lake City's downtown core (Skibine, 2012; Redevelopment Agency of Salt Lake City, n.d.). In 2011, 17 percent of land in the Granary district was vacant (Redevelopment Agency of Salt Lake City, 2011).

The Commons themselves are located at 824 S. 400 West on the former Utah Barrel and Scrap site. Utah Barrel and Scrap was a family-run scrap metal recycling business that operated for three generations on the site, leaving behind a legacy of contamination. In the late 1990s, the Salt Lake City Redevelopment Agency (RDA) prepared a report on existing conditions in the Granary District and adjacent Gateway District, identifying the former Utah Barrel and Scrap site as a high priority for remediation (Utah Department of Environmental Quality, 2011). Following this preliminary report, the Salt Lake City RDA created the Granary District Project Area in 1999, guided by the Gateway District Land Use & Development Plan, the Gateway Specific Plan, and the Granary District Redevelopment Plan. Together, these plans are working to create "mixed-use neighborhoods that support commercial businesses and services by improving public infrastructure, removing blight, preserving historic structures, and reclaiming open space" (Redevelopment Agency of Salt Lake City, n.d.).

Responding to the opportunity created by this policy framework and the city's identification of the Utah Barrel and Scrap as a high priority for remediation, Artspace purchased the site in November 2007 with intentions of remediating and redeveloping it. Artspace is a highly successful not-for-profit corporation that seeks to revitalize and promote vibrant, safe communities in areas like the Granary District by creating affordable housing and workspaces for artists, cultural organizations, and non-profit organizations (Artspace, 2013a).

Project Vision

Artspace Utah was established in 1980 by a collaborative of artists in need of affordable and safe spaces to live and work. Artspace is credited with starting a "real estate revolution" with its first project in 1982, which converted an 80,000 square foot Eccles Browning Warehouse into artist lofts, studio spaces, and offices for not-for-profit organizations. Following the success of this project, Salt Lake City's warehouse district shifted from a "run-down, neglected, crime-ridden area [into] a hip hotspot filled with trendy restaurants, hotels, loft apartments, an upscale shopping mall, and a new train station where commuter rail and light rail trains meet" (Jones, 2010).

Artspace completed three similar award-winning projects before pursuing the Commons (the Artspace Rubber Company 1995, the Artspace Bridge Projects 2001, and the Artspace City Center 2006). These allowed them to solidify their expertise in putting forth the right mix of uses, at the right price point, to successfully develop catalytic, affordable, mixed-use developments in struggling neighborhoods (Artspace, 2013a). While the Artspace Commons largely mirrored the vision that had informed Artspace's previous projects, the Commons added a further dimension of sustainability to Artspace's activities by tackling both brownfield remediation and the successful pursuit of LEED Gold certification.

Ultimately, Artspace's visions of a mixed-use, affordable, dense, and green project contributed to the success of the project by aligning it with Salt Lake City's planning agenda for the Granary District. The RDA's identification of the site as a priority for remediation and the overarching policy framework to revitalize the District into a mixed-use neighborhood created an environment where Artspace could be confident it had public support in pursuing a new iteration of their previously successful vision. The Utah Department of Environmental Quality's Voluntary Cleanup Program and the federal New Markets Tax Credit financing program signaled state and federal support for brownfield remediation. These programs helped to limit the risks associated with a brownfield project by providing progressive financing tools and minimizing risks associated with the removal of contamination.

According to an interviewee, Artspace began looking for a new project opportunity to coincide with the end of the 25-year lease of its founding 1982 project. Initial interest in incorporating green design into a brownfield redevelopment, as well as the decision to build on a brownfield, was motivated by Artspace's desire to do the right thing. However, the confluence of policy between all three levels of government working to support brownfield revitalization, alongside the opportunity presented by an already assembled 3.67-acre property in the Granary District, and the affordability benefits provided by green design features, all provided support for Artspace's decision to pursue the Commons as their first venture into sustainable brownfield redevelopment. Decreased operating costs were particularly important because they are in line with Artspace's mission to keep their units affordable for renters (Jensen, 2010).

Project Characteristics and Development

Artspace Commons features a 102-unit apartment complex with a mix of affordable one- and two-bedroom units, as well as 50,000 sq. ft. of artist studios and commercial spaces for nonprofit organizations and community groups located on the ground floor (Artspace, 2013b). The two Commons buildings are located at 423 West 800 South and 824 South 400 West, approximately two blocks west of the Lincoln Highway (I80 /I15), two blocks east of the closest Trax (Salt Lake City Transit) light rail transit stop, and directly on the 800 South bike path, providing multi-modal access to the site (Artspace, 2013b). Completed in 2010, the Commons was 99% leased by 2013 (Artspace, 2013a), with 12 non-profit tenants such as TURN Community Services serving individuals with developmental disabilities and Bad Dog Arts, a creative arts organization (Jensen, 2010; Skibine, 2012).

Following the purchase of the former Utah Barrel and Scrap site, Artspace received a conditional Enforceable Written Assurance (EWA) from the Utah Department of Environmental Quality (DEQ). The EWA ensured that the DEQ would not bring any enforcement action against Artspace for pre-existing contamination on the site, conditional upon Artspace accepting several obligations to take reasonable steps to remediate contamination. Artspace then successfully applied to the Utah Voluntary Cleanup Program (VCP) and began characterizing the site (Utah Department of Environmental Quality, 2011).

Characterization revealed the presence of lead, arsenic PCBs, PAHs, Petroleum Hydrocarbons, and Benzene (Groundwater Contamination). This informed a Remedial Action Plan, which was put into action in late 2008. Groundwater was treated as part of the plan, and approximately 10,000 tons of impacted soil was removed and disposed of at a regulated facility (Rees, 2011). Removal reduced pollution at the source, preventing further leaching to groundwater and ensuring the site would be protective of human health and the environment (Utah Department of Environmental Quality, 2011). Following the successful cleanup, an environmental covenant was executed, and a VCP Certificate of Completion was granted to Artspace in 2009, allowing the development of the Commons to proceed (Utah Department of Environmental Quality, 2011).

Project Financing

Artspace Commons was a $28 million project, including remediation of the site and the development of new facilities. Financing was very much the result of an innovative and sophisticated partnership that made use of a crucial financing tool for community revitalization – the New Markets Tax Credit (NMTC) financing program. Artspace also ran a successful capital campaign to supplement NMTC financing (National Development Council, 2010).

The NMTC program was enacted by Congress under the Community Renewal Tax Relief Act of 2000 to leverage private investor capital in low-income communities in hopes of catalyzing community and economic revitalization. Administered by the US Treasury Department's Community Development Financial Institutions Fund, the program allows private investors to receive tax credits against federal income tax in return for equity investments in specified Community Development Entities (CDEs) (Business Wire, 2012).

Artspace had previously worked with the National Development Council (NDC) to leverage financing for the Artspace City Center under the NMTC program. Building on this successful partnership, Artspace was able to obtain a $27.1 million NMTC financing package. NDC helped bring two private investors to the table – US Bancorp Community Development Corporation and the American Express Center for Community Development. These investors leveraged the NMTC transaction through two CDEs – Enterprise Community Investment allocated $20 million to the project, and Brownfield Revitalization LLC $7.1 million (Skibine, 2010).

Debt financing was provided by the Utah Community Reinvestment Corporation (UCRC), a local community development lender who made a first-time foray into the NMTC program to make this project happen (National Development Council, 2010). Additional loans were obtained from Ally Bank and Morgan Stanley Bank, with an acquisition loan from the Utah Housing Corporation. In addition to these loans, Artspace raised $4 million through its capital campaign, including donations from the George S. and Dolores Dore Eccles Foundation, Energy Solutions Foundation for environmental mitigation, Rocky Mountain Power Blue Skies, and the Fidelity Foundation (Skibine, 2010).

Sustainability

From an economic standpoint, the project has generated economic success with an estimated 80 construction jobs and 35 permanent jobs associated with the 50,000 sq. ft. of artist studios and non-profit offices. As for community revitalization, Artspace Commons was one of the first redevelopments in the Granary District (Jensen, 2010). By bringing more people and businesses into the area, Artspace Commons is increasing activity in the Granary District (Norie, 2011), which in the long run may spur further redevelopment by attracting more people to, and improving their perceptions of, the District. New redevelopment in the District will, in the long run, have a positive effect on City finances as the City will be able to garner additional income through increased property taxes on other sites. Also, as noted by key respondents, the development is catered to attract members of the creative class and intended to create a cluster of artistic innovation (Jensen, 2010), which will bring additional economic activity and spending power into the District.

One of the most important contributions is the 102 units of affordable housing for households under 80 percent of area median income (Norie, 2011). In 2010, the monthly cost per unit ranged from $960 dollars for a 950 sq. ft., two-bedroom unit, to $770 for a 700 sq. ft., one-bedroom unit. The 650 sq. ft. retail units cost $650 (Jensen, 2010). There is some concern that gentrification will result in the displacement of original residents with further reinvestment in the area (Ellin, 2012). However, units in the Commons are rented by Artspace – which aims to provide affordable housing – meaning that these units at least will continue to be occupied by low-income individuals. This guarantees the community will remain mixed-income going forward, and that original residents of the Artspace Commons need not fear gentrification and displacement.

The residential units in the Commons were constructed using an open concept design and incorporate high-quality materials such as hardwood floors and granite countertops (Jensen, 2010). They also include various amenities such as a washer/dryer in each unit, balconies with views of the Wasatch or downtown, and secure bike storage (Skibine, 2010). The retail units and artist studios contain several amenities as well, such as "sinks, climate control, and natural light" (Skibine, 2010). High-quality construction means future low-income residents will not be living in second-tier housing if the area gentrifies, and that the building will not be a source of neighborhood blight in the future.

The Commons' proximity to a light rail stop, combined with its density, makes it an example of transit-oriented development. By increasing density in the vicinity of public transit, as well as the 800 south bike path, the Commons improves the efficiency of public investment in transit infrastructure and creates more opportunities for multi-modal transit choices. The mixed-use nature of the project means the District will be both a trip origin and destination. This again allows for efficient use of existing transit infrastructure while also creating the potential for some residents to forgo commuting to work entirely by working in the Commons' studios or offices (Skibine, 2010).

The green design features incorporated into the Artspace Commons project led to its designation as a LEED gold-certified building (see Figure 5.1), with some key features including:

- solar window awnings on the building's south side generate 25 kW of electricity annually (installation facilitated by a grant from the Rocky Mountain Power Blue Sky Program) (Norie, 2011);

90 *Residential Redevelopment*

- a solar hot water system provides 70 percent of the year-round hot water needs for the Commons (MJSA Architects, n.d.), in addition to green plumbing fixtures and shut-offs that significantly reduce water use;
- a cool roof and concrete parking lot reflect heat and reduce the heat island (Norie, 2011);
- landscaping designed to curb water use by using native plants (Norie, 2011);
- exterior lighting is designed to reduce light pollution by not going into the sky or off-site;
- waste reduction during construction, with over 90 percent of waste diverted from the landfill (Norie, 2011);
- deck flooring made from recycled tires (Norie, 2011) and the Securock gypsum-fiber roof board made up of 95% recycled content (Willett, 2010);
- the building provides secure bike storage in a locked part of the building (Norie, 2011);
- commercial restrooms include showers for cyclists and others (Norie, 2011);
- high-performance insulation reduces energy consumption (Jensen, 2010; Norie, 2011);
- ENERGY STAR qualified lighting and appliances to reduce energy consumption (Norie, 2011);
- low-emission paints and finishes are used throughout the building to produce a healthy environment;
- interior spaces designed to maximize the penetration of natural light for all occupants; and
- marmoleum used for the bathroom floors is a natural material produced using renewable resources.

Benefits, Barriers, and Lessons Learned

A vital benefit of the Artspace Commons project is its potential to spur further revitalization in the Granary District (see project timeline Table 5.1). As noted by one stakeholder, the hope is that the project will help turn the area into a destination for the creative class, and thereby catalyze further development. Bringing 12 non-profit firms and 35 new jobs associated with the artist studios and offices, as well as 102 new households into the community, was already a significant step in the right direction, as was turning a dilapidated and polluted 3.67-acre site into a model green building project.

Artspace's history indicated a strong possibility that the project would inspire further development. Indeed, the success of Artspace Commons led to further investment in Artspace Solar Gardens soon after. Completed in 2013 on the remainder of the Utah Scrap and Barrel site, the green building contains 10,000 sq. ft. of street-level commercial space and 30 affordable residential units. It also was the first net-zero mixed-use building in Utah, generating enough power to meet the building's needs through 859 onsite solar panels on the roof and surface parking structure. The project was also financed using New Markets Tax Credits and received support from the Rocky Mountain Power Blue Sky program to build its solar panel system (Artspace, 2013c). Artspace and Wasatch Community Gardens (2014), a tenant of the Commons, also partnered to construct a community garden on the site.

Figure 5.1 Artspace Commons, Salt Lake City, Utah, 2011

Despite the positive developments produced by Artspace, additional redevelopment in the Granary district will likely require similar conditions as those that created the Commons and Solar Gardens. A positive sign is that one of the most important conditions which brought the Commons to fruition, according to respondents, was the sizeable pre-assembled parcel of land. Land ownership in the Granary district is somewhat consolidated, with over 50 percent of the properties in several blocks in the District held by fewer than five owners. These blocks encompass over half the land in the Granary District (Redevelopment Agency of Salt Lake City, 2011).

On the other hand, there are issues in the Granary district that may hinder further revitalization, and as such, reduce the catalytic effects of the Commons. Several old buildings sit

Table 5.1 Timeline – Artspace Commons, Salt Lake City, Utah

Year	Description
Utah Barrel and Scrap operates for three generations	What is now the site of Artspace Commons housed a family-run business for three generations; Utah Barrel and Scrap, a scrap metal recycling business. This business created significant contamination on site
Late 1990s	The Salt Lake City Redevelopment Agency (RDA), in a report outlining existing conditions in the Granary District, identified the site as a high priority for remediation
2000	The New Markets Tax Credit (NMTC) financing program was enacted by Congress under the Community Renewal Tax Relief Act
November 2007	Artspace purchased the Utah Barrel and Scrap site
Late 2007	Artspace receives a conditional Enforceable Written Agreement (EWA) and applies to the Voluntary Cleanup Program (VCP)
Early 2008	The Utah Barrel and Scrap site is characterized
May 2008	Artspace holds a green planning charrette with its design and engineering team, property management staff, and consultants
Fall 2008	A remedial action plan is established
Late 2008	Cleanup of the site begins
May 2009	Following the successful cleanup, an environmental covenant was executed and a VCP Certificate of Completion was granted to Artspace. Construction begins soon after
September 2010	Artspace Commons building opens its doors
2013	Artspace Solar Gardens building opens its doors

vacant in the District. The RDA notes that sustained vacancy in older buildings may result in building deterioration producing further blight creation (Redevelopment Agency of Salt Lake City, 2011). Also, there was concern that the lack of community services (e.g., schools, police/fire stations, supermarkets) in the District would reduce residential demand (Redevelopment Agency of Salt Lake City, 2011).

Despite the eventual success of the project at achieving a more sustainable outcome, the Artspace Commons project did face challenges with brownfield redevelopment and the implementation of green building features. With regards to green building features, key informants noted there was a tension throughout the project between affordability and environmental sustainability. The cost of these features and the LEED paperwork proved to be a particular challenge. For example, geothermal technology, though desired, was not used in the Commons because it was considered too expensive and achieving LEED Gold was only possible because of external funding. The Artspace Solar Gardens provides another example in that without the support of the Blue Sky program, Artspace would have only been able to build a system of half the size (Oberbeck, 2013). More financial incentives are necessary, therefore, to promote further sustainability while keeping housing affordable.

Concerning brownfield redevelopment, it is clear that incentives also play a significant role in making projects financially feasible. To an extent, the risks associated with brownfield redevelopment were capitalized into the predevelopment value of the Utah Barrel and Scrap site, as it has been noted, Artspace "negotiated the sales price knowing the property would need environmental mitigation" (Norie, 2011). However, negotiation implies the total cost of remediation cannot always be included in the predevelopment value, and as such, there is a significant role for incentives to play in overcoming this additional cost (or else the developer will attempt to pass it on to consumers at the point of sale). Indeed, the Artspace Commons project received a great deal of support provided by the Utah Department of Environmental Quality's Voluntary Cleanup Program and the federal New Markets Tax Credit financing program. These programs helped incentivize brownfields redevelopment by minimizing risks associated with the removal of contamination and providing progressive financing tools. Also, the RDA provided $450,000 to Artspace through its tax increment reimbursement award (Redevelopment Agency of Salt Lake City, 2009), "which will repay half the project's architectural and engineering design costs" (Norie, 2011). Without these incentives, it is unclear if the project would have gotten off the ground.

Anvil Mountain, Silverton, Colorado

Site History

The Anvil Mountain brownfield redevelopment project consists of an 18.8-acre property, including 8.8 acres of the former Martha Rose/Walsh Smelter. The property abuts the Town of Silverton (population +500) in San Juan County, Colorado, which is nestled between two San Juan Mountain passes and is well known for its scenery and outdoor recreation (see Figure 5.2). The Martha Rose/Walsh Smelter experienced many periods of boom and bust throughout its history. In 1882 Seth R. Beckworth constructed a 20-ton smelting plant on the site and operated it as an ore crushing facility that produced silver, gold, and lead using a coal-fired blast furnace until 1893 when the facility was closed and dismantled (US EPA, 2010). For the next hundred years, the site sat mostly idle, with ownership of the smelter changing hands multiple times. The site is currently jointly owned by San Juan County (57%), Colorado Housing Inc. (22%), and Housing Solutions for the Southwest (21%). The site's history of industrial legacy is a small part of the area's once-thriving mining economy that started in 1876 and ended in 1991, shedding nearly 400 jobs (Singer et al., 2006; US EPA, 2010).

The Rose Walsh Smelter site was singled out for redevelopment in 2002 because of its flat terrain, proximity to the town's infrastructure, and lack of development in the surrounding area. It was deemed an appropriate site for redevelopment as it was a large plot of semi-vacant land in a town where vacant land was on the decline. Many of the homes once owned by miners had been turned into vacation, seasonal, and second homes, resulting in a lack of affordable housing for those living and working in the county (US EPA, 2009a). Given the site's history, however, redevelopment would require dealing with a significant amount of soil contamination and the remains of the former smelting operation, including the old railroad grade and several piles of scrap iron, wood, and slag (URS Operating Services Inc., 2006).

94 Residential Redevelopment

Figure 5.2 Rose Walsh Smelter site, Anvil Mountain, Colorado (Google Earth, n.d.)

Project Vision

The Town of Silverton and San Juan County's vision was to redevelop the entire site into a Planned Unit Development (PUD). The proposed development sought to create a new community consisting of affordable housing units and a mix of single-family and multi-family dwellings. It also aimed to be pedestrian-oriented with an abundant combination of open and green space, as well as architecturally designed to respect the industrial heritage of the site (San Juan 2000 Development Association, 2009).

Initially, the town envisioned placing a county shop on the site with room for residential development. However, this idea received considerable public opposition and was abandoned. The plan was to lay streets, utilities, and infrastructure on the site and then allow the private sector to develop the property. Once environmental assessments were conducted, however, the extent of contamination required a change in the vision. Given the resources needed to remediate the site, it was deemed more financially practical to develop higher density living in the form of multi-family dwellings (Sickmiller, 2009).

The redevelopment was also envisioned to include affordable renewable energy options aimed at reducing emissions and operating costs. The town has a frigid climate, so a significant consideration in housing design is to identify energy conservation options. Technologies such as high-efficiency insulation, roofing, and windows, along with solar energy and geothermal exchange heat pumps are essential given that residents of Silverton often pay as much for heat and utilities as they do for housing. Building affordable housing that is also energy efficient was seen as a way to reduce utility bills and help make it possible for low- to median-income Silverton residents to transition from renters to homeowners. The project also aimed to encourage historical and heritage preservation through architectural design that reflects existing Silverton neighborhoods and honors Silverton's mining legacy (US EPA, 2009b).

Project Characteristics and Development

The initial redevelopment proposal called for building 49 units of housing, ranging from 1,800 to 2,200 sq. ft. in size. There was to be a mix of single-family dwellings, as well as one- and two-bedroom condominiums. The project was planned as an affordable housing development with green and sustainable design innovations integrated into it (US EPA, 2009b).

Environmental site assessments conducted in 2003 and 2004 for due diligence purposes before the county purchased the property identified the presence of contamination stemming from past smelting operations (URS Operating Services Inc., 2006). Levels of lead, arsenic, and barium were detected, and the site was deemed unacceptable for residential use without remedial action. Also, the data gathered was used to evaluate the risk to the health of potential construction workers, residents, recreationists, and onsite workers. The report by URS concluded that contaminants found on the property, if not remediated, could potentially pose a health risk to prospective users of the space (URS Operating Services Inc., 2006).

The remediation of the site began in 2007 and continued well into 2009. It was anticipated that cleanup would be completed in time for construction to commence in late 2009. However, additional soil removal was required in the summer of 2009, and construction was delayed until 2010. The cleanup of the site was administered in partnership with the US EPA and the Colorado Department of Public Health and Environment (CDPHE). The contamination would be buried and capped onsite according to state and federal guidelines to meet the necessary standards for residential use. The repository has since been vegetated, and stairs and a trail installed on top of it. The remediation was funded using a combination of a US EPA Brownfield Cleanup Grant and other matching and leveraged state funds (San Juan 2000 Development Association, 2009).

The EPA was involved in the project since its inception. The EPA aided the town and county by evaluating site conditions and plans, identifying and evaluating energy efficiency options, and providing recommendations regarding potential resources and funding approaches the town may pursue to implement the recommendations. Also, the EPA provided guidance to achieve successful financing and implementation of the development effort. The EPA Brownfields Sustainability Pilot supplied $50,000 in technical assistance to the county to identify and evaluate energy savings and alternative energy options as well as additional funding resources. As part of the pilot, the US Department of Energy's

National Renewable Energy Laboratory developed models of energy conservation strategies that integrate sustainable design concepts (e.g., building orientation, window types, passive solar design) (US EPA, 2010). The redevelopment would also be buffered from the adjacent highway by green space for noise damping and drainage management (San Juan 2000 Development Association, 2009).

Nearly half (44%) of Silverton's homeowners and renters spent 50% or more of their household income on housing costs. To combat this, a portion of the homes built would be offered to people who make 80% of the area's median income, which is approximately $36,000. The history of the site would be preserved through the use of interpretive signage and historical photography. The lower railroad and the Rail Scale structure at the site would also be protected. Furthermore, the architectural design of the dwellings would incorporate Silverton's mining heritage (San Juan 2000 Development Association, 2009).

Throughout the planning process of the Anvil Mountain Neighborhood, numerous open houses and public meetings were organized to both inform the public and gather feedback (Sickmiller, 2009). The town of Silverton has approximately 400 to 500 permanent residents year-round, and the local workforce has very few options to purchase a home in the area. A project like this which aimed to provide locals with opportunities to buy into the housing market and stay in the town was seen as contributing and strengthening the local economy, which is heavily dependent upon tourism in the summer months.

The land use and project characteristics initially desired included 13 single-family dwellings priced at $214,000 each, ten one-bedroom condos at $127,280 each, 33 two-bedroom condos at $147,280 each, worth $26.8 million overall. A skate park and a 2.5-acre community park were also planned. Build out was expected to take place from 2015 to 2020.

In 2016, San Juan County commissioners approved a development plan for the "Anvil Village" workforce housing subdivision that contained over 30 new homes (townhouses, duplexes, and singles), which was set to begin construction sales in April 2016 (Esper, 2016). The project failed to get off the ground, however. Development did commence on two rental apartment buildings, and as of March 2020, the two buildings offer a total of 12 affordable and market-rate units. Thirteen market-rate lots for single-family homes were also put up for sale with the restriction that a home has to be constructed within two years of purchase and that it has to be the purchaser's primary residence or rented to someone who makes it their primary residence. Four of these lots have been purchased, and the remaining are in process, with one home constructed and occupied and a second under construction. There are also ten lots available for the development of "attainable" homes by those earning 80% to 125% of the median income. The county notes a developer has constructed a unit for just under $200,000 that has received interest from a couple of potential buyers, and there has been interest from others to build similar homes (William Tookey, personal communication, March 30, 2020). Unfortunately, the county noted that they have not yet been able to come up with a model that allows for the construction of affordable units for those below 80% of the median income. While it was anticipated that four or five homes would be constructed in the summer of 2020 (and a similar number in 2021), the COVID 19 situation has brought about new uncertainty to the local economy that may cause further delays.

Project Financing

The property cost a total of $279,000 to purchase, with San Juan County paying $200,000 and Housing Solutions for the Southwest and Colorado Housing Inc. contributing the remainder. The total cost per acre was $17,437. The county has mandated that a certain amount of housing must be dedicated to affordable housing for every new subdivision. In 2003, the Durango Mountain Resort (DMR) paid the county "Fees-in-Lieu" so that the Resort may be exempt from providing affordable housing themselves (Sickmiller, 2009). In essence, fees are paid by the developer to "hire" San Juan County or its agents to develop affordable housing, so the developer is not required to build it themselves. According to county regulations, these funds are reserved for investments in affordable housing and were used to purchase the site. The county expects to recover its initial financial investment plus an estimated additional million dollars through property sales and development charges. The county initially planned to sell three wooded lots at a market rate for at least $150,000 each, which will generate $450,000 back to the county. The 43 affordable lots will be sold at an average of $10,000 each, making $430,000 back to the county.

Furthermore, a developer fee ranging from $8,000 to $15,000 will be charged. It was estimated this fund would generate $390,000 back to the county to be invested for future infrastructure and land banking projects (San Juan Development Association., n.d.). That said, the project faced a funding shortage of between $326,000 and $764,000.

The EPA helped with identifying grants and other potential funding sources (US EPA, 2009c). The project continued to receive grants and loans as it progressed. According to the US EPA (2010, p. 2), these included: $686,000 from the Colorado Department of Local Affairs for cleanup and infrastructure; $585,000 from EPA through a Targeted Brownfields Assessment, Brownfields Sustainability Pilot, Brownfields Cleanup Grant and Brownfields Stimulus Grant for site grading; $514,000 from San Juan County for property purchase and matching funds; $124,000 from a Colorado Department of Transportation Enhancement Grant for historical interpretation and landscaping; $100,000 from the Colorado Department of Public Health and Environment for cleanup; $60,000 from Housing Solutions for the Southwest for property purchase; $60,000 from Colorado Housing Inc. for property purchase; and $6,100 from a state Historical Fund Grant for a historic assessment. As a condition for the Department of Local Affairs grant for the subdivision's infrastructure, deed restrictions apply to the subsidized housing units.

Benefits, Barriers, and Lessons Learned

The redevelopment of Anvil Mountain is expected to yield several environmental, social, and economic benefits (see project timeline, Table 5.2). The management of hazardous pollution from the site reduces potential exposure to contamination and creates a cleaner environment. The utilization of green technology in the construction and design will reduce the carbon footprint and emissions of the development while lowering operating costs for residents. The affordable housing component of the redevelopment provides those with fewer means a safe option for living. An interview conducted with someone involved in the project outlined that one of the main benefits of this type of development is the option to purchase

Table 5.2 Timeline – Anvil Mountain, Silverton, Colorado

Year	Description
1882	20-ton smelting plant is constructed on the site and operated as an ore crushing facility
1882–1979	Ownership of facility changes hands several times and capacity is increased and decreased depending on owner
1979–1990	Duane Eggett takes ownership of the property
1990–2004	Lancaster Trust takes ownership of the property
2002	Site is selected for redevelopment
2004 to persent	San Juan County (57%), Colorado Housing Inc. (22%) and Housing Solutions for the Southwest (21%) all own the property
2006	URS Inc. is contracted by EPA to conduct ESAs. Hazardous contaminants are found in the soil
2007–2009	Remediation of contaminants are conducted
2012	Project breaks ground, water and sewer lines installed and site graded
2016	Approval for Anvil Village to construct over 30 new homes, but project fails to get off the ground
2020	Two rental apartments and one single family home constructed, and home lots for sale

an affordable living space as prices have simply been beyond the means of many who wish to reside in the community. Furthermore, construction and remediation will generate employment that will have multiplier effects that add back into the community. Finally, this project is also dedicated to historical and heritage preservation that celebrates the character of the area and the industrial legacy of Silverton.

The Anvil Mountain project has faced many obstacles to redevelopment. The discovery of additional soil contamination initially delayed construction by one year to 2010. Due to the extra volume of contaminated soils, the county was forced to expand the planned repository area, causing at least one lot, which was intended to be a multi-family building, to be sacrificed. San Juan County currently serves as the developer for the project, and it was feared that they might find securing traditional funding a challenge since it had no prior experience building similar developments. Accordingly, the EPA technical assistance team suggested the county hire a developer experienced in affordable housing and sustainable redevelopment as the project moves forward, given that banks prefer to lend to entities with experience (US EPA, 2009b). The consultants hired by the EPA contacted private developers in San Juan County to assess their ability to redevelop the site but found that none had the experience to manage a complicated brownfield project. Throughout the course of the project, unexpected financial considerations arose that forced those in charge to diversify project funding. The county initially counted on funding from the state of Colorado to cover two-thirds of project costs. That funding was no longer available after the state suffered from the national financial crisis. Consultants assisted in identifying grants from other sources to fund supplemental pieces of the project (US EPA, 2009c). Also, in their simulations to determine the most viable energy-conserving design options for the area, the EPA consultants were unable to use local data because it did not exist. As a result, they used weather data from Leadville, CO, which is not the closest geographically but has a climate similar to Silverton (US EPA, 2009c). Lastly, there has also been some backlash to the development of affordable housing in general, as some fear it is subsidizing people who are already overly reliant on government support.

Concerning the EPA's pilot process, the interviewee appreciated the expedited review of the grant application process and noted that a significant amount of staff hours were saved due to the fact they were not preoccupied with grant administration procedures. It was also stressed that proper planning and preparation were essential to the development of the project. Rather than applying broad stroke planning, carefully analyzing and paying attention to the local context is considered crucial to successful redevelopment. While the project has progressed slowly, it has moved incrementally toward its community and sustainability vision.

References

Artspace. (2013a). *Mission and history*. July 27. ArtspaceUtah.org.
Artspace. (2013b). *Artspace Commons*. September 25. ArtspaceUtah.org.
Artspace. (2013c). *Artspace Solar Gardens*. September 25. ArtspaceUtah.org.
Business Wire. (2012). *US Bank and American Express partner on $74 million economic growth investment to create jobs in several southern and western states*. January 12. Business Wire, A Berkshire Hathaway Company.
Ellin, N. (2012). Raze to raise: Polishing gems in Salt Lake's Granary District. *15 Bytes, Utah's Art Magazine*, June Edition, 1, 4.
Esper, M. (2016). Designs released for Anvil Mountain homes. March 17. *Silverton Standard & the Miner*.
Google Earth. (n.d.). Former Rose Walsh Smelter site, Anvil Mountain. 37°48'32" N and 107°40'49" W. December 4, 2020.
Jensen, D. (2010). Salt Lake City's newest, hippest, greenest apartments set to open. September 2, *The Salt Lake Tribune*, sec. Archive.
Jones, R. (2010). Artspace Commons begins the next downtown evolution. September 12, *Examiner.com*, sec. Business & Finance.
McKellar, K. (2013). Festival to help rejuvenate Salt Lake's Granary District. June 2, *Deseret News*, National Edition.
MJSA Architects. (n.d.). *Artspace Commons*. MJSA Architects.
National Development Council. (2010). *Artspace commons opens its doors: Creative new markets tax credits financing helps make it happen*. September 21. National Development Council.
Oberbeck, S. (2013). Rocky Mountain Power funds renewable-energy projects. February 12, *The Salt Lake Tribune*, sec. News.
Redevelopment Agency of Salt Lake City. (2009). *RDA of SLC 2009 Annual Report*. Salt Lake City.
Redevelopment Agency of Salt Lake City. (2011). *West Temple Gateway & Granary District Redevelopment Strategy: Development Guide*. Salt Lake City, 15-20.
Redevelopment Agency of Salt Lake City. (n.d.). *Granary District*. Salt Lake City.
Rees, B. (2011). Utah Department of Environmental Quality Brownfields Community Assistance. *Utah Planner*, 38(3), 1-7.
San Juan 2000 Development Association (2009). *The Anvil Mountain development guide: Merging affordability and community in Silverton*. Economic, Housing and Community Development for San Juan County, Co.
San Juan Development Association. (n.d.). *Anvil Mountain neighborhood and affordable housing: Questions from the community and answers from the project coordinator*. Economic, Housing and Community Development for San Juan County, Co.

Singer, J., Horn, C., & Twitty, E. (2006). *Martha Rose/Walsh Smelter archaeological assessment*. Report prepared by Silverton Restoration Consulting, Alpine Archeological Consultants, and Mountain States Historical, San Juan County.

Skibine, J. (2010). *Artspace Commons to celebrate its grand opening during a ribbon cutting ceremony on September 17 at 4:00 pm*. September 8. National Development Council blog.

Skibine, J. (2012). *Artspace, polishing gems: Prospects for the granary district*. Department of City and Metropolitan Planning, University of Utah.

Thompson, A. (2012). *Salt Lake City's Granary District: Past and Future*. January 9. The University of Utah.

URS Operating Services Inc. (2006). *Analytical results report for targeted brownfields assessment, Rose and Walsh Smelter San Juan County* (Contract No. EP-W-05-050). US EPA Region 8.

US EPA. (2009a). *Energy efficient and affordable homes planned for former mine scarred property* (Report EPA-560-F-09-516). US EPA Region 8.

US EPA. (2009b). *Building a sustainable future: A report on the Environmental Protection Agency's brownfield's sustainability pilots* (Report EPA-560-F-09-500). Office of Brownfields and Land Revitalization.

US EPA. (2009c). *Energy efficiency for affordable housing at a brownfield redevelopment Anvil Mountain Site, Silverton, CO*. Report prepared by SRA International, Inc., Contract No. EP-W-07-023.

US EPA. (2010). *From smelter site to affordable and energy efficient housing in San Juan County, Colorado* (Report EPA 908-F-10-001). US EPA Region 8, Brownfields.

Utah Department of Environmental Quality. (2011). Artspace: Scrap yard to studios and galleries. *Utah Brownfields*, 1, 1–4.

Wasatch Community Gardens. (2014). *Artspace Commons garden*. January 9. Wasatch Community Gardens.

Willett, R. (2010). New construction: Using new roofing products in Utah. September/October, *Western Roofing*.

Interviews

Artspace Commons, Salt Lake City, Utah

- Norie, J. (2011) Executive Director, Artspace.
- Skibine, J. (2011) Director of Development, Artspace.

Anvil Mountain, Silverton, Colorado

- Sickmiller, A. (2009) Town and Country Planner, Town of Silverton Colorado.
- Tookey, W. (2012, 2020) San Juan County Administrator, San Juan County Colorado.

6 Green and Community Space Redevelopment

Although land recycling is increasingly accepted as part of the urban development process, brownfield reclamation projects initially tended to overlook the potential of parks and community space as infrastructure for ecological and social functions. The five case studies examined in this chapter – Moran Center in Burlington, Vermont, Haynes Recreation Center/Chacon Creek in Laredo, Texas, Elmhurst and Freshkills Parks in New York City, and plans for the former Allen Morrison facility in Lynchburg, Virginia – demonstrate the challenges and transformative benefits of redeveloping brownfield properties as parks and public spaces. The case studies offer an alternative approach to brownfield reclamation focused on real estate and economic development. Each case study describes how collaboration, innovation, and sustainable design are transforming urban blight into public assets while contributing to broader public policy objectives.

Moran Plant, Burlington, Vermont

Site History

In the middle of the 19th Century, Burlington, Vermont, was one of the largest lumber ports in the nation. As was common practice at the time, extensive filling of the shoreline created new land to expand industrial activity along the water. Filling of the waterfront continued well into the 1950s and was permitted through the state-mandated Public Trust Doctrine because the employment it supported was seen as a significant benefit to the public. In addition to lumber processing, Burlington's waterfront supported an array of industrial uses, such as the Moran Generating Plant constructed in 1954 to supply electricity and a bulk petroleum facility to store fuel for shipment in barges through the Hudson River/Champlain Canal system.

By the late 1980s, the filled lands along Burlington's waterfront had fallen into decay, and the remarkable shore of Lake Champlain became mostly inaccessible to the public (see Figure 6.1). The 2.8-acre Moran Generating Plant site, built on land that had previously housed railroad, lumber, and petroleum businesses, was decommissioned in 1986 and sat idle except for a small sailing center that uses part of it for storage (US EPA, 2009a).

Project Vision

In the late 1980s, the city of Burlington used the Public Trust Doctrine in court, but this time as an argument for reclaiming the filled lands along the waterfront for public use. In

Figure 6.1 Moran Plant, Burlington, Vermont, 2009

a noteworthy Vermont Supreme Court ruling, the petroleum storage and rail siding properties were found not to be beneficial to the general public. The Vermont legislature defined Public Trust Lands as those reserved for: *"indoor or outdoor parks and recreation uses and facilities including parks and open space, marinas open to the public on a non-discriminatory basis, water-dependent uses, boating, and related services"* (city of Burlington, 1994). After the Supreme Court ruling, the city acquired over 60 acres of waterfront land, including the Moran property, which became the focal point of waterfront revitalization planning efforts. The overall goal of this effort was to make the waterfront "a vital, year-round part of the community, providing safe and environmentally sustainable cultural, recreational, social, and economic opportunities that are accessible to all regardless of income, ability or lifestyle" (Burlington Community and Economic Development Office, 2007).

Focus on the site emerged through a public process that unfolded over a decade wherein the community identified the Moran plant as a vital piece of a much larger vision for the waterfront. Indeed, the city acquired the plant in 1986 because it was the only place where locals could physically access the water, given that everything else was fenced off. When the Moran plant was about to be decommissioned, it inspired numerous, passionate ideas about the future of the waterfront and became a focal point for community action.

Burlington voters approved the city's Waterfront Revitalization Plan in 1990, but despite community desires to revitalize the site, the city encountered extreme difficulty identifying a suitable end-use. Many ideas were proposed but failed to materialize, including a center for science and arts, an aquarium, a recreation center, a baseball stadium, and a brewery and concert hall. A Request for Letters of Interest in 1993 yielded several proposals, all with inadequate funding or programming plans. The city issued a second request for proposals in 1995, and a project by the University of Vermont's Fleming Museum was selected (Burlington Community and Economic Development Office, 2007). After several years of planning, however, the Fleming Museum chose not to move forward. Reasons for the failure of past proposals are varied but seem typical for highly visible brownfield projects aiming to reclaim hulking industrial buildings (i.e., high costs and unrealistic terms related to addressing site conditions, design and engineering, development and parking, and project operation over the long run). After a lively and well-publicized public debate around the creation of a new YMCA and expanded Lake Champlain Sailing Center that failed to materialize, it was felt that more public consultation was needed (city of Burlington, 2010).

A more robust public participation process was initiated in 2005 by Burlington's Community and Economic Development Office (CEDO) that involved several steps, commencing with a survey of community desires and redevelopment options. Every household in the city was mailed an "Idea Card," and from these, an Idea Review Committee identified over 30 "Idea Categories" for further exploration. Over 140 citizens attended three public forums in the fall of 2005 to provide feedback on the Idea Categories. A survey was also mailed to every household, asking residents to rank the Ideas and essential factors for redevelopment. Survey results highlighted citizen preference for passive open space and recreation-center type uses, followed by a middle-tier of tourism, retail, and private-recreation uses, and a lower tier of institutional, residential, and commercial (e.g., hotel, office) uses (Burlington Community and Economic Development Office, 2008).

From the information collected, the city generated a Waterfront Advisory Survey: Moran Plant Ballot (dated March 7, 2006) that asked for more specific reuse ideas and about approaches for managing the Moran building. Nearly 10,000 people turned in their ballots. Upon review of the results, the city Council offered seven concepts for further discussion by the community: (1) a waterfront park (demolish the building and extend Waterfront Park); (2) a community and recreation center; (3) a community sailing center; (4) an outdoor concert bandshell; (5) a maritime museum; (6) a combination of uses with part of the Moran; and (7) a mix of uses in the Moran (Burlington Community and Economic Development Office, 2008). In September of 2006, the city held a Moran Open House to review the results of the ballot and allow for feedback on the seven concepts.

After synthesizing the results from the intensive two-year public process, the city proposed a multi-use redevelopment. The Mayor set up three groups to develop and assess the Moran redevelopment concept. The Moran Advisory Group, made up of business, citizen, and park committee members, was charged with evaluating project feasibility and the public process. The Moran Users Group, made up of organizations that could occupy the building, assisted the Advisory Group with tenancy issues. The Moran Technical Advisory Committee, made up of city departments, sorted through the technical details associated with the project. On March 4, 2008, after over two years of consultation, the process culminated in a town meeting day vote in which Burlington voters approved by a two-to-one margin an advisory referendum endorsing the proposal for renovating the plant.

Community members and the local government were determined from the outset to incorporate sustainability elements into the project. The Mayor and the city Council Parks, Arts & Culture Committee put forward fundamental principles to guide the redevelopment of the Moran Plant to:

- ensure permanent public ownership and control;
- create year-round use;
- create and extend elements of the Waterfront Park;
- minimize undue traffic and parking issues;
- retain the Lake Champlain Sailing Center;
- provide the opportunity for new public and private partnerships;
- utilize the existing building shell where cost-effective;
- retain historical elements when possible;
- generate income for operations and maintenance;
- keep development costs reasonable; and
- utilize the highest standards in energy conservation and green building construction (Burlington Community and Economic Development Office, 2008).

The city noted that it has been undertaking environmentally sustainable green building for over 20 years, even before the introduction of LEED green building standards. The community was demanding things be done better environmentally, and virtually all city projects currently involve green building concepts.

Project Characteristics and Development

The Moran Plant building is about seven stories high, with a gross floor area of 44,142 sq. ft. The structure sits on a solid reinforced concrete pad located below lake level that allowed water to enter the building for the coal-fired boilers and cooling of generator components. Most of the interior space consists of neglected industrial infrastructure. The main floor features ceiling heights of approximately 20 feet, while the land surrounding the facility is mostly undeveloped.

As the project coordinator noted, Burlington Electric, the former owner of the site, did a good job of decommissioning the property, dealing with waste oils, asbestos, transformers, and most other equipment. That said, the first phase of the project was to assess whether the building could physically support any use. Preliminary building evaluation started in 2006, and the corrective action plan for the building exterior was completed soon after. Interior cleaning and dewatering planning commenced in 2007.

Early on, the Vermont Downtown Program provided CEDO with a grant to conduct geotechnical, structural, environmental, and wetland analyses at the Moran Plant site. A historic building assessment and structural analyses were also completed (New England Preservation Collaborative Inc., 2006). The building was found to be historically significant because it is older than 50 years and one of the few remaining coal-fired power plants from that era. The structural assessment found the building to be generally sound and capable of being renovated. A wetlands analysis performed on the property revealed a wetland had resulted from the removal of a sizeable above-ground storage tank in the late 1980s. The investigation found two connected wetland complexes, classified as Class III wetlands, storing 2.7 acre-feet of water (Heindel & Noyes Inc., 2006).

Much of the brownfields work - contaminant identification, delineation, and initial remediation - was complete, and site-specific standards for cleanup of remaining soil contamination were determined. Remediation work for the remaining asbestos and lead paint in the building's interior was to be finished once final designs were completed. Phase I and II ESAs found the presence of lead paint and asbestos in the building. Most asbestos was removed during decommissioning, but traces still covered the interior floor and walkways. The Vermont Department of Environmental Conservation (VT DEC) agreed to wait for a redevelopment plan before requiring a mitigation plan for the interior.

From the outset, the city and state worked closely to identify and address short-term risks while the revitalization plan was under development. Shallow soil on site was contaminated with arsenic levels above state standards and PAHs above US EPA's risk-based guidance level for residential use. Both contaminants are high in areas where coal storage and coal conveyor belts were located. Waite Environmental Management in 2006 recommended developing site-specific risk-based cleanup levels for shallow soils, taking future use into account (Waite Environmental Management LLC, 2010). VT DEC agreed to a site-specific arsenic guideline, which limits the area of concern to a portion of a grassy area north of the plant where coal had been stored. The city capped the area with clean fill to prevent contact and remove any risk to the lake. The only impact on deeper soil was trichloroethylene (TCE) contamination found at a 16-foot depth at only one place north of the building, where groundwater contamination was also found. Remediation of deeper soil is only recommended if the new development requires excavation.

In March of 2008, voters approved the city's proposed redevelopment plan for the site. By October of that year, members of the Moran Users Group signed Memoranda of Understanding to participate in the project. The project would retain the building shell and create a multi-use facility with public access and activities. Construction and operations would be supported by private and non-profit ventures integrated into the tenant mix (Burlington Community and Economic Development Office, 2008).

The site would be designated as an extension of the Waterfront Park, to which pedestrians and other amenities will be linked. An ice rink, water play area, and a skate park were proposed for the outside. The building would continue to house the Community Sailing Center, along with a children's museum, indoor rock/ice climbing center, restaurant, café, fitness center, meeting rooms, community space, public restrooms, and observation deck. The project was to be completed by the summer of 2010, but a more comprehensive financial examination necessitated by the 2008 recession delayed the project.

The desire for green elements was essential for project proponents and the community. In August 2008, the US EPA selected the Moran Center for a Brownfields Sustainability Pilot award and provided technical assistance to assess the feasibility of implementing various green building elements into the project, including onsite renewable energy production, energy and water conservation, innovative stormwater treatment techniques, and ecological enhancements. The comprehensive report provides detailed design options for the building and infrastructure design, as well as for the project's integration with the surrounding uses (Vita Nuova LLC, 2009). The project aimed for LEED Gold certification.

In October 2008, Freeman French Freeman, an acclaimed local architecture firm, was hired in a competitive process to provide architectural and engineering services for the Moran project, and their design was approved by the city of Burlington Development Review Board in August 2010 (Burlington Community and Economic Development Office, 2020). The proposal contained numerous green building features, including a lake-water-cooled water-source heat-pump system with a high-efficiency condensing boiler heating system, high-efficiency lighting, stormwater management via wetlands restoration and a green roof, public transit connections, bicycle parking, and pedestrian access.

The Waterfront Revitalization Plan positioned the plan as a catalyst for economic growth for the city. Burlington's stated Sustainable Economic Development Strategies included financial and technical assistance to small and large businesses and targeted assistance to employers with livable wage jobs, and companies playing a pivotal role in downtown vitality. The goal of the project is to create 500 construction and 80 permanent jobs.

Among the most critical elements of the project were its community-oriented features. In addition to rehabilitating a derelict property that blighted the waterfront, the project planned to add numerous amenities related to public education, community gathering, access, recreation, and relaxation.

Project Financing

Despite the momentum surrounding the project, the city had acted in a fiscally conservative manner to ensure it would be feasible over the long term. On April 26, 2010, Burlington's city Council passed a resolution to appoint a Moran Blue Ribbon Committee charged with reviewing the financial structure of the project in terms of how it protects taxpayers during a downturn, the financing model applied, and the financing plans of the tenants.

Given that the project is community-based, the committee concluded that the $16 million Moran redevelopment project would not be viable using traditional financing but required an array of "non-traditional" vehicles to be successful. The committee focused on various risks within the project's scope. It felt that environmental risks had been mitigated. Still, it worried about financial risks associated with the redevelopment, such as potential cost overruns due to inadequate budgeting, scope, quality changes, and hidden conditions, and the failure of the contractors to complete the project. The committee recommended additional cost estimates be made before construction plans move forward (city of Burlington, 2009).

According to the committee's final report, most of its attention focused on the complex financial structure of the proposed redevelopment. It highlighted four major financial components of the proposal: (1) tax revenues from the Waterfront TIF district, not the project, would be used to pay the debt service on a $2.1 million loan from HUD's Section 108 program; (2) the project would require additional debt to be paid from TIF revenues of up to $6.6 million to complete the redevelopment as proposed unless other significant funding sources could be accessed such as; (3) Historic Tax Credits and Federal Rehabilitation Investment Tax Credits valued at $1.3 million based on qualified rehabilitation expenses of $6.6 million;

and (4) New Market Tax Credits (city of Burlington, 2010). The report advised the city to only move forward with the transaction when all of the financing components were secured and not replace any of it with debt. It should be noted that the city had already secured over $1.5 million from a myriad of other smaller funding sources – third-party grants and project subsidies.

While there was some concern expressed about the ability of the tenants to secure funds, it was noted that the city had structured the project such that the tenants' success was not critical to the project's success. This is because the TIF and not the tenants would pay the project's debt. Tax credits from the project would continue to flow to the investors should one or more of the tenants fail. Interestingly, the committee also pointed out that specific funding opportunities might be lost if the Moran project did not proceed, and the city would then be stuck with a multi-million-dollar demolition cost as well.

Eventually, the financing challenges associated with the Moran Center would lead the project in a new direction. In 2012, a new mayoral administration assumed office and promised to cancel the previous project, but continue with surrounding waterfront area improvements (Weinberger, 2012). The new Mayor stated, "the city will not go forward with the former administration's plan to have the city of Burlington serve as the developer of a complicated, speculative, commercial real estate venture" (Weinberger, 2012).

The administration created a Public Investment Action Plan (PIAP) to replace the project through a competition to evaluate proposals for the Moran Center with the finalists put to a public vote (Burlington Community and Economic Development Office, n.d.). The competition was won by New Moran Inc., a local non-profit created to redevelop the site. New Moran proposed mixed-use development, including a concert hall and farmer's market, and signed a memorandum of understanding with the city in 2014 (True, 2016). This proposal was eventually scaled back from a $33 million to a $15 million development due to funding challenges, which eliminated amenities such as an art gallery and market space (Baird, 2017). New Moran Inc. and the city administration had come into conflict over whether the project was viable, and the city gave the organization "one last chance" to submit a viable project (True, 2016). New Moran Inc. provided a detailed project outline in December 2016. However, it was rejected in September 2017 by the city, and the building was slated for demolition (Jickling, 2017).

In 2017, the city charged its Community Economic Development Office (CEDO) with developing the Moran Municipal Generating Station Deconstruction and Demolition Study. The study provides detailed information regarding the costs for multiple demolition and redevelopment scenarios that ranged in price from approximately $4 to $11 million. In late 2018, CEDO presented a plan to fill in the basement of the old structure, remove the brick exterior, and leave the steel skeleton of the building in place. Burlington's city Council approved the plan in early 2019. The city started conducting more detailed assessment work to characterize the hazardous building materials, which revealed levels of asbestos, lead paint, and PCB laden coatings that drove up demolition, abatement, and remediation costs (Burlington Community and Economic Development Office, 2020). Despite this, in February 2020, Burlington's city Council approved moving forward with the first phase (1a) of the so-called Moran-FRAME project budgeted at $6.55 million (markedly lower than the $15 million plan rejected in 2017) (Burlington Community and Economic Development Office, 2020). This first approved phase will begin construction in 2020 to provide a clean, safe frame that is open to the public. Once completed, the city hopes to get the next phase (1b) of the construction approved to add finishes and public park amenities, such as restrooms, lighting, paths, utilities, roofing, and more. On August 19, 2020 the city broke ground on the Moran FRAME project designed by Freeman French Freeman, Inc. (see Figure 6.2), which is expected to be completed by the end of 2021 and will be managed by the Waterfront division of Burlington Parks, Recreation & Waterfront (Burlington Community and Economic Development Office, 2020). While the FRAME concept does not contain all of the features of earlier proposals, it does provide a more affordable start to realizing critical community objectives (i.e., site remediation, public waterfront access, historic preservation). It also creates a platform for possible future projects such as elevated viewing decks, a winter ice rink, summer stage, large children's playground (Burlington Community and Economic Development Office, 2020).

Figure 6.2 Moran FRAME, Burlington, Vermont (courtesy of Freeman French Freeman, Inc., 2020)

Benefits, Barriers, and Lessons Learned

The Moran project faced numerous hurdles from its inception. Achieving public buy-in for a site that had become an iconic symbol of the city's waterfront required a very robust public participation initiative to break the logjam (see project timeline Table 6.1). Nevertheless, concerns about project funding and risk continued to derail the process. Other barriers included the financial resources required to build green (anticipating costs and generating resources), physical design challenges associated with remediating and preserving a power plant building

Table 6.1 Timeline – Moran Center, Burlington, Vermont

Year	Description
1954–1986	Coal-fired power plant was built and operated
1990	City of Burlington voters approved the urban renewal plan for the Waterfront Revitalization District
2005	After several failed proposals, the city acted to ensure strong public engagement • Mails "Idea Card" to every household • Idea Review Committee organizes results • Survey and public forums used to rate ideas
2006	Waterfront Advisory Survey: Moran Plant ballot distributed to voters to rate top ideas
May 2007	• Finance Board and City Council actions directing CEDO to conduct feasibility study • Presentations to Neighborhood Planning Assemblies • Update to Parks Commission • Moran Users Group (MUG) develops needs of tenancy
Summer 2007	Conceptual development – refinement: Moran Advisory Group (MAG) meetings Feasibility: MAG and MUG meeting to evaluate and refine information
Fall 2007	Presentations and community feedback on the MAG and MUG work on the draft feasibility report to Neighborhood Planning Assemblies and other community groups
January 2008	City Council decides whether to place the Moran on a March ballot
March 4, 2008	• Advisory Ballot vote on Town Meeting Day • Continued public process, including open studio
October 1, 2009	City secures $3 million federal financing package
December 21, 2009	Moran Plant financing plan presented to City Council
May to July 2010	Moran Blue Ribbon Committee established to evaluate the financial implications of the project on the city and its taxpayers. Completes final report in July
2012	As part of the Moran Revisioned process, the City launches the Waterfront and Downtown Public Investment Action Plan
2013	The Public Investment Action Plan Process identifies a project known as New Moran Inc.
2017	The Mayor terminates the Moran re-visioning effort due to lack of progress and CEDO is tasked with developing the Moran Municipal Generating Station Deconstruction and Demolition Study
2018 December	CEDO proposes the FRAME concept to Council
2020	Burlington's City Council approves advancing phase 1a of the Moran-FRAME project with a budget of $6.55 million

and incorporating public access and green elements, rationalizing the high energy demand of tenants versus the goal of energy efficiency, and regulatory permitting.

Public officials at all levels worked diligently to overcome many of these obstacles throughout the process in response to keen public awareness and their desire to see the project succeed. The ongoing role of Mayors and government agencies, such as CEDO, has also kept the process moving forward for almost three decades. While short- and long-term contamination-oriented barriers have been worked out via collaboration between the city and state agencies, accessing a myriad of financial tools has often been too challenging to turn the project into reality. As such, the city seems to have finally found a cost-effective and creative solution to remediate, green, and retain the historical legacy of the site that will improve waterfront access and trigger further waves of revitalization.

In all, the Moran project provides an interesting case study for addressing a challenging industrial property that lies in the public spotlight. Broad public participation identified community desires for the property, and information from public ballots allowed decisions to be made and moved forward despite several false starts. While the project proposal abandoned in 2017 was more ambitious from a sustainability perspective (i.e., reducing waste, preserving energy embedded in the structure), a valuable lesson that can be drawn is the need to have realistic and sustainable funding to make any redevelopment happen. After three decades, one could say that for the Moran Plant, there is a direct correlation between the energy embedded in the site and the energy the community has devoted to preserving its legacy.

Elmhurst Park, New York City

Site History

Elmhurst Park is a six-acre community green space situated between Grand Avenue and the Long Island Expressway in the borough of Queens. The park replaces an industrial storage facility owned by KeySpan Energy Corporation (now part of National Grid USA) that consisted of two above-ground gas tanks. While the gas tanks were perceived as an eyesore by the surrounding community, they reflected the evolution of energy production and distribution in New York City. Gas was used to illuminate city streets beginning in the early 1800s. While methane from coal combustion fueled the earliest street lamps, KeySpan relied exclusively on natural gas to generate heat and electricity by the 1950s. The Elmhurst Gas Tanks date back to the 1970s when problems in the supply chain from international sources threatened local service delivery. This necessitated the construction of storage tanks throughout the city to ensure an uninterrupted supply of gas to businesses and residents. Investment in new storage and distribution technologies, however, prompted KeySpan to abandon the Elmhurst Gas Tanks sometime in the 1980s (Greene, 2008). Until they were dismantled in 1996, the idle 'white-and-red' gas tanks, both 275-feet in diameter, temporarily served as a local commuter landmark (Hughes, 2006; Lopes, 2011). KeySpan then used the vacant site to store its fleet of company vehicles.

The underutilized property stood in contrast to the changing demographic of the surrounding neighborhood. Elmhurst became a popular destination for new immigrants in the 1980s and 1990s with all the benefits of a mixed-use community. While the private sector quickly responded to the influx of residents – notably through the conversion of single-family homes into multi-family apartment complexes and co-ops, as well as the emergence of multicultural grocers and restaurants – public institutions were slower to adapt (Hughes,

2006). There was consequently a need to expand public services and amenities to keep pace with the increasing population and density, but little developable land to do so.

In September 2001, KeySpan began remediating the property to sell it for redevelopment based on a New York State Department of Environmental Conservation Voluntary Cleanup Agreement (Lopes, 2011; No Author, 2009). Shortly after KeySpan announced its plans to sell the property, residents collaborated through the Juniper Park Civic Association (JPCA) and Citizens of Maspeth and Elmhurst Together (COMET) to voice their concerns and promote their interests.

Project Vision

As is sometimes the case with parks constructed on brownfields, civic action and intervention from elected representatives were required to contest other proposals and secure a park on the KeySpan site. At a meeting between the JPCA and KeySpan in August 2002, also attended by elected officials, three preliminary plans were initially put forward: (1) a residential development, (2) a 34-store mall and parking lot with a capacity for 1,200 cars, and (3) a big box retail establishment (No Author, 2003). JPCA opposed commercial development and requested the land be donated to the community for use as a public park. KeySpan felt that granting the land, worth $13 million at the time, was not feasible according to regulations established by the Public Service Commission.

Between August 2002 and November 2003, several meetings between the JPCA, KeySpan, private developers, elected officials, and local planning boards were held to negotiate the fate of the vacant property. While there was some divergence concerning the preferred type of redevelopment, residents overwhelmingly prioritized public amenities and services to private ones. For instance, a survey administered by the JPCA to residents living within a quarter mile radius of the Elmhurst Gas Tanks site revealed that "of the surveys returned, 367 people wanted a park, 79 wanted residential, 18 wanted a mall, and only 10 wanted a superstore" (No Author, 2003). Other civic groups advocated for the development of "a school, post office, a library, and a 9/11 memorial" (No Author, 2003).

In November 2002, private developers Mattone Group and Starwood Ceruzzi approached KeySpan with an offer to purchase the property for big-box development. Several months after the offer was tentatively accepted, in March 2003, elected officials requested a delay of the sale while they determined if municipal funds could be raised to purchase the land. Although KeySpan agreed to the delay, it also proceeded to complete contract negotiations with the Mattone and Starwood joint venture. In the meantime, local councilors Melinda Katz and Dennis Gallagher successfully secured $3 million to facilitate the public acquisition of the property (No Author, 2003).

Between July and September 2003, representatives of the Mattone Group informed elected officials and the JPCA of their deal with KeySpan to purchase and develop a big box center anchored by Home Depot, as well as a self-storage facility and a bank on the property. Subsequent communications between stakeholders became increasingly hostile, with accusations that KeySpan had been deceitful throughout the negotiation process. Residents began organizing a protest scheduled for November 8, 2003, at KeySpan's Brooklyn-based headquarters, and also "demand[ed] that elected officials pressure KeySpan" to abandon the deal (No Author, 2003).

In October 2003, a sequence of meetings between elected officials escalated to the Mayor's office, where it was agreed that the city should buy the land. Mayor Bloomberg contacted the CEO of KeySpan to negotiate the acquisition. An announcement was made days before the scheduled protest that the "contract for the building of a Home Depot would be deemed null and void and that the city intends to purchase this land for placement of a passive park" (No Author, 2003). KeySpan sold the Elmhurst Gas Tanks property to the city's Department of Parks and Recreation in 2005 for $1.

Planning of the new park was completed in 2006, with input from local residents. The final project vision for the park includes a playground, recreational pathways, public art, and landscaping based on the site's pre-industrial land characteristics.

Project Characteristics and Development

The park plan was implemented in three phases between 2007 and 2012 to distribute the financial cost of the development over several budget cycles as funding, approximately $20 million, was provided through the Mayor's capital budget. Phasing also prioritized infrastructure projects that addressed site-specific considerations relating to its former brownfield status. The park's characteristics and development reflect an integrated approach that considers local heritage, interpretive design, and sustainability.

Development

KeySpan began remediating the property in 2001, after deconstructing the two above-ground storage tanks. Remediation was completed using the "grid method," which involved "subdividing the entire area into blocks, and then digging, cleaning, and testing each one individually" (No Author, 2009). The assessment revealed "that the entire site was covered by soil contaminated with lead," necessitating the removal of 18,000 tons of topsoil (Department of Environmental Conservation, 2012). The New York State Department of Environmental Conservation (DEC) approved the remedial course of action "and signed off on a soil management plan" (No Author, 2009). The property was subsequently remediated to meet state requirements for residential development (No Author, 2009).

Phase One of the Elmhurst Park project focused on preparing the site for further development. As per the soil management plan, 4,000 cubic feet of clean fill material was used to cap the property. Warning mats were laid below the clean fill material to alert prospective developers about the property's condition. Future projects that necessitate digging beyond the layer of warning mats will require permission from the DEC.

A stormwater management system was also implemented to capture runoff from storm events on site and to prevent precipitation from draining into the city's sewer infrastructure. Rainfall "is collected over approximately half the site in an underground retention system consisting of perforated pipes and broken stone wrapped in filter fabric" (Lopes, 2011). Stormwater is also collected in 23-foot-long underground storage tanks and used to irrigate the park's landscaping.

Phase One also implemented the park's infrastructure through the construction of sidewalks, utilities, fencing, and landscaping (Lopes, 2011). Design strategies inspired by Olmsted's approach to landscape architecture such as curving pathways and differential grading were used to give park users the impression of a more extensive green space (No Author, 2009). Nearly 500 trees were planted on the denuded property to renew ecological functions and create a park-like atmosphere. Landscaping was limited to native shrubs and plants "resistant to the Asian Longhorn Beetle" (No Author, 2009). Phase One was completed in late 2008 at the cost of $5 million (No Author, 2009).

Phase Two of the redevelopment focused on the construction of the park's playground and recreational amenities (see Figure 6.3). The playground was designed in part to promote energy literacy among children through experiential and interpretive features, with a nod to the park's industrial heritage. In addition to conventional playground equipment, such as swings and slides, "children can pedal [one of three] stationary bike[s] to provide a light effect on a nearby column" (Lopes, 2011). A decorative fountain, benches, and lighting were also installed, and an existing building, previously occupied by KeySpan, was retrofitted for the park's maintenance staff. Additional landscaping and another 150 trees concluded the second phase of the park's development.

Figure 6.3 Elmhurst Park playground, Queens, New York, 2011

The construction of a new comfort station, completed in 2012, marked the final phase of Elmhurst Park's development. Although praised for its innovative design, the project did draw some criticism for its costly $2.3 million price tag.

In June 2017, an announcement was made that a $2.85 million Queens Vietnam Veterans Memorial was going to be erected at the northeastern corner of Elmhurst Park. The semicircular memorial was completed in 2019 and dedicated to the 371 residents from Queens who died fighting in the war.

The remediation of the property was regulated and enforced primarily by the New York State Department of Environmental Conservation. In contrast, zoning and site plan requirements were addressed by the city's Department of Parks and Recreation and Department of City Planning. The consensus among interviewees was that complying with multiple rounds of regulatory requirements to transform the industrial storage facility into a park increased project costs and contributed to delays. A streamlined approach and inter-agency collaboration were considered essential for expediting future municipally led brownfield redevelopments.

Sustainability

Elmhurst Park is profiled as a brownfield revitalization best practice in part because of the integrated approach to park planning that emphasizes sustainability. Individual project components, such as financing, local ecology, and community needs, were considered simultaneously. The objective was to "merge" the site's challenges and opportunities to create a functional and resilient community green space. As conveyed by the Department of Parks and Recreation's Senior Project Manager for Sustainability, "there was no distinction between park design and sustainable park design" (Compton, 2011).

Particular attention was paid to the site's ecology. As noted earlier, the property had been cleared of vegetation, dramatically altering its ecology. Renewing the site's ecosystem functions involved reconciling two competing objectives: brownfield remediation and sustainable landscape design. For instance, stormwater runoff had to be managed onsite, without allowing the water to percolate and discharge contaminants into the municipal system. These requirements increased the redevelopment costs and also affected the project's claim of being sustainable, as soil capping requires a substantial amount of clean fill material, "which has a highly negative impact on sustainability" (Compton, 2011). An innovative response to the challenge included recirculating stormwater in the park's fountain, as well as utilizing stormwater collected in underground storage tanks to irrigate the park's landscaping. To address the need for clean fill material, city departments collaborated to develop a soil exchange program to limit long-distance transport (Ilan, 2011).

The Sustainable Sites Initiative also influenced the design of Elmhurst Park. Like LEED, it provides a framework for landscape design that allocates points to project components that preserve and enhance ecosystem processes based on performance benchmarks and offers a tool to assess project sustainability.

The Elmhurst Park case study demonstrates the many ways that converting brownfields into public assets can contribute to social sustainability. To begin with, the community pressure that prioritized neighborhood park space required an extraordinary amount of collaboration and cooperation between residents, politicians, and stakeholders in the private sector. The display of civic action was celebrated by municipal staff and elected officials, including the Mayor at the park's opening (Lopes, 2011). The redevelopment also fulfills city targets to increase access to public park space in dense neighborhoods. The redevelopment added infrastructure to enhance quality of life, promote physical recreation and provide "psychological respite from dense urban neighborhoods" (Department of Parks and Recreation, 2010). The redevelopment also highlights ongoing efforts by the municipality to respond to community needs. The fact that the park is "heavily used" and "jam-packed with people" speaks directly to these benefits (Ilan, 2011).

Freshkills Park, New York City

Site History

The area referred to as Freshkills Park located on Staten Island's western shore remained mostly undeveloped until the mid-20th century when it became New York City's largest landfill. Before this, the area's landscape was characterized by coastal marshes, estuarine creeks, and lush hillocks formed by geological processes with natural resources used by Native Americans and early European settlers for hunting, agricultural, and recreational purposes (Department of Parks and Recreation, n.d.; Field Operations, 2006). The name Freshkills was initially used by Dutch settlers in the 1600s to refer to the area's fresh waters (Department of Parks and Recreation, n.d.). Although industrial activities followed early settlement on Staten Island, they were limited in scale or located at the periphery of Freshkills due to marshy conditions that could not support development.

In 1948, New York City initiated landfilling operations at Freshkills to dispose of municipal solid waste and to reclaim land (Department of Parks and Recreation, n.d.). Landfilling was considered a temporary measure to prepare the site for future use, given that marshland was not suitable for construction. After three years of landfilling, the plan conceived by Robert Moses, New York City's Parks Commissioner, was to develop a "residential community ... and an industrial zone" (Department of Parks and Recreation, n.d.).

Despite the temporary intentions, Freshkills operated as a landfill for 53 years. It became the city's main landfill for solid waste disposal (Department of Parks and Recreation, n.d.). The dump was organized into four areas that occupied 45 percent of the 2,200-acre site (Department of Parks and Recreation, n.d.). Waste dumped in each quadrant created "four landfill mounds, which range in height from 90 feet to 225 feet" (Department of Parks and Recreation, n.d.). At the pinnacle of its operations in the mid-1980s, 29,000 tons of waste was deposited at Freshkills each day. By the 1990s, it was renowned as the world's largest landfill (Department of Parks and Recreation, n.d.). The residual landscape not employed in the landfill's operations consisted of "creeks, wetlands and dry lowlands" that continued to support ecosystem functions and features but were negatively impacted (Department of Parks and Recreation, n.d.).

A combination of regulatory interventions and public pressure led to the landfill's closure in 2001. Federal and state legislation directing landfill "siting, design, operation, closure, and monitoring" were introduced in the 1970s (Department of Parks and Recreation, n.d.). The landfill was retrofitted in the early 1990s with infrastructure designed to contain leachate and odors. In 1996, however, a state law mandated the closing of the landfill on December 31, 2001. By the end of 2002, "two of the four mounds were closed and covered with a thick, impermeable cap" (Department of Parks and Recreation, n.d.). The two remaining mounds stopped accepting waste in March 2001 but were temporarily re-opened to permit the disposal of debris following the September 11 attacks on the World Trade Center (Department of Parks and Recreation, n.d.). Throughout the landfill's operations, Staten Islanders endured the stigmatization associated with its presence. In turn, they contributed to efforts to ensure public health and reduce environmental contamination, and eventually "the landfill's closure" (Sugarman, 2009).

In 2001, an International Design Competition was launched by NYC's Department of City Planning as part of a master planning process to reclaim the brownfield site. The goal of the competition was to "generate ideas and innovative designs that would meet the needs of the city's communities, and respond to the natural and constructed history of the site" (Department of Parks and Recreation, n.d.). The competition's winning submission, *lifescape* by the landscape architecture firm Field Operations, was chosen for its reinterpretation of Freshkills as a publicly accessible ecological landscape.

Project Vision

Between 2003 and 2006, Field Operations led a multidisciplinary team of consultants in the production of the Draft Master Plan. At the beginning of the planning process, it was unclear what kind of land use would reclaim Freshkills. A confluence of factors contributed to the project vision as a public park. To begin with, site-specific considerations, including the area's ecosystem functions in addition to technical aspects associated with its historical use, precluded most forms of development. Contrary to the plan initially put forward by Robert Moses, the site's history as a landfill protected it from real estate development (Field Operations, 2006).

Consultations and charrettes throughout the master planning process with policy-makers, designers and residents revealed an explicit preference for the development of a mixed-use, urban park (Sugarman, 2009). Community aspirations and concerns captured throughout the consultation process aim to:

- maintain the site's natural and passive characteristics;
- preserve the sites open spaces;
- include recreational trails for walking, cycling, and horseback riding;
- make the shoreline publicly accessible;
- restrict commercial activities to the center of the site;
- improve the site's connectivity and circulation through new roadways;
- include amenities for sports and active recreation;
- include renewable energy; and
- utilize ecological techniques of land reclamation (Field Operations, 2006; Sugarman, 2009)

Green and Community Space Redevelopment 117

The participatory approach to planning utilized did more than reveal a preference for recreational amenities or sustainable landscape practices; it also contributed to consensus building within the community and ultimately encouraged support for the reclamation, facilitating the project's development.

The completed Draft Master Plan submitted to the city in 2006 is an expression of the community's needs and aspirations that seeks to reconnect the area's human and natural systems. Accordingly, the park's design incorporates a systematic approach to "programming, wildlife, and circulation" (Department of Parks and Recreation, n.d.). The project vision, therefore, describes "an ecologically robust landscape, not as a pastoral refuge from the city, but as an active agent within it" (Department of City Planning, n.d.). In addition to offering amenities that support a diversity of active and passive recreational opportunities, Freshkills Park will renew and enhance the area's ecological functions and utilize innovative strategies to promote sustainable landscape design (see Figure 6.4).

Figure 6.4 Freshkills Park, Staten Island, New York (Google Earth, n.d.a)

The framework established in the master plan organizes the park into five areas (or five parks in one) – the Confluence, North Park, South Park, East Park, and West Park. Each park will have its own "distinct character and programming approach, developed in response to site opportunities and constraints, public meeting and stakeholder input, agency input, operation and maintenance concerns, and feasibility of implementation" (Department of Parks and Recreation, n.d.). The resulting site plan is reminiscent of Ian McHarg's approach to landscape design, layering a site's physical, ecological, and cultural features to extract the highest and best use. With the completion of the Draft Master Plan in 2006, the Department of City Planning transferred the responsibility of realizing the project vision to the Department of Parks and Recreation. It amended Field Operations' original design proposal slightly with input gathered from meetings and workshops between the project team and local stakeholders. Goals emerging from the outreach efforts and integrated into the park's design include roads to ease traffic congestion surrounding the Freshkills site, active recreational uses such as kayaking, horseback riding, and sports fields, and projects generating and using renewable energy (New York City, Department of City Planning, 2009).

Project Characteristics and Development

A particularly important element of the project vision is the idea of Freshkills Park as "a place and a process" (Field Operations, 2006). Accordingly, *lifescape* presented a design strategy to guide the evolution of Freshkills Park incrementally over three decades. At 2,200 acres, the development is "one of the most ambitious public works projects in the city's history" (Department of City Planning, n.d.). The project is organized into three ten-year phases, given its spatial scale and the technical issues that complicate its redevelopment. Each phase consists of projects to improve the park's systemic functions and features – programming, habitat, and circulation – while ensuring flexibility to meet the needs of the surrounding community.

Phase One, initiated in 2007, established the framework for the park's physical development. As conveyed in the Draft Master Plan, Phase One also set the tone for the project's evolution and aimed to "build momentum and secure investment for subsequent phases" (Field Operations, 2006). Essential Phase One projects to be implemented independently or simultaneously included: preparation of North Park, South Park, and Confluence for public access; improve circulation within the park (Loop Drive) and connectivity to adjacent transportation systems (West Shore Expressway) and neighborhoods; completion of select recreational amenities and facilities; installation of public art and September 11 monument; ecosystem renewal; capping of East and West landfill mounds; and programming to attract visitors (Field Operations, 2006).

A substantial amount of front-end public investment was necessary to initiate the site's transformation and attract future investment given real and perceived land-use concerns about its history as a landfill. Accordingly, NYC has allocated $100 million for Phase One of the development (Field Operations, 2006). The annual cost to operate Freshkills Park at build-out is estimated between $15,000 and $30,000 per acre (Field Operations, 2006). Admittedly, financial resources to maintain public parks are limited, compelling the park's proponents to coordinate projects to minimize costs and to investigate a combination of revenue-generating programming, services, and or attractions.

Phase Two proposed to enhance spaces for cultural events and programming as well as continue the site's environmental reclamation. It was anticipated the second phase of development would attract non-profit and commercial operations such as "an ecological golf course, outdoor amphitheater, marina, cultural and educational center or meeting hall," thereby expanding the programming (Field Operations, 2006). The third scheduled phase of development would enhance previous interventions to improve the functions and features of the park. By this time, the complete decomposition and associated gas production and settlement of the landfill's buried waste were anticipated. The park's build-out, scheduled for 2036, aimed to align with the transformation of the site's natural features into a mature ecosystem (Field Operations, 2006).

Construction and programming of the park have progressed well, although most of the site remains closed to the public. Activities are well documented by both the city's Parks Department and by the Freshkills Park Alliance (Freshkills Park, 2019). The park's edges are opening first, with priority given to projects that provide a direct connection to adjacent communities. Some that have already opened include:

- Schmul Park, which abuts the former landfill, opened in September 2012 and contains handball and basketball courts as well as a colorful playground;
- Owl Hollow Soccer Fields consist of four pitches, a pathway, parking, and lawn space opened in 2013, with a LEED-certified Park House currently under construction that will contain public restrooms, outdoor seating, a small NYC Parks Maintenance & Operation facility, parking, and an electric vehicle charging facility; and
- the 3.3-mile New Springville Greenway along the eastern edge of Freshkills Park opened in 2015.

Construction of North Park Phase 1 is currently underway. This 21-acre swath of land will connect visitors to views of Main Creek and the William T. Davis Wildlife Refuge via divided walking and high-speed paths that lead past seven acres of native seed plots. The $22.9 million construction contract was awarded for Phase 1 in 2017, and it is expected to be open in summer 2020. Also, the South Park Anchor Park project is currently in design, with plans for multipurpose fields and trails adjacent to Owl Hollow. In planning are: East Park, a 482-acre site that will be programmed with six miles of walking trails, a 3.5-mile bike loop, wetland overlooks, educational programming, and improvements to the road system that will provide access to the different areas of the park and create a connection to major roadways in the area (Freshkills Park, 2020).

Regulatory Framework

Several overlapping land-use requirements produced a highly regulated environment for the project, given its scale, history, and function. Complying with federal, state, and municipal regulatory standards were cited as a challenge to the park's development (Grassi, 2011). The regulations apply to four policy areas: landfilling, air, water, and soil to ensure human health and environmental protection (Department of City Planning, n.d.).

Landfilling: Regulations governing the "closure and post-closure operations" of a landfill site are enforced by the New York State Department of Environmental Conservation (DEC) (Department of City Planning, n.d.). The post-closure requirements are outlined in the "New York State Codified Rules and Regulations, Part 360, 'Solid Waste Management

Facilities,' specifically subsection 360-2.15, 'Landfill Closure and Post Closure Criteria" (Field Operations, 2006). In addition to capping the remaining two landfill mounds, the regulatory requirements contain measures to control landfill gas, collect and treat leachate, and a 30-year plan coordinating the landfill's post-closure operation and maintenance (Department of City Planning, n.d.). These regulatory measures are implemented by the NYC Department of Sanitation (DSNY).

Air Quality: Federal and state regulations regarding air quality include standards and "emissions guidelines for municipal solid waste landfills" (Department of City Planning, n.d.). These standards and guidelines can be found in the National Ambient Air Quality Standards (NAAQS), made under the Clean Air Act and in the New York State Codified Rules and Regulations, Part 275 (Department of City Planning, n.d.). While air quality is addressed in part by capping the waste with an impermeable layer, further measures are required to manage the accumulation of landfill gas produced by decomposing waste (Department of City Planning, n.d.). Flaring was used initially, but landfill gas is now collected and distributed for residential heating on Staten Island and represents one sustainable innovation strategy (Department of Parks and Recreation, 2010).

Water Quality: The Federal Water Pollution Control Act establishes standards that are, in turn, used by state regulators to "set allowable concentrations of pollutants in groundwater and surface water" (Department of City Planning, n.d.). A total of 238 groundwater monitoring wells and 14 surface water sampling stations throughout Freshkills test water quality and ensure human health and ecosystem functions are not affected (Department of City Planning, n.d.).

Soil Quality: Soil quality is addressed through a combination of federal and state legislation on a contextual basis. "Screening levels" are used by the EPA and DEC to determine a threshold for pollutant concentrations "below which there is unlikely to be a concern" (Department of City Planning, n.d.).

Sustainability

The redevelopment of Freshkills represents a new model for park planning and landscape design based on the principles of environmental sustainability. Goals outlined in PlaNYC 2030, the city's long-term vision for sustainable development, will also be realized by the project. Innovative land-use practices, onsite renewable energy production, and conservation measures are the strategies being used to promote sustainable park development. Examples include the recovery of landfill gas for residential heating, rain gardens and infiltration trenches to capture stormwater, eco-friendly comfort stations, complimentary waste reduction strategies, and the creation of an onsite native plant and seed nursery. These efforts contribute to the renewal of ecosystem functions while ensuring the long-term sustainability of the park's operations. The result is a public park that also serves as a "laboratory for sustainable land practices and infrastructure" (Sugarman, 2009).

In terms of social sustainability, the transparent and collaborative approach adopted throughout the development of Freshkills Park is a best practice for public engagement in planning. While public participation was facilitated through meetings, workshops, and charrettes, a Community Advisory Group comprising representatives from recreational, environmental, cultural, and youth organizations was also established to ensure that a cross-section of community needs are addressed in the park's development. In contrast to the case study of Elmhurst Park, proactive public engagement contributed to a positive planning process.

Elmhurst Park and Freshkills Park – Benefits, Barriers, and Lessons Learned

Reclaiming brownfield properties is both an opportunity and a challenge, particularly in dense urban environments where the supply of land is limited. In a built-out municipality like New York City, recycling brownfield properties is one of the only options available to obtain developable land. This is especially true of efforts to acquire properties for parkland development, given that brownfield reclamation is often used as an economic development strategy. According to New York City's Department of Parks and Recreation, brownfields "are the future for new parks" as they are relatively cheaper than "shovel ready" properties, which make them affordable options for municipal acquisition. The opportunity is in the potential to transform urban blight into a public asset. However, the financial and regulatory uncertainty associated with the reclamation of these properties challenges the potential to fulfill broader public policy objectives. Through a pro-active approach, new regulatory tools and procedures were developed to facilitate future brownfield reclamation projects in New York City, based on lessons learned from the Elmhurst Park and Freshkills Park projects (see timelines for both projects in Table 6.2 and 6.3).

Two primary benefits are associated with the development of each park: (1) reclaiming underutilized, contaminated property, and (2) fulfilling broader public policy objectives. Remediating each property addressed the contamination incurred by decades of industrial land-use, recycling a valuable resource while simultaneously ensuring public health and renewing ecosystem functions.

The redevelopment of each park also corresponds to public policy objectives in the city's long-term vision for sustainable development, referred to as PlaNYC. Initially released in 2007, the vision outlines the city's goals to promote economic growth, address climate change, and enhance the quality of life of its residents through an integrated approach. Concerning parks, PlaNYC recognizes that "the need for parks and public space will only become more acute as our population increases" (Department of Parks and Recreation, 2010), and establishes a goal to improve quality and access to parks. The objective is to ensure all residents live within a ten-minute walk of a public park. In this regard, the addition of Elmhurst Park and Freshkills Park, and the amenities they offer, to the city's network of parks and green space realize the goals set out in PlaNYC. These goals are further supported by the Green New Deal recently announced by the city to mitigate climate change and create healthier communities.

Overall, these benefits of parks and open spaces, while not always quantifiable, incur several spillover effects that contribute to sustainability in dense urban areas such as:

- Economic
    - urban renewal and revitalization;
    - enhancing property values and economic well-being of surrounding neighborhoods;
    - investing in local and regional assets;
    - employment development.

- Environmental
  - brownfield remediation and reclamation;
  - infrastructure for ecosystem functions (stormwater management, urban heat island);
  - increasing public education and awareness through interpretive design strategies;
  - demonstration project to showcase the benefits of remediation and sustainable landscape design;
  - laboratory for renewable energy technologies.
- Community/Society
  - fulfill public policy objectives to improve public amenities to keep pace with population growth and urban intensification;
  - infrastructure for social functions (recreation, relaxation);
  - responding to community needs.

Several barriers, however, complicated the acquisition of these benefits. Site-specific barriers involved reconciling competing objectives to fulfill broader development goals. For instance, managing stormwater was noted as a challenge to park implementation in both case studies. Addressing precipitation onsite is a priority for the city to prevent storm events from overwhelming municipal infrastructure and to mitigate flooding (Department of Parks and Recreation, 2010). This is particularly significant given that more than "half the city is served by a combined [storm and] sanitary sewer system" (Department of Parks and Recreation, 2010). Addressing stormwater onsite, however, had to be reconciled with the need to prevent contamination from decades of industrial use from spreading through the hydrological cycle. Although satisfying both objectives required site-specific interventions that increased front-end project costs, the results are being showcased as demonstration projects to promote future brownfield initiatives.

Obtaining city, state, and federal approvals for each park's redevelopment required an extraordinary level of collaboration and communication between project proponents and stakeholders, which was also a challenge. A streamlined approach would have facilitated redevelopment from a regulatory perspective, especially for municipalities interested in advancing brownfield reclamation projects. The existing (state and federal) regulatory framework was designed to promote privately led brownfield redevelopment projects after the introduction of CERCLA created financial and regulatory uncertainties and financial tools are sometimes not available for municipally or non-profit-led projects.

The lessons learned from the Elmhurst Park and Freshkills Park redevelopments contributed to the development of proactive regulatory procedures and tools to facilitate future brownfield redevelopment initiatives and sustainable park planning. Both originally evolved from opportunities identified in PlaNYC to promote sustainable development and are summarized below.

1. **New York City Brownfield Cleanup Program** – This initiative represents the first municipal brownfield program recognized by the US EPA that has the ability to approve cleanup. It is overseen by the Office of Environmental Remediation launched in 2010

with a mandate to facilitate the redevelopment of contaminated properties through a streamlined process (Office of Environmental Remediation, n.d.). The significance of this program is that it fills a gap in the regulatory system governing brownfield remediation by providing financial and technical resources to non-profit developers or owners of "light to moderately" contaminated properties that would not be eligible for state or federal assistance. The New York Brownfield Cleanup Program does not replace state and federal brownfield programs. Instead, it operates in conjunction with them, referring severely contaminated and complex privately led projects to their state and federal counterparts (Ilan, 2011). Successfully remediated properties are released of future liability or remedial action from the city and the state DEC through a Notice of Completion. The Office of Environmental Remediation utilizes its application process to identify properties with little development potential that could be converted into park space and acknowledges that economic development is only one component of sustainable development.

2. **High-Performance Landscape Guidelines** - This manual is a planning tool to guide the design, construction, and maintenance of NYC's public parks into the 21st century (Department of Parks and Recreation, 2010). The Department of Parks and Recreation recognizes the value of a comprehensive framework for park planning that translates best practices that critically assess a park's ecological, social, and economic impact into performance standards. Best practices and performance standards that cover the different elements in the park planning process are complemented by case studies, including examples of parks developed on brownfield and reclaimed sites. The Guidelines, developed in partnership with the NYC-based Design Trust for Public Space, establish a precedent in sustainable park planning that will be referred to as a model by other municipalities.

Table 6.2 Timeline – Elmhurst Park, Queens, New York

Year	Description
1970s	Construction of above ground storage tanks to ensure the uninterrupted delivery of natural gas to businesses and residents
1980s	Above ground storage tanks are superseded by investments in new technologies for natural gas distribution. The Elmhurst Gas Tanks left idle
1996	KeySpan dismantles the Elmhurst Gas Tanks and tells the neighboring community it will use the land to store company vehicles
2001	KeySpan voluntarily begins remediating the property with intentions to sell it for redevelopment
2001	Public meeting held due to community concerns regarding plans to redevelop the property
2001–2003	Meetings between project proponents and stakeholders are held to decide the fate of the KeySpan property. Civic action, with assistance from elected officials including Mayor Bloomberg results in the public acquisition of the property for redevelopment as a park

(Continued)

Table 6.2 Continued

Year	Description
2004	KeySpan sells the property to NYC's Department of Parks and Recreation for $1
2005	Land officially transferred to the city
2006	Completion of park planning and design
2006-2008	Phase One, consisting mainly of infrastructure projects, to prepare the site for redevelopment completed
2008-2010	Phase Two of the park redevelopment concludes with the installation of recreational amenities
2009	NYC's Department of Parks and Recreation honored with the Big Apple Brownfield Open Space Award for its work on Elmhurst Park
2012	Phase Three, the construction of the park's new comfort station completed
2012	Elmhurst Park officially opens to the public
2019	The Queens Vietnam Veterans Memorial dedicated

Table 6.3 Timeline – Freshkills Park, New York

Year	Description
Pre-European Settlement	Freshkills' landscape characterized by coastal marshes, estuarine creeks, and lush hillocks formed by geological processes thousands of years ago
17th Century	Freshkills landscape used by Native Americans for subsistence, and by early European settlers for agricultural and recreational activities
19th Century	Industries begin to locate on the edges of the Freshkills landscape. The area resists development until the mid-20th century
1948	Freshkills landfill begins receiving residential and municipal solid waste. It was intended to be a temporary landfill but rescheduled for residential and industrial development after three years
1990	Freshkills renowned as the world's largest landfill
1990s	Landfill retrofitted to comply with recently enacted federal and state regulations governing the operation of solid waste facilities
1996	Landfill scheduled to permanently close on December 31, 2001 as per state directives
1997	Two of the four landfill mounds closed and sealed with an impermeable cap
2001	International Design Competition launched to develop a master plan for future land use in Freshkills
2001	The two remaining mounds stop accepting waste in March, but temporarily re-opened to permit disposal from the World Trade Center following the September 11 attacks
2003	Field Operations, a landscape architecture firm based in New York, wins design competition and draft master plan announced
2004-2006	Public consultation, facilitated by the Department of City Planning and team of consultants through meetings and workshops
2006	The draft master plan (lifescape) for Freshkills Park released in April outlining a phased approach to the park's development over a 30-year timeframe
2006	New York City Department of Parks and Recreation assumes responsibility for implementing the project and will use the draft master plan as a conceptual guide
2007	Phase 1 begins with capping of East Mound
2012	Schmul Park and Visitor Center open

Year	Description
2013	Owl Hollow Fields opens and Main Creek Restoration Complete
2014	West Mound capping begins
2015	Springville Greenway complete
2017 to present	North Park Phase 1 breaks ground, South Park Anchor Park in design, and East Park and road improvements are in planning

James & Maria Luisa Haynes Recreation Center at Chacon Creek, Laredo, Texas

Background and History

In the 1980s, Laredo, Texas (pop 260,000) was one of the fastest-growing cities in the US, and planners worried that growth would encroach into sensitive environments if not appropriately managed. Before development, the site of what was to become the Haynes Recreation Center lay within Laredo's ecologically rich but historically neglected Chacon Creek watershed. Chacon Creek was considered the last unaltered tributary to the Rio Grande in

Figure 6.5 James & Maria Luisa Haynes Recreation Center at Chacon Creek, Laredo, Texas (Google Earth, n.d.b)

Laredo and had tremendous potential to become a valuable environmental, recreational, and educational asset (Porter, 2017). Over the years, however, many unregulated industrial businesses and land users abused the creek, resulting in high levels of debris and pollution (US EPA, 2008).

The city and its partners strategically brought together various initiatives and resources to address pollution along Chacon Creek to restore the watershed. These included the development of a Master Plan, an in-depth study of the floodplain, a brownfield assessment, the creation of a hike-and-bike trail, and the construction of a community recreation center next to a reclaimed lake at the center of its restoration story (see Figure 6.5).

Project Vision

The revitalization of Killam Lake and the construction of a community center emerged from a confluence of initiatives that started in the mid-1990s. The city's Chacon Creek Master Plan process began in 1998 (completed in 2001) and called for the preservation of natural areas along the creek and development of a network of trails and recreational facilities from Lake Casa Blanca at its northern point to the Rio Grande in the south (Carter & Burgess, 2001). It consisted of the following project goals that were anticipated to take ten years and approximately $36 million to realize (Pescador & Mia, 2007):

- flood and erosion control;
- creating buffer zones along creeks and streams;
- improvement of water quality;
- wetland and ecosystem restoration;
- natural habitat conservation (babbling brooks and native vegetation);
- linear park development along the creek (Hike and bike trail system);
- creating "people spaces;"
- crime prevention;
- environmental education;
- environmental justice to low-income residents; and
- development of eco-tourism (bird and nature watching activities).

To support the development of the Master Plan the city also worked with the Army Corps of Engineers and other consultants to study floodplain issues in the Chacon watershed (Brown and Root Services, 1999). This would justify acquiring property in high-risk areas and provide direction for engaging in wetland enhancements to manage flood risk. The feasibility study would also support the city's requests for federal support.

While the city's environmental services department provided the initial push for the Master Plan and greening of the watershed, the local community became increasingly active in the early 2000s to address its park space deficiency. A local citizen's advisory committee also worked with the city to put forward a Green Spaces Preservation Ordinance in 2004 that requires buffer zones along creeks and streams, which affected all new development in Chacon Creek and other watersheds in Laredo (Mia, 2007).

The city, state, and EPA were also conducting brownfields assessment and cleanup initiatives with funding from a Brownfields Assessment Demonstration Pilot awarded to Laredo in 1995 (US EPA, 2000). The initial purpose of the funds was to investigate a 100-acre site owned by the city further from the downtown core. Finding no contamination at that site, however, funding was redirected to inventory and assess brownfields along the creek to create a green corridor between the US-Mexican border for improving water quality, spurring commercial development, preventing crime, and increasing interest in environmental cleanup (US EPA, 2000). Phase I site assessments along the creek identified 18 potential brownfields. The city was quickly able to clean up most sites, littered mainly with illegally dumped construction waste, except for one, Killam Lake. The lake was a rather large (18 acres) and attractive wetland, except for the thousands of tires illegally dumped into it over time. Interest in acquiring the site for the Chacon Creek Master Plan was high, so the city asked if the Killam family would donate the land in exchange for cleaning it up. The Killam family agreed but requested that it be renamed to Chacon Creek Lake.

In 2005, the city also obtained $3.3 million in transportation funds for a hike-and-bike trail system that would become a vital component of the Chacon Creek Master Plan (Pescador & Mia, 2007). The initial desire was to start the trail at Lake Casa Blanca in the north and have it run 13 miles along Chacon Creek to the Rio Grande. Given that $3.3 million would not fund the whole trail, it was proposed that Chacon Creek Lake be the central hub from which other trails could be built. A council member from the district liked the idea and felt a recreation center could be built on the site to complement the "environmentally themed" Master Plan and create a hub of activity for the local community, which could include canoeing, fishing, gym facilities, and indoor sports.

Project Characteristics

The community facility, which came to be called the James and Maria Luisa Haynes Health and Wellness Center, sits on a nine-acre site adjacent to Chacon Creek Lake. It is a multi-use facility designed around the core idea that recreation and environment go hand in hand in the health of an individual and a community (Frank Architects Inc., 2017). The center has typical elements of a recreation center (e.g., gymnasium, fitness area, lounge, and concessions, indoor and outdoor tracks, outdoor pool) and incorporates an array of green features to allow citizens to interact with nature and learn about green design (Papakos et al., 2010). The 45,000 sq. ft. building, completed in 2012, is the first in Laredo to have a green roof. Other green features include a community garden, rain collection system, and a recycling and composting center (Frank Architects Inc., 2017). While the city contemplated LEED certification for the project, it did not go forward with it due to cost. The Center is run by the city's Parks and Recreation Department with a critical goal of providing affordable programming (annual memberships = $50 per person; $40 for seniors).

In between the recreation center and the restored lake is an alternate parking lot that was planned to serve both the recreation center and the hike-and-bike trail. The parking lot incorporates numerous Low Impact Development (LID) design features including porous concrete, pavers with grass surfaces and flat curbs, rain gardens and bioswales for bioretention, and infiltration trenches (Papakos et al., 2010; Tetra Tech, 2009; US EPA 2009b). The project was built to serve as a demonstration for other parking facilities throughout the city. Funding for research on green building and LID elements was awarded to the city of Laredo Environmental Services Department from the EPA's Sustainable Brownfields Pilot program.

In response to its Master Plan, the city began to conduct numerous projects to reclaim riverfront property and develop a network of nature trails and wildlife sanctuaries along the creek. By 2007, the city completed Phase I of a restoration project funded by the EPA in lower Chacon Creek and a network of trails with funds from Texas Parks and Wildlife (Mia, 2007). The city also received a grant from the EPA, under the Wetlands Protection grant program, to carry on with the second phase of exotic species removal and erosion control. Another related initiative located where the Rio Grande meets the Chacon Creek watershed is the River Bend Ecosystem Restoration Project. Army Corps of Engineers completed a feasibility study of the River Bend Ecosystem Restoration Project in 2001 and aimed to secure $2.66 million for project design and construction (Mia, 2007). Construction began in 2016 to restore the 77-acre riparian ecosystem, which involved removing exotic plant species, stabilizing significant erosion areas, reforestation, and excavating historic gravel pits to expand the wetland area and create islands (iNaturalist, 2020).

Since 2011 the city has been seeking congressional authorization to complete the Chacon Creek Study by the US Army Corps of Engineers in the central and northern part of the watershed. The flood risk management component of the project will consist of the permanent evacuation of 73 residential structures along Chacon Creek, as well as 16.75 acres of wetland restoration and 401 acres of riparian restoration (Porter, 2017). As of 2014, the project has a near-completed draft report ready to be released for public comment but is unable to do so due to the lack of a study authority. The city moved forward with completing the report under Section 203 of WRRDA 2014 and requested congressional inclusion in the next Water Resources Development Act for construction funding (Porter, 2017).

In 2008, the city of Laredo partnered with the Texas Department of Transportation to build the Chacon Creek Hike & Bike Trail system. Phase I of the project connecting the Haynes Recreation Center to Eastwood Park (about a half-mile north) was completed in August 2011. In 2016 a second phase was opened, connecting the Recreation Center to state Highway 359 about two miles south. Phase III of the project began in 2016 to join the trail north to Highway 59, but progress has been delayed by landowner issues. Interestingly, what was initially planned to be Phase IV of the project, connecting Highway 359 to the Rio Grande, was the first to be constructed as part of the restoration in lower Chacon Creek.

Site Remediation

The Phase II site assessment for the Chacon Creek Lake revealed lead and cyllinium (which is associated with the natural soil content of the area) at levels below state standards. The firm responsible for cleanup examined multiple options for dealing with the discarded tires and debris. Leaving the tires in place was considered a low-cost alternative, but raised concerns related to water contamination, combustion, and stagnant water. Burying tires under clean fill material could deal with some of the pollution mobility issues but might also cause flooding upstream, and fill material might be displaced over time. The consultants focused, therefore, on removing the tires for disposal or recycling, ultimately choosing the former because the city did not have easy access to recyclers, and even if they did, recyclers are not interested in dirty tires that can damage equipment. As such, the 18-acre wetland lake had to be painstakingly cleaned-up by hand to comply with federal requirements under the Clean Water Act that regulate the removal of vegetation and disturbance of the soil in such waters (Carter and Burgess, 2007).

Funding and Financing

Tracking the funding and financing for the numerous initiatives is a challenge. As mentioned, funds in the amount of $36 million were being sought in the early 2000s to provide the necessary improvements outlined in the ten year Master Plan that includes flood control, habitat conservation, and linear park development (Pescador & Mia, 2007). The material costs for the Haynes Recreation Center were estimated at $8 million and were to be funded by the city via bonds. The green parking lot project design was funded by the EPA through their Sustainable Brownfields Pilot grant ($25,000) and constructed by the city's Environmental Services Department with funding from a stormwater fee. All 50 plus properties acquired in the watershed for the restoration process were obtained from the Stormwater Improvement fund, except for donations. Brownfield site assessment costs were funded, in part, by the US EPA Brownfield Assessment Demonstration Pilot Grant (US EPA, 2000). Funding for the Hike and Bike Trail came from a US Transportation Bill (TEA -LU) Transportation Equity Act - $3.3 million (Pescador & Mia, 2007). Funding for the work of the Core of Engineers feasibility study, Stormwater Improvement fund and ACE was $2 million. The River Bend Ecosystem Restoration Project was estimated to cost approximately $4.1 million, with 65% cost-shared by the federal government and 35% by the city (Mia, 2007).

Project Impacts and Lessons Learned

One of the main benefits associated with the development of the recreation center and restoration of Chacon Creek lies in getting stakeholders and the public to see value in the protection, restoration, and development of green space (see project timeline, Table 6.4). Even the parks department, which historically focused on active recreation and sports, has seen benefits in aligning traditional organized athletic activities with the active and passive opportunities provided by the hike and bike trail. The shift from grey infrastructure to green infrastructure at the micro-scale with the parking structure and the macro-scale with the watershed also highlights the benefits of greener approaches. The hope is that the restoration and green development that has already snowballed throughout the creek will influence the surrounding area and the entire city.

Local representatives did note that having an incentive to promote sustainability, like the EPA Sustainable Brownfield Pilot funds, did make it easier to explore and implement greener alternatives to traditional development, with the added possibility of getting consumers and builders interested in these methods. Lower municipal fees or faster approval might also be a way to incentivize buy-in.

130 Green and Community Space Redevelopment

Table 6.4 Timeline – James & Maria Luisa Haynes Recreation Center at Chacon Creek, Laredo, Texas

Year	Description
1995	EPA Brownfields Assessment Demonstration Pilot announced
1998	Chacon Creek Master Plan process initiated
1999	Publication of watershed and flood risk studies
2000	EPA Brownfields Assessment Demonstration Pilot begins to assess brownfields in Chacon Creek
2001	Army Corps of Engineers completed a feasibility study of the River Bend Ecosystem Restoration Project
2005	Congress approved $3.3 million dollars in funding through the US Transportation Bill, (TEA-LU) Transportation Equity Act: Legacy for Users to enhance and extend the Chacon Creek trail system
2007	Tire Cleanup Plan prepared for Chacon Creek Lake
2008	EPA Brownfields Sustainability Pilot awarded for the Laredo Recreation Center
2011	The Army Corps of Engineers Fort Worth District preparing the Chacon Creek Study for public review and comment, but work suspended due to lack of study authority
2011	Hike and Bike Trail connecting Eastwood Park to the Haynes Community Center completed
2012	James & Maria Luisa Haynes Recreational Center completed
2016	Hike and Bike Trail connecting Haynes Recreational Center to State Highway 359 is completed and Phase 3 begins
2016	River Bend Ecosystem Restoration Project begins construction
2017	The City of Laredo continues to seek congressional authorization to complete the Chacon Creek Study by the US Army Corps of Engineers for the purpose of providing flood control, natural habitat conservation and linear park development

The project has faced several challenges, especially when working on initiatives that involve many simultaneous projects, scales, and partners. As one interviewee noted, "getting everybody on the same page tends to be difficult." A challenge related to green and sustainable projects is that they do not always align with traditional building and zoning regulations. There was also some resistance to the Green Space Ordinance from the development community, particularly from smaller landowners wanting to maximize the use and density of their sites and not provide green space.

Despite these challenges, the promotion of a greener vision for the watershed via the Master Plan process has brought together multiple partners, resources, and projects to share in that vision. The restoration of the sizeable blighted brownfield lake and the development of a recreation center acted as a focal point for the revitalization of the long-neglected watershed and the community.

Allen-Morrison Pilot, Lynchburg, Virginia

Site History

In 1996, the Allen Morrison Sign Company declared bankruptcy and abandoned its 16.9-acre property about 2 miles west of downtown Lynchburg, Virginia. The property had a

Green and Community Space Redevelopment 131

long industrial history, and before sign manufacturing, part of the site was used by the Thornhill Wagon Company, once the largest independent manufacturer of farm wagons in the eastern US (US EPA, 2009c). Other businesses that had occupied Allen-Morrison's buildings included the Ferrum Veneer Company, Metallo Chemicals, and Lynchburg Dry Kilns (US EPA, 2009c). Two primary building facilities stood on the diamond-shaped site bisected by Rutherford Street, including the Allen-Morrison Facility (87,800 sq. ft.) to the north and the Thornhill facility (86,400 sq. ft.) to the south (US EPA, 2009d). A creek flows behind the Thornhill property buffering it from single-family homes to the southwest. The residential neighborhood of Fort Hill bordering the property to the west and south is a diverse community with lower-income working-class residents underserved by recreational facilities. A rail corridor and various industrial uses lie to the southeast. Seven acres of industrial land lie along the eastern boundary housing the former Schenkel farm that specialized in rose production and contains two acres of indoor space in nine greenhouses (five constructed in 1919) (van Ness, 2014). To the northwest of the farm is a baseball stadium and football complex initially built for professional teams in 1939 (see Figure 6.6). Allen-Morrison came to the city's attention as a result of several code violations. When city officials inspected the site, they found suspicious barrels in one of the warehouses and contacted the Virginia Department of Environmental Quality (VDEQ), who then informed the EPA. The city was

Figure 6.6 Allen-Morrison, Schenkel Farm, and Lynchburg City Stadium, Virginia (Google Earth, n.d.c)

very concerned about the health and safety of the citizens and the potential for fire but worked slowly at first because they were not owners and were leery of shouldering taxpayers with the cleanup costs.

Project Characteristics

The city acquired the abandoned Allen-Morrison and Thornhill facilities through eminent domain in 2003 with plans to build a park (Lynchburg Parks & Recreation, 2020). In 2002, three conceptual park designs were put forward in the city's Comprehensive Plan for both the Allen-Morison and Schenkel Farm properties. Two of the designs incorporated the restoration of some historic structures along with the development of green space, parking, athletic fields, a community center, and other passive and active recreational uses. The site has been managed primarily by the Parks and Recreation Department since the city assumed ownership. Also, in 2003, plans began for a $6.5 million renovation to the Lynchburg City Stadium and its parking and plaza areas.

In the same year, community members began to search for new garden space and set their sights on Schenkel Farm's greenhouses that had been closed in 1999. The Schenkel family was intrigued by their interest in urban farming and preserving the greenhouses. Lynchburg Grows was formed as a non-profit, and a deal was structured to make it possible for it to raise funds and turn the farm into the H. R. Schenkel Urban Farm and Environment Center (Hardy, 2007/2008). Lynchburg Grows provides opportunities for the disabled and disadvantaged to garden and encourages active and healthy living. The appeal for volunteers to preserve the site raised significant interest from the community who helped replant surviving rose bushes, build compost beds, and repair the greenhouses. Those involved were also very keen to clean brownfields and address soil pollution from historic greenhouse activities through organic means.

The city partnered more closely with Lynchburg Grows in 2008 to develop a comprehensive master plan with opportunities for remediation by design, shared resources and facilities, and neighborhood engagement in the redevelopment process (US EPA, 2009c). Both viewed the project as an opportunity to educate and engage citizens in sustainability through design, construction, educational interpretation, and historical preservation (Fraser, 2009). The city is keen to facilitate active recreation by linking the park to the city's extensive trail system. The park also aims to increase tree canopy and use green management strategies like green roofs and rain gardens for stormwater management (Mishkovsky, 2018). In addition to recreation and environmental goals, the city leadership is very interested in supporting economic development and healthy living by connecting the Allen Morrison project to Lynchburg Grows and the city Stadium (Fraser, 2009). While plans are still in development, the hope is to include recreation and athletic fields, a skate park, community center, walking trails, and tot lots.

Concerning brownfield issues, the site had seen many industrial uses throughout its history, including Allen-Morrison, which manufactured paints and solvents. A joint site assessment was conducted in 1998 by the US EPA Region III, VDEQ, city of Lynchburg, and the city's Deputy Fire Marshal, revealing numerous drums and containers with flammable and corrosive liquids (city of Lynchburg, 2013). The EPA removed the hazardous materials in

March 1999 and also sampled the soil and groundwater to find that the site was not severe enough to recommend for the National Priorities List. Before taking ownership in 2003, the city conducted a Phase 1 ESA that identified the historical use of hazardous material and petroleum-based products, underground storage tanks not properly managed or closed, and other historical environmental conditions identified by the EPA. A targeted assessment conducted by VDEQ in 2006 gathered and analyzed soil, groundwater, and air samples throughout the site finding that most contaminants were not seen as posing a concern under an industrial/commercial scenario. In 2010, additional site characterization work was performed with financial support from the EPA to develop corrective actions needed to use the site for recreational purposes. Three alternatives were evaluated, including: (1) no action; (2) capping; and (3) excavation with disposal. Despite being the costliest option ($250,000), excavation with disposal was recommended because it addressed necessary risks (unlike option 1) and did not require the annual monitoring and maintenance needed for the capping option (estimated at $175,000). A Certificate of Satisfactory Completion was issued by VDEQ for the Allen Morrison property in May 2017 (with groundwater and residential use restrictions recorded), and one was also issued to Lynchburg Grows in November 2018 (with groundwater, residential use, and dig restrictions recorded). Interestingly, both projects were enrolled and officially became eligible for Virginia's remediation program in fall 2005.

Through the Brownfields Sustainability Pilots program, the EPA provided the city of Lynchburg with $25,000 in technical assistance to devise a strategy for the deconstruction of the Allen-Morrison site. This included developing a building materials inventory tool, assessing the feasibility of building deconstruction, and identifying building materials that could be sold through reuse and recycling markets or reused onsite as part of redevelopment (US EPA, 2009d). The assessment determined that the Allen Morrison buildings to the north, and the materials therein, were not suitable for reuse and that demolition with mechanical separation to salvage recyclable materials (mainly scrap metal, brick, and concrete) was more cost-effective. The Thornhill facility, on the other hand, could be deconstructed, and a quantitative inventory of materials was generated to identify recoverable materials with high market value potential, materials suitable for reuse in the proposed redevelopment that promote sustainability and industrial heritage, and any that could be used by Lynchburg Grows (US EPA, 2009d).

While the park was initially slated to open in 2011, the "eco-friendly" demolition of the Allen-Morrison property only commenced in 2010. The goal of recycling 75 percent of all materials was exceeded by another ten percent (Petska, 2010). The contractor treated wood, brick, and concrete recovered from the building for reuse, and the city also used some of the salvaged materials for local projects (Petska, 2010). With the Allen-Morrison demolition complete, the city intended to move on to the Thornhill Wagon Co. buildings to the south. The project has since run into delays. According to the most recent posting on the Lynchburg Parks & Recreation website (2020), once final demolitions are completed, and the site is clean-closed by VDEQ (which occurred in 2017), the entire site will be planted with grass and land banked by the city until funding becomes available for Master Planning of a new park. The Parks and Recreation Department still hopes to incorporate some of the Thornhill Buildings into the new design. There currently is only a site plan for the property.

Table 6.5 Timeline – Allen-Morrison Pilot, Lynchburg, Virginia

Year	Description
April 2003	Site acquisition by city of Lynchburg
2004	Initial site reconnaissance
2006	Targeted brownfields assessment
2008	Site received $25,000 for brownfields sustainability project
November 2012	Site Screening Report and Corrective Action Work Plan Update submitted to VDEQ
2015	Cleanup alternatives

Project Impacts and Lessons Learned

As with many brownfield to green space projects, one of the critical challenges faced by the city early on was concern regarding the cost of acquiring the property, remediating it, and undertaking long-term development for public use, especially given that the city is one of the most fiscally stressed in Virginia (see project timeline, Table 6.5). Being able to devise and translate a vision for the project has been essential for moving it forward, especially when alternative uses were also being considered early on. The project coordinator also noted that this was one of the first brownfield projects that the city engaged in, so it took time to familiarize themselves with regulations and processes, to overcome the fear of risk, and to build relationships with non-profits and others to move it forward.

The EPA notes that benefits derived from the technical assistance were that it helped build local capacity to deal with large deconstruction projects, and it showed how a full-cost accounting could reduce uncertainty about its viability (US EPA, 2009d). In terms of building capacity, the project also paved the way for the city to deal with brownfields and incorporate sustainability into its activities. Media stories, for instance, point to the city's success in managing the Allen Morrison project as a critical reason for their success in acquiring future brownfields grants from the EPA (Draper Aden Associates, 2015).

Overall, the project, while still a few years away from completion, looks to provide a valuable, sustainable redevelopment for residents in an area facing environmental and social inequality challenges. A key sustainability feature is the aim to reuse and recycle the materials from demolition. The assessment and cleanup of the brownfield will put formerly unusable land back into productive use. The incorporation of green space and additional amenities seeks to enhance the quality of life of area residents and promote active living. The development of a community center also aims to build social capital in the neighborhood.

References

Baird, J. B. (2017). Moran developers face demolition deadline. January 24, *Burlington Free Press*, sec. News.

Brown and Root Services. (1999). *Chacon Creek Watershed flood insurance study update* (Report prepared for the city of Laredo). Brown and Root Services.

Burlington Community and Economic Development Office. (2007). *Consolidated annual performance & evaluation report: Neighborhood development goals, strategies and funded activities*. City of Burlington.

Green and Community Space Redevelopment   135

Burlington Community and Economic Development Office. (2008). *Moran Center at waterfront park: guide to the redevelopment of the Moran Plant*. City of Burlington. 6, 7, 9, 12.

Burlington Community and Economic Development Office. (2020). *The Moran Plant*. September 29. City of Burlington.

Burlington Community and Economic Development Office. (n.d.). *Public investment action plan (PIAP)*. City of Burlington.

Carter and Burgess. (2001). *Chacon Creek final conceptual master plan, Laredo, Texas*. (Report prepared for the City of Laredo). Carter and Burgess.

Carter and Burgess. (2007). *Tire cleanup plan Chacon Creek Lake*. (Report prepared for City of Laredo, Environmental Services Department). Carter and Burgess.

City of Burlington. (1994). *Zoning ordinance, Article 9: Special overlay district, Part 1: Public trust district*. City of Burlington.

City of Burlington. (2009). *Moran Center sources and uses budget*. Report prepared by White + Burke Real Estate Investment Advisors, Inc., City of Burlington.

City of Burlington. (2010). *Moran Blue Ribbon Committee final report the Burlington City Council*. City of Burlington.

City of Lynchburg. (2013). *Analysis of brownfields cleanup alternatives – preliminary evaluation: Contaminated soil and groundwater site 300, 329, and 500 Rutherford Street, Lynchburg Virginia, State Tracking Number VRP00423*. City of Lynchburg.

Department of City Planning. (n.d.). *Freshkills park project*. New York City.

Department of Environmental Conservation. (2012). *Newtown –Elmhurst former gas holder*. New York State Department of Environmental Conservation.

Department of Parks and Recreation. (2010). *High performance landscape guidelines*. Design Trust for Public Space and City of New York Parks and Recreation.

Department of Parks and Recreation. (n.d.). *Freshkills Park press kit*. City of New York Parks and Recreation.

Draper Aden Associates. (2015). *Lynchburg wins 2015 EPA brownfields assessment grants*. July 17. Draper Aden Associates blog.

Field Operations. (2006). *Freshkills Park: Lifescape, Staten Island, New York, draft master plan, March 2006*. Report prepared by Field Operations for the city of New York City and the New York City Department of City Planning.

Frank Architects Inc. (2017). *James & Maria Haynes recreational center*. Frank Architects.

Freshkills Park. (2019). *Landfill-to-park timeline*. December 12. Freshkills Park, The Freshkills Park Alliance, Freshkillspark.org.

Freshkills Park. (2020) *Design + construction updates*. February 19. Freshkills Park, The Freshkills Park Alliance, Freshkillspark.org.

Google Earth. (n.d.a). *Freshkills Park, New York City, New York*. 40°34'23" N and 74°11'05" W. December 4, 2020.

Google Earth. (n.d.b). *James & Maria Luisa Haynes Recreation Center at Chacon Creek in Laredo, Texas*. 27°30'52" N and 99°27'16" W. December 4, 2020.

Google Earth. (n.d.c). *Allen-Morrison, Schenkel Farm, and Lynchburg City Stadium*. 37°23'28" N and 79°10'35" W. December 4, 2020.

Greene, C. (2008). Elmhurst gas tanks park taking shape. October 2, *The Forum Newsgroup*, 9.

Hardy, H. (2007/2008). Lynchburg Grows: An organic community garden where people meet and gain a deeper understanding and mutual respect. January 8, *The Virginia Sportsman*, 60-63.

Heindel & Noyes Inc. (2006). *Former Moran plant, Burlington, Vermont, wetland delineation report*. Report prepared by Heindel & Noyes (H&N), Inc.

Hughes, C. J. (2006). Polyglot haven awaits a 'Gas Tank Park'. September 3, *The New York Times*, Living In, 9.

iNaturalist. (2020). *Laredo riverbend*. April 3. iNaturalist.org.

Jickling, K. (2017). No new Moran: Burlington ends old plant redevelopment talks. September 1, *Vermont's Independent Voice: Seven Days*.

Lopes, P. (2011). *Mayor Bloomberg opens Elmhurst Park in Queens*. June 6. New York City.

Lynchburg Parks & Recreation. (2020). *Improvement projects, master plans, Former Allen-Morrison Brownfield Site*. August 15. Lynchburg Parks & Recreation.

Mia, R. (2007). *Conservation easements and restoration projects* (Fact Sheet). City of Laredo.

Mishkovsky, N. (2018). Healthy makeover. In Gonzalez III, J. J., Kemp, R. L., & Rosenthal, J. (Eds.), *Eminent domain and economic growth: Perspectives on benefits, harms and new trends* (pp. 102-103). McFarland, P.

New England Preservation Collaborative Inc. (2006). *Assessment of historic electric generating facilities on the Burlington waterfront*. New England Preservation Collaborative.

New York City, Department of City Planning (2009) *Fresh Kills Park project, draft master plan, community input*. Wayback Machine Internet Archive. https://web.archive.org/web/20091124082134/http://www.nyc.gov/html/dcp/html/fkl/fkl4b.shtml

No Author. (2003). Timeline of the Elmhurst gas tanks property. December, *Juniper Berry Magazine*, *Juniper Park Civic Association*, 2-6.

No Author. (2009). *Gas tank park: Queens creates green space at former gas storage facility*. New York Construction, 1-2.

Office of Environmental Remediation. (n.d.). *NYC Brownfield Cleanup Program*. New York City.

Papakos, T. H., Gould, M., & Brunner, J. (2010). Redeveloping brownfields with LID design. In S. D. Struck & K. H. Lichten (Eds.), *Low Impact Development 2010: Redefining water in the city* (pp. 1684-1697). American Society of Civil Engineers.

Pescador, M., & Mia, R. (2007). *Chacon Creek master plan funding* (Fact Sheet). City of Laredo.

Petska, A. (2010). Allen-Morrison building teardown nears an end. December 28, *The News & Advance*.

Porter, J. (2017). *Rio Grande basin – Chacon Creek – funding: federal legislative agenda 2017*. City of Laredo.

Sugarman, J. (2009). Environmental and community health: A reciprocal relationship. In L. Campbell & A. Wiesen (Eds.), *Restorative Commons: Creating health and well-being through urban landscapes Vol. 39*, (pp. 138-153). USDA Forest Service.

Tetra Tech. (2009). *Technical memorandum: Brownfields sustainability pilot conceptual design drawings – Haynes Recreation Center* (Report prepared for US EPA Office of Solid Waste and Emergency Response, Office of Brownfields and Land Revitalization). Tetra Tech.

True, M. (2016). *Burlington ends pact for Moran plan redevelopment*. July 21. VT Digger: Business and Economy.

US EPA. (2000). *Brownfields assessment demonstration pilot, Laredo, TX* (Fact Sheet EPA 500-F-00-267). Office of Solid Waste and Emergency Response.

US EPA. (2008). *Brownfields sustainability pilot fact sheet Laredo recreation center* (Report EPA 560-F-08-268 5105T). Office of Solid Waste and Emergency Response.

US EPA. (2009a). *Building a sustainable future: A report on the environmental protection agency's brownfields sustainability pilots* (Report EPA-506-F-09-5002009a). Office of Brownfields and Land Revitalization.

US EPA. (2009b). *Low impact development parking lot for a new recreation center* (Report EPA-F-09-508). Office of Solid Waste and Emergency Response.

US EPA. (2009c). *Technical memorandum: Brownfields sustainability pilot – Allen-Morrison site, Lynchburg, Virginia*. Office of Brownfields and Land Revitalization.

US EPA. (2009d). *Deconstruction and building material reuse to foster community redevelopment in Lynchburg* (Report EPA-560-F-09-513). Office of Brownfields and Land Revitalization.

Van Ness, M. (2014) *The story of Lynchburg Grows*. H. R. Schenkel Urban Farm and Environmental Education Center, Slideshare.

Vita Nuova LLC. (2009). *City of Burlington, Vermont sustainability pilot: Recommendations for sustainable infrastructure final report*. US EPA Office of Solid Waste and Emergency Response, Sustainable Brownfields Pilots program.

Waite Environmental Management LLC. (2010). *Additional brownfield site investigation report, Moran Generating Plant, Lake Street, Burlington, Vermont*. April 15. Waite Environmental Management.

Weinberger, M. (2012). *Moran open letter*. July 2. Office of the Mayor, city of Burlington, Vermont.

Interviews

Moran Center, Burlington, Vermont

- Warner, N. (2010). Community Economic Development Office, city of Burlington, Vermont

Elmhurst Park and Freshkills Park, New York City

- Compton, N. (2011). Senior Project Manager for Sustainability, New York City Department of Parks and Recreation.
- Grassi, C. (2011). Freshkills Park Outreach Manager, New York City Department of Parks and Recreation.
- Ilan, L. (2011). Chief of Planning, Mayor's Office of Environmental Remediation, city of New York.
- McIntyre, M. (2011). General Counsel, Mayor's Office of Operations, Office of Environmental Remediation, city of New York.
- Ogrinz, H. (2011). Sr. Landscape Architect, New York City Department of Parks and Recreation.

James & Maria Luisa Haynes Recreation Center at Chacon Creek in Laredo, Texas

- Porter, J. (2011). Assistant Director Environmental Services Department, city of Laredo.

Allen-Morrison Pilot, Lynchburg, Virginia

- Fraser, K. (2009). City of Lynchburg, Parks and Recreation Department.

7 Corner Gas Station Brownfields

The brownfields that often frustrate communities the most are the abandoned gas stations that linger on corners and advertise a sense of neighborhood blight to all who drive past. Our love of the automobile and their thirst for gas has resulted in numerous fuel station brownfields that are typically small parcels of land that may contain a range of pollutants. Consequently, the environmental costs of cleanup sometimes exceed the redevelopment value of the small plot, leaving them idle as landowners wait for the market to pick up. Fortunately, there is interest in redeveloping these sites because of their prominent location on street corners. Stakeholders have begun to seek guidance on how to address redevelopment barriers, navigate reuse, and prioritize parcels in a manner that attracts the market and enhances community sustainability. The similarities of these brownfields in terms of both problems and characteristics also make it possible to plan for them in a more holistic fashion that considers fates beyond redevelopment or nothing. The consideration of beautification measures or interim uses (e.g., gardens, farmers markets, and open space) can help activate sites without penetrating the ground. The case studies examined here – June Key Delta Community Center and Tabor Commons in Portland, and Green Avenue in Greenville – tell the story of three fuel station projects, two led by non-profits and one by a municipality, that provide valuable lessons for communities seeking to recharge these brownfields sustainably.

June Key Delta Community Center, Portland, Oregon

Site History

Through the June Key Delta Community Center project in Portland, Oregon, the members of a sorority sought to not only improve the condition of a brownfield property but also to enrich the lives of local citizens. Chartered in 1945, the Portland Alumnae Chapter of Delta Sigma Theta Sorority is a non-profit public service organization of professional African American women. With over 800 chapters throughout the US and abroad, the sorority's "Five-Point Programmatic Thrust" places emphasis on: (1) economic development; (2) educational development; (3) international awareness and involvement; (4) physical and mental health; and (5) political awareness and involvement.

For decades, the Portland chapter of the sorority has engaged in numerous activities that target minorities, such as conducting workshops and seminars on physical and mental health, tutoring children, and working on affordable housing issues (Portland Delta Sigma

Corner Gas Station Brownfields 139

Theta Alumnae Chapter, 2020a). In the late 1980s, members of the sorority wanted to establish a more permanent home in Portland, and over a dozen of the sorority sisters donated $100 each to initiate a search. Through the efforts of June Key, a member of the sorority, the organization purchased an old ARCO gas station and convenience store in 1992 (see Figure 7.1). The 15,090 sq. ft. property, located at 5940 North Albina Street in North Portland, sits in a culturally diverse neighborhood with a mix of residential and commercial uses. It lies on a prominent corner, not only for the locals but for those visiting Portland's Peninsula Park Rose Garden.

Figure 7.1 ARCO Gas Station, Portland, Oregon, 2010

Upon purchasing the site, the Neil Kelly Construction Company, which has a showroom a few blocks away, donated survey work and created a blueprint for the property (Bingham, 2010). The building was painted and patched up through voluntary efforts, put into immediate use as a meeting site for the group, and became the nucleus of its community outreach activities. The building itself was maintained on a shoestring budget until funds could be raised to realize a more inspiring vision, which started to be explored in earnest in 1997.

Project Vision

From the outset, the vision for the building was for it to serve as the sorority's headquarters and a hub for community outreach and tutoring services. Planning and development committees were established in 1999 to explore new ideas and to ensure that the property was maintained. More formal development steering committees were set up in the early 2000s, and funds were raised to help the sorority lay the groundwork for property development (Portland Delta Sigma Theta Alumnae Chapter, 2020a).

A Delta House Construction Committee was founded at the end of 2000, and members of the sorority met with representatives of the city of Portland's Office of Sustainable Development in 2002 to explore ways of making the project sustainable. The simple goal was to create a vibrant corner with an innovative building that could act as a demonstration project for other non-profits. In the spring of 2003, students from the University of Oregon's School of Architecture prepared and presented several green designs, of which one laid the foundation for the site's future development.

As noted by the project coordinator and soror, Chris Poole Jones, the vision that evolved was of a green building demonstration project that would provide a safe, nurturing environment for children and seniors to gather for academic, mental, and social development. Following Delta's program thrusts, the facility was envisioned to include activities such as afterschool mentoring and educational development programs for middle to high school teens, low- or no-cost meeting space for neighborhood and community organizations, as well as support for the physical and mental health needs of the community.

One key challenge to the vision early on was the growing interest in the property and repeated offers from developers to purchase it. The difficulty was whether to take the funds and put them back into the sorority's programming or to retain the central location in the community and move forward with the vision. Once the decision was made not to sell and to stay the course, the group unanimously moved forward.

Project Characteristics and Development

The property had been occupied by a gasoline service station from 1963 to approximately 1989 and listed by the Oregon Department of Environmental Quality (DEQ) as a leaking underground storage tank site (WorleyParsons Komex, 2009). In 1989, the site was screened, and five underground storage tanks were excavated. Five soil borings undertaken during the investigation detected significant petroleum hydrocarbons in the soil in the area of the tanks. Approximately 20 cubic yards of impacted soil was excavated from the tank area to a depth of 14 feet below grade. Deeper excavation of impacted soil was reportedly not conducted due to the proximity of building structures.

On August 9, 1990, the DEQ provided ARCO, the owner of the property, with a No Further Action (NFA) letter based on the following: the tanks and accessible contaminated soils had been excavated and removed from the site; the venting of deeper gasoline contamination had been accomplished per the Corrective Action Plan for the site; the soils aerated at the surface were tested and found to be within the appropriate cleanup standards for gasoline and diesel; there was little concern that groundwater could have been influenced by the contamination due to its depth; and natural degradation appeared capable of reducing any residual pollution to near background levels without adverse impacts. An analysis performed in 2008 revealed that petroleum hydrocarbon concentrations were well below the cleanup goals for gasoline, diesel, and heavier range hydrocarbons due to previous corrective action measures and natural attenuation. Based on the fate and transport properties of the remaining contamination levels, it was considered unlikely that such isolated and low-level contamination would migrate to groundwater as a result of future onsite rainwater infiltration actions (WorleyParsons Komex, 2009).

The sorority formed a non-profit corporation in 2005 – The Peninsula Rose Corporation, Incorporated – to create design priorities for property renovation, and initiated extensive fundraising activities. The Delta Project was a multi-phase development. According to the environmental consulting firm Vita Nuova, Phase I of the comprehensive development plan for the June Key Delta House: (1) increases the usable area from 876 to 2,700 sq. ft.; (2) provides a 120-seat "assembly" space; (3) adds 1,335 sq. ft. of usable landscaped exterior space; and (4) provides for the future development of the project site (Vita Nuova LLC, 2009).

Sustainability

Initially, a conventional development model was contemplated for the site, but there was great interest in applying greener concepts. Two critical goals put forward for the project were to use 50 to 70 percent recycled resources and to implement sustainable strategies that could qualify the project under the "Living Building Challenge" sustainability program. The Living Building Challenge is run by the Cascadia Region Green Building Council and is considered to be one of the most challenging green building programs globally. It aims to have projects that make a "positive" regenerative contribution to the environment as opposed to green and high-performance buildings that focus on making less of a negative environmental impact compared with code-compliant ones. Using the analogy of petals in a flower, the Living Building Challenge is comprised of seven performance categories (Petals = place, water, energy, health & happiness, materials, equity and beauty) that are subdivided into 20 Imperatives that can be applied to almost every building project at any scale or location. All Imperatives are mandatory (although some may be given 'temporary' exceptions due to market limitations), and certification is based on actual, rather than modeled, performance, which requires projects to be operational for at least 12 consecutive months before evaluation (International Living Future Institute, 2020). There are three levels of certification: Living Certification, whereby a project attains all 20 Imperatives; Petal Certification, where at least three of seven Petals Imperatives are achieved (one of which is either water, energy, or materials); and Net Zero Energy Certification that requires four specific imperatives to be met and 100% of the building's energy needs to be supplied by onsite renewable energy.

The sorority made plans to reuse the existing building, expand it using shipping cargo containers, and employ 90% salvaged recycled materials for interior finishes so that the approximately 2,400 sq. ft. facility could demonstrate numerous options for materials reuse (No Author, 2007). As for sustainable site design, funds from the US EPA's Brownfields Sustainability Pilots program were used to investigate the development of a rainwater harvesting and reuse system for the property to provide non-potable water for flushing toilets and irrigation. Rainwater landing on the roof and awnings of the building is directed into a cistern for storage. Any overflow from the cistern is directed to the site's stormwater management system and allowed to infiltrate into the ground. The 1,000-gallon cistern proposed by the consultants was anticipated to contain enough water for approximately 600 toilet flushes when full and is supplemented by city water when empty. Other sustainable site design features include brownfield redevelopment and site cleanup (including asbestos inside of the building), public transportation (including bike racks, Zipcar lot), urban redevelopment, open space (native plantings and permeable area), and zero VOC products for improving indoor air quality. Setting an example for sustainable energy use was also considered significant because of the former use of the property. Plans were made for passive solar daylighting, sun shading specific to orientation, geothermal heating and cooling, and net-zero renewable energy production using solar PV panels.

The June Key Delta Community Center pursued the Living Building Challenge's stringent requirements with an emphasis on the brownfield transformation, productive urban gardens, net-zero energy consumption, stormwater stored and processed to potable standards and reused onsite, blackwater effluent treated and infiltrated onsite, the installation of non-toxic and sensitively sourced and recycled materials, and equitable hiring and training opportunities created throughout construction (see Figure 7.2) (Portland Delta Sigma Theta Alumnae Chapter, 2020b).

Figure 7.2 June Key Delta Community Center, Portland, Oregon, 2016

The sorority secured a $70,000 grant from Pacific Power's Blue Sky renewable energy program to install 62 solar panels in the building in 2013 (Parks, 2013). The 18.36-kw solar energy system generates enough energy to power all the facility's electrical needs. With the solar panels, the building achieved six of the seven "Petals" required to earn the Living Building designation (Parks, 2013).

In addition to the green building goals, the community-oriented goals of this project have also been realized. It removed blight, provides a space for mentoring, tutoring, culturally based activities (e.g., an art gallery for people of color), and community members to meet. It also serves as a destination project to show sustainability on a small scale and highlight the work of non-profits. The members of the sorority also feel that the green economy/movement is not well incorporated into communities of color, so the building helps introduce the community to these ideas. The sorority also used minority contractors and worked with local apprentice programs to train the community in green building techniques (e.g., Oregon Tradeswomen, Verde landscaping, Constructing Hope).

Project Financing

A primary objective of the project was that the Delta Sigma Theta Sorority be debt-free when it was completed. The sorority embarked on an ambitious fundraising effort to obtain grants and donations for every aspect of the project, from site acquisition to development. Their list of supporters includes over one hundred grants and donations provided by Delta Sorors, public sector agencies, private agencies, community groups, and non-profits. This includes early contributions, such as survey work donated by the Neil Kelly Construction Company that created a blueprint for the property and recycled glass from Benson Industries Glass Division of $57,000.

By spring 2010, the sorority had spent $131,000 on property acquisition, brownfield work, design, and engineering. With grants and savings, they had another $300,000 to devote to the estimated $755,000 needed for the project going forward, leaving them with a $455,000 gap for which to raise funds. When the community center opened on August 10, 2011, a fundraising campaign was still underway to raise $100,000 to assist with the development of community-based programming and to help retire the construction debt (June Key Delta Community Center, 2011). A series of fundraising events had been organized to pay off the debt. Names of contributors are etched on glass windows, doors, or bricks on the center's grounds to acknowledge contributions. In 2015, the sorority was deep in its "Burn the Mortgage" campaign, which was selling bricks to raise the last $50,000 needed to pay off the debt.

Benefits, Barriers, and Lessons Learned

The Delta House project faced numerous barriers throughout the redevelopment process that were overcome by the tenacious perseverance of the project coordinator and the sorority members. Efforts to raise funds were a constant concern and challenge throughout. The sorority also had some difficulty getting the project off the ground and determining the best use for the site. The zoning and permitting process was considered very complicated, especially concerning using the Living Building Challenge criteria for the site renovation.

In its project summary, the US EPA notes additional challenges related to incorporating sustainability features (US EPA, 2009a). For instance, the city of Portland required further analysis to show that the stormwater management and reuse techniques would not mobilize residual contamination. The high-level stormwater management and green building features also did not conform to local regulations, and a few specialty materials did not satisfy the Living Building Challenge's requirement for local materials.

Despite these challenges, the desire to bring to fruition the benefits of the project pushed the sorority, and the volunteers and donors it inspired, forward. The coordinator felt that to promote similar projects in the future, more needs to be done to galvanize groups to embrace sustainability, and more information is needed to understand the long-term cost-effectiveness of these approaches. What eventually emerged was the first African American owned Living Building in the country, which is a testament to what is the most inspiring aspect of this project, the women who championed it. This included June Roe Runnells Key (the soror for which the building is named) who came up with the idea in the early 1990s and pushed for it among the local community but died before it happened, and Christine Poole-Jones, the soror who provided vision and steadfast leadership in getting it built, who sadly passed in 2014. The work of these individuals, along with the other sorors and community partners who aided in the project, is encapsulated in a humble quote located on a memorial to Christine at the front of the community center, which reads, "May the work I've done speak for me" (Portland Delta Sigma Theta Alumnae Chapter, 2020a).

Much of the timeline below (Table 7.1) was graciously provided by Chris Poole Jones on October 25, 2011. Certain vital events are bolded; however, the table is mainly left unmodified to show the complexity of actions involved in planning and development, as well as the scope of involvement and fundraising required by inspiring people to realize an inspiring project.

Table 7.1 Timeline – June Key Delta Community Center, Portland, Oregon

Year	Description
August 9, 1990	- **Brownfield report – "conditions at the site do not appear to pose an environmental threat (ARCO)"**
Purchase Property	- Purchased from ARCO Products Company under the leadership of Soror June Key
1992	- Neil Kelly Construction Company donated survey work on property and created a site blueprint
1992–1994	- Site cleanup and fix-up – painted, repaired tiles
	- Keith Edwards and Donna Hammond volunteered to get electrical circuits in working order
	- Vera Pool recruited men from the Inverness Jail to clean and repair
1995	- Fence built with money from an anonymous donor
1996	- Fundraising for maintenance
1997–1998	- **Exploring site construction options**
1999–2000	- Delta House Planning Study (Emmons Architecture)
	- Created development planning committees
	- Repaired light fixtures, installed ceiling tiles, patched back wall
2000–2001	- House Development Steering Committee, chaired by Lois Washington
	- Application for Peninsula Rose Corporation (2001)
	- Peninsula Rose House Development (Stuart Emmons, AIA) (2000)
	- Delta House Pledges

December 2002	- **Met with Greg Acker, Michael O'Brian (City of Portland Office of Sustainable Development) and Tom Kelley (Neil Kelly Construction) on development** - **Created House Construction Committee**
Spring 2003 Summer 2003 Fall/Winter 2003	- **Met with University of Oregon School of Architecture instructor, Greg Acker, and his graduate students** - **Students presented five "green designs"** - Sorority selected a design by Toni Garza - Created groundwork for developing site
2004	- **Peninsula Rose Corporation Incorporated, 501(c) established (Marian Gilmore, Board President)**
2005	- Peninsula Rose Corporation Board 501(c)(3) established - **Created design priorities for house renovation** - Worked with William Hart, Carleton Hart Architecture Company, in submitting Green Investment Fund (GIF) Grant Proposal
2006	- GIF Grant Proposal submitted (City Office of Sustainable Development) – not granted - Architect Bob Belcher volunteered to work on plan and development - Belcher submitted design to obtain building permits - **Fundraising stepped up to high gear** - Pledges, silent auction
2007 June Key Delta Community Center Demonstration Project	- **Started building permit process** - Continued internal fundraising - **Peninsula Rose Corporate/Portland Delta Alumnae Chapter developed partnership cooperation for nonprofit fundraising** - Benson Glass donated (Richard K. Woodling) - Submitted GIF Grant (City Office of Sustainable Development) - GIF Grant (Greg Acker, Richard K. Woodling, Bob Belcher, D'Norgia Price, Chris Poole-Jones) - Watershed Grant (D'Norgia Price, Greg Acker, Chris Poole-Jones) - Nike Grant (D'Norgia Price, Chris Poole-Jones) - Portland Development Commission (PDC) Grant (Greg Acker, Richard K. Woodling, Bob Belcher, Leslie Unthank, Aletha Chavis, Chris Poole-Jones) - Community Benefit Opportunity (CBO) Grant (Chris Poole-Jones, Greg Acker, D'Norgia Price) - Umpqua Bank opened up bank account for house construction funds - Met with Richard R. Harris, CPA to work with construction accounts - Partnered with Sienna Architecture for design and construction - Topographic Survey-Centerline Concepts, Inc. (7/15) - Summer meeting with construction committee and team partners - Selected lead contractor and secondary contractor: Lead, CJ Jackson Construction Inc.; Secondary, Orange, Green Design Contractors - Asbestos Testing – MESA Environmental LLC – results: Building clear except for kitchen sink fixtures (11/19) - Met with Carl Talton/ Chris Hasle Portland Family Fund on tax credit funding - Met with Serena St. Wesley, Community Coordinator Legacy Emmanuel Hosp. – will publish brochure (11/28)

(Continued)

Table 7.1 (Continued)

Year	Description
	- Albina Rotary ($1,000) – submitted a grant proposal
	- Met with Sue Arbuthnot and Richard Wilhelm on video-DVD of project (12/11)
	- Met with Debbie Casselton, City Environmental Services, on CBO grant contract (12/11)
	- JL Jackson Construction Co. – brought in electrical and drywall contractors for project bid (12/12)
	- Met with Susan Kuhn and Becki Marsh of Portland Development Commission to review budget and process of project
	- Sienna Architecture Co. presented preliminary construction design (12/7)
	- CL Jackson Construction Com. presented Description of Work and Schedule of Values cost sheet (December)
2008 June Key Delta Community Center Demonstration Project www.dstportland.org	- Grant Award: Albina Rotary (January)
	- Preliminary construction design plans given to CJ Construction Company (February)
	- Met with Susan Kuhn and staff of PDC and Sienna Architects (Greg Acker, Mark Nye) (3/20)
	- Bureau of Developmental Services renewed Conditional Permit (February) Pre-Application Conference (3/27)
	- Met with Stephen Shacketon (Watershed Grant) (4/1)
	- House Construction Committee Strategy Planning (4/4)
	- Pre-Application Conference Summary Report Case File EA 08-112436 (4/22)
	- TMR Consulting Engineers (proposal) structural site evaluation (4/23)
	- Project Enrollment form 510E sent to EnergyTrust (4/24)
	- Submitted GIF progress report to Kyle Dreisner (Office of Sustainable Development) (4/25)
	- Met with Dr. Algie Gatewood, President PCC Cascade on parking for large events (4/28)
	- Met with architect Bob Belcher, updating him on project progress (5/1)
	- Met with architect Greg Acker (Sienna Architecture) on Kresge Grant (5/7)
	- Marketing Committee meeting create develop marketing plan (5/20, 5/31, 6/7, 6/19)
	- Roofing assessment Delta House pre-construction inspection (Reuben) (5/22)
	- Evan du Pont, Energy Trust Program Manager, enrolled project in the New Building Fund (5/28)
	- Met with Clark Henry (Environmental Services) – agency will assist with brownfield issues (5/30)
	- Met briefly with Serena Wesley on Emmanuel Legacy Foundation (6/9)
	- CJ Jackson Construction Company construction bid (6/11)
	- Met with Michael Sur (Suh's Equipment, Inc.) on heating and cooling components (6/11)
	- Contract for Consulting Engineer, TM Rippey, engineering analysis (6/12)
	- Signed contract with TM Rippey Consulting Engineers for structural engineer services (6/18)
	- Met with Tim Hill (McMenamins historian), updated on Delta Project work on corporate support and launching project (6/23)

- Met with PDC on progress of project (6/24)
- Signed contract for geotechnical engineering services for site (6/30)
- Signed contract Site Access Agreement with Bureau of Environmental Services for technical assistance for additional environmental assessment working with US Environmental Protection Agency (Seattle) (7/3)
- Met with Richard Harris, CPA on finances of construction (7/9)
- **U.S. Environmental Protection Agency Technical Assistance Grant ($25,000) (7/29)**
- Mark Nye submitted Conditional Use Documents to the Bureau of Development Services (8/5)
- Met with Loretta Smith of Senator Ron Wyden's Office (8/5)
- Jean Loomis, Robin Robertson updated Portland Delta website: www.dstportland.org (8/6)
- Submitted Black United Fund Grant (8/14)
- Umpqua Bank Line of Credit letter (8/22)
- Timothy Agnew, TM Rippey Consulting Engineers' structural study initiates (8/28)
- Received email that project qualified for a PDC Storefront Grant (9/5), will submit (9/10)
- Met with Faye Burch (National Association of Minority Contractors) (9/5)
- Signed contract with Sherry Lenard, PDC Storefront Grant (9/15)
- **Environmental soil testing hydrogeology provided by Bureau of Environmental Services (Worley Parson) (9/16)**
- PDC meeting with Susan Kuhn/Beckie Marsh update on project (8/17)
- EPA Region 10 phone conference with Nuova Vita Architecture on EPA work (9/18)
- PDC meeting with Sherry Lenard, signed Storefront grant contract (9/26)
- Delta Marketing Committee fundraiser at World Trade Center (10/5)
- Teleconference (EPA Grant) SRA International/Nuova Vita Architects for Green Landscape Plan (10/6)
- Site visit by Damon I. Turner of the Black United Fund (10/16)
- Portland Community College, Dr Algie Gatewood/Pat Dickerson signed MUD Parking Doc. (10/16) (9/11)
- GIF Grant report (10/16)
- Black United Fund Grant Award (11/8)
- **Vita Nuova, Regina Winters, landscape architect (EPA Grant) site visit (12/11-13)**
- Bureau of Developmental Services: Conditional Use Posting (12/12)

2009-2010 "Living Building Challenge"
- Bureau of Developmental Services: Conditional Use Hearing (1/28/09)
- Decision of the Hearings Officer: Approved on condition (2/12/09)
- Mark Nye, Architect, contract for project (2/9/09)
- Mark Nye and Calvin Jackson CJ Construction meet to develop working plans for construction (2/18/09)
- Roslyn Hill assigned as a mentor for the project by a PDC contract (2/19/09)
- Bureau Developmental Services Permit application approval documents filed (April 2010)
- Asbestos roof inspection (4/24/10)

(Continued)

Table 7.1 (Continued)

Year	Description
	- Presentation to Humboldt Neighborhood Association (5/12/09) Mark Nye, Pat Dickerson, Chris Poole-Jones - Delivery of cargo containers (3) (5/27/09) - Groundwork Foundation Portland (Andea Hamberg, Exec. Dir.) granted 10 hours consultant services (6/11/09) - **Development Plan Project (Sept-Dec) Elizabeth Nye (July 2009)** - Contract Selection Committee selected Colas Construction Committee's bid for the project (July 2009) - Energy Trust Pilot Project Grant (August 2009) Evan deDupont - Ground Breaking (10/7/09) - Permit Granted (10/20/09) Submitting Bond for Permit - Piedmont Neighborhood Association meeting project presentation (10/29/09) - Energy Trust Award, Design Charrette (December 2009) - IEBW (Minority Workers) and Oregon Tradeswomen, Inc. volunteered skilled workers for the project (December 2009) - Hare In the Gate Productions (Sue Arbuthnot/Richard Wilhelm) – video to document the project - Meeting with Multnomah County Commissioner Jeff Cogen (12/17/09) - Holiday Fundraiser (12/19/09) - **Project Charrette (12/28/09)**
June Key Delta Community Center 2010	- Path to NetZero Pilot Project (January) - Oregonian Article on Project – front page (2/5) - Portland Development grant and loan (April) - Energy Studies in Building Laboratory (ESBL) University of Oregon Seminar (April) - Cascadia Region Green Building Council "Living Future Program" Conference, Seattle, WA (May) - Met with Oregon Electrical Construction Corp on Solar Array (June) - Insurance Bond, Assurity Northwest Insurance (7/22) - Bureau of Developmental Services Commercial Building permit (7/23) - Colas construction contract signed (7/26) - **Construction began (8/9)** - Site visit Spirit Mountain Fund (8/31) - Community Hard Hat Walk Around (10/30) - Northeast Neighborhood Coalition small grant (11/3) - House party fundraiser Marian and Gar deBarleban (11/7) - Meeting with Larry Dortmund, CFO McMenamins Pubs and Breweries (11/9) - Spirit Mountain Community Fund Award (12/2) - Bethel Foundation Kids robotic school hard hat walk around with Andrew Colas (12/4) - Met with Pat Daniels, Exec. Dir., Construction Hope – working on a partnership (1/4)
2011 "Living Building Challenge"	- Rebuilding Center grant for building materials (1/6) - Ainsworth Church Grant (1/14) - Portland Trail Blazer Community Outreach (3/1)

	- Spirit Mountain Community Fund Workshop (3/4)
	- Mt. Hood Community College video production Leigh Oliver Host (3/9)
	- East Multnomah County Water and Soil Conservation (small grant application) (4/15)
	- Met with Gina Binole, GBM Communications (4/19)
	- Community Hard Hat Walk Around (4/23)
	- East Multnomah County Water and Soil Conservation District Grant for community garden project (5/5)
	- Metro awarded 25 gallons of paint for project (5/20)
	- Clariner Boston and Bobbie Foster fundraising house party (5/22)
	- JKDCC Garden Planting Party (5/29)
	- Joan Brown Kline and Kay Toran fundraising house party (5/29)
	- Alec Mesdag (Oregon Electric Group) presentation of MDU Resources Foundation grant (6/3)
	- East Multnomah County Water & Soil Conservation District Green Street grant (6/5)
	- Region 10 Environmental Protection Agency tour and grants presentation (6/7)
	- Bureau of Planning & Sustainability (6/10&13) Desiree Williams Raja; Leslie Lum; Tony DeFalco (ctr for diversity in the environment)
	- Group Tour Bull Run Water Shed from JKDCC (7/7)
	- PDC planning meeting Sara King, Susan Kuhn, Becki Marsh (7/19)
	- PDC matching grants (signage, management, construction) (7/28)
	- Interior Design Committee Walkthrough (7/28)
	- Delta Sorority Walkthrough (8/8)
	- **JKDCC Grand Opening & Community Open House (8/10)**
	- Received City of Portland Office of Sustainability "Rethink" Grant (September)
	- Center for Livable Future Conference panel (9/22)
	- Featured in City of Portland Green Building Tour (9/24)
	- EcoDistricts Summit Panel (10/27)
2013	- Installation of solar panels moves the project 1 step closer to Living Building Certification
2015	- Memorial and ceremony for Christine Poole-Jones

Tabor Commons, Portland, Oregon

Site History

The Tabor Commons site, located at 5633 SE Division St., contained a small property (14,040 sq. ft.) with a one-story (967 sq. ft.) structure and a tool shed in a quiet residential neighborhood in southeast Portland directly across the street from two local schools. It was used as a gas station from the late 1920s to the 1980s and, after that, was owned by a series of different members of the same family who ran a variety of businesses, including mini-markets, a video arcade, and a used car lot. Community members were increasingly concerned about recurring criminal activity on the property, which included drug deals, loitering, a stabbing, laundering of food stamps, vandalism, arson, and the sale of cigarettes to minors.

Project Vision

In the early 1990s, the principal of the elementary school across the street championed the idea of turning the site into a community gathering place. The opportunity to realize this vision came in 2003 when federal agents arrested the property owner for illegally selling pseudo-ephedrine to local methamphetamine labs. The community immediately contacted the US Attorney's office in Portland to work on having the property transferred to community ownership. The US Marshals Service took ownership of the property on February 7, 2005, when the owner was sentenced. The Southeast Uplift Neighborhood Program took ownership from the Marshals on behalf of the Atkinson Parent Teachers Association and Mt Tabor and South Tabor Neighborhood Associations, with the condition that it obtain adequate liability insurance for the property (US EPA, 2009b).

In November 2004, before site acquisition, a series of community meetings were organized to come up with a vision for the property. In April of 2005, community members, local design firms, government officials, and urban planning students from Portland State University further explored and refined the community's vision for designing the site and buildings. The project received extensive coverage in the local media. The project vision aimed to create a vibrant and active facility that fosters relationships between the school and residents, including low-income and immigrant families. Community members identified three priorities for the project: (1) community center/gathering place; (2) activity space and meeting rooms; and (3) showcase for innovative environmental design features (Leistner, 2005). Part of the vision also involved green job training by a local non-profit, Oregon Tradeswomen, on building construction, mechanical, technical, and utility fields.

The coordinator for the project noted that the community pressed for an innovative environmental design that reflected the culture of the neighborhood. He also stated that "this is just how things are done in a progressive place like Portland." A few minor but significant barriers to the project did arise during the visioning process. Unknown environmental liability was considered the principal challenge early on, but this was dealt with via the negotiation of a prospective purchaser agreement with Oregon's Department of Environmental Quality (Oregon Department of Environmental Quality, n.d.). Obtaining insurance for the property also proved to be costly, but this was mitigated somewhat through the management of environmental liability. Another concern included some pushback from the local business association about community ownership of a commercial property, which was managed by working with the support of the association's president to ease the concern of members. Last but not least, the project was faced with the typical brownfields challenge of identifying funding to pay for remediation.

Project Characteristics and Development

Soon after the US Marshals seized the property in June 2004, the city of Portland's Bureau of Environmental Services conducted a preliminary investigation of the site to examine past uses, obtain any relevant documents, and assess the likelihood of contamination. The Bureau sent a letter to the Justice Department stating that cleanup costs for the site might exceed $200,000, which dropped the value of the property below $50,000. This made it possible for the parcel to become part of the Federal Department of Justice's Operation Goodwill initiative, which allows the Marshals Service's Asset Forfeiture Division to transfer property to state and local government agencies or their designated non-profit organizations.

A limited Phase II ESA conducted in December of 2004 found petroleum-contaminated soils, and consultants working with the city's Brownfield Program prepared an analysis of cleanup alternatives (GeoEngineers, 2007a). Neighborhood leaders worked with the Portland Brownfield Program and Oregon's Economic and Community Development Department to secure grant resources for environmental cleanup. Project coordinators also attempted to raise funds via an insurance archeologist but abandoned this effort once funding became available from the state of Oregon. In 2008, underground storage tanks and 200 tons of petroleum-contaminated soil were removed from the site using funds from the US EPA, Oregon Economic and Community Development Department, and Portland's Bureau of Environmental Services (GeoEngineers, 2007b). Oregon's Department of Environmental Quality granted a Notice of Completion of Remedial Measures on April 30, 2009. Even though the cleanup process went very smoothly, the application and reporting process required to obtain the necessary approvals and reimbursements from the state government were considered very complicated for a community non-profit to navigate.

Opsis Architecture and GreenWorks, a Portland-based design firm, worked with community members to generate concepts for a two-phase redevelopment of the Tabor Commons site. The first phase, completed in summer 2010, transformed the original structure into the Café au Play coffeehouse/community center and replaced the asphalt with sustainable landscape features and a public terrace. Phase II would have added a community building on the eastern portion of the site to accommodate meetings, classes, events, conferences, and receptions, but was never constructed.

Sustainability

The green design was central to the community's vision for the property, and essential to planning and implementation were the developer, community members, the city Bureau of Environmental Services, and the city stormwater program (in addition to state and federal involvement with site remediation). Given that the site lies in a combined-sewer neighborhood, one of the primary desires was to have the property manage stormwater and help educate about the issue. The project replaced impervious surface with green and porous pavement, increased canopy cover, and installed bioswales to capture stormwater generated onsite and from adjacent streets.

Project leaders hoped initially to qualify for LEED Gold Certification but later abandoned this goal due to cost. The project still involved the recycling of renovation materials, installation of bicycle parking, energy-efficient lighting and appliances, and incorporated many visible environmental education components like the bulletin board with a green roof. A radiant floor and eco-roof were contemplated but not built due to the cost and limited strength of the structure.

The primary goal for the project was to create a community gathering space and to remove the negative impact of the property on the neighborhood. Having the planning and development process administered by a community-based non-profit with a steering committee made up of several local groups kept this mission front and center. In addition to providing a meeting space, the building had hosted a variety of community-oriented education activities, such as classes in prenatal and infant care, child development, positive parenting techniques, nutrition, finance/budgeting, conflict resolution, and career exploration. There were also various community support groups for parents, as well as workshops in arts and crafts, and yoga. The building and outdoor area also provided space for local artists and musicians to put on exhibits and performances.

In addition to facilitating community economic revitalization, another primary objective was to provide a model of community development and ownership, with local and sustainability principles. Neighborhood groups worked with local businesses to manage initial resistance to the idea of community-ownership of both the project and retail venture. The main building housed Café au Play, a non-profit organization that operated a coffeehouse with play areas and activities for kids, caregivers, and the community (see Figure 7.3). Proceeds from the coffee business helped provide funding for the Café (originally projected to have four employees), patrons would design and lead activities, and families could connect to services and support networks. In the summer of 2011, Café au Play also started a weekly Saturday community farmers' market on the site.

Figure 7.3 Café au Play, Portland, Oregon, 2010

Another economically oriented function of the project was workforce training via the local high school in non-profit business management, child care, and the creation of family-focused businesses. This seven-week program was free, and each week participants spent one day in the classroom, one "hands-on" day in the field, and one field trip day where they apply their newly acquired skills. Café au Play had also created the "Volunteer Barista" program that trained high school students in the skills needed to work in a coffee shop, in exchange for their volunteer help. Through the Brownfields Sustainability Pilots program, the EPA supported a consultant to help develop a green job training curriculum with Oregon Tradeswomen, a non-profit founded to help women gain economic self-sufficiency through careers in the trades (US EPA, 2009b; US EPA, 2009c). The curriculum covered topics such as energy efficiency, passive solar design, solar panels, green roofs, solar thermal panels, stormwater management, the effects of water pollution, natural resource conservation, and building life cycle. Job training participants were also instructed on green building certifications and green building elements such as recycled materials, installing energy-efficient heating and cooling, weatherization, and avoiding volatile organic compounds. The curriculum covered necessary job skills, potential employers, as well as information on how to identify sources of financial support for integrating green features into site planning (International City/County Management Association et al., 2009). Oregon Tradeswomen piloted the curriculum on a group of over 20 people and then offered additional classes. During the training, participants practice their skills on properties owned by non-profits such as Tabor Commons. Indeed, students from this program built the eco-roof on the existing informational kiosk in front of the site.

Unfortunately, Café au Play ceased operations in 2015, mainly because the business model was unsustainable (SE Uplift Neighborhood Coalition, n.d.a). Other contributing factors, as outlined in a note posted by the Café au Play Board, included the departure of their long-term manager, over-reliance on a small group of "dedicated but burnt out" volunteers, the challenge of attracting non-profit board members, the difficulty of hiring café management and staff in a competitive job market, and the difficulty of realizing their non-profit mission while being "submerged" beneath the weight of managing a café. A community visioning process was initiated by the Southeast Uplift Neighborhood Coalition to help figure out a "new evolution" for the Tabor Commons site. After extensive consultation, a new tenant with a social mission was found in April 2017. The building was leased to Vibe of Portland, an organization created to provide art and music education to students regardless of economic means affected by the elimination of funding for such programs in Metro Portland schools. Opened in May of 2017, the new Vibe Art Studio offers weekly classes, summer camps, workshops, family engagement events, and other activities year-round, all lead by local professionals (SE Uplift Neighborhood Coalition, n.d.b).

Project Financing

In terms of project financing, the initial $50,000 to purchase the site was raised via local individuals, businesses, and a local philanthropist. Additional costs consisted of payment to US Marshals for their costs ($8,000), Multnomah County back property taxes ($26,000), insurance ($5,000), utilities ($2,000), and a contingency ($12,000). Grant funds were also obtained from various groups to pay for a variety of elements, including:

- underground storage tank cleanup, $60,643 from the state of Oregon Business Development Department and $14,043, city of Portland Bureau of Environmental Services;

- city of Portland Brownfield Program (BIF fund), $34,000;
- green job curriculum, $25,000, US EPA Brownfields Sustainable Pilots grant and Brownfields Job Training grant;
- building renovation, $12,000, city of Portland "Vision into Action" grant;
- bio-swales and landscape features, $37,000, city of Portland Bureau of Environmental Services;
- replacement of asphalt parking lot with pervious pavers, $22,000, East Multnomah (County) Soil and Water Conservation District;
- expansion of the capacity of stormwater swales to handle runoff from public streets, $8,294, city of Portland Bureau of Environment Services Community Watershed Stewardship Program;
- eco-roof on the garbage/recycling structure, $375, city of Portland Bureau of Environmental Services as part of the city's $5/sq. ft. eco-roof incentive; and
- decommissioning of unused driveways from the former drive-through operation and to channel stormwater runoff from the public street under the sideway and into the stormwater swale system on the site (scheduled for February 2012), $47,000, city of Portland Bureau of Environment Services "1% for Green" Program.

Services were also donated by a litany of volunteers who provided labor, in-kind resources, and professional services, including legal advice, electrical, plumbing, civil engineering services, concrete work, installation of doors and water heaters, and who performed many other tasks.

Benefits, Barriers, and Lessons Learned

Information gathered for this case study reveals obstacles encountered at virtually every stage of the redevelopment process, from site acquisition to business programming (see project timeline, Table 7.2). Several barriers appeared during the project visioning stage when members of the local business association were skeptical about community ownership and operation. Community members, however, were able to overcome this by working closely with the association to build support for the project, although time did prove that community management of an ongoing operation can be a lot for volunteers to bear. Another critical barrier early on was the difficulty of obtaining insurance for a contaminated property, which was managed somewhat via the negotiation of a prospective purchaser agreement with Oregon's Department of Environmental Quality.

The primary obstacles identified for the Tabor Commons project overall include the complexity of the cleanup and redevelopment process, the difficulty of obtaining insurance for a contaminated property, and challenges in gaining ownership of the site. Another challenge was the community organization's capacity to administer the process, which required a significant learning curve and long-term commitment. Nevertheless, patient and committed leadership from community leaders and the long-term dedication of project champions kept the process moving forward in a manner consistent with the community's sustainability vision. Strong support from multiple community groups helped enhance the groups' overall capacity to deal with issues and enhanced support networks. Site acquisition would have

Table 7.2 Timeline – Tabor Commons, Portland, Oregon

Year	Description
1999	Community members successfully oppose the liquor license application of the property owner after he is caught several times selling cigarettes to minors
June 2003	Police raid the property as part of an investigation of a multi-state drug ring that acquires pseudoephedrine and distributes it to meth labs. Community members contact US Attorney's office to express interest in gaining community ownership of the property. MTNA, STNA and Atkinson PTA and other community members form a steering committee to pursue community ownership of the property
June 2004	The US Marshals Service seizes the property
September 2004	City of Portland Bureau of Environmental Services examines the site
October 2004	US Department of Justice considers Goodwill Initiative
November 2004	Community Forum held to determine goals/vision for the property. Neighbors hold community meetings to discuss using the site as a community center in the future and to share ideas of how to redevelop the property
December 2004	City of Portland Bureau of Environmental Services completes limited Phase II Environmental Site Assessment report
February 2005	Property owner pleads guilty and is sentenced to 135 months in federal prison. The US Marshals take formal ownership of the property
April 2005	Community Forum held
Summer 2005 to Spring 2006	Neighbors successfully raise $49,000 in donations to cover the costs of the property transfer and initial holding costs, securing it as a community-owned space
Winter 2005	Portland State University student team studies the cleanup and makes recommendations
Fall 2005 to 2006	Prospective Purchaser Agreement (PPA) negotiated
2006	Intensify search for underground tank cleanup funding via insurance archeologist and government programs
June 2006	PPA filed with county government. US Marshals transfer ownership of site to Southeast Uplift Neighborhood Coalition
July 2006	Neighbors clean up, paint and renovate building and hold an open house. White House "Drug Czar" visits site and presents Community Anti-Drug Excellence awards to the Mt Tabor and South Tabor Neighborhood Associations, Atkinson Elementary PTA, and Southeast Uplift Neighborhood Coalition
October 2006	Community Forum held
2007	Some funding acquired to assess and remediate the site
February 2008	Additional grants awarded
2008	Site remediation carried out
May 2009	State DEQ formally states SEUL met PPA requirements
August 2010	Grand Opening Community Celebration event attended by over 800 community members
2015	Café au Play closes and community consultation for future use initiated
2017	New lease signed with Vibe of Portland which opens in May 2017

been impossible without the federal government's Operation Goodwill program, which allows the Marshals Service's Asset Forfeiture Division to transfer property to state and local government agencies or their designated non-profit organizations. It should be noted, however, that the program's rules could focus less on the price of a property and more on the community benefits associated with redeveloping it.

Implementation of many environmental features, including remediation and stormwater management, required significant administrative and financial support from government agencies at all levels. Portland's progressive Bureau of Environmental Services was very active in supporting and facilitating the project via its Sustainable Stormwater Program, which has received international praise for its efforts to integrate stormwater into building and site development. The "culture of support" from city agencies in Portland, in particular, helped move individual components of the project forward. This allowed the community to overcome the permitting process, which often stifles the implementation of innovative sustainability features in favor of conventional measures.

The project coordinator noted that the primary benefit associated with redeveloping this brownfield more sustainably was to establish a model that incorporates community partnerships, non-profit leadership, and more environmentally conscious redevelopment. He also added the provision of environmental educational opportunities, more social sustainability, and providing an opportunity for individuals to volunteer. A grant proposal written for the project offers a comprehensive list of benefits that different partners felt the project would bring (Leistner, 2005). The local elementary school believed the property would be useful for meetings, environmental education, and adult language programs. The building could also be a place where community members could access computers, library books, and garden produce offered via existing community programs. The direct benefits to the community included the creation of a meeting and gathering place for events, an environmental education opportunity, and a potential space for affordable office incubator space and/or affordable housing on one or more upper floors. As for broader community benefits, the proposal lists enhancing relationships, quality of life, and the pedestrian environment, as well as support for the local economy, ecological design, and environmental sustainability.

To facilitate the inclusion of sustainability in future brownfields efforts, those involved with this project pointed to: the need for case studies and best practices outlining how to do it (with information on real risks and action); education of the private sector about brownfield risks; modifications to the permit process to foster innovative measures; enhancement of the capacity of the city to support and facilitate community-led development; the continuation of the EPA's Pilot process for linking brownfields and sustainability; and additional technical and financial support.

In all, the Tabor Commons project is a model for the community-led and sustainable redevelopment of small brownfield sites. However, the closure of Café au Play and subsequent signing of a new tenant highlights the importance of long-term financial sustainability of operations to be considered when redeveloping brownfields. Since the site was already remediated and the structure was renovated, Southeast Uplift was able to find a new use for the site, which would not be possible if funding ran out during the initial stages of the project instead of later in its operation. Although the goals of the new tenant are narrower compared with those outlined in the original grant application and delivered by Café au Play, the arts and music mission still offers community benefits. Vibe also continues to host some community events, such as a tree lighting event and tree sale fundraiser, and a community Artisan fair. Socially, the redevelopment brought the community together to provide a gathering space and numerous educational opportunities (e.g., green jobs, language, now music, and art). Environmentally, the project continues to showcase an array of green technologies and features that improve the site and the surrounding neighborhood. Economically, the project removes blight and brings positive activity back to a derelict space. The project also adds to a growing list of sustainable brownfield projects in Portland that all point the way for other interested community groups and developers, which is music to everyone's ears.

Green Avenue, Greenville, South Carolina

Site History

The Greenville Sustainability Brownfields Pilot site is located on a one-acre former commercial property in Greenville, South Carolina. The property is in the western quadrant of the city, one mile southwest of the city center, in the Green Avenue neighborhood. The history of the west part of the city is reminiscent of the boom and bust economic cycles that brought commercial and residential development supported by industrial growth to predominantly agricultural settlements beginning in the late 1800s. Following the end of the civil war, warehouses and textile mills expanded in this area as cotton came into production on upstate farms. In response to economic decline and the relocation of textile mills outside the central city at the turn of the century, commercial activity gradually shifted to the production and packaging of soft drinks. The invention and widespread proliferation of the automobile in the early 1900s encouraged the creation of service stations and repair shops that also enhanced economic activity in the western quadrant. The Great Depression, however, affected this renewed economic development until World War II, when the construction of an Air Force Base in South Greenville contributed to an improvement of the city's economy (city of Greenville, 2012). The allure of suburban development in the 1950s–1960s, however, claimed residents and businesses.

Economic decline and the community's industrial past resulted in a concentration of brownfield properties in the western part of the city. Many of these properties sat vacant or under-utilized due to the uncertainty regarding their environmental condition and the potential cost of environmental remediation (US EPA, 2012). This uncertainty acted as a disincentive to future commercial or industrial redevelopment as developers base their decisions on market transparency. In addition to brownfields, land use in the western part of the city was affected by the limited availability of affordable housing in good repair and outdated infrastructure. The minority population, made up 66% African Americans in the mid-2000s, was also struggling with 12 percent unemployment and 40 percent of families living at or below the poverty line (US EPA, 2008).

Following the successful revitalization of downtown Greenville, the city began investigating strategies to renew the western part of the city starting in the early 2000s. The city of

Greenville's 2002 Green Avenue Master Plan (i.e., Green Avenue Revitalization Strategy) focused on the Green Avenue neighborhood, a historically vibrant African-American district experiencing hard times resulting in boarded-up properties, vacant lots, a deteriorating housing stock, and crime (city of Greenville, 2002). The revitalization strategy, developed with the Green Avenue Neighborhood Association, sought to build on past renewal efforts by creating a mixed-income neighborhood with a variety of residential opportunities. This included the creation of 36 market rate and 71 affordable units and 68 owner- and renter-occupied homes designed to architecturally complement the existing housing stock and to target existing residents to minimize displacement. The city was very concerned with the brownfield sites in this area and secured funding through a combination of granting programs offered by the US EPA to finance the administrative and technical costs of environmental assessments. In this regard, the proposed Green Avenue redevelopment is part of a coordinated effort by the city of Greenville to assess and remediate brownfield properties to encourage urban revitalization in the area. The majority of assessed properties did not require remediation, bringing an end to the uncertainty that had impeded redevelopment in the community (US EPA, 2008).

Project Vision

Initial plans for this site called for affordable workforce housing with sustainable landscape features adjacent to a detention pond to support the city's stormwater infrastructure. This pilot project was tied to the existing neighborhood Master Plan. By the spring of 2010, the city had acquired properties around McLeod Street and Green Avenue for the project. However, as new residential units were built in the neighborhood, the city and the Green Avenue Civic Association determined that the pilot site and one directly across the street from it would provide an opportunity for a passive park and green space. Instead of housing, plans for a green space commenced in late 2011, and construction began in mid-April, 2012, and completed later that year.

From the outset, the city of Greenville was motivated to incorporate sustainable design features into the project vision for a variety of reasons. The first was to remediate the brownfield property and enhance its appeal to prospective developers and residents. Promoting sustainable design and energy efficiency on the property was initially considered to be a way of reducing energy and water consumption and their associated costs, both of which contribute to affordable living (Tetra Tech, 2009)

The integration of more intensive sustainable design features in the site plan to deal with stormwater was also used to increase the property area available for development. Sustainable landscape features such as grass pavers, bioswales, and rain gardens would make it possible to reduce the size of a detention pond, which would otherwise have occupied half the site (Tetra Tech, 2009). Tetra Tech, the consultant for the Sustainable Brownfields Pilot, initially developed a conceptual residential and sustainability plan for the site based on the parameters put forward by the city (i.e., appropriate residential design, stormwater pond, maintaining 18 onsite monitoring wells). The original site plan consisted of six detached single-family houses overlooking green space and designed to provide sustainable and environmentally friendly living

(Tetra Tech, 2009). The significant sustainable landscape features proposed in Tetra Tech's site plan included "community gardens, a passive park with a plaza and native landscaping, rain gardens, a bioswale, infiltration trenches, filter strips, pervious paving, rain barrels, and solar panels" (Tetra Tech, 2009). In terms of the development of the larger area, the intention was to encourage walkability and social interaction between residents, particularly children walking to nearby schools. The city was also planning for the addition of 40 single-family homes to the neighborhood as a whole. The houses would be a mix of affordable and market residences ranging from $95,000–$150,000 to support a diverse community.

Project Characteristics and Development

Environmental tests on the Greenville Workforce Housing Project site revealed the presence of a range of contaminants from the previous land uses. The area designated for the project was initially two adjacent but separately owned properties that were combined when the city acquired them in 2007 (Tetra Tech, 2009). One was formerly a BP service station, whereas a Thriftway supermarket occupied the second property. Each property was approximately half an acre. The BP service station began operating in 1964. It included "a service garage, station, fuel oil dispenser island, nine underground storage tanks for petroleum fuel products, one above-ground storage tank, parking areas, and an office building" (Tetra Tech, 2009). The Thriftway supermarket consisted of a 6,250 sq. ft. building, which also opened for business in the 1960s. Both the BP service station and the Thriftway supermarket ceased their operations sometime in 2002 (US EPA, 2009d).

A Phase I Environmental Assessment completed by the city in November 2002 found asbestos in the former Thriftway building structure and recommended further testing on both sites. Soil sampling was performed in December 2006, followed by groundwater sampling in February 2007 (Tetra Tech, 2009). Analysis of the groundwater indicated the presence of several contaminants of concern, including benzene/toluene/ethylbenzene/xylenes (BTEX), methyl tertiary-butyl ether (MTBE), ethylene dibromide (EDB), and naphthalene. Concentrations above detection limits were localized, with a significantly high concentration of 26,000 micrograms per liter (µg/L) for MTBE found at one sampling location on the site near Green Avenue (Tetra Tech, 2009)

Working with the US EPA and the South Carolina Department of Health and Environmental Control, the city of Greenville decided upon monitored natural attenuation, permitting naturally occurring processes to filter the toxic potential of present contaminants, as the remedial course of action for the site. The sustainable design features initially proposed by the team of consultants from Tetra Tech were selected to minimize stormwater runoff and its associated impacts, as requested by the city of Greenville. Onsite stormwater management can be achieved through low-impact development practices designed to absorb or distribute the runoff (Tetra Tech, 2009). Collectively, the proposed design features encourage sustainability by reducing energy and water consumption while providing space for public gathering and interaction.

The conceptual site plan proposed the numerous sustainable design interventions for stormwater management (i.e., erosion and sediment control, permeable pavement, rain barrels, bioswales, vegetated curb extensions, native landscaping), community gardens for public engagement, solar panels for energy conservation, and compost bins for waste reduction. The city of Greenville was receptive to most of the recommendations but acknowledged early on that it may not be possible to implement all of the proposed sustainable design features.

While the original vision for the Greenville Workforce Housing Project initially proceeded without difficulty, its implementation was ultimately blocked by the economic realities facing the housing market (Tetra Tech, 2009). Indeed, the developer identified by the city was forced out of business by the decline in the housing market. As the city contemplated the next steps, a review of the 2001 Green Avenue Master Plan revealed that plans for parks and green space had not been adequately addressed. The city and the Green Avenue Neighborhood Association worked together to design a passive park space that would allow long-time Green Avenue residents and new neighbors to create a gathering place for events, picnics, and neighborhood activities. Although there was consensus that new homes would make an excellent addition to the community, residents also wanted a beautiful space where they could socialize with their neighbors, take their children and grandchildren, and re-introduce green spaces into the neighborhood.

Project Financing

The city of Greenville secured financing for the environmental assessment and technical site plan assistance through a combination of US EPA grants. The first grant awarded in 2000, the EPA Brownfields Assessment Grant with a value of $200,000, was used to complete environmental assessments on several brownfield properties in West Greenville, including the Green Avenue site. The removal of underground storage tanks (UST) in West Greenville, including the Green Avenue site, was made possible through an EPA grant of $100,000 to the South Carolina Department of Health and Environmental Control under the Agency's USTfields Program in July 2002 (US EPA, 2008). The EPA also financed the technical assistance provided by Tetra Tech to develop a site plan with sustainable design features through a $25,000 Technical Assistance grant. The city used the available grants effectively by coordinating the assessment and remediation of multiple brownfields simultaneously. Acquiring the site in 2007, however, was paid for by the city; the combined cost of the properties was $225,000. The city also bore the cost of constructing the passive park (estimated at $100,000).

Benefits, Barriers, and Lessons Learned

Implementing the proposed site plan for the Greenville Workforce Housing Project presents opportunities and challenges that may prove to be insightful to other cities interested in initiating similar projects.

The redevelopment of an underutilized brownfield property in West Greenville provides the surrounding community with a variety of benefits (see project timeline, Table 7.3). To begin with, the environmental assessments and the demolition of dilapidated structures throughout the neighborhood have eliminated the uncertainty related to property condition and opened the way for future redevelopment. The intersection on which the project site is located is an important node within the community, and its revitalization has stimulated further development and investment in the neighborhood. This, in turn, has supported the local economy through job creation and an increased tax base.

The interrelated benefits of this Brownfield Sustainability Pilot project have enabled the city to encourage sustainable community development in the Green Avenue neighborhood. The demolition of under-utilized and dilapidated buildings has put an end to illegal activities on the property and contributed to an increased sense of security in the area (Tetra Tech, 2009). Given that the proposed redevelopment is part of a city effort to re-urbanize the Green Avenue neighborhood, the realignment of the McLeod Street and Green Avenue intersection along with the addition of sidewalks and crosswalks have made it safer for pedestrians. Community development, on a broader level, was also achieved as the project vision and design process required collaboration between several stakeholders, including the US EPA, HUD, the Green Avenue Neighborhood Association, the city of Greenville, and Upstate Forever (a non-profit that advocates species protection and smart growth).

An important lesson, however, is that despite technical support, community buy-in, and progressive planning, brownfield plans cannot be implemented if market conditions are unfavorable. From the outset, the city was mindful of the market challenges and how this might affect the implementation of sustainability features in both the housing and green space components of the original vision. An interview with a city employee noted that the costs of the project needed to be maintained at a reasonable level to encourage buy-in from developers. Sustainable design interventions are not necessarily affordable and can escalate project costs, which are, in turn, transferred to the homebuyer. The malaise in the housing market caused by the recession resulted in a rethinking of the project. Still, the sustainability visioning and technical support did "plant a seed" in terms of visioning a greener future for the property. Indeed, the central location of the property, the availability of other buildable lots throughout the neighborhood for housing, and the need for porous surfaces for stormwater management all seem to support the park function that was ultimately developed at the site.

In recognition of National Community Development Week, the city of Greenville hosted a community celebration of the Green Avenue Revitalization Project on Wednesday, April 3, 2013. In the new park, the Mayor, city staff, and members of the Green Avenue Neighborhood Association celebrated the new space and the implementation of the various projects undertaken since 2001, including streetscape work and the construction of 28 affordable homes in the area by the city's development partner. They also announced the remaining components of the plan, such as the construction of approximately 30 more homes, neighborhood gateway signage, additional streetscape work, and the naming of the two parks. In 2019, Green Avenue Memorial Park was dedicated in memory of Officer Allen Jacobs and in honor of neighborhood leaders (Velma Gooch, Etta Patterson, and Shirley Gambrell) for their efforts to improve the community (see Figure 7.4).

162   Corner Gas Station Brownfields

Figure 7.4 Green Avenue Memorial Park, Greenville, South Carolina, 2019

Table 7.3 Timeline – Green Avenue, Greenville, South Carolina

Year	Description
1960s to 2002	Functioned as gas station and supermarket
2002	Nine underground storage tanks and one above ground storage tank were removed from the site
November 2002	City of Greenville conducted a Phase I Environmental Assessment
December 2006	Soil and ground water sampling
February 2007	Soil and ground water sampling
2009	Structures demolished; natural attention chosen as method of remediation
2011	Plans developed for the park 2011
2012	Construction begins on the park in mid-April with completion anticipated by June 15, 2012
2013	Green Avenue Neighborhood Celebration takes place on the newly constructed site to celebrate the Green Avenue Revitalization Strategy (www.youtube.com/watch?v=GM4QbFuaDzs)
2019	Green Avenue Neighborhood Association dedicates the Green Avenue Memorial Park in honor of Officer Allen Jacobs, a Greenville police officer who was killed in the line of duty, and other neighborhood leaders

References

Bingham, L. (2010). Gasoline station being reborn as community center by African American sorority in North Portland. February 5, *The Oregonian*.

City of Greenville. (2002). *Green avenue neighborhood revitalization strategy (green avenue master plan)*. Community Development and Relations Division.

City of Greenville. (2012). *City of Greenville, South Carolina Brownfields Program*. January 4. City of Greenville.

GeoEngineers. (2007a). *Analysis of brownfield cleanup alternatives former service station 5633 SE Division Street Portland Oregon*. City of Portland Bureau of Environmental Services.

GeoEngineers. (2007b). *Proposal for remediation of petroleum-contaminated soil; Oregon Department of Environmental Quality 2006 prospective purchaser agreement*. GeoEngineers.

International City/County Management Association, Oregon Tradeswoman, Flying Hammer Productions. (2009). *Tabor Commons green jobs program*. US EPA, Brownfields and Land Revitalization.

International Living Future Institute. (2020). *Living Product Challenge Certification: Certification Overview*. April 10. International Living Future Institute.

June Key Delta Community Center. (2011). *June Key Delta Community Center*. August 9. www.key-delta-living-building.com

Leistner, P. (2005). *Application for property transfer under the operation goodwill initiative, 57th and division school/neighborhood community center Portland, Oregon: Southeast uplift neighborhood program*. US Federal Department of Justice.

No Author. (2007). *Living building challenge*. Poster for LBC competition provided by Chris Poole Jones.

Oregon Department of Environmental Quality. (n.d.). *Prospective purchaser agreements*. Oregon Department of Environmental Quality.

Parks, C. (2013) June Key Delta Community Center closer to becoming first african-american owned living building. November 18, *The Oregonian*.

Portland Delta Sigma Theta Alumnae Chapter. (2020a). *JKDCC housing history*. March 5, Portland Deltas.

Portland Delta Sigma Theta Alumnae Chapter. (2020b) *June Key Delta Community Center: Green sustainable building*. March 20. Portland Deltas.

SE Uplift Neighborhood Coalition. (n.d.a). *Tabor Commons*. www.seuplift.org

SE Uplift Neighborhood Coalition. (n.d.b). *New Tenant at Tabor Commons*. www.seuplift.org

Tetra Tech. (2009). *EPA brownfields sustainability pilot, conceptual site design for sustainable redevelopment green avenue sites, Greenville, SC*. US EPA Office of Solid Waste and Emergency Response, Office of Brownfields and Land Revitalization.

US EPA. (2008). *In Greenville, SC, coordinating resources from two EPA programs maximizes their effectiveness and results* (Report EPA-560-F-239). US EPA Office of Solid Waste and Emergency Response.

US EPA. (2009a). *Nonprofit using sustainable design to convert a former gas station into a community center solid waste* (Report EPA-560-F-09-511). US EPA Office of Solid Waste and Emergency Response.

US EPA. (2009b). *Building a sustainable future: A report on the environmental protection agency's brownfields sustainability pilots* (Report EPA-506-F-09-500). US EPA Office of Brownfields and Land Revitalization.

US EPA. (2009c). *Green jobs training curriculum for nonprofit in Portland* (Report EPA-560-F-09-509). US EPA Office of Solid Waste and Emergency Response.

US EPA. (2009d). *Sustainable housing and stormwater infrastructure on a former gas station and supermarket* (Report EPA-560-F-09-506). US EPA Region 4 Brownfields Team.

US EPA. (2012). *Brownfields sustainability pilots fact sheet, Greenville workforce housing project*. (Report EPA 560-F-08-276). US EPA Region 4 Brownfields Team.

Vita Nuova LLC. (2009). *Recommendations for sustainable site design: Green landscape plan final, June Key Delta House*. US EPA Office of Solid Waste and Emergency Response Office of Brownfields and Land Revitalization.

WorleyParsons Komex. (2009). Additional site assessment report for property located at 5940 N. Albina Avenue, Portland, OR. In Vita Nuova LLC (Ed.), *Recommendations for sustainable site design: Green landscape plan final, June Key Delta House* (Appendix E, pp. 25-121). US EPA Office of Solid Waste and Emergency Response Office of Brownfields and Land Revitalization.

Interviews

June Key Delta Community Center, Portland, Oregon

- LaJewel, L. (2020). President, Portland Alumnae Chapter of Delta Sigma Theta Sorority.
- Poole-Jones, C. (2009, 2011). Project Coordinator, Portland Alumnae Chapter of Delta Sigma Theta Sorority.

Tabor Commons, Portland, Oregon

- Leistner, P. (2009, 2011). Project Coordinator, Chair, Tabor Commons Steering Committee Neighborhood & Program Coordinator, Office of Neighborhood Involvement, city of Portland.

Green Avenue, Greenville, South Carolina

- Stroud, Ginny. (2010, 2012) Community Development Advisor, City of Greenville.

8 Main Streets, Neighborhoods, and Towns

While most think of brownfields as individual parcels, small or large, to be addressed one at a time, some think of their impact and potential opportunity more comprehensively and holistically. The four case studies examined in this chapter – Focus HOPE in Detroit, Michigan, the Jackson Square Redevelopment Initiative in Boston, Massachusetts, the Commercial Street Historic District in Springfield, Missouri, and Samoa Town in Humboldt County, California – look at efforts by developers, non-profits, and local governments to work at a larger scale to address brownfield problems and undertake projects with the hope of sparking sustainable brownfield and community development.

Focus: HOPE, Detroit, Michigan

Site History

Focus: HOPE is a non-profit organization in Detroit, Michigan, established in 1968 to unite a community sharply divided along racial and economic lines and shaken by severe rioting the year before. Its efforts to build community and overcome racism, poverty, and injustice by providing education, training, and other services for underrepresented minorities are both extensive and inspiring. Over the last few decades, it has been working with local partners to redevelop several brownfield properties along Oakman Boulevard, which is considered a gateway into the mostly African-American community. Although the US EPA's Sustainable Brownfields Pilot focused on green streetscape efforts, it is crucial to see this project and others in this chapter as seeking to either initiate or contribute to broader revitalization efforts. In the 2000s, Focus: HOPE, acting both as the community organization and developer, began to take on multiple catalytic projects, including: (1) the recycling of an automotive site; (2) the construction of affordable housing; (3) the revitalization and redevelopment of park space; and (4) the conversion of a historic commercial building (the Bell Building) into a mixed-use building (US EPA, 2009a). A fifth element of the process was a "green streets" component to weave it all together, supported by the US EPA's Sustainable Brownfields Pilot process.

Project Vision

The area where the green street is to be located is adjacent to the Focus: HOPE campus and several redevelopment efforts that they and their community partners were undertaking.

The projects, described in more detail below, have come together piece-by-piece, and the green street intends to unite them. According to the Project Coordinator Deborah Fisher, Focus: HOPE was interested in the project at two levels. First, on a broader scale, its mission takes into consideration a radius of about a hundred blocks and is focused on a holistic set of activities, from education to safety, all of the elements that go into making a sustainable community. As for the specific cluster of properties, these act as an entryway into the Oakman area, a 30-block zone where they wish to see more new development and rehabilitation. Sustainability has historically been a focal point for Focus: HOPE and its efforts to be at the forefront of change and innovation to benefit the community.

Focus: HOPE conducted a neighborhood analysis in 1997 following a tornado that negatively impacted the community. It started planning projects around 2005-2006, but Detroit's economic downturn delayed progress. Focus: HOPE learned of the Brownfields Sustainability Pilot program in 2008 while presenting its brownfield reuse efforts at the national brownfields conference in Detroit. The Pilot was initially supposed to focus on green building design elements for commercial and residential projects, but Focus: HOPE and its partners determined that there was a greater need to incorporate sustainability approaches along the street to link multiple projects and improve community aesthetics and walkability. The EPA's technical assistance to Focus: HOPE included the development of the Green Streetscapes Study for Oakman Boulevard (US EPA, 2009a). The study consists of an introduction to green streetscape concepts, sample specifications, and construction details to support implementation by developers, designers, and policymakers. Although many of the green streetscape components outlined in the study may be applied to other properties, the research focuses on those being redeveloped along the half-block area of Oakman Boulevard. The EPA technical assistance team identified six green streetscape design objectives to improve air quality, reduce the heat island effect, improve water quality, enhance the urban forest and wildlife habitat, reduce light pollution, and mitigate/rehabilitate brownfield conditions. It put forward design guidelines and developed project concepts to meet the six objectives related to sustainable stormwater management practices, native landscaping, bike facilities, and furniture and fixtures. The study also provides a conceptual design for the redevelopment to illustrate the feasibility and provide a roadmap for implementation.

While stakeholders supported the green vision, challenges faced in 2010 with persuading the city to approve sustainable treatments that were not seen as meeting requirements caused the project to take a back seat to other initiatives. An early project was the recycling of a two-acre abandoned automotive facility for reuse as a parking lot to support a planned mixed-use development on adjacent property. US Real Estate donated the site to Focus: HOPE Revitalization, established in 2002 as a non-profit through its Community and Economic Development department to work on neighborhood revitalization. EPA assessment grant funding was received through Wayne County and EPA cleanup funding through the city of Detroit's Revolving Loan Fund (RLF) program (US EPA, 2008). Phase I and Phase II ESAs revealed PCB, asbestos, mercury, sodium hydroxide, and residual PNA contamination that required cleanup. Cleanup and demolition activities commenced in August 2005 and were completed in December 2005. A more sustainable approach to remediation and demolition waste recycling made the parking lot project feasible by reducing the total project cost by

20 percent, a savings of $150,000, made possible by recycling approximately 1,200 tons of materials and over 13,000 gallons of liquid wastewater (US EPA, 2008).

On February 14, 2007, Focus: HOPE then opened the Village of Oakman Manor, a new senior living community located on the eastern edge of Focus: HOPE's campus. The four-story, 55-unit building was sponsored by Presbyterian Villages of Michigan in collaboration with Focus: HOPE and was the first new development in the area in over 50 years. Each one-bedroom apartment in the $6.2 million structure includes a full kitchen, combined living/dining room, barrier-free bathroom, and a walk-in closet. Community rooms and activities encourage residents to mingle, and rent is set at 30 percent of adjusted gross income, which typically ranges from $200 to $275 per month, given that many residents live below the poverty line. Funding for the project came from HUD, the Nonprofit Facilities Center, Michigan State Housing Development Authority, city of Detroit, Wayne County, and MASCO Corporation. (Focus: HOPE, 2007). The Focus: HOPE project was also considered in Michigan's Cool Cities Neighborhoods program (Cool Cities, 2010).

Focus: HOPE was also involved in several green space projects, including the revitalization of a local park, the development of a pocket park on its campus, and a neighborhood park converted from a former parking lot. In 2005, the park at the corner of Ford and LaSalle, just two blocks south of Focus: HOPE's offices, had dilapidated and antiquated play equipment that attracted unsafe uses. Focus: HOPE and community residents formed the Ford/LaSalle Park Revitalization Committee to refurbish the site, which now includes a safe playscape, picnic area, and basketball court (Focus: HOPE, 2010). Also, the HOPE Community Park (aka Cool Cities Park) is a community public space on Oakman boulevard created on the site of a former service station with funding from the Cool Cities Initiative and the Local Initiatives Support Corporation, along with trees donated from Greening of Detroit and plants from Lowes and other contributors (see Figure 8.1). In response to community desires and through an activity fund grant of $4,500, Focus: HOPE hosted three grand-opening events at the park in 2009. Cool Cities park has become a neighborhood hub anchoring the corridor and, in 2018 and 2019, hosted the city's first outdoor photography festival featuring work by local youth complete with a light show and large-scale projections on the adjacent Bell Building (Fisher, 2020).

The Bell Building, well-known locally for its iconic Yellow Pages sign, was rehabilitated in 2012 to include 155 fully furnished one-bedroom apartments for formerly homeless adults and to serve as the headquarters of the non-profit Neighborhood Service Organization (NSO). The building, constructed in 1929–1930 as a warehouse, garage, and office space, required extensive remediation for residential use that included the removal of underground storage tanks, remediation of contaminated soil, mitigating soil vapors, and removing lead-based paint and asbestos (O'Brien Construction Company Inc., 2020). The building was bought in 1996 by Focus: HOPE and acquired in February 2011 by NSO and took $52 million to refurbish (CBS Detroit, 2013). The eco-sensitive restoration salvaged and restored many existing elements and returned the facade to its original historic look. Financing was complicated by the market crash of 2008, with NSO submitting Low Income Housing Tax Credit applications for three years before finally securing a reservation in 2009/2010. Following this, two years of meetings took place between the builder, architect, NSO staff, accountants, consultants,

Figure 8.1 HOPE Community Park, Detroit, Michigan, 2016

and government representatives to shape the project and financing (O'Brien Construction Company Inc., 2020). Funding for the development came from equity financing, donations from individuals, tax credits, and loans and grants. The stakeholders involved include HUD, Michigan State Housing Development Authority, city of Detroit, Wayne County, The Kresge Foundation, The McGregor Fund, The National Trust Community Investment Corporation, Bank of America, Corporation for Supportive Housing, Local Initiatives Support Corporation, and the Opportunity Resource Fund (CBS Detroit, 2013). The hugely successful NSO Bell Building has won numerous awards since its redevelopment, including the Governor's Award for Historic Preservation, Michigan's Historic Preservation Network's Building Award, the National Trust for Historic Preservation Award, and the National Housing and Rehabilitation Association's Judges Award: Most Advanced Financial Structure category of the 2013 J. Timothy Anderson Awards for Excellence in Historic Rehabilitation (O'Brien Construction Company Inc., 2020).

Success with individual projects continued to fuel momentum with Focus: HOPE'S sustainability efforts. In 2010, it partnered with the Graham Sustainability Institute at the University of Michigan on the HOPE Village Initiative, which seeks to "ensure that, by the year 2031, 100% of neighborhood residents will be educationally well-prepared, economically self-sufficient, and living in a safe, supportive environment" (University of Michigan, 2012). The partners conducted a Sustainability and HOPE Village Initiative Integrated Assessment that led to Focus: HOPE becoming the first of two EcoDistricts in Detroit in 2016. The EcoDistrict program supports the identification of opportunities and the development of community-driven plans, studies, and activities aimed at fostering neighborhood regeneration and sustainability. In addition to pressing forward with the streetscape plan, the program advanced projects and plans related to open/vacant space, social perceptions, housing, education, built environment, and economic development. While the Graham Institute's collaborative study ended in 2014, project teams developed many proposals that Focus: HOPE could submit to potential funders. The EcoDistrict program also continues to move forward with notable accomplishments in the neighborhood, including: (1) local gardens and food systems work that supports new and existing gardens, a farmers market, and a food academy for training middle schoolers; (2) community-led projects such as the Clements Street Rain Garden and the installation of renewable energy-generating playground equipment at Glazer Elementary School; and (3) placemaking and community art initiatives that have added over 100 new pieces of art in Hope Village. Another notable project is the LaSalle Eco-Demonstration home, Detroit's First LEED Platinum Home Rehab development intended to serve as a demonstration site for green technologies, host an art gallery, and provide meeting space for the community (Ecodistricts.org, 2017; Enterprise, 2018).

In 2019, Focus: HOPE announced that it was spinning off its community development non-profit to refocus on its historic core mission of workforce development, early childhood education, and its senior food program (Nagl, 2019). Focus: HOPE Revitalization (established in 2002) and the Hope Village Initiative (launched in 2009) would be renamed Hope Village Revitalization, registered as a separate non-profit, and operate as a community development corporation. It will occupy part of the LaSalle Eco-Demonstration home as its headquarters and be led by long-time director Debbie Fisher, three paid staff, two volunteers, and a 12-member board made up of neighborhood stakeholders and one member from Focus: HOPE. The new organization will allow for sharper focus and community control to pursue equity and sustainability-oriented activities such as building a community-based fresh and local food system with multiple community gardens, operating a weekly Farmers Market, revitalizing parks and brownfield properties, creating affordable housing, installing solar panels through a community-owned cooperative venture on multifamily structures and potentially homes in the area, and working with the city of Detroit to convert an abandoned rail corridor into a 26 mile "Joe Louis Greenway."

Project Impacts and Lessons Learned

Innovative green and sustainable ideas have been advanced and supported by an array of dedicated local volunteers and city-wide groups, all committed to realizing Focus: HOPE's mission (see project timeline, Table 8.1). As with most non-profits involved in sustainable brownfields redevelopment, Focus: HOPE is often challenged by limited capital for community and affordable development and must seek and piece together multiple sources of funding to cover project costs (e.g., government funding and private funding such as grants from foundations, equity investments, and market-rate loans). This requires maintaining a strong ongoing relationship with city leaders and agencies, who may change staff and priorities over time. Raising funds has been a particular challenge for green streets work because it is less well defined than parcel-specific projects and requires collaboration among many stakeholders with their

Table 8.1 Timeline – Focus: HOPE, Detroit, Michigan

1996	Landmark 14-story former Yellow Pages building purchased by Focus: HOPE
1997	Tornado hits community
2005	Recycling and development of former automotive facility
2007	Construction of a 55-unit apartment building for low-income senior citizens
June 2009	Redevelopment of HOPE Community Park (aka Cool Cities Park)
2010	Focus: HOPE and the Graham Sustainability Institute launch the HOPE Village Initiative
2013	NSO Bell Building Completed
2016	HOPE Village becomes the first of two EcoDistricts in Detroit
2019	HOPE Village Revitalization registers as a separate non-profit and now operates as a community development corporation

funding challenges and priorities. It also requires consulting teams to align their ideas with community desires and with other consulting teams representing multiple projects to create synergies (US EPA, 2009a). Novel green street design and infrastructure may also not align with local policies and existing infrastructure (e.g., cable and gas lines). Despite these challenges, Focus: HOPE has tenaciously pursued sustainable brownfields reuse throughout the community to remove blight, provide affordable spaces to live, work, and play, and increase the long-term viability of projects and the community as a whole. It is for this reason that it is safe to bet that a green street will one day link the green community.

Samoa Town/Humboldt County, California

Background and History

In the late 19th century, people from the town of Eureka in northern California formed the Samoa Land and Improvement Company and purchased 270 acres of land along the Samoa Peninsula (an ecologically rich 9.5-mile-long and 1-mile-wide coastal bar between Humboldt Bay and the Pacific Ocean). A sawmill was constructed and became a major draw with promises of jobs, a beach-style atmosphere, and a comfortable climate. By 1901, the Samoa sawmill was considered the world's largest sash and door factory (Samoa Pacific Group, 2002). With the redwood logging industry booming, sawmill owner AB Hammond Lumber Company began to buy up homes and other property in the area to form a company town. Business remained stable throughout the middle of the 20th century, and in 1956, Georgia Pacific purchased the entire site to build a newer, automated lumber mill. The logging industry began to decline, however, and majority ownership of the business switched hands several times, ending with the Simpson Timber Company in 1998.

By 2001, the Simpson Timber Company no longer wanted to manage the town. It sold 65 acres at auction for around $3 million to the Samoa Pacific Group, comprised of the Sun Valley Group and Dan Johnson, president and CEO of the Danco Group and lifetime resident of Humboldt County. The town came complete with 99 homes, a restored hostelry, the popular Samoa Cookhouse, gift shop, post office, vacant gas station, various other buildings, and a sewer system in a leaky condition. The historic homes were in poor condition but leased year-round, while most of the commercial properties lay vacant. The Samoa Pacific Group bought an additional 150 acres of industrial and dune lands soon after and retained an option to purchase an additional 200 acres to the north (Samoa Pacific Group, 2002).

As noted by Vita Nuova, the firm providing technical assistance for the EPA Pilot: "the majority of Samoa's physical structures were built between 1892 and 1923 and reflect the social, physical, economic, and cultural characteristics typical of northern California company-owned lumber mill towns." Many of its historic structures remain intact, and the homes and commercial buildings reflect the planning and hierarchy of mill operations. The Hammond Lumber Company limited building types and controlled building details, resulting in a neighborhood with visual coherence and significant historical character that demanded preservation (Vita Nuova, 2009a). As such, Samoa is one of the best examples of a Company Town remaining in California and, at the time, was one of only 13 company towns remaining in the country (Johnson, 2017).

Vision and Planning

Between 2001 and 2007, various activities were undertaken by the Samoa Pacific Group (2007) to advance the vision for the town. A market-evaluation was conducted in 2001 exploring multiple reuse options, including demolition and the construction of a new resort and convention center. Still, the analysis and the developers landed on reclaiming the existing community. In 2002, developers worked with the PLANNING Studio and the County of Humboldt to generate a Master Plan for 174 acres in Samoa and some adjacent county lands (see Figure 8.2). The historic town was seen as lacking activity and a sense of place, with housing, infrastructure, and public buildings in disrepair and few business and employment opportunities (Samoa Pacific Group, 2007). In March 2003, a Master Environmental Impact Report was initiated, but suspended while revisions were made to the Master Plan. Both were completed in 2006 and, along with a Tsunami Evacuation Plan, were recommended for approval by Humboldt's Planning Commission later that year. Public consultation was initiated in 2007 with residents, local and state government agencies (e.g., Humboldt County, city of Eureka, California Coastal Commission), and environmental and historic preservation groups. The Samoa community is considered to be very politically active, particularly with regard to ecological and historic preservation issues, so it was no surprise that they wanted a project that could deliver opportunity while not impacting the environmental or historical significance of the town.

In January 2008, the Master Plan was approved by the Humboldt County Planning Commission. The development would draw upon Samoa's cultural heritage and historic assets to guide the rehabilitation of existing structures and the design of new places to turn the town into an attractive model for "contemporary village living" akin to New Urbanism. The image of Samoa as a seaside destination and a sustainable community with historical and cultural integrity was considered vital (Samoa Pacific Group, 2007). The plan proposed a 19-acre business park at the southern end and 35 acres of natural resource area on the western side of town along New Navy Base Road that runs along the Pacific. In the center, 57 acres of mainly

172 Main Streets, Neighborhoods, and Towns

Figure 8.2 Samoa, California (Google Earth, n.d.)

low-density residential, 4 acres of public recreation space, and 5 acres of historic commercial core were proposed. To the east of town, the plan called for 35.5 acres of industrial use to abut the former pulp mill along Humboldt Bay, and 10 acres of commercial recreation space wrapping overtop the mill in the so-called Samoa Block along the Bay to the northeast.

The development would unfold in four phases and was anticipated to start in spring 2009. Phase 1 would involve the preservation of natural and recreation space, renovation of historic homes in the north-central part of town, and restoration of the existing cookhouse to add a boutique hotel on the upper floor and turn the gift shop into a Maritime Museum. Phase 2 would see infrastructure improvements (new sewage facilities and road renovations), development of the business park, modern recreational facilities in the northwest, and new and restored residential/workforce housing and vacation rentals. New residential development would continue in Phases 3 and 4, with the latter also seeing the revitalization of the historic core for commercial and community uses, such as a new Post Office, reconstructed gas station, and the conversion of the old Post Office and two residential structures into commercial use.

The vision to incorporate sustainability and build green was advanced by the community's strong environmental conscience and the Samoa project's constant interaction with the EPA through grants and loans (Whitney, 2009). In 2004, Humboldt County received a Brownfields

Hazardous Substances Assessment Grant from the EPA to conduct Phase I and II site assessments on parcels comprising the Town of Samoa. The studies identified multiple potentially impacted sites affected by lead from historic paint and other chemicals from past mill operations. While a few cleanup efforts were initiated, the Samoa Pacific Group also had plans to apply to the county's Brownfields Revolving Loan Fund to help remediate soil surrounding the homes (US EPA, 2009b).

The EPA Brownfields Sustainability Pilots program provided Humboldt County with technical assistance that resulted in the production of two reports evaluating sustainable options for the town's Master Plan (US EPA, 2009b). The first, entitled *Recommendations for Sustainable Site Analysis*, considers the town's Master Plan in relation to two green rating systems (Vita Nuova, 2009a). The study found that the Master Plan scored well enough to achieve a silver rating under the LEED's Neighborhood Development (ND) Rating System because of brownfields redevelopment, building restoration, wetlands and habitats, walkable streets, access to public spaces, and stormwater management (among other criteria), although it lost points for low density and limited public transit. The project scored at the gold level, however, under the Land and Natural Development (LAND) Code rating system created by faculty at Yale University. It was praised for producing an integrated development that avoids impacts to a delicate ecosystem (dunes) and includes compact lots, low impact parking and plantings, and transit access; but it loses points for its proximity to the shore and few green design features (e.g., green roofs, renewable energy, pervious paving) (Vita Nuova, 2009a). The second report, *Sustainable Solutions for Historic Houses in Northern California*, is a voluntary green code and green rehabilitation manual for homeowners on how to rehabilitate Victorian-style wood-framed homes built in the early 1900s (US EPA, 2009c). The manual addresses issues related to preserving the interior and exterior of the structure, insulation, heating and ventilation, lighting and electrical systems, sustainable materials, and appropriate landscaping.

Despite approval from the Humboldt County Planning Commission in 2008, the project took another four years and $6.5 million in research to gain support from the California Coastal Commission in 2012 (Johnson, 2017). This was considered a significant milestone for a project believed to be the largest ever permitted by the Commission. In 2013, however, the developer proposed amendments through the County and Coastal Commission to revise the Master Plan and project phasing to facilitate the acquisition of a $3.5-million-dollar infrastructure grant to upgrade the wastewater treatment facility for the community and support the development of low-income multifamily housing (granted in 2014). The new Master Plan is similar in scope to the original, shrunk slightly in terms of project size (from 174 acres to 170 acres) and the number of proposed residential units (from 293 new and 98 existing residential units to 88 of 99 existing units remaining residential plus 198 new units, including 80 multifamily). The phasing of the plan has been altered most significantly with phase 1 (anticipated to begin in fall 2019) involving the development of a new wastewater treatment facility and upgrading of utilities on one of the main streets in "old town" (Vance St.), additional soil and groundwater cleanup, construction of affordable multifamily housing, and renovation of all existing historic structures. Once complete, later phases will involve the development of "new town" residential and non-residential uses. Interestingly, historic preservation groups preferred to keep the "new town" distinct from the "old town," which differed from initial plans to meld the designs together (Humboldt County, 2019). While some restoration and redevelopment had already commenced by 2017 (i.e., on the Women's Club, the Gymnasium, and the Humboldt Bay Maritime Museum), the developer anticipated in 2017 that the project would receive all approvals and commence phase 1 by fall of 2019, then take eight years to build out (Johnson, 2017).

Project Impacts and Lessons Learned

In all, the Samoa project seeks to restore and reclaim an entire town in a way that preserves its historical character, protects the coastal environment, and maintains affordability (see project timeline Table 8.2). While the project meets many of the criteria for LEED-ND and LAND rating systems, sustainable objectives are derived more from the remediation, preservation, and redevelopment of the existing community rather than the application of green building design and technology elements. In 2017, Dan Johnson, who has managed the project from its inception, took pride in the fact that all but one building in the old town was able to be preserved and that the rest would be restored and the town added to the Historic Register upon completion. He also discussed the importance of upgrading utilities and the old housing stock in a way that would not price out existing residents and allow them to afford

Table 8.2 Timeline – Samoa Town/Humboldt County, California

Year	Description
2001	Samoa Pacific Group purchased town of Samoa and ERA conducts market evaluation
July 2002	The PLANNING Studio completes Samoa Town Master Plan
March 2003	Planwest Partners begins Environmental Impact Report
August 2003	E.I.R. suspended and Master Plan revision started
April to October 2004	Master Plan revision and Draft E.I.R. completed
February 2006	Master E.I.R. completed
March 2006	Obtained Planning Commission recommendation of approval
December 2006 to September 2007	Tsunami review and revisions to Master Plan completed
2007	Revised and recirculate EIR and begin public hearings
January 2008	Humboldt County Planning Commission – Approved
May 2012	California Coastal Commission – Approved
November 2014	$3.5 million infrastructure grant – Approved
February 2015	Humboldt County Planning phasing amendment – Approved
May 2017	CPD for Vance Avenue reconstruction. Affordable housing design review – Approved
2017 anticipated	Development agreement and Treatment system permit
2018 anticipated	Community services district active
	Major infrastructure improvement (water, sewer, vance, end services to 28 existing homes)
	Construction of 80-unit affordable housing
2019	Begin phase 1 including sale of serviced existing homes

to purchase their homes. New single-family homes would also be kept at a reasonable price, and new affordable housing would be constructed. Indeed, renderings have been generated, and applications are already being accepted for the Phyllis Rex Samoa Coast Townhomes containing 80 affordable units for families and those with disabilities. It should also be noted that the Master Plan is already having some spillover effect, with the EPA recently awarding $300,000 to Humboldt County to complete the cleanup of five sites at the historic railroad Roundhouse Property adjacent to the Cookhouse and Maritime Museum. These funds will allow the non-profit Timber Heritage Association to take ownership of the property, cleanup the contamination, and enable the public to access the site (US EPA, 2020a).

While the dedicated developer continues to lumber forward with the support of the community and the county, the project has faced many challenges. Soon after the site was acquired, the property market dropped, and then again in 2008. Costs of dealing with lead contamination affecting historic buildings and soil were also higher than anticipated. As the developer noted in a presentation in 2017, one of the significant constraints has been the complexity and time that it has taken to gain "approvals and blessings" from 37 different agencies, particularly the California Coastal Commission. One could see that the delays had taken their toll on the community-oriented developer who noted that the investors, who already had $15 million tied up in the project, would *not* have done it if they knew how challenging approvals would be. This would not have benefited the town or the contaminated and derelict coastal brownfield. Another important lesson from this project is the need to consider the economic costs and benefits associated with applying modern green techniques and technologies to historic buildings, especially when the developers and residents are trying to keep them affordable and preserve their historic appeal.

Jackson Square Redevelopment Initiative, Boston, Massachusetts

Background and History

Jackson Square is located on the edge of two neighborhoods in Boston: Jamaica Plain and Roxbury. Jamaica Plain was initially part of Roxbury until Boston annexed both in the late 1800s (Wikipedia, 2010). Jamaica Plain became one of the first streetcar suburbs in America and, by 1900, had a significant immigrant population lured by large factories and other employment opportunities. In the 1970s, an interstate project planned for the neighborhood was halted due to community opposition. By then, however, many buildings had been demolished for the project leaving empty spots throughout the district. The decision by Boston banks to cut mortgage lending (redline) in the area also advanced property disinvestment and abandonment (Wikipedia, 2010). Urban Edge, founded as a non-profit real estate firm in 1974, found it necessary to recruit volunteers to physically take possession of empty properties in the neighborhood to prevent vandalism and arson.

Fortunately, community and anti-redlining efforts started to bear fruit, which helped real estate prices stabilize and investment to return. The area's low rent attracted students, artists, musicians, and a vibrant lesbian and gay community. In the mid-1980s, the city, along with Urban Edge and other local non-profits, began working together to bring employment opportunities back. Urban Edge also initiated a four-year community visioning and planning initiative in the mid-1990s to examine housing, retail, and infrastructure needs for both public and private lands. While non-profits like Urban Edge and the Jamaica Plain Neighborhood Development Council (established in 1977) began to purchase rundown houses and vacant lots to create opportunities for low-income residents, other properties in the neighborhood, like the former Plant Shoe Factory that burned in 1976, were being redeveloped for retail and other uses. Gentrification pressure began to intensify in the 1990s as Boston's hot real estate market increased the value of housing in Parkside, Pondside, and Sumner Hill neighborhoods to the southwest and fueled the conversion of large properties into condominiums (Wikipedia, 2010).

It was at the prominent, but blighted, intersection known as Jackson Square, where the non-profits, the city, and other partners envisioned a more harmonious mixed-income, mixed-use, and sustainable transit-oriented community. The area comprised 14 acres of industrial land parcels around the intersections of Centre Street and Columbus Avenue. At its center lay the Jackson Square Transit stop surrounded by five acres and nine parcels of publicly owned land that had been cleared of industry and gas stations decades earlier (CEDAC, 2016). Boston's Mayor, Thomas Menino, was a vital proponent of the project and once referred to the area as "a dead spot in the community" that had a reputation for gang and drug activity. Not only was the area considered unsafe, but it also unhealthy, posting the highest rates of asthma in the state of Massachusetts.

Vision and Planning

In the summer of 1999, the Mayor, through the Boston Redevelopment Authority (BRA), appointed a Jackson Coordinating Group made up of representatives from numerous community groups, non-profit agencies, for-profit developers, and government officials. A participatory and comprehensive planning process unfolded over the next five years bringing residents and partners together at over 80 public meetings. In 2005, the BRA designated Jackson Square Partners (JSP) as the Master developer; bringing together Urban Edge, Jamaica Plain Neighborhood Development Corp., and Hyde Square Task Force, with Mitchell Properties and Gravestar Inc. (groups initially competing for the right to build) (CEDAC, 2016). Once the developers were teamed up, a new public process was initiated to firm up the development plans.

The plan put forward by Jackson Square Partners in October 2006 aimed to transform the parcels of public and private land into a new neighborhood center with distinctive places to live, work, play, eat, and shop, a broad mix of housing opportunities, transit and pedestrian-friendly spaces integrating green and sustainable design, and job and business opportunities (Jackson Square Partners, 2006). It was the most extensive planned development in Boston at the time, proposing more than 400 new housing units (60% for those earning below 80% of AMI) to be built in four phases, along with a youth and family center, three acres of open space, five acres of brownfields cleanup, green roofs, alternative energy generation, and 60,000 sq. ft. of retail, generating 185 permanent jobs, $1 million in new property tax, and $800,000 in new annual sales taxes (Jackson Square Partners, 2008) (see Figure 8.3).

Main Streets, Neighborhoods, and Towns 177

Figure 1-5: Preliminary Site Plan and Building Map

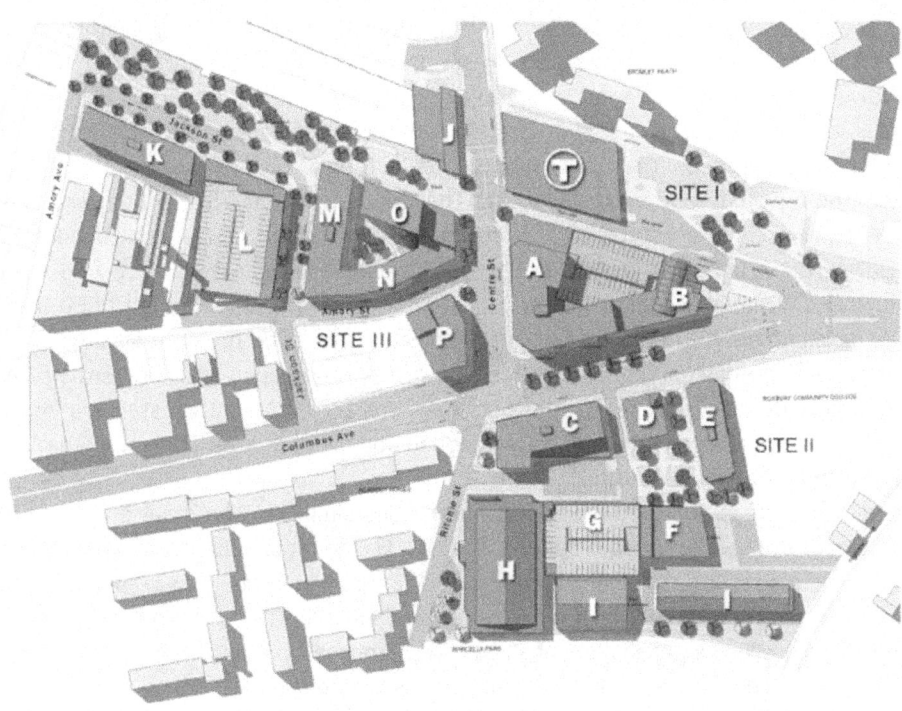

A - 225 Centre Street (94 Rental Units)
B - Youth and Family Center (19,810 SF Recreation)
C - 1562 Columbus Avenue (42 Condo Units)
D - 1542 Columbus (Webb Building: 13,500 SF Office)
E - 1522 Columbus Avenue (36 Rental Units)
F - DYS Facility (19,800 SF)
G - Parking Facility
H - Indoor Recreation (30,000 SF)

I - DPW Facilities
J - Incubator Retail (3,500 SF)
K - 50/70 Jackson Street (19 Condos/36 Rentals)
L - 32 Jackson Street (16 Rentals)
M - 15 Jackson Street (36 Rentals)
N - Amory Street Artisan (23 Condos)
O - 250 Centre Street (75 Condos)
P - 240 Centre Street - NSTAR Site (54 Rentals)

Figure 8.3 Preliminary Site Plan and Building Map, Jackson Square, Boston, Massachusetts, 2006 (Jackson Square Partners, 2006)

Phase 1 was to see $115 million invested in five buildings near the intersection of Centre Street and Columbus Avenue, including: (Building A, see Figure 8.3) 103 rental units, retail, and parking adjacent to the Jackson Square transit station; (B) a 30,500 sq. ft. Jackson Square youth and family center; (C) 37 affordable condos and 14,000 sq. ft. of retail at 1562 Columbus Avenue; (D) 13,500 sq. ft. of office space in the restored Webb Building; and (F) a 13,500 sq. ft. 25 bed facility for young men under the temporary custody of the commonwealth (note: E was initially part of phase 4) (Jackson Square Partners, 2008). Groundbreaking for the first phase occurred in June 2008 when the governor announced $3.1 million in state funding for the project, and it was hoped that the entire project would be fully completed by 2013 at an estimated cost of $250 million.

The project was to be a model for smart growth development linking environmental justice and neighborhood revitalization (Massachusetts Government, 2020). An interviewee involved with the project noted that the city of Boston had very rigorous building standards, so adding green and sustainable elements was not considered that much more of an investment. Indeed, the city of Boston had just introduced Zoning Article 37 in 2007, requiring private developers to adhere to the standards of the LEED rating system for all building projects over 50,000 sq. ft. The aim for Jackson Square was for all buildings to be LEED-certified. In 2008, the Master Plan was included as a pilot for the LEED-ND program, which was initiated in 2007. The project would go on to become the first LEED-ND certified development in the northeastern United States, meeting the prerequisites for Silver designation by remediating brownfields and incorporating open space, renewable energy, and access to various modes of transportation. The project also addressed economic sustainability through investment in an abandoned and blighted area, and equity through the provision of affordable housing.

In 2008, Urban Edge received a Brownfields Sustainability Pilot grant of $25,000 from the EPA to evaluate green roof options. The goal was to reduce the street-level stormwater infrastructure required to meet government guidelines, which would also reduce the volume (and cost) of contaminated soil needing removal (US EPA, 2009d). EPA's technical assistance provided a preliminary evaluation of all buildings proposed in the four phases of the project, finding that redevelopment could potentially yield more than 95,000 sq. ft. of green roof area when the project was complete (US EPA, 2009d).

As for brownfield issues, environmental site assessments were conducted by the Boston Department of Neighborhood Development using EPA funding. They revealed a variety of contaminants in the redevelopment area, including petroleum contamination, underground storage tanks, lead, arsenic, petroleum hydrocarbons, naphthalene, VOCs, polycyclic aromatic hydrocarbons, non-aqueous phase liquid, and heavy metals. The project coordinator noted that the preference was to employ risk-based measures and institutional controls to manage contamination onsite, so as not to export the problems elsewhere. The city of Boston obtained funding from the EPA ($400,000), half to cleanup 1540 Columbus Avenue, and the other half 1542R Columbus Avenue (US EPA, 2020b).

Project Sites

Constructed

225 Centre Street
The property at 225 Centre Street (Building A) had hosted many uses over the years, starting with a blacksmith shop in the late 1800s, followed by a machine shop and a paint shop, a filling station and auto repair shop by the mid-1900s. The buildings were torn down in 1980 to put up a parking lot for state transit authority (Vita Nuova, 2009b). Using funding from the EPA, the Boston Department of Neighborhood Development conducted Phase I and II ESAs

on the site, finding lead, arsenic, and petroleum-related contaminants that were remediated to acceptable levels (Vita Nuova, 2009b).

The $53.2 million mixed-use building was developed by The Community Builders (one of America's leading non-profit real estate developers headquartered in Boston), along with a team that included Mitchell Properties, JPNDC, and Urban Edge. To help finance the six-story building, MassHousing (an independent, quasi-public agency charged with providing financing for affordable housing in Massachusetts) provided $31.4 million in loans, while the AFL-CIO Housing Investment Trust (HIT), and its subsidiary Building America, provided a combined total of $15.4 million (MassHousing, 2012). The project also included first-floor commercial space and parking that was partially financed through $5.5 million of New Markets Tax Credits provided by Building America (MassHousing, 2012). Completed in 2013, the prominent building at the northwest corner of Centre and Columbus and east of the Jackson Square MBTA station contains 103 rental units (one, two and three bedrooms), 33 of which are affordable rental housing. The transit-oriented, mixed-income, mixed-use development is also LEED Certifiable and Energy Star compliant. While there is no green roof, it does have a cool white roof with solar panels covering about 50% of the surface.

1540 (Building D) - 1544 (Building E) Columbus Avenue (Jackson Commons) (see Figure 8.4)

Property on the northeast side of Columbus and Centre also had a long history, hosting a stable in the early 1900s, then a plumbing warehouse, an automobile dealership, repair shop, and garage for the city of Boston Department of Public Works. Since the 1970s, part of the site was used as a minimum-security correctional facility, while other parts were vacated (Vita Nuova, 2009b). Funding from the EPA was used by the Boston Department of Neighborhood Development to conduct a Phase I and II analysis, which revealed petroleum contamination onsite, as well as elevated levels of lead and arsenic that required remediation.

The development of Jackson Commons by Urban Edge was the second building slated for completion under the Jackson Square Redevelopment Initiative. It consisted of the

Figure 8.4 Jackson Commons and Urban Edge, Boston, Massachusetts (Google Street, n.d.a)

renovation of the 100-year old Webb Building plus a newly constructed four-story addition. In 2010, Jackson Square Partners modified the original plan for the area because the Department of Youth Services was no longer able to fund the Youth Treatment Facility building. As such, Building F was eliminated, while the Webb Building (D) was expanded with a new four-story addition to the north side (proposed initially as Building E) with parking to the rear of the site. The development, completed in 2015, consists of 37 mixed-income rental apartments, 21 affordable to households earning up to 60% AMI, eight for extremely low-income families who are transitioning out of homelessness (up to 30% AMI), and eight workforce housing units affordable to different AMI levels (Urban Edge, 2015). The building also has 13,000 sq. ft. of ground-floor retail and office space hosting Urban Edge's offices and several initiatives, such as asset and wealth building programs, a youth leadership academy, a food pantry, resident-led education activities, and space for other non-profits to use.

Funding for this LEED Gold development came from an array of sources including state, federal, and New Market Tax credits, Massachusetts Department of Housing and Community Development, Neighborhood Housing Trust and HOME funds from the city of Boston, IDP funds from the Boston Redevelopment Authority and state Historic tax credits from the Massachusetts Historic Commission. Furthermore, the Hyams Foundation, the Vincent Mulford Foundation, and MassDevelopment gave money for environmental remediation and infrastructure work (Urban Edge, 2015).

75 Amory Avenue (Building K)

The four-story LEED certifiable building, completed in 2017, contains 39 affordable apartment units and 27 parking spaces (Urban Edge, 2015). All of the apartments are rented to households earning no more than 60% of the AMI (BLDUP, 2017). It received $400,000 funding from the Community Economic Development Assistance Corporation (CEDAC) in predevelopment financing, as well as $600,000 in state CBH funding (CEDAC, 2016).

270 Center Street

Although not technically part of the Jackson Square master plan, the first affordable housing project that contributed to the vision for the area was built at 270 Centre Street by JPNDC. It acts as a western gateway from Jamaica Plain into Jackson Square (above Building J in Figure 8.3) (CEDAC, 2016). With a predevelopment loan from Massachusetts' Community Economic Development Assistance Corporation, as well as over $965,000 in Housing Innovation and Facilities Consolidation funds, JPNDC built 30 new units of affordable housing for residents earning between 30 and 60% of AMI, and almost 1400 applications were received (Heath, 2015). Completed in 2011, the LEED-certifiable and transit-centered development across the street from Jackson Square Station also includes 8,000 sq. ft. of street-level retail space and a white (cool) roof, a quarter of which is covered by solar panels (JPNDC, 2020).

Proposed/Under Construction

Phase 1 of the Jackson Square plan proposed that the property at 1531 Columbus Avenue (B) be used for the creation of a Youth and Family Center. The EPA awarded Urban Edge a $200,000 Brownfield Cleanup Grant in 2008 to fund excavation, transportation, and disposal of up to 1,400 cubic yards of contaminated soil and support community involvement activities. Regrettably, however, Urban Edge announced in 2019 that they would no longer move ahead with the project due to the high cost associated with building and operating the center in a manner that would "ensure it was an affordable and accessible community resource" (Urban Edge, 2019). As such, the site continues to be used as a parking lot.

Together, the properties at 250 Centre and 25 Amory Street (Buildings M, N, O, L) form a large triangular parcel of land sandwiched between the new developments at 75 Centre Street to the west (on the opposite side of the transit tracks), 75 Amory Avenue to the south, and the transit station and 225 Centre St Apartments to the North. The two new buildings recently approved for development by the city include Building M at 25 Amory Street with 44 affordable residential apartments and Building N at 250 Centre Street with 112 residential rental apartments (30% affordable) in a six-story structure with 2,400 sq. ft. of ground-floor retail (Shanley, 2017). The project will also create a bike path and green area along the rail tracks to the west, plus a public plaza space along Centre Street. The Community Builders (TCB) is heading up the development of the larger building, which will contain both income-restricted and market-rate units, while the Jamaica Plain Neighborhood Development Corporation is managing the smaller affordable development. Building N has been awarded funding by the city of Boston Department of Neighborhood Development and the Neighborhood Housing Trust (city of Boston, 2020a, 2020b).

The buildings from the original plan that have not materialized include:

- Buildings C and F were initially meant for 37 affordable housing units with ground-floor retail (C) and a DYS treatment program (F), but the state agency pulled out of the project in 2008. Urban Edge submitted plans in 2011 to build an indoor skating rink and recreation center in the area of Building C and H, but the site remains a parking lot;
- Building B, the original location of the Jackson Square Youth and Family Center remains a parking lot;
- Building I remains DPW Facilities with a new Salt Storage Building in area G; and
- Building J Incubator Retail was not constructed and will be part of public space for the 250 Centre and 25 Amory Street projects.

Project Impacts and Lessons Learned

The Jackson Square project is an inspiring case study of dedicated stakeholders working together over time to erase blight and promote sustainable redevelopment in a manner that not only brings about greener buildings but ensures that redevelopment guards against gentrification and provides housing and opportunities for lower-income residents (see project timeline, Table 8.3). Although the plan has been modified and taken longer to build than expected, the dedicated non-profits, developers, and stakeholders have continued to forge ahead and realize most of the projects put forward in 2006. Early obstacles related to high remediation and financial costs, managing the economic downturn, and mustering the resources and energy to sustain project planning and administration over the long term. Incorporating sustainability and green building are also considered a standard practice that conforms with city and state requirements. Brownfield redevelopment was seen as essential

Table 8.3 Timeline – Jackson Square, Boston, Massachusetts

Year	Description
1970	Plans to extend I-95 from Canton north into downtown Boston resulted in the demolition of many houses and commercial buildings that left a scar through the community when the project was cancelled
1974	A group of community activists from Jamaica Plain and Roxbury come together to create Urban Edge, a community development corporation
1977	Founded in 1977, the Jamaica Plain Neighborhood Development Corporation pursues the mission of promoting equitable development and economic opportunity in Jamaica Plain
1980s	Local community groups and city begin planning the future of the area. As part of a city-wide effort, Boston Main Streets districts were named (Hyde/Jackson Square, Egleston Square, and Centre/South), bringing city funds and tools of neighborhood revitalization to local business owners
July 8, 1999	First meeting with the community advisory group to begin planning of Jackson Square
2002	The city, state and MBTA agree that the parcels of land could be developed together
July 2, 2004	City issues a request for proposals
2005	Urban Edge partners with Jamaica Plain Neighborhood Development Corporation and a developer
June 1, 2005	Mayor Menino announces the chosen developers for the project, designating Jackson Square Partners as Master developer and bringing together Urban Edge, JPNDC, Hyde Square Task Force, and Mitchell Properties
2005	JSP Begin a more detailed study of environmental conditions to identify hot spots and estimating total cleanup costs in $3 million range
October 31, 2006	Project Notification and Master Plan for the Jackson Square submitted by Jackson Square Partners to the Boston Redevelopment Authority
2008	USGBC awards a silver rating to the Jackson Square Neighborhood Development Master Plan, making it the first ND certified project in the northeastern United States
2008	The US Environmental Protection Agency (EPA) recognizes Urban Edge as one of five winners of a 2008 National Award for Smart Growth Achievement
February 2009	Developers ask city for permit extension
2010	JSP submits a notice of project change regarding Jackson Commons Project
2011	Although not technically part of the Jackson Square master plan, the first affordable housing project that reflects the vision for the area is built at 270 Centre Street by JPNDC's, which acts as a western gateway from Jamaica Plain into Jackson Square
2013	The apartments at 225 Centre Street (the first development in phase 1 of the Master Plan) are constructed east of the Jackson Square MBTA station
2015	The Jackson Commons project is completed adding new and renovated affordable rental apartments and office space for Urban Edge
2017	The four-story building development at 75 Amory Avenue is completed, adding 39 affordable apartment units
2019	The proposal in Phase 1 of the Jackson Square plan to build a 30,500 ft. sq. Youth and Family Center at 1592 Columbus Avenue is officially canceled due to high development and operating costs
2019	Approval is granted for Building M at 25 Amory Street that will comprise 44 affordable residential apartments and Building N at 250 Centre Street with 112 residential rental apartments (30% affordable) and 2,400 sq. ft. of ground-floor retail. This represents a significant parcel in the build out of the development plan

for erasing decades of blight and restoring neighborhood health. From the outset, proponents saw the sustainable transit-oriented development of a central location 20 minutes from the city's downtown as a way to reduce carbon impact and improve access to employment and infrastructure. The project is also considered a "symbolic statement that communities like this can do it, and non-profits can do it" (Hacobian, 2009).

Commercial Street Historic District, Springfield, Missouri

Background and History

In 1870, the Atlantic and Pacific Railroad arrived at Springfield, Missouri. The line and rail depot bypassed the center of town and located a mile to the north with a commercial district sprouting up along what came to be called "Commercial Street" (Commercial Club, 2020). The area officially became part of Springfield in 1887, and Commercial Street led a business and population boom in Springfield until the 1960s when a decline in rail travel resulted in a decrease in population and business growth. Interest in loft development and the listing of the district on the National Register of Historic Places in the 1980s did bring about some interest in rehabilitation but not enough to combat the decline. By the early 2000s, the district was perceived as lacking relevance in the regional economy, with few active businesses on the first floor and only a 32% occupancy rate leading to the area being labeled as blighted according to the city statute (city of Springfield, 2005, p. 2). It was, therefore, agreed that city plans and strategies take a more comprehensive approach to foster reinvestment in the area (Hough, 2009).

Vision and Planning

To breathe new life into the district, the city produced the *Commercial Street Historic District Strategy for Success*, which was accepted by City Council in February 2006. It built upon similar ideas being applied in downtown Springfield in its *VISION 20/20 Comprehensive Plan*. The 300-acre revitalization plan for Commercial Street (or Historic C-Street as it came to be called) focused on a six-block area and proposed to use live music venues to re-energize the street and lure people back. According to the vision statement (city of Springfield, 2005, p. 1):

> The future Commercial Street District will be a safe and inviting mixed use area with live music, restaurants, office, and retail, while providing a quality environment for residential living, both in the district and the surrounding neighborhoods. It will be built on the current regional market opportunities while drawing on historic elements of the past to play a unique role in the growing regional economy. It will appeal to a diverse customer base and be "everybody's neighborhood" as envisioned for Center City in Vision 20/20 providing a memorable experience for all. The district will be unique and creative as well as progressive while adhering to its authentic historic roots. It will be beautifully landscaped with trees and plants creating vibrant public space which is inviting for outdoor dining. Social services agencies and their clients will be integrated into the fabric of the street and provide a positive contribution to the economy. There will be strong physical and visual connections to downtown, Jordan Valley Park, and the rest of the community.

The Commercial Street TIF Redevelopment Plan approved in 2008 (expires 2031) will support the strategy and help fund the revitalization of the ten-block area around Historic C-Street. The TIF supports public improvements related to blight elimination, infrastructure, economic development, and historic preservation, estimated at $5.5 million. A Commercial Street Community Improvement District (CID) was also established in 2009 operating with funds generated through private donations, as well as a supplemental sales tax of 0.375% voted into effect in 2010 (Commercial Club, 2020). City initiatives were supported by the work of the Commercial Club, a non-profit and the city's oldest civic organization, founded in 1928 to support local efforts.

In the mid-2000s, the city was in close contact with the EPA's regional office to discuss possible grant funds for the initiative. It was determined that the project was eligible to become a Brownfield Sustainability Pilot based on the number of service stations that littered the area (Hough, 2009). A "Green Resolution" adopted by the city in 2006 for public buildings and supported by the Commercial Club committed to protect, restore, and sustain the historic street. While there was some initial concern about cost, funding, and the complexities associated with aligning green and historic preservation elements, the foundation was laid for sustainable brownfield development to occur.

Pilot funds were awarded to the city in 2008 to provide green design recommendations for three selected properties (a microbrewery, a professional massage training center, and the historic Commercial Club building owned by the city) and to convene a Sustainable Design Peer Workshop on sustainable design and construction options (US EPA, 2009e). The report provided to owners examined and recommended green options related to process engineering, daylighting, energy-efficient lighting, insulation, green materials, water conservation, and greywater systems (Vita Nuova, 2009c). At the Workshop, project teams and EPA consultants fine-tuned design and construction plans, and an open house allowed the public to discuss project progress and learn about green design (Vita Nuova, 2009d). All three properties also received funds from the EPA to conduct Phase I and II ESAs. These found contaminants below non-residential standards at the massage training and Commercial Club sites but did identify storage tanks and floor tiles containing asbestos at the microbrewery property that would require remediation (US EPA, 2009e).

The microbrewery building at 505 W. Commercial Street was constructed in 1924 to store coal and was then used for an array of other purposes, including a peanut butter plant, automotive repair shop, filling station, and metal fabrication business before becoming vacant in 2003. The building was purchased in 2007 and, after privately financed remediation and renovation, opened in 2012 as the White River Brewing Company (US EPA, 2016). The building applied some of the green building recommendations suggested by the Pilot, such as the skylights for daylighting and a light-reflective roof resulting in lower heating and cooling costs (US EPA, 2009e).

The property at 233 E. Commercial Street, constructed in 1954, had been the site of a print shop, a filling station, and an appliance-retail building. The building was renovated in 2011 and adjoined to the Day Spa and Professional Massage Training Center. While the spa closed in 2015, the building currently hosts the Wellspring School of Allied Health. It is not known whether green building recommendations were applied.

The distinguished two-story red brick Commercial Club building at 299 E. Commercial Street was constructed around 1910 and is owned by the city (see Figure 8.5). The first floor of the building is used as a police station and the second floor by the Commercial Street Historic District and the Commercial Club for public use. Renovation of the building and a new light-reflective roof was supported through a $250,000 HUD redevelopment grant. The front of the building also had green landscaping and public art.

Figure 8.5 233E (left) and 299E Commercial Street, Springfield, Missouri (Google Street, n.d.b)

These projects have played a central role in sparking the revitalization of Historic-C Street. An article by Wheeler (2018) traces efforts by investors, the city, and the Commercial Club since the mid-2000s to restore buildings and transform the street into a vibrant district. The article tells the story of pioneering businesses, including White River Brewing Company, as well as plans by companies such as Burning Tree Consulting, who have purchased over a dozen buildings in the area with plans to initiate a "cultural shift towards authentic, community-focused housing and shopping experiences." Wheeler highlights the importance of the Commercial Club in rallying support and advocating for the district, as well as the importance of government support and funding for purchasing land, restoring historical structures, and building affordable housing (e.g., New Market Tax Credits). The article ends by noting that eight businesses opened on Commercial Street in 2017 alone and that the area looks poised for further growth.

An inclusionary and supportive approach has been vital to the revitalization process. The city had not spent any TIF funds collected by 2015 and initiated a process to decide upon proposals for TIF revenues (city of Springfield, 2015). In 2018, city staff hosted a public meeting to discuss several proposed projects (e.g., a parking lot, pedestrian walkway, an alley project, and a facade loan program) to be funded with two-thirds of the captured revenues ($520,000), as well as options for the uncommitted funds (e.g., banking for future projects, public art, landscaping, signage, land acquisition, etc.). The city has since moved forward with the community to construct enhancements at two pedestrian alleyways and a public parking lot funded through the TIF and pending approval of final designs. Project construction is anticipated in 2020 (city of Springfield, 2020).

The city has also revised the Commercial Street Design Guidelines from 1982 to preserve the historical significance of the area. The new 2019 version (pending approval) includes guidelines on commercial frontages, parking, and streetscapes. It also encourages the preservation of historical materials and decorative facade elements that accentuate the area's history and guides new construction (city of Springfield, 2019). While a lot of attention is given to urban design principles (i.e., unity, building heights, materials, windows, alignments, spaces between buildings, color, streetscape, and public realm) and individual building features (i.e., windows, facades, doors, awnings, materials), there is no mention of green infrastructure or LEED. Furthermore, sustainable design and energy efficiency improvements are permitted, as long they do not "affect the appearance and fidelity of historic elements" (i.e., solar panels are not visible from the street).

Project Impacts and Lessons Learned

Technical support provided early on was essential for helping the city and stakeholders learn about the viability of integrating sustainability into historic preservation through green design (see project timeline, Table 8.4). It also pointed to potential benefits and cost savings associated with green technologies and sustainability approaches that could inform future

Table 8.4 Timeline – Commercial Street Historic District, Springfield, Missouri

Year	Development
Late 1800s	Commercial Street (C-Street) created by the Frisco Railroad Co.
1970s	Vibrancy ends and disinvestment begins
1980s	Commercial Street home to many social service offices creating an "unsafe" public perception, and blight (ten abandoned gas stations)
2004	Adoption of the Vision 20/20 plan and citizen desire to extend the emphasis given in downtown Springfield to the Commercial Street area. City staff began to engage with stakeholders to create a socially inclusive economic revitalization plan for the district
2006	*Commercial Street Historic District Strategy for Success* adopted by City Council "Green Resolution" adopted in 2006 by the city for public buildings
2008	Commercial Street TIF Redevelopment Plan approved
2009	Commercial Street Community Improvement District (CID) established
June 25, 2009	Workshop of the City of Springfield Sustainability Pilot for the Commercial Street Historic District
2011	Property at 233 E. Commercial Street renovated and adjoined to day spa
2012	White River Brewing Company opens microbrewery building at 505 W. Commercial Street
	Commercial Club building at 299 E. Commercial Street
2015	City begins process to develop proposals to spend TIF revenues
2017	Historic C-Street revitalization gaining momentum
2018	City staff host public meetings to discuss proposed projects and examine options for uncommitted funds
2019	*Commercial Street Design Guidelines* updated and pending approval
2020	Pending final approval, the city will move forward to enhance two pedestrian alleyways and a public parking lot funded through the TIF

activities, even when costs for those activities are perceived as low (US EPA, 2009e). The case of Commercial Street in Springfield provides a great example of the collaborative efforts of public, non-profit, and private partners to address blight and disrepair, reverse the shrinking city, and preserve and celebrate history. Although there is sustainable benefit in preserving neighborhood history, adding new jobs, and repairing and reusing existing structures, this case shows some of the cost, aesthetic, and practical challenges associated with incorporating green innovation with the preservation of historic places. This is definitely something that the EPA and the National Parks Service should work together to figure out so that the preservation of historic space celebrates and sustains antiquity, but doesn't have the same impacts.

References

BLDUP. (2017). *75 Amory Avenue*. May 21. BLDUP.com.
CBS Detroit. (2013). Iconic Michigan bell building rededicated as center for homeless. October 23, 62 *CBS Detroit*.
CEDAC. (2016). *Jackson Square: Connecting communities, creating a new neighborhood*. Community Economic Development Assistance Corporation.
City of Boston. (2020a). *Building N (250 Centre Street)*. Department of Neighborhood Development.
City of Boston. (2020b). *125 Amory Street Development*. July 8. Boston Planning and Development Agency.
City of Springfield. (2005). *Commercial Street Historic District Strategy for Success*. Department of Planning and Development in cooperation with the Commercial Club, Urban Districts Alliance, staff and local community input; approved by City Council February 6, 2006.
City of Springfield. (2015). *Tax increment financing, 2015 annual report*. Planning and Development Department.
City of Springfield. (2019). *Commercial Street historic district design guidelines*. City of Springfield & Commercial Club.
City of Springfield. (2020). *Commercial Street projects*. July 14. www.springfieldmo.gov
Commercial Club. (2020). *Historic c-street history*. July 14. Commercial Club, www.historiccstreet.com
Cool Cities. (2010). *Project 15*. August 3. Cool Cities.
Ecodistricts.org. (2017). *ECO-D case study: Detroit, MI, USA* (Case study report). August 3. ECO-D.
Enterprise. (2018). *ECO-D every Detroit neighborhood becoming green, eco-d initiative overview*. Enterprise Sustainability Exchange 2018.
Focus: HOPE. (2007). Opening of senior housing is valentine's gift to seniors. Spring/Summer, *Hope in Focus Newsletter*.
Focus: HOPE. (2010). *Community*. March. Focus: HOPE.
Google Earth. (n.d.). Samoa California. 40°49′55″ N and 124°13′21″ W. December 4, 2020.
Google Street. (n.d.a). Jackson Commons, 1540 Columbus Avenue, and Urban Edge, 1542 Columbus Avenue, Roxbury, MA. December 4, 2020.
Google Street. (n.d.b). 233 East and 299 East Commercial Street, Springfield Missouri. December 4, 2020.
Heath, R. (2015). Last major piece of Jackson Square would bring MIT-style architecture to J.P. November 18, *Jamaica Plain News*.
Humboldt County. (2019). *Samoa Town master plan: Draft supplemental master environmental impact report, July 2019* (Report State Clearinghouse # 2003052054). Humboldt County Planning and Building Department.
Jackson Square Partners. (2006). *Jackson Square: Project notification form*. Boston Redevelopment Authority Pursuant to Article 80 of the Boston Zoning Code.
Jackson Square Partners. (2008). *Jackson Square: Building together*. Boston Redevelopment Authority Pursuant to Article 80 of the Boston Zoning Code.
Jackson Square Partners. (2010). *Notice of project change, submitted pursuant to article 80 of the Boston zoning code, Jackson Square, Jackson Commons project*. Boston Redevelopment Authority Pursuant to Article 80 of the Boston Zoning Code.

Johnson, D. (2017). *Samoa development - danco part 1 and part 2*. Public presentation made to residents of Samoa Town. July 17. Youtube.

JPNDC. (2020). *Jackson Square project status*. April 10. www.jpndc.org

Massachusetts Government. (2020). *Case studies - environmental justice (EJ): Jamaica Plain, Massachusetts*. July 24. Massachusetts Government.

MassHousing. (2012). 225 Centre Street development receives funding. February 16, *MultifamilyBizz.com News*.

Nagl, K. (2019). Focus: HOPE spins off community development non-profit to refocus on strengths. November 3, *Crain's Detroit Business*.

O'Brien Construction Company Inc. (2020). *NSO bell building*. April 29. O'Brien Construction Company Inc.

Samoa Pacific Group. (2002). *Samoa Town master plan, draft 1*. Prepared by the Planning studio and the Samoa Pacific Group for Humboldt County.

Samoa Pacific Group. (2007). *Samoa Town master plan*. Presentation slides, The Planning studio.

Shanley, P. (2017). Real estate today: ZBA approves 250 Centre St. September 29, *Jamaica Plain Gazette*, sec. News.

University of Michigan. (2012). *Sustainability and the hope village initiative*. Graham Sustainability Institute.

Urban Edge. (2015). *Urban edge opens Jackson Commons, JPNDC starts construction on 75 Amory Avenue as part of Jackson Square redevelopment initiative (JSRI)*. October 2. Urban Edge.

Urban Edge. (2019). *An important announcement about the Jackson Square recreation center*. August 7. Urban Edge.

US EPA. (2008). *C&D success story: Recycling at former automotive site spurs revitalization* (Report EPA-560-F-08-001). US EPA Office of Solid Waste and Emergency Response.

US EPA. (2009a). *Nonprofit creates model green streetscape design to enhance community: Brownfields sustainability pilot* (Report EPA-560-F-09-502). US EPA Office of Solid Waste and Emergency Response.

US EPA. (2009b). *Sustainable options for a former United States lumber company town: Brownfields sustainability pilots* (Report EPA-560-F-09-503). US EPA Office of Solid Waste and Emergency Response.

US EPA. (2009c). *Sustainable solutions for historic houses in Northern California: A voluntary green code and green rehabilitation manual*. US EPA Office of Solid Waste and Emergency Response.

US EPA. (2009d). *Brownfields sustainability pilots: Evaluating green roof potential in the Jackson Square redevelopment project* (Report EPA-560-F-09-507). US EPA Office of Solid Waste and Emergency Response.

US EPA. (2009e). *Brownfields sustainability pilots: Historic district properties lead the way for green buildings in Springfield* (Report EPA-560-F-09-504). US EPA Office of Solid Waste and Emergency Response.

US EPA. (2016). Springfield, MO, recognized for 17-year history of successful use of EPA brownfields assistance to spur redevelopment. June 13, *News Releases from US EPA Region 07*.

US EPA. (2020a). US EPA announces $300,000 for additional cleanup, reuse effort in California's Humboldt Bay Harbor district. June 11, *News Releases from US EPA Region 9*.

US EPA. (2020b). *Massachusetts brownfields funding history (1994-2020)*. July 7. US EPA Brownfields Program.

Vita Nuova. (2009a). *Town of Samoa, California sustainability pilot, recommendations for sustainable site analysis, final report*. March 2. US EPA Brownfields Program and Humboldt County.

Vita Nuova. (2009b). *Jackson Square redevelopment initiative sustainability pilot: Recommendations for green roof planning*. May 4. US EPA Office of Solid Waste and Emergency Response.

Vita Nuova. (2009c). *City of Springfield, Missouri environmental protection agency sustainability pilot: Recommendations for sustainable design and adaptive reuse: Commercial Street Historic District*. March 20. US EPA Brownfields Program.

Vita Nuova. (2009d). *Workshop analysis and outcomes: City of Springfield, Missouri, Commercial Street sustainability pilot*. US EPA Brownfields Program.

Wheeler, V. (2018). Hot spots: Rising developments in downtown Springfield, Commercial Street and Galloway. January–February, *BIZ 417*.

Wikipedia. (2010). *Jamaica plain*. Wikipedia.

Interviews

Focus: HOPE, Detroit, Michigan

- Fisher, D. (2009, 2020). Executive Director, Hope Village Revitalization, Detroit, MI.

Samoa Town/Humboldt County, California

- Whitney, A. (2009). Economic Development Specialist, Humboldt County, CA.

Jackson Square Redevelopment Initiative, Boston, Massachusetts

- Hacobian, M. (2009). President, Urban Edge, Boston, MA.
- Maslan, N. (2009). Director of Real Estate, Urban Edge, Boston, MA.
- Stoddard, L. (2009). Resource Development Manager, Urban Edge, Boston, MA.

Commercial Street Historic District, Springfield, Missouri

- Hough, O. (2009). Brownfields Coordinator, Department of Planning and Development, city of Springfield, MO.

9 Mixed-Use Complete Communities

Mixed-use development incorporates many uses into a single urban project rather than segregating them. Models such as Transit-Oriented Development (TOD) and New Urbanism aim to provide a dense and pedestrian-friendly environment as compared with traditional sprawling suburban neighborhoods where land uses are separated, and a car is necessary for many activities. Many cities and developers seek to erase blight and revitalize their cities by taking large dilapidated brownfields and building new neighborhoods that combine higher density housing, office, and retail activities close to transit and along restored waterways. The case studies examined in this chapter – Atlantic Station in Atlanta, Georgia, South Waterfront in Portland, Oregon, Langdale and Riverdale Mills in Valley, Alabama, and The Waterfront in Allentown, Pennsylvania – all aim to create mixed-use complete communities that incorporate sustainability, green building, and ecological restoration. Their goals are often as extensive as their projects. They include desires to improve accessibility and public safety, increase transit ridership, reduce rates of Vehicle Miles Travelled and pollution, conserve land use and open spaces, enhance economic development, and add more mixed and affordable housing options for the residents in the neighborhood.

Atlantic Station, Atlanta, Georgia

Site History

The story of Atlantic Station's development begins with the decline of the Atlantic Steel Company. Established in 1901 as the Atlanta Hoop Company, the mill specialized in the manufacture of "wagon wheels and cotton bales" (city of Atlanta, 2005). By the 1920s, production expanded to include "nails, barbed wire, plow shears and galvanized steel," which was reflected in the company's new name, Atlantic Steel (Western Pennsylvania Brownfields Center, 2008). When production peaked in the 1950s, more than 2,300 people were employed at the mill, manufacturing 750,000 tons of steel products a year (Western Pennsylvania Brownfields Center, 2008). In 1979, the mill was purchased by Ivaco Inc., a steel manufacturer based in Montreal, Canada. Atlantic Steel was subsequently forced to scale back its operations as the domestic steel industry collapsed in response to foreign competition in the early 1980s (Bacon et al., 2008). The de-industrialization of the mill continued into the 1990s. By 1997, only 400 people were employed, with operations ceasing the following year.

Three conditions guaranteed the property would eventually be redeveloped: (1) its size; (2) its location; and (3) the rapid population growth in Metropolitan Atlanta. Atlantic Steel's manufacturing complex was developed on 138 acres west of Midtown Atlanta, and the size of the property, considered to be the nation's largest brownfield redevelopment at the time, presented an unparalleled opportunity for development near Atlanta's downtown core. The site is also adjacent to major transportation infrastructures such as the Norfolk Southern Railroad and Interstate 75/85, which serve as its northern and eastern boundaries.

While the site was situated at the edge of Atlanta's urban core when it was first developed, three residential neighborhoods – Home Park, Loring Heights, and Ansley Park – had come to surround the property by the time the mill closed in the 1990s. Over time, the Heavy Industrial zoning designation of the Atlantic Steel property became incompatible with the residential character of the surrounding neighborhoods.

Despite the decline of Atlantic Steel, Metropolitan Atlanta was experiencing an unprecedented level of population growth as people began to move back into the urban core for the first time in 50 years. Atlanta was the fastest growing city in the southeast (US EPA, n.d.). And while the decline of Atlantic Steel contributed to the loss of thousands of jobs, it also presented a tremendous opportunity to develop a new urban neighborhood (US EPA, n.d.).

While the confluence of these conditions generated interest amongst developers, the property's brownfield status discouraged many from investing in it. Even in the context of "aggressively sought after real estate opportunities," developers did not want to assume the financial risk of being liable for the environmental remediation that likely followed decades of heavy industrial activity (Dagenhart et al., 2006). By 1997, however, a contract between Jacoby Development Inc. (JDI) and Ivaco Inc. was made to remediate and redevelop the Atlantic Steel property. The site was subsequently rezoned in 1998 as "Commercial and Mixed-Use" by the city of Atlanta in anticipation of its redevelopment. By then, JDI had partnered with AIG Global Real Estate to finalize the project vision.

Project Vision

While Atlantic Station has become known as a trendsetter "for its live-work-play environment" based on a mixed-use New Urbanist and TOD model of development, this was not the original project vision (US EPA, 2008a). JDI's reputation as an entrepreneurial developer was attributed to its "success building conventional suburban big-box projects" (Miller, 2006). The original Master Plan put forward in 1997 perpetuated the "suburban model of land use compartmentalization, with the Master Plan proposing three distinct development areas – a retail mall, a multifamily residential complex, and an office park – separated by landscaped buffers and linked together by a new arterial street crossing the Interstate 75/85 on the east to connect to Midtown Atlanta" (Bacon et al., 2008). The three areas would be developed independently by different developers. The original project vision "concentrated on moving people in and out as quickly as possible. It was large-scale, mass-market-oriented, and included gated garden apartments and industrial uses" (Miller, 2006). This particular project vision, however, conflicted with the broader public policy objectives that the city of Atlanta was pursuing to manage population growth sustainably (US EPA, n.d.). It would, therefore, take four Master Plans for the site to detail the evolving project vision.

The city of Atlanta was considered one of the least dense metropolitan areas in the US at the time (Atlantic Regional Commission, 2009). It was acutely aware that developing a low density, suburban-style community would just exacerbate existing challenges caused by sprawl (city of Atlanta, 2005). The city was, therefore, considering a new approach to development, based on the principles of Smart Growth that would encourage sustainable growth while addressing congestion and air pollution. This was particularly important given that Atlanta's population was projected to continue growing by an additional 2.5 million in 25 years (US EPA, n.d.). The original Master Plan was incidentally not well received by the city of Atlanta or the Midtown Alliance, a coalition of stakeholders, prompting JDI-AIG to revise it.

JDI-AIG's Master Plan revision benefited from the ideas of Brian Leary, the President and CEO of Atlanta Beltline Inc. from 2009-2012. As the Master Plan was being drafted, Leary was a graduate student in the Georgia Institute of Technology's City Planning program. He presented his master's thesis "Atlantic Station: A Place to Live, Work and Play" to Mr Jacoby of JDI and was subsequently hired to steer the project's zoning applications. According to Leary, "the Master Plan went from big-box site, to a sort of 'macro mixed-use'... to broken-up superblocks with pedestrian areas... Bike lanes were added to the streets, and wider streets will eventually accommodate a dedicated transit line" (Miller, 2006).

The revised Master Plan addressed the criticisms against the first Master Plan, although the original concept was mostly preserved. According to Bacon et al. (2008), the plan also "reflected the influence of... stakeholder voices that became involved in the process through the city's Neighborhood Planning Unit development review framework." The plan also integrated "Smart Growth principles [which] led to the use of higher densities, mixed uses, and increased pedestrian and transit accessibility" (Bacon et al., 2008). While segregated land uses persisted, a new mixed-use district, as well as an "expanded street network... to improve connectivity" distinguished the revised proposal from the original Master Plan. The significant change was the placement of an 8000-car parking deck under the entire retail district, which was put forward as a logical step to cap part of the contaminated soil on the site and provide a plinth [base] for a traditional town-like retail district on top (see Figure 9.1) (Dagenhart et al., 2006).

While the revised JDI-AIG Master Plan was considered an improvement to the original, a third independent plan was commissioned by the US EPA. The EPA intervened in the project shortly after the city of Atlanta approved zoning for the construction of the arterial bridge that would travel over the I-75/85. Although the site is adjacent to the I-75/85 freeways and nearby transit routes, the nature of Atlantic Steel's operations precluded the development of multi-modal access. As a result, the property is physically isolated, with limited connectivity to surrounding neighborhoods. The proposed bridge would address, in part, the site's physical isolation and limited connectivity while offering a direct route to Midtown Atlanta. The EPA's intervention, however, was based on Atlanta's non-compliance with the Federal Clean Air Act, which triggered a mandatory multi-year planning process and the implementation of programs and actions to reduce pollutants (Dagenhart et al., 2006). As a non-compliant area, Atlanta was prohibited from constructing new roads, freeways, or bridges, and the additional people, cars, and pollution sources projected for the new Atlantic Station development became a key factor for the need to plan the project in a more sustainable manner.

Mixed-Use Complete Communities 193

Figure 9.1 Atlantic Station atop the parking deck, Atlanta, Georgia, 2010

The EPA subsequently hired Duany Plater-Zyberk (DPZ), consultants specializing in New Urbanism, to facilitate a three-day public design charrette. The charrette led to the creation of "an alternate Master Plan" that "abandoned the idea of land use compartmentalization and instead created a street network based on the traditional urban subdivision, continuing the adjacent Home Park neighborhood block format into the Atlantic steel site" (Bacon et al., 2008). The DPZ Master Plan suggested an entirely mixed-use development that promoted connectivity at the local scale and prioritized the public realm, rather than private development space, as a framework for redevelopment. JDI-AIG integrated several recommendations from the DPZ model into its revised Master Plan, which allowed it to gain regulatory approval from the city, state, and the EPA to allow the project to proceed. Despite this, some feel the Smart Growth interventions were too modest and that too much of the design and character of the original Master Plan prevailed (Dagenhart et al., 2006).

Project Characteristics and Development

The final Master Plan organized Atlantic Station into three development areas – the District, the Commons, and the Village. The District, opened in March 2004, is the mixed-use section of the development and is located on the east side of the property. This area is comprised of several mid-rise office buildings, retail stores, restaurants, and apartment units (US EPA, n.d.). The Commons, situated west of the District, is the residential section of the development. It features mid-rise homes surrounding a large pond and park. Historical attributes from the steel mill, such as pressed steel sculptures and smokestacks, have been displayed in the park to preserve the site's industrial heritage. The Village is located on the far west side of the property and contains a combination of mixed-income housing and an existing two-story 336,000 sq. ft. IKEA store (Miller, 2006). Construction of Phase One of the project overlapped with the site remediation and cleanup phase of development, which began in 2001 (US EPA, n.d.). Once completed, the redevelopment was to consist of "six million square feet of Class A office space; 3,000 to 5,000 residential units (for-sale and for-rent); two million sq. ft. of retail and entertainment space, including restaurants and movie theatres; 1,000 hotel rooms; [and] 11 acres of public parks" (Miller, 2006). The redevelopment aimed to leverage $2 billion in public and private investment and continues to be built out as of 2017 with new office space planned for construction (Kahn, 2017).

Redevelopment was initiated in 1998, prioritizing site remediation and cleanup. Atlantic Steel partnered with JDI to remediate the property's contaminated soil and groundwater (city of Atlanta, 2005). A $10 million remedial action plan was created following a risk-based site assessment framework to determine the level of cleanup required (US EPA, n.d.). The plan was administered by The Atlantic Station, LLC, and was approved by the state of Georgia Environmental Protection Division (GAEPD) in December of 1999. Remediation involved the removal of approximately 165,000 tons of steel slag contaminated soil (the equivalent of 9,000 dump truck loads) for management at state-approved landfills removed from the site (US EPA, n.d.).

The remedial action plan necessitated the removal of 180,000 cubic yards of steel slag contaminated soil (Western Pennsylvania Brownfields Center, 2008). A groundwater collection and treatment system was also installed on the property to monitor and treat contaminated groundwater before discharge to the city's sewer system (Western Pennsylvania Brownfields Center, 2008). Roughly 132,000 cubic yards of construction debris, mainly concrete from the steel mill's underground support structures and foundations, were reused as backfill, in combination with some clean fill material to cap the entire site (Miller, 2006). The Georgia Environmental Protection Division (GA EPD) monitored the site remediation process, and in December 2001 issued a Plan Certification Report declaring the property remediated (US EPA, n.d.). The state of Georgia subsequently issued a No Further Action (NFA) letter for the property, indicating that it was ready for redevelopment.

Changing the zoning designation proved to be the least complicated planning approval required for the redevelopment given the city's desire to re-purpose the underutilized brownfield and catalyze investment, and the industrial site's incompatibility with residential uses that came to surround it. In 1998, the city of Atlanta rezoned the entire property as commercial and mixed-use in support of the Atlantic Station redevelopment (city of Atlanta, 2005). The rezoning was completed before the final sale of the property to JDI in 1999.

Although regulatory approvals pertaining to brownfield remediation at the state level were more complicated, they were facilitated through cooperation among project stakeholders. Steps were taken to streamline the cleanup and redevelopment processes. For example, the

GAEPD designated one person to make decisions, thereby expediting responses for review and approval. The owner and developer used the same consultant to address both remediation and redevelopment issues. The presence of these members at face-to-face meetings with authority to make real-time decisions kept the project on track and reduced the administrative costs of working with governmental agencies (US EPA, 2007).

Transportation planning requirements at the federal level were initially a regulatory challenge but ultimately contributed to a more sustainable final project vision. A vital feature of the redevelopment is the 17th Street Bridge as it provides a direct connection between Atlantic Station and nearby transportation and transit routes. The bridge was mandated by Atlanta's zoning requirements to improve accessibility to the site and was prioritized by the Georgia Regional Transportation Authority (GRTA) (Dunn, 2010; US EPA, 2008a). As mentioned, construction of the bridge would contravene federal regulatory conditions due to Atlanta's non-compliant status with the Clean Air Act (CAA) and proscribed by the EPA (Miller, 2006). At the time, the city of Atlanta had been noncompliant with the CAA since the early 1980s for failing to develop a 20-year regional transportation plan (RTP) and for exceeding ground-level ozone air quality standards (city of Atlanta, 2005). The city was prohibited, therefore, from building any new roads, bridges, or freeways that require federal approval unless it could be argued that they will improve air quality (US EPA, n.d.). Also, federal subsidies for transportation projects were suspended in non-compliant areas. Without the bridge, however, the redevelopment project was not viable and was effectively quashed.

An innovative solution was reached through a collaborative process between JDI-AIG and the EPA, as well as other stakeholders (city of Atlanta, 2005). While the move by the EPA initially precluded the redevelopment plan, JDI-AIG applied for regulatory flexibility by suggesting that as a Smart Growth project, Atlantic Station was, in effect, a Transportation Control Measure (TCM). Even in a non-compliant area, plans that offer the benefits of a TCM can be provided with an exception to proceed (US EPA, 2008a). Regulatory flexibility was achieved through Project XL, a "program promoting environmental eXellence and Leadership (XL)" (US EPA, 1999). Project XL allows "states and local governments, businesses, and federal facilities" to partner with the EPA to achieve broader environmental and public health policy objectives (US EPA, n.d.). In its Project XL application, JDI-AIG reasoned that population growth in Atlanta is projected to continue, primarily through low-density greenfield development, which would be particularly true if the Atlantic Station redevelopment were not approved. As an urban infill project, the Atlantic Station redevelopment offered the occasion to promote Smart Growth and effectively reduce vehicle miles traveled (VMT).

The rationale put forward by JDI-AIG prompted the EPA to conduct its empirical analysis to test the benefits of compact, mixed-use, transit-oriented development. Data indicated that "the smart growth aspects of the redevelopment would help reduce air pollution, among other environmental benefits" (US EPA, 2008a). The EPA recognized, however, that while the location of the proposed development influences VMT and emissions, site design is equally significant. The EPA subsequently "evaluated the original Jacoby site design, and determined that [it] could be improved to reduce driving and emissions." The EPA hired DPZ at this point in the project to leverage opportunities to reduce VMT and emissions in the proposed Atlantic Station site plan. The EPA approved the Project XL agreement after JDI-AIG revised the site plan based on DPZ's recommendations to enhance the project's congestion and air pollution mitigation effects through diversity, design, and density (city of Atlanta, 2005; US EPA, n.d.). With the necessary planning and regulatory approvals in place, the project was able to proceed.

Financing and Economic Development

The scale of the Atlantic Station redevelopment, which included significant brownfield remediation and cleanup, necessitated a public-private partnership between JDI-AIG and the city to secure the $2 billion needed for project financing. With authorization from the Georgia Redevelopment Powers Act, the city of Atlanta established the Atlantic Station Brownfield Tax Allocation District (ASBTAD) to generate financing for the redevelopment. A Tax Allocation District (TAD) is a tax increment financing overlay that utilizes incremental property tax revenues to finance site remediation and infrastructure improvements (Smith & Russell, 2004; US EPA, 2008a).

The TAD was established in 2001 to coincide with phase one of the project and is set to expire in 2026 (US EPA, 2008a). Organizing the project into three phases prioritized infrastructure projects while distributing the financial cost of the redevelopment over several years, with the city's total TAD contribution to the development initially set at $170 million (city of Atlanta, 2005). Phase one initiated in 2002, would cost $210 million, with $110 million from the TAD for environmental remediation ($25 million), capping (environmental, $25 million), roads and utilities ($30 million), and parking ($30 million), $50 million from the developer for the right-of-way, and $50 million from state and federal sources for the bridge. Thirty million from the TAD would fund parking ($15 million) and roads and utilities ($15 million) in phase two initiated in 2005 and another thirty million for similar expenditures in phase three (no date set). While the city of Atlanta initially agreed to allocate $170 million in TAD funds for the redevelopment, JDI-AIG also contributed $25 million toward site remediation and preparation. The majority of redevelopment, however, was financed by the private sector. The projected investment was considered a significant boost for the city. Before the reconstruction, Atlantic Steel paid approximately $300,000 a year in property taxes (Western Pennsylvania Brownfields Center, 2008). The economic impact of the redevelopment project was nearly immediate as the estimated incremental increase in tax revenues for 2006 (over the 2001 base year) was $8,347,722 (Smith & Russell, 2004). The redevelopment in 2008 generated nearly $30 million in property taxes per year, plus retailers in the new development contributed $10 to 20 million per year in Special Interest Local Option Sales Taxes.

A more recent review of TIF in Atlanta written by the Center for State and Local Finance at Georgia State University (Layton, 2016) notes, however, that the Atlantic Station TAD has faced challenges. The study points out that Atlanta issued $75.5 million in tax allocation bonds for phase one infrastructure in 2001 and another $166.5 million in subordinate lien TIF bonds in 2006 for phase two infrastructure. Although most of the proposed building development was completed, absorption by homeowners, shoppers, and office workers ground to a halt in late 2007 and 2008, during which time interest payments on the TAD continued, but principle payments deferred. Tax increment collections continued to fall but turned around in 2015. As Layton (2016, p. 24) notes, however, "with $151.4 million in principal still outstanding, rising interest costs, and fewer than nine years remaining before the bonds are due, a default in the payment of these junior lien obligations could occur without substantial and sustained growth in Atlantic Station tax increments and the application of those taxes to bond payments between now and December 1, 2024."

A presentation by Invest Atlanta (2019, p. 12) optimistically reports that the Atlantic Station TAD collected $22 million in tax increment in 2018 and that principle payments were being made. It mentions a total TAD investment of $256 million to support a total project cost of $1.6 billion and an economic impact of $2.3 billion, with a return on investment of $7.81 (ROI= [Economic Impact - TAD Investment]/TAD Investment). Other projects and accomplishments highlighted include 12,465 direct jobs, 3,600 residential units (23% affordable), 1.3 million retail sq. ft., 1.0 million office sq. ft., 101 hotel rooms, 7,200 structured parking spaces, 1.35 miles of streetscape and connectivity improvements, and an assessed value of $650 million in 2019 (up from $445 million in 2008 and a base value of $7 million).

Sustainability

As mentioned, regulatory requirements compelled the developers to integrate sustainable design principles into the project to address Atlanta's air quality concerns. The Green Star Environmental Plan that was created focused on five areas affected by the redevelopment – land, air, water, green buildings, and smart growth. Georgia's State Energy Program provided over $80,000 to support the initial concept and the Energy Phase of Atlantic Station's Green Star Environmental Plan to help it compete for federal green bond financing, which required plans to achieve aggressive energy and environmental goals (Bhedwar, 2006).

As an EPA XL project, JDI-AIG had to provide the EPA with an annual report identifying whether the redevelopment meets the conditions and targets established during the planning phase. The progress report includes data on VMT and emissions, density and mixed-use, and efforts to promote broader public policy objectives. Based on the progress report submitted by JDI-AIG for 2008, the EPA reports that "the average vehicle miles traveled (VMT) for residents and employees of Atlantic Station is significantly lower than the rest of the region." The regional average VMT for individuals is about 34 miles per day, while Atlantic Station residents average 14 miles per day, and employees working at Atlantic Station travel 12 miles. Furthermore, while single-occupancy vehicle trips constitute more than 60 percent of trips in the region, in Atlantic Station, about half the trips made by residents and employees are in single-occupancy vehicles (US EPA, 2008a).

A key strategy of the Green Star Environmental Plan was to recycle under-utilized land in the city to protect Atlanta's greenfield areas. As an urban infill project, Atlantic Station repurposed a 138-acre brownfield site in Central Atlanta, while conferring other environmental benefits. In addition to remediating the contaminated property, the project also promoted compact, mixed-use, and multi-modal transit development as a means to reduce automobile dependency (US EPA, 1999). Indeed, it has been estimated that Atlantic Station protected over 1,000 acres of greenfield from being developed (California Energy Commission, n.d.). Concerning air quality, an empirical analysis by the EPA comparing the proposed Atlantic Station redevelopment with similar developments on greenfield sites indicated the redevelopment would reduce VMT by 34 percent and Nitrogen Oxide (NO) emissions by 45 percent relative to the greenfield developments (US EPA, 2005). Site-specific and regional water concerns were also factored into the redevelopment. As part of the remediation process, an interceptor system was installed to treat contaminated groundwater before it is discharged into the municipal system and to prevent contaminated groundwater from migrating to adjacent areas. The redevelopment also upgraded water infrastructure by separating stormwater, sanitary, and sewer lines (Green, 2010). A two-acre pond in the Commons also serves as a stormwater management strategy, while addressing regional watershed concerns. Site design, grading, and drainage interventions also ensure that finite water resources are managed sustainably (city of Atlanta, 2005).

The Green Star Plan also establishes a commitment to promote sustainable building design and provide a national model for green development. Atlantic Station intended to develop 100 percent of the project's commercial buildings to LEED standards. Completed in 2004, the development's first commercial building, 171 17th Street, was designed and constructed to achieve LEED certification. The 500,000 sq. ft. building became the first office tower in the world to be certified Silver in LEED's Core and Shell Development Program (Atlantic Station LLC, n.d.). A 2012 performance update of Atlantic Station found that the project is home to 1.4 million sq. ft. of LEED-certified office space, with 840,000 sq. ft. certified Gold (Atlantic Station Master Owners Association, 2011). Although not originally planned, many of the residential buildings are also being developed using green building techniques. Developers found that green design principles were compatible with conventional building practices and that economies of scale could be achieved for installing renewable energy technologies, such as a geothermal heating and cooling system, in a new development. New green buildings and spaces continue to be added, including the Atlantic Yards office complex (700,000 sq. ft.) that broke ground in 2018 and a timber-framed T3 West Midtown office building (230,000 sq. ft.). Several new green retail buildings have also been announced, along with upgrades to Central Park that double the existing green space and expand the pedestrian space.

Benefits, Barriers, and Lessons Learned

Atlantic Station was honored as "the nation's best brownfield redevelopment" with the EPA's Phoenix Award in 2004 (see project timeline, Table 9.1) (Dagenhart et al., 2006). As one of the earliest and most significant examples of best practice in brownfield remediation and redevelopment, Atlantic Station serves as a model of the benefits that can be realized through urban revitalization projects. The privately led redevelopment project was commended by those interviewed for remediating the property's contaminated soil and groundwater after decades of substantial industrial activity and addressing regional stormwater management concerns through onsite measures. The redevelopment also contributed to Atlanta's economic development by increasing property tax values and restoring jobs that were lost as Atlantic Steel declined.

According to a public sector representative, Atlantic Station also prompted a dramatic shift in the culture of urban and regional development in Atlanta. As an urban infill project, the Atlantic Station prioritized compact, high-density, mixed-use and multi-modal development over the conventional lower-density, single-use, auto-dependent sprawl that was partially responsible for Atlanta's congestion and air quality issues. The redevelopment, therefore, leveraged the use of existing infrastructure while enhancing community amenities and ensuring employment, housing, and recreational opportunities for a cross-section of Atlanta's population. As a result, Atlantic Station also serves as a Transportation Control Measure to mitigate congestion and air pollution. Indeed, a performance report in 2010 examining Atlantic Station's progress toward achieving the environmental goals found that Atlantic Station's cleaner modes of commuting reduced vehicle miles traveled by 316,466, volatile organic compounds by 340,093 grams, and commuting costs by $158,233 in 2010 (Atlantic Station Master Owners Association, 2011).

The features applied in the Atlantic Station project have influenced the character of other New Urbanist and Transit-Oriented development projects built on brownfields throughout the city, including:

- **Glenwood Park:** A 28-acre brownfield located a couple of miles from downtown that was turned into a model community linking environmentally sustainable and New Urban design concepts;
- **Inman Park:** A National Historic District where various industrial buildings have been adapted to office, residential, retail, and other uses that are home to an array of artist and creative businesses;
- **the Atlanta Beltline:** Using an existing 22-mile historic rail corridor that encircles the city, the Atlanta BeltLine aims to link 45 inner suburban neighborhoods with pedestrian-friendly rail transit and multi-use trails sparking economic growth, sustainable development, and TOD;
- **Westside Urban Market:** Developers turned Atlanta's derelict original meatpacking district into a modern urban market with an exciting mix of boutique retailers and restaurants;
- **The District at Howell Mill:** Located near one of Atlanta's many historic mills, developers demolished an abandoned and condemned structure and removed debris from a former dump on the site to pave the way for a mixed-use retail and residential development; and
- **Lindbergh City Center:** This transit-oriented development was constructed on approximately 50 acres surrounding the Metropolitan Atlanta Rapid Transit Authority's Lindbergh Station and consists of 4.8 million sq. ft. of development, 2.7 million sq. ft. of office space, 330,000 sq. ft. of retail space, 566 apartments, 388 condominiums, and a 190-room hotel.

Several significant challenges did affect redevelopment. In addition to the size of the property, the scale and scope of the project were unprecedented. The former Vice President of Atlantic Station noted that implementing the project vision was a challenge from day one, citing "the remediation plan, the bridge approvals, the economy, 9/11" as delays (Miller, 2006). Increasing connectivity and accessibility to the site was more complicated than constructing an arterial bridge as initially planned.

The overlapping complexity of local, state, and federal planning and regulatory approvals highlights the importance of collaboration between project stakeholders. For instance, dialogue between the EPA and JDI-AIG ensured that environmental and economic considerations of the project would be addressed in the revised Master Plan. Congestion and air pollution were addressed by increasing diversity, design, and density in the site plan. The EPA, however, was also sensitive to the development pro forma, and hired DPZ as a consultant "for the firm's expertise in mixed-use, infill development, but also because its projects are commercially successful" (US EPA, 1999). In fact, interviewees for this case study indicated that the EPA was particularly pleased with the results of the Project XL Agreement that was achieved and gave the agency confidence to engage in more public-private partnerships.

While the redevelopment of Atlantic Station evolved to address Atlanta's broader societal needs, community consultation throughout the Master Planning phase incurred both support and resistance for the project. Multiple public meetings, group discussions, individual contacts, and a full public notice and review process were held during the rezoning of the property (Western Pennsylvania Brownfields Center, 2008). At a macro level, community members and stakeholders supported enhancing the city's economic, environmental, and recreational opportunities by transforming the under-utilized brownfield. At a micro level, however, an interviewee noted that the adjacent residential neighborhoods were displeased by the scale of the redevelopment "and wanted controls to isolate themselves." Resistance was attributed to "a difference in perspective and wealth," particularly given that Atlantic Station represented a considerable amount of change in the middle of an established, 80-year-old community.

Residents from these neighborhoods used engagement and public participation events to persuade the developer to limit change. Loring Heights, for instance, opposed extending its neighborhood's streets into the development to improve access and circulation, and successfully lobbied to limit connectivity. The same is true of Home Park, although some residents did advocate for connectivity. Ansley Park, a particularly affluent neighborhood in Atlanta, was considered "very adversarial." Ansley Park residents did not participate in community consultation events until later in the Master Planning process, and resisted aggressively, threatening the developers with legal action. Considerable public outreach and education efforts by JDI-AIG and the city were essential to overcome perceived negative impacts and civil resistance to the project.

Brownfield developers sometimes cite regulatory delays in slowing the pace of their projects. As noted above, in this case, although regulatory approvals on brownfield remediation at the state level were complicated, to simplify the approval procedure for site remediation, the GAEPD designated one person to make decisions, thereby expediting responses for review and approval. The owner and developer also facilitated the process by using the same consultant to address both remediation and redevelopment issues. The presence of these members at face-to-face meetings helped to keep the project on track, and, as described above, regulatory flexibility was achieved through the EPA's Project XL, in which various entities can partner with the EPA to achieve broader environmental and public health policy objectives.

While Atlantic Station has been celebrated for the benefits, it is not without reproach. Critics point to the limitations of the final Master Plan design, which they maintain should have integrated more of DPZ's recommendations. They also contend that the project retained the single-use character from the original project vision and that internal and external connections are poorly structured (Dagenhart et al., 2006). In this respect, city-approved urban design guidelines would have provided a blueprint for development on the site.

Table 9.1 Timeline – Atlantic Station, Atlanta, Georgia

Year	Description
1901	Atlantic Steel Company is established
1974	Atlantic Steel employs 2000 people and produces 750,000 tons
1979	Atlantic Steel is acquired by Ivaco Inc.
1997	Atlantic Steel property is contracted to Jacoby Development Inc. (JDI)
1998	Atlantic Steel Mill closes
1999	JDI closes on Atlantic Steel property and forms partnership with AIG Global Real Estate Investment Corporation
1999	Deconstruction and site remediation of Atlantic Steel property begins
2001	Site remediation completed; No Further Action letter issued by the state
2001	Phase one of the Atlantic Station redevelopment begins
2004	17th Street Bridge, connecting Atlantic Station to midtown Atlanta, is completed
2004	Atlantic Steel Redevelopment is recognized "for excellence in Brownfield redevelopment" through the EPA's Phoenix Award
2005	The District (phase one) of the Atlantic Station redevelopment officially opens
2005	Atlantic Station appears in the Sierra Club's 2005 America's Best New Development Projects listing
2010	North American Properties and CB Richard Ellis Investors purchase Atlantic Station's retail component, which had languished due to the recession, and launch a revitalization strategy
2015	Atlantic Station's retail core was officially sold to Hines Interest Limited Partnership
2018	Renovation of the central green space and new retail space; construction begins on Atlantic Yards office development; announcements for two new hotels and a residential apartment building
2020	Microsoft announces 1500 job expansion and Macy's 630 job technology hub at Atlantic Station

Project partners and critics concede that the "goal was to figure out how to take a behemoth project and stitch it into the fabric of the city," acknowledging that urban redevelopment is a process, not an end in itself (Bacon et al., 2008; Miller, 2006). Whether comments about Atlantic Station are positive or negative, they emphasize the importance of collaboration and partnerships between stakeholders early in the redevelopment process to ensure the project objectives do not compromise the interests of the community. The lesson here is that while "developers have come to expect significant public assistance" in "large scale brownfield redevelopment projects," this is ultimately a trade-off to meet broader public policy objectives (Dagenhart et al., 2006).

South Waterfront, Portland, Oregon

Site History

The South Waterfront District redevelopment project is the largest urban renewal initiative in Portland's history, transforming an underutilized and isolated brownfield into a mixed-use, transit-oriented neighborhood that reclaims public access to the Willamette River. Situated within the North Macadam Urban Renewal Area (447 acres), the South Waterfront Plan District is located south of downtown Portland on 140 acres of former industrial land. The

Willamette River forms a natural boundary on the east side of the district and offers 1.2 miles of waterfront access. Marquam Bridge and the I-5 freeway serve as the northern and western boundaries of the area, while Hamilton Street forms its southern edge (Portland Bureau of Planning, 2002).

Industrial activities characterized the landscape in the South Waterfront District for most of the 20th century, before technical innovation and the unintended impact of land use interventions contributed to the eventual decline of the area (Portland Bureau of Planning, 2002). The Portland Lumber Company was one of the first businesses to establish in the area. It supplied heat and electricity to Portland's downtown core beginning in the 1880s (The Center for Brownfields Initiatives, 2003). Followed by the development of Power's Lumber Mill shortly after, South Waterfront appealed to businesses that relied on river-frontage, as well as road and railway access. Other companies that contributed to the industrial character of the South Waterfront area, while supporting its timber and shipping trades, included a metal fabrication plant, chemical manufacturers, an aluminum smelting operation, and various salvaging facilities. By 1910, these businesses had permanently transformed the resource-rich riparian forest that had sustained Oregon's indigenous population and first European settlers into an industrial hub. By the 1960s, however, South Waterfront's industrial development began to decline as technological innovation in several sectors started to displace older industrial practices. The construction of two freeways, Harbor Drive in the 1940s and the I-5 in the 1960s, compounded the area's industrial decline by creating a physical barrier that limited railway, waterfront, and local access to the district, consequently leading to its isolation (Portland Bureau of Planning, 2002). Waste from industrial activities disposed of directly into the adjacent lands and water contributed to the South Waterfront's status as a brownfield (Portland Bureau of Planning, 2002).

Efforts to revitalize the South Waterfront District began in the late 1970s with the removal of Harbor Drive. The Portland Development Commission (PDC), now Prosper Portland, acquired 73 acres in the district in 1978 and made provisions for their redevelopment in the Portland Downtown Urban Renewal Plan (The Center for Brownfields Initiatives, 2003). This was followed by the creation of several other long-term revitalization plans, including the South Waterfront Redevelopment Program (1979), the Central City Plan (1988), the North Macadam Urban Renewal Plan (1999), and the South Waterfront Plan (2002) (Portland Bureau of Planning, 2002; The Center for Brownfields Initiatives, 2003). While the South Waterfront remains a sub-district of the North Macadam Urban Renewal Area, the name of the redevelopment plan was officially changed from North Macadam to South Waterfront by Portland City Council when the 2002 plan was adopted.

Project Vision

Since the adoption of the Central City Plan in 1988, the South Waterfront District has been envisioned as an urban mixed-use neighborhood (Portland Bureau of Planning, 2002). While the precise details of the vision evolved incrementally, adapting to meet Portland's changing economic and social needs, the primary objective that remained consistent within each successive plan was to re-establish connectivity between the South Waterfront District and the neighboring communities. Transforming the Willamette River waterfront into a public amenity with opportunities for recreational and civic activities also persisted as a cornerstone of this vision. This vision was influenced by the principles of Smart Growth that emphasized:

- compact growth to reduce demand for greenfield, agricultural and forest lands;
- creating communities with a strong sense of place;
- transit-oriented development offering public transit, cycling, and pedestrian options;
- mixing land uses integrating housing, commercial and retail uses;
- providing a range of housing size and price options;
- encouraging economic development opportunities that result in new jobs, businesses, services, and improved local tax base;
- restoring and conserving open space, natural beauty, and critical environmental areas and habitats; and
- utilizing environmentally friendly and sustainable site-development practices, building designs, and construction techniques (Portland Development Commission, n.d.a).

Despite the environmental remediation and infrastructure investment challenges, the city recognized it had an unparalleled opportunity to contribute to Portland's urban planning legacy while implementing public policy objectives through the creation of a Master Planned community (Portland Development Commission, n.d.a). These public policy objectives include affordable housing, job growth, new greenways and parks, new transportation options, sustainability, and smart growth practices, and enhancement of the city's research universities (Portland Development Commission, n.d.a). As an interviewee pointed out, the project vision for South Waterfront is based on the renewal potential of its locational assets, which include waterfront access, proximity to downtown, views to Ross Island, and utilizing Oregon Health and Science University (OHSU) as an economic development anchor. Key stakeholders, project partners, and landowners in the South Waterfront Redevelopment included: the Portland Development Commission (PDC), charged with coordinating and guiding the development of the South Waterfront Plan Area on behalf of the city per the vision and goals of the South Waterfront Plan; the Oregon Health and Science University (OHSU); and three Limited Liability Corporations (River Campus Investors, North Macadam Investors, and Block 39).

Visioning for the South Waterfront Master Plan began in 1997 with details evolving incrementally through weekly meetings between stakeholders that built consensus and support for the initiative while balancing their individual needs and objectives (Brown, 2010; US EPA, 2012). For instance, OHSU constrained by its location on Marquam Hill, which rises just west of the South Waterfront site, was considering expansion in Portland's suburbs (Williams, 2010). The redevelopment of the South Waterfront brownfield area would provide OHSU with the land base needed to expand its research, teaching, and service facilities within the renewal area while acting as a catalyst for economic development and retaining jobs within the city. An aerial tram for staff and students between the existing and planned OHSU campuses was part of the vision. Williams and Dame Development, a real estate developer, consulted during the visioning process, was the first to suggest that OHSU should serve as an economic development anchor to facilitate the city's employment objectives. The integration of sustainable design and green building techniques in the Master Plan vision was advocated for by Gerding Edlen, a real estate investment and development firm (Wilde, 2010).

The final Master Plan vision comprised a three-phase development program to transform the Project Area into a vibrant, sustainable mixed-use neighborhood to include open space and commercial, retail, institutional, and educational facilities as well as a range of housing options at various levels of affordability (Portland Development Commission et al., 2003). The objective was to create 10,000 jobs, 3,000 housing units, inclusive of 788 affordable housing units by 2019 (Portland Bureau of Planning, 2002). The phased approach was based on improvements to buildings and infrastructure, rather than geographic areas within the South Waterfront District. The first phase of redevelopment was, however, directed to the Central District, a 31-acre zone within the South Waterfront plan area (Portland Development Commission, n.d.b), with phases two and three being directed to the north and south respectively. The 2002 South Waterfront Plan affirmed the project vision established in previous renewal plans with policies and urban design standards to guide its implementation. The companion South Waterfront Central District Project Development Agreement describes and allocates development responsibilities between the project partners.

Project Characteristics and Development

Based on experience with other urban renewal projects, the Portland Development Commission (PDC) recognized that redeveloping the South Waterfront District necessitated public leadership and assistance to generate private interest and investment. Environmental assessment and cleanup activities were prioritized to prepare for redevelopment. The PDC utilized funding awarded through a $200,000 US EPA Brownfields Assessment Project grant to complete a Phase I area-wide assessment between 2003 and 2004 (Abuaf, 2010). The EPA facilitated the assessment and remediation efforts in partnership with the Oregon Department of Environmental Quality (DEQ), and properties within the South Waterfront plan area were among the first to participate in the DEQ's Voluntary Cleanup Program.

Several properties did not have any identifiable environmental concerns, whereas others situated mostly in the northern reaches of the district required Phase II assessments and remediation, according to those interviewed. As is the case with most brownfield redevelopment projects, the intended end-use of a property determines, in part, the course of action for remediation or cleanup efforts. Redevelopment in the South Waterfront District, therefore, addressed the necessary cleanup and remediation requirements on a site-by-site basis. For instance, the immediacy of the Willamette River presented challenges to the assessment and remediation stage of project sites adjacent to the waterfront due to overlapping regulatory requirements (The Center for Brownfields Initiatives, 2003). There was also a concern that contaminated groundwater below the redevelopment area of individual projects would leach into the river. Although groundwater flow modeling indicated this was unlikely, the DEQ prescribed "a 5-year groundwater-monitoring program" in combination with the "installation of a riverbank stabilization system" (The Center for Brownfields Initiatives, 2003).

Phase one of the South Waterfront redevelopment concentrated in the Central District plan area and was initiated in 2003, overlapping with the environmental assessment and remediation efforts. The key phase one redevelopment projects, as described in the South Waterfront Central District Project Development Agreement, included the transportation, open space, housing, and economic development elements. Multi-modal transportation options were prioritized early to address the physical isolation of the district and re-establish connectivity with surrounding neighborhoods. By prioritizing access to public transit, as well as bicycle and pedestrian pathways, the intent was to encourage alternative modes of transportation while reducing dependency on automobile use. Infrastructure improvements included an extension of the Portland Streetcar, which was completed in October 2006 and follows a 7.5-mile loop with three stops in the South Waterfront District, one of which serves as a transfer point to the aerial tram (Portland Development Commission, n.d.c). The construction of an aerial tram linking OHSU's existing campus on Marquam Hill with its new facilities in the South Waterfront District travels 22 miles/hour to complete a one-way trip in three minutes, and operates at a 99.8 percent reliability rate (Oregon Health & Science University, n.d.b). This, according to an interviewee, ensures OHSU's medical and research staff can travel quickly between the campuses without compromising patient care and service delivery. The construction of the tram in 2006 was financed through public and private funds and cost approximately $60 million to build (Go by Tram, 2010). Public investment in the tram ($8.5 million) will be recaptured over time through property tax increases in the renewal area (Go by Tram, 2010). While the tram is owned and operated by the city of Portland Office of Transportation, maintenance and operating costs are shared with OHSU. Other infrastructure projects of note include the Gibbs Street Pedestrian Bridge (opened in July 2012) connecting the South Waterfront District with Lair Hill over I-5, Tilikum Crossing and Bridge of the People (opened in September 2015), and a TriMet bridge for the MAX Orange Line that carries only pedestrians, bicyclists, and public transit vehicles between South Waterfront and Hosford-Abernethy.

Declining water quality and habitat degradation in the Willamette River, as well as a shortage of public space in the district, motivated the city to explore efforts to renew the river ecology while providing public access and parkland. Extending the Willamette River Greenway from downtown Portland through the South Waterfront District will facilitate connectivity between the renewal area and surrounding neighborhoods. Set-back an average of 125 feet from the riverfront, the 38-acre South Waterfront Greenway offers alternative transportation routes, as well as passive and active recreational opportunities. Development of the greenway had been complicated by overlapping regulatory permits required to address stormwater runoff and leachate into the river from former industrial areas. Phase one of the construction involved removing contaminated soil and restoring shoreline habitat through public investment at the cost of $10.5 million (Portland Parks & Recreation, 2012). The southern section was completed in 2015 while the 'north reach' project is currently ongoing as of writing and coincides with phase two redevelopment of the area (Portland Parks & Recreation, n.d.). A two-acre neighborhood park in the Central District, formally known as Elizabeth Caruthers Park, was completed in 2010 on land once utilized as a public storage facility (US EPA, 2012). Funding through an EPA Brownfields Grant enabled the PDC to assess and remediate the parkland between 2004 and 2006. The development of the park leveraged ten jobs for cleanup and 39 jobs for construction and cost approximately $3.95 million to acquire the land, remediate, and develop (US EPA, 2012). The completed park offers active and passive recreational opportunities, while its re-naturalized landscape is designed to absorb and treat stormwater runoff. It is considered a 'focal point' for civic activity in the Central District.

206 *Mixed-Use Complete Communities*

The renewal plan for the South Waterfront District called for the development of 3,000 residential units offering market-rate, affordable homeownership and rental options. Developers pursued LEED-ND certification, making the renewal area one of the densest and sustainably designed communities in the country (US EPA, 2012). Sustainable design strategies include orienting buildings to optimize solar radiation, district heating, onsite stormwater management, mixed-use, and transit-oriented development. The LEED-ND certification was seen by interviewees as a way to validate the commitment to Smart Growth and sustainable development adopted by the project partners during the project visioning (see Figure 9.2).

Figure 9.2 South Waterfront, Portland, Oregon, 2010

Several condominium projects were completed during the first phase of development, including the Meriwether, John Ross, and Mirabella buildings. Market volatility in the late 2000s, however, led to high vacancy rates forcing developers to auction off units to recover construction costs (Mirk, 2010). The recession also led to the cancellation of the first affordable housing development with 400 units, referred to as Block 33. A second affordable housing project with 200 units was initiated in 2010 and completed in the fall of 2012 (Koffman, 2012).

As for economic development, the project included strategies to promote "a mix of occupations and wage levels that provide a range of employment opportunities" (Portland Development Commission, n.d.d). In particular, OHSU was identified as an anchor to spark the development of a biotechnology cluster as part of Portland's efforts to encourage economic growth and diversification. Expansion of the OHSU campus in the South Waterfront District takes advantage of "an existing industry base" while serving as an incubator for industry growth (Portland Development Commission, n.d.e). The completion of the 16-storey Center for Health & Healing in 2006 provided OHSU with 400,000 sq. ft. of additional research and clinic space. The developer, Gerding Edlen, also pursued LEED certification and integrates several sustainable design features such as daylight harvesting, 100 percent wastewater treatment and recycling, and "a large-scale onsite microturbine plant" (Natural Resources Defense Council, 2012). The building utilizes 60 percent less energy and 55 percent less water than a comparable facility built to code (Natural Resources Defense Council, 2012).

Phases two and three

Phase one public projects were largely complete (Prosper Portland, n.d.) by 2012. Phase two projects in the North District included the 26-acre expansion of the OSHU Schnitzer Campus with three new buildings commencing construction in 2016. An agreement to redevelop Zidell Yards (a 33-acre site) in 2015 recently fell through due to infrastructure costs, inclusionary zoning and other factors (Marum, 2016; Oregon Health & Science University, n.d.a). Another recently announced project, the Landing at Macadam, is a four-block development proposal with 1,079 residential units, 926 vehicular parking spaces, and 27,259 sq. ft. of retail. The project is subject to the city's inclusionary housing rules, which require the provision of affordable housing or the payment of a fee-in-lieu.

Zoning and Urban Design Guidelines

Since 1990, the South Waterfront District has been zoned as CX (Central Commercial), which permits a wide variety of office, retail, and housing uses at urban densities (Portland Bureau of Planning, 2002). Based on the existing site conditions and characteristics of the South Waterfront District, assumptions about the relative location of office and research, housing, and public space uses were made. For instance, office and research facilities are expected to locate near the existing transportation infrastructure and the I-5 freeway in the northwest portion of the district (Portland Bureau of Planning, 2002). Residential uses would be clustered between the office and research facilities and along the Willamette River, offering views of downtown Portland and the waterfront. Retail would locate on an east-west axis at grade-level throughout the district. The greenway adjacent to the Willamette River ensures public access to the waterfront while serving as an alternative transportation route to downtown Portland.

While the redevelopment maintains the CX zoning designation, urban design guidelines specific to the South Waterfront District were introduced to achieve the desired urban form and mix of uses in the plan area. The urban design guidelines refer to building scale, orientation, and height, ultimately influencing site planning, development, and investment in the plan area. Moreover, the district was subdivided into "blocks" in a grid-like pattern to emulate urban form.

As an example of how the urban design guidelines influence the pattern of development within the district, east-west view corridors to the waterfront are preserved and enhanced by requiring buildings to "'step back' from the street, for the portion of the building over

50 feet in height" (Portland Bureau of Planning, 2002). Setbacks for buildings at grade are also required, to a maximum of "12 feet from the sidewalk," in combination with "active ground floor uses, including retail, office and housing," which facilitate an attractive and visually interesting pedestrian environment (Portland Bureau of Planning, 2002). Trade-offs in building height and density had to be made to achieve the 125-foot setback for the waterfront greenway desired by the Mayor at the time. The urban design guidelines, therefore, allow "building heights of 125–250 feet," while buildings up to 325 feet may be permitted in exchange for density bonusing or financing for projects that benefit the public (Portland Bureau of Planning, 2002). The prescribed residential density was also increased from "at least 1 unit per 2,900 sq. ft. of net site area" as required by the zoning code to "1 unit per 1000 sq. ft. of net site area" to enable other project goals such as generating ridership to support public transit development (Portland Bureau of Planning, 2002).

Project Financing

The redevelopment of Portland's South Waterfront District is being financed through a 20-year funding strategy established by the PDC (Portland Development Commission, n.d.d). The basis of this strategy is a public-private partnership between the PDC and the stakeholders noted earlier in the Project Vision. This approach leverages public and private resources to generate investment and development in the plan area that would otherwise not be feasible. Moreover, given the district's industrial heritage, public intervention was necessary to reduce the environmental and economic costs of development and to encourage private investment in support of broader policy objectives. A report prepared for the PDC by E.D. Hovee & Company analyzing the anticipated return on investment of the South Waterfront District plan found that a public-private approach would achieve more of the policy objectives in the plan area than private mechanisms alone (E.D. Hovee & Company, 2003). For instance, a market-only approach would have resulted in $352 million of investment compared to the $1.9 billion of public and private investment currently projected by build-out in 2020. Under this second scenario, $1.7 billion is from private investors with the balance coming from public sources ($131 million from TIF, $23million Other public, $64million Potential public), leading to an estimated ROI of $7.71 (E.D. Hovee & Company, 2003). Performance indicators for housing, jobs, transportation, retail, and parks and open space also demonstrate higher quantitative measures through the public-private approach, allowing the redevelopment project to move from a conventional to a more sustainable one.

The public-private partnership is governed by the South Waterfront Central District Project Development Agreement, first signed in 2003 and updated through multiple subsequent amendments. The Development Agreement specifies the terms and conditions of the partnership while allocating the redevelopment responsibilities between the project partners. The Development Agreement also specifies "a 20 percent aspirational contracting goal for minority-owned, women-owned and emerging small business participation" (Portland Development Commission, n.d.d).

Public projects are administered and managed by the PDC. Approximately $131 million of the phase one public funds were sourced through Tax Increment Financing (TIF), to pay for "urban renewal bonds." Other public sources were earmarked to contribute $23 million at the time (E.D. Hovee & Company, 2003). Public sector financing prioritizes investment in infrastructure such as "street and utility construction, extension of the Portland Streetcar, and [the] riverfront Greenway," to prepare the plan area for private investment (Portland Development Commission, n.d.d). A significant share of the public funds for phase one, $53 million, was allocated for transportation projects, followed by $28 million for affordable housing and parks, and $17 million for additional infrastructure and job investment programs (E.D. Hovee & Company, 2003). In 2006, Portland City Council adopted a TIF Set Aside Policy to establish a consistent and predictable level of funding for affordable housing pegged at 30% of TIF resources, which contributed to the Grove Apartments and numerous other projects (Resolution No. 36404). Private investment, on the other hand, was being directed to the development of office and research facilities, retail establishments, and market housing in the district. Through a condition specified in the Development Agreement, the private sector partners are obligated to pay the TIF difference, or revenue gap, if their projects do not proceed as scheduled, according to an interviewee. This ensures the urban renewal initiative progresses as planned and that the city does not incur a loss over the long term due to unexpected delays to the redevelopment.

Despite the recession in the late 2000s and its impact on the US real estate market, the PDC reported that the South Waterfront redevelopment was well-positioned to repay the $62 million borrowed through the TIF (Mirk, 2010). According to the PDC's account in 2010, the annual property tax revenue incurred through the redevelopment is $7.2 million and exceeded the estimate provided by E.D. Hovee & Company by $2.2 million (Mirk, 2010).

Benefits, Barriers, and Lessons Learned

Portland's South Waterfront District offers an exemplary case study in brownfield remediation and renewal (see project timeline, Table 9.2). The project vision for the Master Planned community reflects the planning approach utilized by the PDC (now Prosper Portland) that integrates economic, environmental, and social sustainability. Several policy tools and mechanisms enable this integrated approach, affirming the public's commitment to the principles of Smart Growth.

The Master Planned vision for a mixed-use, multi-modal, 21st-century urban neighborhood emerged from the need to address several interrelated challenges, including industrial decline and Portland's decreasing land supply. De-industrialization beginning in the 1960s contributed to significant unemployment in Portland while the area's subsequent brownfield status and physical isolation discouraged private investment. Regional planning directives limiting greenfield development through an urban growth boundary have encouraged Portland to be creative with the use of its limited land supply. While the South Waterfront District represents less than one percent of the city of Portland's area, it was projected to "assume 4.7 percent of the city's job growth, 2.5 percent of housing and residents and potentially more than 4.4 acres" of public open space (Portland Development Commission, n.d.d). Benefits of the urban renewal initiative included:

- Economic
    - increased property tax base;
    - employment retention, development, and diversification with a projected total of 10,000 new jobs upon full redevelopment;

- expansion of a highly regarded research and educational institution;
- job support for ethnic minorities and women through the construction and development phases of the urban renewal initiative.
- Environmental
  - renewing the Willamette River ecology;
  - brownfields remediation and land reuse
    - clean-up strategies included: "riverbank stabilization, site capping, off-site soil disposal, and ground-water monitoring" (Portland Development Commission, n.d.e).
  - South Waterfront Plan Code and Design Guidelines to establish a smart growth and sustainable vision and ensure implementation;
  - pursuing LEED Neighborhood Development Gold Certification;
  - LEED Gold requirement with an aim for the most LEED-certified residential towers of any neighborhood in the country (EPA Brownfields ECP);
  - integrated stormwater management system.
- Community/Society
  - infill development and urban revitalization;
  - new high-density housing options, with 3,000–5,000 rental and ownership units anticipated, including 788 affordable units (of which only 209 units had been built by 2018);
  - public access to the William River waterfront;
  - expanding Portland's network of parks and open space;
  - multi-modal transportation options (streetcar, aerial tram, pedestrian and bicycle network).

The confluence of Portland's economic and land use needs may have contributed to the project vision for the South Waterfront redevelopment. However, implementing this project vision would not have been feasible without enabling policy tools and mechanisms that support broader public objectives. For instance, the South Waterfront Urban Design Guidelines prescribe the form and function of development to satisfy housing, employment, and public open space targets, while the Development Agreement ensures that the appropriate stakeholders and resources are in place to see the project through to completion. Portland's culture of sustainability, the adoption of Smart Growth principles, and public leadership also account for the South Waterfront's status as an exemplary case study of brownfield remediation and urban renewal.

This is not to say that the implementation of the South Waterfront Plan has been without criticism or challenges. For instance, the South Waterfront redevelopment illustrates that while public-private partnerships leverage benefits to the public, benefits may also accrue to private stakeholders to secure investment. An example, in this case, is the tram that links the OHSU campuses. While citizens perceive the tram as an inefficient use of public funds, it was a critical component of the Development Agreement, which made it possible for OHSU to serve as an economic development anchor in the district. The lesson here is that trade-offs are inherent in any public-private partnership, particularly to achieve broader public policy objectives.

While support for the urban renewal initiative generally gained momentum as the project developed, community consultation revealed concerns about building heights and the eventual increase in demand for existing traffic and transportation routes. Community members also voiced concerns about potential health and safety issues associated with brownfield redevelopment. Given that Portland's urban planning legacy is based on a transparent and collaborative approach, however, these concerns were addressed through education and outreach activities led by the PDC. Communication tools such as fact sheets and maps in combination with information meetings provided the general public with a better understanding of environmental issues in the South Waterfront District (Abuaf, 2010).

Financial constraints and market volatility presented significant challenges, particularly concerning the project's environmental and affordable housing objectives (Mirk, 2010). Some of the ecological goals were also in direct conflict with each other. For instance, onsite stormwater management in a brownfield area adjacent to a river is challenging enough considering the overlapping jurisdictional and regulatory requirements but was further complicated by the objective to create a new habitat for the Willamette River's fish population. As an interviewee pointed out, capping the site would address stormwater runoff, but not the river ecology; dredging the site would also negatively impact the river (Abuaf, 2010). Reconciling the opposing objectives by removing the contaminated soil was achieved in a "hybrid concept" plan primarily through inter-governmental cooperation and resources. Phase one of the riverbank restoration was started in 2012 (Portland Parks & Recreation, 2012) and completed in 2015 (Portland Parks & Recreation, n.d.).

Efforts to implement the affordable housing targets established for the South Waterfront redevelopment have been constrained by funding, further compounded by the recession in the late 2000s. For instance, while the city invested $16 million toward the development of 400 affordable housing units, "the deal fell through with the market crash" (Mirk, 2010). Fortunately, progress was made to secure the development of a six-story, 209-unit affordable housing Gray's Landing building for households earning 60% of median family income that was completed in fall 2012. Interviewees acknowledged that Prosper Portland had been criticized for the way the affordable housing portfolio has been managed, especially given the number of luxury, market-rate condominium units that have been developed in South Waterfront. The recent impasse with the Zidell Yards project, reportedly due in part to land for affordable housing among other infrastructure costs, shows that this is still a challenge. Urban revitalization in the community has incidentally increased the need for affordable housing units, as gentrification begins to displace marginal populations to other areas.

Global and regional market conditions also impacted the district's market housing and office development. High vacancy rates prompted developers to auction off condominium units, while vacancy rates in office buildings downtown and in the surrounding metropolitan area indicated "the need for private office tenancy drops to less than one-half of the level previously planned" (E.D. Hovee & Company, 2003; Mirk, 2010). This may explain, in part, why job creation did not keep pace with projected targets early on. It also indicates that all areas of the project are susceptible to external market influences.

While financial constraints and market volatility have led to project delays and cancellations in some cases, challenges are to be expected in any redevelopment project, with this one being no exception. The unprecedented scale of the South Waterfront redevelopment, in terms of time and space, increases the risks and thereby challenges associated with the urban redevelopment initiative. Moreover, given that the project is still in progress, perhaps the most essential lessons that Portland's South Waterfront District has to offer have yet to be learned. It is clear that development has picked back up since 2015.

Despite some challenges, however, it is essential to note that the South Waterfront project is not a "one-off" best practice, but one of a growing portfolio of brownfield projects in Portland that incorporate sustainable elements. Indeed, Prosper Portland, the city of Portland's Bureau of Environmental Services (which manages the city's brownfields program), along with other government agencies, non-profits, and private developers are taking a proactive and progressive approach to brownfields redevelopment, targeting sites throughout the city and incorporating sustainable elements. A map of 74 brownfield projects funded by Portland's Brownfields Program from its inception in 1998 to 2019 notes the support provided for affordable housing projects (10), community and other gardens (13), along with an array of additional housing, non-profit, small business, retail, temporary and other uses (Environmental Services, 2019). The list below outlines just a few of the exemplary sustainable brownfield projects that have been developed in the city.

- June Key Delta Community Center
    - a small corner gas station and convenience store converted by a female African American sorority into a green building where community outreach and tutoring services are provided (see Chapter 7).
- The Yards and Union Station
    - this EPA Phoenix Award-winning project converted a former rail yard into a LEED rated redevelopment with affordable family housing.
- The Watershed at Hillsdale
    - a former auto wrecking, rail stop, and barn in Southwest Portland converted into a 51-unit senior affordable housing project with extensive building efficiency and stormwater management features.
- Hacienda Community Development Corporation
    - an Earth Advantage certified office building that will house Hacienda CDC, a non-profit organization that provides affordable housing, homeownership support, economic advancement, and educational opportunities for low-income residents.
- Dharma Rain Zen Center (Dharma Rain Zen Center, 2020)
    - this 14-acre former landfill located in a low-income neighborhood is being transformed via: stormwater management; methane mitigation systems; ecological Master Plan projects that involve removal of invasive species, planting an oak savannah, restoring an overgrown ravine and planting native species; linkages to a local greenway; the development of a traditional Zen temple that will include a meditation hall, ceremony hall, dormitories, office, classrooms, and community gardens; and

a 31-unit residential community. More than 20 neighborhood groups, educational institutions, religious groups, environmental non-profits, and government entities have contributed labor, funding, or in-kind support for the project that will act as a "living" campus for area schools to study conservation/ecology and to conduct field research.
- Songbird (North Williams)
    - with funding from the EPA and the city, this project is converting the site of a former battery company into 61 affordable apartments with about two-thirds of the units receiving Project-Based Section 8 subsidy.
- The Pearl District
    - often considered the project that set the tone for Portland's brownfields success, this former warehouse/industrial area began revitalization into a vibrant mixed-use neighborhood in the mid-1980s.

Table 9.2 Timeline – South Waterfront, Portland, Oregon

Year	Description
1880s	Industrial development of South Waterfront landscape begins
1960s	Period of industrial decline contributed to rise in vacant lots and brownfield sites
1966	Completion of I-5 freeway through Portland (created a physical barrier to the South Waterfront area)
1976	Portland City Council votes to remove Harbor Drive (six-lane expressway); first step in reclaiming waterfront for public benefit
1978	Portland Development Commission acquires South Waterfront Redevelopment Project area
1979	City of Portland adopts the South Waterfront Redevelopment Program
1980s–1990s	South Waterfront devolves into a blighted area and becomes disconnected from the city
1997	Visioning process led by the city to reclaim and renew the waterfront area
1999	North Macadam Urban Renewal Area established by Portland City Council
2003	Public-Private Development Agreement reached between the Portland Development Commission, Oregon Health and Science University and North Macadam Investors, River Campus Investors, and Block 39
2003	EPA Grant for a Phase I area-wide assessment
2004	EPA Grant for Phase II assessment of the future Elizabeth Caruthers Neighborhood Park
2006	Clean-up and remediation of Elizabeth Caruthers Neighborhood Park completed Completion of the LEED Platinum OHSU Center for Health & Healing
2007	Oregon Department of Environmental Quality issues a No Further Action letter
2010	Block 33 affordable housing unit project cancelled
2011	Eight residential towers, including one affordable housing development and a senior living community

(Continued)

Table 9.2 (Continued)

Year	Description
2012	Phase one of South Waterfront Greenway river restoration begins and completion of the Gibbs Street Pedestrian Bridge
2014	The Joseph E. Robertson, Jr Collaborative Life Sciences Building, jointly owned and operated by Portland State University, Oregon Health & Science University, and Oregon State University, opens on the Schnitzer Campus. This 650,000 sq. ft. complex consists of several buildings and is LEED Platinum certified due to a host of sustainable features including green roofs, a storm water collection system for non-potable water, energy-efficient climate control and lighting, and extensive use of recycled and sustainable materials
2015	Tilikum Crossing bridge opens to carry pedestrians, bicyclists and public transit vehicles between the South Waterfront and Hosford-Abernethy
2019	The Gary and Christine Rood Family Pavilion, run in partnership with Ronald McDonald House Charities, opened in 2019 with a five-story guest house atop six levels of parking and holds 38 suites for pediatric patients and their families and 38 for adult patients and their families

Langdale and Riverdale Mills, City of Valley, Alabama

Site History

The city of Valley, Alabama (pop. 9,000+) was formed in 1980 by incorporating the four textile mill towns of Langdale, Riverdale, Shawmut, and Fairfax (Hand, 2007). The Langdale and Riverdale Mills, located three miles apart, were built in 1866, coinciding with the beginning of the southern textile revolution and the end of the Civil War (Hand, 2007). Both mills harnessed the power of the Chattahoochee River, where it flows between Alabama and Georgia, to manufacture textiles from cotton. Villages developed adjacent to the mills provided workers with housing, stores, churches, schools, and recreational facilities (Hand, 2007). The Langdale and Riverdale Mills were acquired by the West Point Manufacturing Company during the 1880s. Two other mills, Shawmut and Fairfax, were built by the Company in the early 1900s (Hand, 2007). All four textile villages are registered on the National List of Historic Places and the Alabama Historic Register as valued historical and cultural heritage landmarks (Hand, 2007).

Both the Langdale and Riverdale Mills ceased operations in the late 1990s (US EPA, 2008b). Valley municipal staff recognized the need to preserve the cultural heritage of the mills while promoting new forms of economic development as both mills had served as the economic and cultural foundation of the community (US EPA, 2009a). The city of Valley purchased the Langdale Mill in 2004 at a bankruptcy sale. Subsequently, in 2006, the city acquired the Riverdale Mill intending to redevelop both properties into a mix of commercial, recreational, residential, and cultural facilities and amenities (US EPA, 2008b).

Both mills are ideally situated for redevelopment as they are easily accessible by two major highways: I-85 and Highway 29 (Hand, 2007). Moreover, each is surrounded by significant cultural and environmental assets and waterfront access (Hand, 2007). The Langdale

Mill lies on a 25-acre site with over 500,000 sq. ft. of building space (a two-/three-story main building and five smaller buildings), and 900 feet of waterfront access on the Chattahoochee River (see Figure 9.3). The Riverdale Mill is on 14 acres of riverfront property and includes 220,000 sq. ft. of building space (a four-story main building) (Hand, 2007; MACTAC Engineering and Consulting Inc., n.d.).

Figure 9.3 Langdale Mill, Valley, Alabama (Google Earth, n.d.a)

Project Vision

The closure of the Langdale and Riverdale textile mills in the late 1990s gave rise to vacant, underutilized properties with historical and economic value. Valley also lost a significant source of employment and economic activity. In an attempt to preserve the legacy of the textile industry, the city began to explore options to redevelop the sites and put them back into productive use. The project vision was based on two primary objectives: (1) to preserve the historical and cultural heritage of the mills while protecting them from decay; and (2) to promote local economic development. Preliminary efforts to redevelop the mills began in 1999 when the city hosted design charrettes to vision an appropriate and sustainable development of the properties (US EPA, 2009a). As a result of the charrettes, the city outlined the need to assess the environmental condition of the sites and remediate any potential contamination. The city of Valley purchased the mills, with the full support of the city council, in recognition of their role in the community's history with a vision of the potential they offered to the community's future.

The original intention was to dismantle the existing structures and preserve the history of the location. According to an interviewee, however, it shifted toward revitalization and adaptive reuse to cut costs and adhere to the principles of sustainability. Once Valley acquired the mills, an architectural firm was hired to create a Master Plan for the redevelopment. The Master Plan took approximately one year to complete and put forward a mixed-use project consisting of residences, commercial and office spaces, recreational and tourist-based amenities, as well as a conference center and community garden. During the Master Planning, the city of Valley explored funding opportunities to finance the project while simultaneously maintaining the mill properties to prevent further degradation.

When the decision to redevelop the sites was made, city staff contacted the US EPA for technical support. The city was encouraged by its partnership with the EPA to integrate the principles of smart growth and sustainability into the project vision, based on the economic, environmental, and social benefits they offer. The redevelopment of the Langdale and Riverdale Mills qualified for financial and technical assistance through the EPA Brownfields Sustainability Pilots program to advance these principles.

Project Characteristics and Development

With the conceptual planning stages in progress, Phase I and II ESAs were initiated in 2006 and 2007 via the Alabama Department of Environmental Management (MACTAC Engineering and Consulting Inc., n.d.). The city received EPA Brownfields Assessment and Brownfields Cleanup grants to begin remediation and redevelopment activities at both the Langdale and Riverdale sites (US EPA, 2009a). The ESAs revealed the presence of asbestos-containing materials and contaminated storage tanks, but they were not expected to affect the redevelopment of the mills negatively, according to the city. In 2008, the EPA provided the city with technical and financial assistance through the Brownfields Sustainability Pilots program to generate a material reuse inventory tool for the Langdale Mill property. The tool was used to document and quantify the potential value of building material, including lumber, metal for scrap or reuse, brick, concrete, and other items with monetary or industrial heritage value. The inventory estimated that "109,000 board feet of lumber, 209,000 pounds of metal, and 63,000 bricks could be recovered for recycling or reuse" through the deconstruction of the Langdale Mill (US EPA, 2009a). The approximate value of the building materials was projected at $150,000 (US EPA, 2009a).

Given that the inventory outlines the potential resale value of each item, the city can consider alternative uses for the recovered contents versus recycling or reusing them to preserve the mills' industrial heritage (US EPA, 2009a). The inventory tool, therefore, provided alternative options to conventional demolition practices. A mill deconstruction feasibility assessment was also performed for each property, during which building conditions and safety were also evaluated. This included "building dimensions, accessibility, and complexity;

entanglement; asbestos and hazardous materials; materials and salvage potential; mobilization; garbage; and labor" (US EPA, 2009b).

The Master Plan for the Langdale Mill Redevelopment was to be carried out in three phases. Each phase addresses a specific portion of the site, with each subsequent stage increasing in size and complexity. Income generated from services as each step is completed and becomes operational was to be used to finance the next development phase (Hand, 2007). The target markets of the Langdale Mill redevelopment included historic- and eco-based tourism, active seniors, small conventions, small businesses, and local and regional residents. Phase one was to involve developing the riverfront and a Discovery Center and Café. Phase two would see the construction of a live-work community with new residences introduced to the site. And phase three the development of a Hotel and Convention Center, as well as the introduction of commercial space (MACTAC Engineering and Consulting Inc., n.d.)

The Riverdale Mill property is roughly half the size of the Langdale site. Unlike the Langdale plan, the Riverdale Mill Redevelopment Master Plan focuses on recreation and conservation. The vision was to conserve natural heritage along the Chattahoochee River and provide Valley residents with recreational amenities such as nature trails and parks that link to a more extensive network of green space, providing connections to the other mill villages of Langdale, Fairfax, and Shawmut. Amenities include river access, outdoor recreation, retail, and dining. The main characteristics of the redevelopment offered a multi-state water resource management center, a warehouse for research and meetings, a recreational river trail, park and boat launch, nature preserve, fishing and recreation park, cabins for camping and research staff, and the Riverdale school archives and arts center (MACTAC Engineering and Consulting Inc., n.d.)

Work on phase one of the Langdale Mill redevelopment began on January 23, 2012, starting with the deconstruction of several non-historic warehouse buildings (city of Valley, 2012). The materials recovered from the deconstruction of the warehouse buildings were to be reused in the redevelopment of the mill or sold to offset project costs. The inventory tool created with technical assistance from the EPA valued the building material from these warehouses at $163,400 (city of Valley, 2012). As of 2018, demolition activity has continued on the north side of the Langdale Mill site, with 11 of 12 separate buildings deconstructed. The intention is to continue to remain on plan and retain some critical buildings with historic and aesthetic value to incorporate them in the development of residential apartments (Clark, 2018). Interestingly, the company involved in the reclamation and redevelopment also owns a flooring company located in a refurbished cotton warehouse nearby and sells the reclaimed wood to many customers interested in the history of the product. The ultimate goal is to add residents to the area, attract a major grocer, and help the area make it past a population tipping point to initiate the envisioned plan (Clark, 2018). No activity seems to have commenced on the Riverside Mill site.

The city explored many funding and financing options and was able to obtain funding early on from the EPA for assessment ($200,000 in 2008), cleanup ($135,000 for Langdale and $100,000 for Riverdale), and Pilot activities in 2008, as well as funds from the Appalachian Regional Commission ($50,000 in 2005), the United States Department of Agriculture ($32,000 in 2007), and an appropriation by US Representative Mike Rogers for $150,000 (in 2008) (city of Valley, 2008). Council also approved a bond for early demolition work.

Benefits, Barriers, and Lessons Learned

The redevelopment of the Langdale and Riverdale Mills should result in several sustainable outcomes when finalized (see project timeline, Table 9.3). The off-site remediation of contaminated storage tanks will safeguard natural resources and prohibit any further environmental degradation. The adaptive reuse and recycling of existing building materials in the redevelopment has been cost and resource-efficient. The proposed redevelopment also provides an abundance of parks and natural space.

Adaptive reuse of the mills continues the tradition of historical preservation that recognizes the importance of the city of Valley's industrial legacy to its past and future economic development. The redevelopment of these mills also encouraged the city council and staff to seek out partnerships to investigate opportunities to incorporate green and sustainable design into the development process. The recent establishment of a community garden and farmers market serve as forums of social exchange, which will cultivate social capital and increase community capacity through collective interaction.

Historic dependence on textile manufacturing in the region has limited the local workforce's ability to adapt to changing economic conditions and led to population decline. Prioritizing mixed-use development will allow the city to offer diverse employment, recreational and cultural activities, and the potential to withstand future economic fluctuations. It should also help it benefit from large-scale investments in job creation in neighboring municipalities through tourism, employment, and population growth. Kia Motors, for instance, constructed a new manufacturing plant in West Point, Georgia, 4.5 miles northeast of the city of Valley with 3,000 employees. As part of the development agreement, 700 to 800 of these jobs will be reserved for Alabama residents (Hand, 2007).

Financing the redevelopment of the Langdale and Riverdale Mills has been an ongoing obstacle to the redevelopment. One of the main priorities is to secure additional funding to offset the costs of demolition and construction. The city of Valley keeps seeking additional funding to carry out further studies about the redevelopment. Valley's population may also not be large enough to support a redevelopment of this scale. As noted by commentators early on, demand for the commercial and recreational facilities offered by the project is affected by the proximity of competing facilities that provide similar amenities and services (Hand, 2007).

There was some uncertainty with regards to land use zoning for the mixed-use plan envisioned for the redevelopment given that both properties did not have a zoning classification until 2013. Two zones were created for the sites: RD (Redevelopment District) in the northern portions permits mixed-use development, while RP (River Park District) along the southern part permits recreational uses along the Chattahoochee River.

An interviewee noted that the planning framework used for the design of the Langdale and Riverdale Mills was practical and useful, once support from the local council had been acquired. Furthermore, the EPA's technical assistance and Brownfield Pilot Process were beneficial and provided a useful planning tool that can be applied in future development projects. Additional technical support will likely be required to ensure the integration of sustainable development principles into the project's planning and development process as

Table 9.3 Timeline – Langdale and Riverdale Mills, City of Valley, Alabama

Year	Description
1866	Cornerstones for both mills laid on the same day
1980	Valley Alabama becomes incorporated
Late 1990s	Both Langdale and Riverdale Mills cease operations
1999	Design Alabama holds visioning charrette
2004	City of Valley purchased Langdale Mill
2004	City of Valley holds open house for Langdale Mill
2005	KPS Group holds workshop for community feedback on reuses of Langdale Mill
2005	Langdale Mill project presented at National Brownfields Conference
2006	City of Valley purchased Riverdale Mill
2006	Alabama Department of Environmental Management performs Phase I Environmental Study
2006	Auburn University Architectural Department holds design charrette
2006	Langdale Mill project presented at ARC National Conference
2006	"Twin Mills on the Chattahoochee" project presented at National Brownfields Conference
2007	Alabama Department of Environmental Management performs Phase II Environmental Study
2008	"Twin Mills on the Chattahoochee" project design charrette
2012	Implementation of Phase 1 of Langdale Mill redevelopment begins
2018	Demolition of buildings in the north end of the mill site continues

it moves forward. City officials acknowledged that this would also need to involve a heavy emphasis on sustainability education and outreach within the various city departments and the general public as well.

The Waterfront, Allentown, Pennsylvania

Site History

The Lehigh Structural Steel Company was founded in 1919 and, over time, built a vast industrial complex along the Lehigh River in Allentown, Pennsylvania. The company fabricated steel for everything from bridges and airplane hangars to high-rise office buildings, employing over 500 workers in the 1960s (Hernan, 1992). The company began facing stiff competition in the 1970s and shuttered the plant 1983. Two large contracts resuscitated the company in 1984, but competition forced it to close its doors again in 1989 and to sell the Allentown complex to local investors the following year (Hernan, 1992).

In the spring of 2005, the newly founded Dunn Twiggar Company (DTC) first eyed the property. While to most, it was just a collection of industrial buildings containing a random assortment of businesses, DTC focused on what was behind the old buildings: one of the most-navigable stretches of the Lehigh River. The company knew something better could be done with the site and wanted to reorient it toward the water and build something that was pedestrian-friendly, environmentally responsible, and socially interactive that would encourage public gathering and provide "a sense of place."

220 *Mixed-Use Complete Communities*

Project Vision and Planning

The land wasn't advertised for sale, but its owner LSS Realty Corporation was willing to talk. By August 2005, they had a deal for 26-acres of the site, which was to be finalized that summer if the property was rezoned for riverfront development (selling price not disclosed) (see Figure 9.4). DTC made public its initial plans for an attractive, lively, and sustainable mixed-use waterfront community in early 2007, and the city introduced a new zoning ordinance, the Riverfront Redevelopment Overlay District, to accommodate the new development. DTC felt it was essential that community stakeholders be included from the outset of the project. It presented "the Waterfront" project at several neighborhood meetings that were credited with improving public buy-in. Additionally, DTC brought on as a partner the area's leading conservation group, the Wildlands Conservatory.

Figure 9.4 The Waterfront site, Allentown, Pennsylvania (Google Earth, n.d.b)

In regards to contamination, DTC successfully worked with the Lehigh Valley Economic Development Corporation to obtain grants for a Phase I ESA. Previous assessments revealed that much of the site was built on fill material comprised primarily of steel slag and gravel (US EPA, 2009c). It also identified past citations related to the improper disposal of demolition waste, discharges into the Lehigh River, and removal of underground fuel tanks. Field tests performed at the site identified some localized areas of contamination. As part of a separate project for EPA Region 3, contractors sampled soil and groundwater at the property in July

2008, finding metals likely from leachate of slag fill material (US EPA, 2009c). The contractor also conducted a site visit in December 2008 to assess the condition of the riverbank and found it to be stable enough to sustain development, in large part due to the presence of large trees and other vegetation.

The original vision for the project forwarded by DTC called for a half mile of unobstructed frontage along the Lehigh River and over 1,200,000 sq. ft. of occupied buildings, including over 550 residential townhomes, condominiums, and apartments, over 100,000 sq. ft. of office space (400 jobs), a 90+ room hotel with conference facilities (60 jobs), and 65,000+ sq. ft. of retail space (150 jobs). The hope at that time was for site construction to begin in 2010 when the existing tenants' leases expired.

Initial interest in advancing green and sustainable elements was prompted, according to DTC, by the EPA's Sustainable Brownfield Pilot grant, which the developers learned about via the local economic development corporation responsible for the brownfields program. Their primary interest was to use it to work through how to give the community access to the riverfront and promote the historical, cultural, and environmental prominence of the Lehigh River. EPA's technical assistance focused on conceptual design drawings for the master plan to account for the site's location in the floodplain and to make recommendations for low impact development (LID) stormwater management practices (US EPA, 2009d). It recommended green techniques (e.g., silt fences, turbidity barriers, sedimentation basins, inlet protection) for controlling sediment during construction, and an erosion control blanket and a seeded buffer zone to reduce soil movement during construction and site reuse (US EPA, 2009d). LID features (e.g., a living wall, naturalized detention areas, and a riverwalk with pervious pavement) were proposed to protect the riverbank from flood damage (US EPA, 2009d). Technical assistance also suggested methods for controlling stormwater entering the river from the new development, such as porous pavement, bioretention areas, rain gardens, green roofs, cisterns, and rain barrels. While DTC noted that the $25,000 Sustainability Pilot grant was a "drop in the bucket," it provided symbolic direction and allowed them to put more funding toward examining best practices for the riverside trail and riverbank development. One interviewee noted the developer's initial renderings were overly paved, and it was hoped that porous paving or more plantings would be better options. At the same, the EPA also encouraged DTC to use LEED or another "green" rating system to inform the development, even though there was hesitation in the local development community about the potential costs this might add.

The cost of the project at the time was estimated at approximately $175 million. Government funding support announced before 2011 included a $5 million grant from the state Governor to the city of Allentown for redeveloping the riverfront through the Redevelopment Capital Assistance Program ($3 million directed to site preparation at the Waterfront project riverfront) and a $25,000 grant from the EPA for stormwater management.

While DTC and government partners worked diligently to get the site rezoned, another barrier was the delay in constructing the long-promised American Parkway bridge linking Route 22 and downtown Allentown, which would provide crucial access and exposure to the property. After 60 years in the making, a new bridge finally opened to the public in late 2015. Another issue raised during the interviews was that DTC was a young company formed by two keen individuals who had never attempted a project of this magnitude. This may explain why it formed a partnership (The Waterfront Development Company – WTC) in 2012 with a large local developer, Jaindl Properties. At this time, the new collaboration anticipated full engineering and architectural plans under development to move through the approval process in 2013 and construction to start in 2014 with initial occupancy beginning in 2016 (Barry Isett & Associates Inc., 2013).

Despite delays, WTC commenced demolition activities in 2014 on buildings located within the Phase I project area near the southern end of the site, along with ground infrastructure placement. It also unveiled its first development, an eight-story office building with street-level retail and restaurants along a signature River Walk that offers walking and running paths, programmable amphitheaters, and two floating docks. WTC also acquired a nearby property expanding its site by approximately 7% (Jaindl Enterprises, 2014).

In 2015, WTC purchased three and a half miles of railroad on the western side of the river to develop a new roadway that would improve access to the project. It would also make it possible for WTC to unite two significant legs of the Delaware and Lehigh Heritage Rail Trails that comprise of over 165 miles of bike and walking paths serving the Lehigh Valley (Jaindl Properties, 2015a). WTC officially broke ground in November on the 26-acre mixed-use project that was now projected to cost $400 million at full build-out. Lehigh Valley's Economic Development department was praised as a partner through its Lehigh Valley Land Recycling Initiative, which provided federal environmental assistance to the effort. The project would introduce, in two phases, over eight years, six brand new office buildings, three residential complexes, three parking structures, a vibrant main street, and a signature half-mile River Walk. Among the announcements was an update of the site's Master Plan to reflect the rail land acquisition, road development, and the linking of the heritage trails (Jaindl Properties, 2015b). The project is expected to generate some 2,900 permanent jobs and $3.8 million in annual real estate taxes. There is no indication of whether green buildings will be developed.

In December 2017, all 26 acres of The Waterfront property was placed within Allentown's Neighborhood Improvement Zone, and Jaindl Enterprises received full site approval through the Allentown Neighborhood Improvement Zone Development Authority. The so-called NIZ is a special taxing district created by the state in 2012 to encourage development and revitalization in Allentown's city center and along the Lehigh River. The zone benefits The Waterfront by driving down office and residential lease costs with all local and state non-property taxes generated by the development of property within the zone going toward paying down project debt for up to 30 years, with the developer vowing to pass the benefit to tenants through subsidized rent (Backover, 2019). In 2013, the LVEDC also received a $468,000 Growing Greener grant from the Pennsylvania Department of Environmental Protection to help restore the river bank and install infrastructure (McEvoy, 2015). Most recently, LVEDC performed environmental assessment work on parcels of land that will become Riverside Drive.

In 2018, Dunn Twiggar dropped out of the partnership to pursue other opportunities. Jaindl Enterprises became the sole developer of the project and started to pursue office tenants from outside the Lehigh Valley more aggressively. By 2018, it was reported that the developer had already invested $19 million into the project, including utilities. Jaindl's objective was not to build until the office space was 50% leased (anticipated for the end of 2019) and to construct the new office, residential, and garage projects at the same time to give the project critical mass (Backover, 2019). Unfortunately, the economic impact of COVID-19 on the local market might cause the project to stall once again.

Table 9.4 Timeline – The Waterfront, Allentown, Pennsylvania

Year	Description
1977	Lehigh structural steel cited for disposing demolition waste
1985	Lehigh structural steel cited for disposing fuel oil
September 1989	Environmental Site Assessment Phase I and II
Early 2007	Dunn Twigger Company make public its plans for the site
April 2007	Zoning for site approved
August 2008	Mayor allocates $3 million for site clean up
2009	Tetra Tech Environmental report
2012	The property is fully acquired
2014	The Waterfront commences demolition
2015	The Waterfront purchases 3.5 miles of railroad to allow for better access and rejoin the North and South legs of the D&L Trail, and enhance open space
2015	The Waterfront breaks ground and unveils an updated Master Plan
2015	The new American Parkway Bridge is officially opened
2016	WTC designs the first of three onsite apartment complexes
2018	Jaindl Enterprises becomes the sole developer on the project
2019	Infrastructure work continues and developer seeks office tenancy of 50% to begin construction on preliminary office, residential, and parking properties

Project Impacts and Lessons Learned

As with other projects examined in this chapter, re-connecting people to the water was considered a genuine opportunity for both developers and the city (see project timeline, Table 9.4). The experience of the project reveals an effort to provide and expand such access and to understand ways to reclaim the waterfront using progressive and more natural green techniques. Public-private partnerships have been essential for both understanding and implementing measures for reclaiming the riverfront thus far. They have also been essential for providing key infrastructure both onsite and off-site to support the project. While there seems to be little appetite for green buildings due to cost fears, the project reveals a healthy desire for the renaturalization of our waterways from both the public and private sectors. And hopefully, the riverfront revitalization and expansion will draw attention, people, and eventually sales, to The Waterfront.

References

Atlantic Regional Commission. (2009). *2009 livable centers initiative implementation report*. Atlantic Regional Commission.
Atlantic Station LLC. (n.d.). *Green star environmental plan: Green buildings*. Atlantic Station LLC.
Atlantic Station Master Owners Association. (2011). *Atlantic Station transportation control measures 2010 performance update*. Office of Environmental Accountability, US EPA Region IV.
Backover, J. (2019). Selling the waterfront: Jaindl highlights Lehigh River waterfront's potential. October 16. *WFMZ-TV 69 News*.
Bacon, K. L., Dagenhart, Jr. R., Leigh, N. G. and Skach, J. (2008). The economic development – urban design link in brownfield redevelopment. *Economic Development Journal*, 7(2), 30-39.
Barry Isett & Associates Inc. (2013). *Waterfront takes shape in Allentown, PA*. January 8. Barry Isett & Associates Inc.

Bhedwar, C. (2006). *Georgia SEP update*. Georgia Environmental Facilities Program.
California Energy Commission. (n.d.). *Energy aware planning guide: Smart growth development*. California Energy Commission.
City of Atlanta. (2005). *Atlantic steel brownfield redevelopment plan & tax allocation bond district*. Office of Planning, City of Atlanta.
City of Valley. (2008). *Twin mills on the Chattahoochee – Langdale Mill & Riverdale Mill fact sheet*. City of Valley.
City of Valley. (2012). *Langdale mill redevelopment project*. February 29. City of Valley.
Clark, W. (2018). Langdale Mill demolition carries on throughout rain. November 13, *The Times-News*.
Dagenhart, R., Leigh, N. G, & Skach, J. (2006). Brownfields and urban design: Learning from Atlantic Station. *WIT Transactions on Ecology and the Environment*, 94, 185-194.
Dharma Rain Zen Center. (2020). *Project overview*. March 5. www.dharma-rain.org
E.D. Hovee & Company. (2003). *North Macadam urban renewal area return on investment (ROI) analysis update*. Portland Development Commission.
Environmental Services. (2019). *Portland brownfields program: Funded projects*. City of Portland.
Go by Tram. (2010). *Frequently asked questions*. Go by Tram Portland.
Google Earth. (n.d.a). Langdale Mill Pumping, Valley, Alabama. 32°48'01" N and 85°10'11" W. December 4, 2020.
Google Earth. (n.d.b). The Waterfront, Allentown, Pennsylvania. 40°37'10" N and 75°27'11" W. December 4, 2020.
Hand, P. (2007). *View to the future: Feasibility study for urban and architectural redevelopment of the Langdale Mill in Valley, Alabama*. Richard, Wittschiebe and Hand.
Hernan, M. (1992). End of a legend: Lehigh Structural Steel closes chapter in Lehigh Valley. November 1, *The Morning Call*.
Invest Atlanta. (2019) *Community development/human services committee tad quarterly and opportunity zone update*. Atlanta City Council.
Jaindl Enterprises. (2014). *The waterfront commences demolition*. July 24. Jaindl Enterprises.
Jaindl Properties. (2015a). *The waterfront purchases 3.5 miles of railroad*. February 3. Jaindl Properties.
Jaindl Properties. (2015b). *The waterfront breaks ground*. November 12. Jaindl Properties.
Kahn, M. (2017). Atlantic Station plans call for three new office buildings. April 24, *Curbed Atlanta*.
Koffman, R. (2012). Gray's landing, first affordable housing development in south waterfront, is nearing completion. September 4, *The Oregonian*.
Layton, D. (2016) *Effects of the great recession on tax increment financing in the United States, Georgia, and Atlanta* (Report No. cslf1909). The Center for State and Local Finance, Andrew Young School of Policy Studies, Georgia State University.
MACTAC Engineering and Consulting Inc. (n.d.). *Twin Mills on the Chattahoochee Valley, Alabama*. MACTAC Engineering and Consulting Inc.
Marum, A. (2016). Zidell Yards unveils south waterfront development plan. December 15, *The Oregonian*.
McEvoy, C. (2015). *Allentown waterfront groundbreaking marks 'beginning of a rebirth*. November 12. Leigh Valley Economic Development.
Miller, J. (2006). Evolution of a brownfield. *New Towns* (Spring), 1, 4.
Mirk, S. (2010). We built this city. *Portland Mercury*, 10(49), 13.
Natural Resources Defense Council. (2012). *Case studies: OHSU's center for health and healing*. July 10. Natural Resources Defense Council.
Oregon Health & Science University. (n.d.a). *Campus development*. OHSU.
Oregon Health & Science University. (n.d.b). *Portland aerial tram*. OHSU.
Portland Bureau of Planning. (2002). *South waterfront plan*. City of Portland.
Portland Development Commission. (n.d.a). *Introduction to smart growth*. PDC.
Portland Development Commission. (n.d.b). *South waterfront within the urban renewal area*. PDC.
Portland Development Commission. (n.d.c). *South waterfront district FAQs*. PDC.
Portland Development Commission. (n.d.d.) *South waterfront central district diversity in contracting & workforce training report fiscal year 03/04*. PDC.
Portland Development Commission. (n.d.e). *South waterfront park redevelopment area, region 10 phoenix award winner 2003*. PDC.

Portland Development Commission, Oregon Health & Science University, River Campus Investors, LLC, North Macadam Investors, LLC, and Block 39, LLC. (2003). *South waterfront central district project development agreement*. August 23. PDC.

Portland Parks & Recreation. (2012). *South waterfront greenway – central district*. July 9. City of Portland.

Portland Parks & Recreation. (n.d.). *South waterfront greenway – north reach*. City of Portland.

Prosper Portland. (n.d.). *South waterfront central district development agreement: Exhibit J- eighth amendment*. Prosper Portland.

Smith, G., & Russell. (2004). Tax increment financing. *SGR Insights*, Issue 10 (Winter).

The Center for Brownfields Initiatives. (2003). *EPA region 10: South waterfront redevelopment project, Portland, Oregon*. University of New Orleans.

US EPA. (1999). *Project XL and Atlantic Steel: Supporting environmental excellence and smart growth* (Report EPA-231-R-99-004). US EPA Office of Policy, Urban and Economic Division.

US EPA. (2005). *What are brownfields? Revitalizing southeastern communities, a brownfields toolkit*. US EPA Region 4.

US EPA. (2007). *Atlantic Steel*. US EPA.

US EPA. (2008a). *Atlantic Station (Atlantic Steel site redevelopment project)*. US EPA Smart Growth.

US EPA. (2008b). *Brownfields sustainability pilot fact sheet: Langdale and Riverdale Mills* (Report EPA 560-F-08-275). US EPA Office of Solid Waste and Emergency Response.

US EPA. (2009a). *Brownfields sustainability pilot: Deconstruction and building material reuse in former textile mills* (Report EPA-560-F-09-514). US EPA Office of Brownfields and Land Revitalization.

US EPA. (2009b). *Building a sustainable future: A report on the environmental protection agency's brownfield's sustainability pilots* (Report EPA-560-F-09-500). US EPA Office of Brownfields and Land Revitalization.

US EPA. (2009c). *Technical memorandum brownfields sustainability pilot: The Waterfront, Allentown PA.* (Report Contract No. EP-W-07-023). Prepared by Tetra Tech and SRA International for the US EPA Office of Brownfields and Land Revitalization.

US EPA. (2009d). *Brownfield sustainability pilot: Managing stormwater through low impact development techniques* (Report EPA-560-F-09-510). US EPA Office of Brownfields and Land Revitalization.

US EPA. (2012). *Brownfields at-a-glance: Elizabeth Caruthers Park* (Report EPA 560-F-12-013). US EPA Region 10 Brownfields.

US EPA. (n.d.). *Atlanta, GA turns Dixisteel into Atlantic Station*. US EPA Region 4.

Western Pennsylvania Brownfields Center. (2008). *Atlantic Station*. Carnegie Mellon University.

Interviews

Atlantic Station, Atlanta, Georgia

- Diamantides, M. (2010). Vice President and General Manager, Jones Lang LaSalle, Atlanta, GA.
- Dunn, B. S. (2010). External Relations, Transportation Planning Division, Atlanta Regional Commission, Atlanta, GA.
- Green, S. (2010). Senior Principal Operations Engineer, Georgia Regional Transportation Authority, Atlanta, GA.
- Leary, B (2010). President & CEO, Atlanta Beltline, Atlanta, GA.
- West, B. (2010). Environmental Scientist, Office of Environmental Assessment, Environmental Protection Agency, Atlanta, GA.
- Woodward, M. (2010). Deputy State Property Officer, Georgia State Financing and Investment Commission Construction Division, Georgia Building Authority, Georgia State Properties Commission.

South Waterfront, Portland, Oregon

- Abuaf, L. (2010). Development Manager, Portland Development Commission, Portland, OR.
- Bateschell, M. (2010). Senior Land Use Planner, Metro: Portland Metropolitan Area, Portland, OR.
- Bildersee, J. (2010). Brownfield Coordinator, City of Portland Brownfield Program, Portland, OR.
- Brown, M. (2010). Development Manager, Williams and Dame, Portland, OR.

- Gibb, M. (2010). Manager, Metro: Portland Metropolitan Area, Portland, OR.
- Mirk, S. (2010). Reporter, Portland Mercury, Portland, OR.
- Wilde, D. (2010). Architect, Gerding Edlen, Portland, OR.
- Williams, M. (2010). Associate Vice President, Campus Development and Administration, Oregon Health & Sciences University, Portland, OR.

Langdale and Riverdale Mills, city of Valley, Alabama

- Cato, M. (2010). City Clerk, City of Valley, AL.
- Jones, J. (2010). Executive Director, Valley Community Development Corporation, Valley, AL.

The Waterfront, Allentown, Pennsylvania

- Twiggar, A. (2009). Principal, Owner and Co-founder, Dunn Twiggar.

10 Brightfields

Commonly referred to as "brightfields," efforts to locate renewable energy facilities (solar, wind, landfill gas, or biomass) on brownfields have received increasing attention in the United States. While solar and wind remain the most common focus, the idea of producing energy crops for biomass on brownfields is also "growing." A primer on the subject by the National Association of Local Government Environmental Professionals in 2012 provides a comprehensive overview of renewable energy options, as well as tools for evaluating their economic feasibility and a review of issues regarding zoning, permitting, and liability. The US EPA's (2019) RE-Powering America's Land Initiative has also been instrumental in advancing and monitoring brightfields redevelopment, reporting in an October 2019 study 352 renewable energy projects on 327 contaminated properties, landfills, and mine sites. Also, 91% of these projects are solar, and 64% are on former landfills, with all projects generating a cumulative installed capacity of 1,710.2 megawatts. Massachusetts continues to lead the nation in siting solar on landfills and other brownfield sites with roughly one-third of all installations in the US. There are close to 200 others in various stages of development or have been suggested in public meetings (Trevizo, 2019).

Brockton Brightfield, Brockton, Massachusetts

Site History

The Brockton Brightfield is owned by the city of Brockton, Massachusetts. Located about 20 miles south of Boston, the city has an ethnically diverse population of approximately 95,000. It is home to Heavy-Weight Champion Rocky Marciano and the world's first centrally powered electrical station constructed by Thomas Edison in 1883, giving Brockton the nickname "city of Firsts" and "city of Champions." It is fitting, therefore, that one of the nation's first brightfields was constructed here and that the Brockton's Brightfield retained its title as New England's largest photovoltaic facility from when it was completed in 2006 to 2010.

The 3.7-acre brightfield is installed on a 27-acre parcel of land abutting an industrial area near the downtown core and is the site of the former Brockton Gas Works manufactured gas plant operated from 1898 until 1963 (Ribeiro, 2007). The community surrounding the current brightfield had a median annual household income below 65% of the statewide median, and a large portion of the local population was foreign-born or minority (Ribeiro,

2007). The community was also affected by substandard housing, abandoned buildings, crime, and high unemployment rates.

In 1989, following some investigative work by the Massachusetts Department of Environmental Quality Engineering, it was determined that the soil was contaminated with an array of VOCs, such as benzene, toluene, and xylene (Hersh, 2010). In 2000 the neighborhood, whose residents were already burdened by a demolition debris transfer station, a wastewater treatment plant, and a foundry, was declared a state Environmental Justice Area. A proposal to construct a tire-recycling plant provoked opposition in the community, and it was clear that a different path had to be taken to shake the city's emerging image as the "Commonwealth's dumping ground." Given that 97% of the city is built-up, redeveloping a brownfield was vital to the economic development of Brockton. The Bay State Gas Company is the property owner (on a 30-year lease) and one of several responsible parties.

Project Vision

According to Lori Ribeiro, who served as project director and wrote a thesis about the development, the city of Brockton started to take steps in the late 1990s to shed the negative image of the community. It developed an application for the US EPA's Sustainable Development Challenge Grant in 1999 proposing a virtual eco-industrial park with a place-based approach emphasizing its energy history. The city initiated its brownfield to brightfield project to develop a photovoltaic (PV) array as a Solar Energy Park in 2000 with the following goals and objectives: redevelop brownfields in an environmentally friendly manner; develop a new local and clean energy source for city use; expand the city tax base; enhance Brockton's image; attract PV manufacturers to Brockton; and to promote the "Brockton Solar Champions" concept and build on the "city of Champions" image by making Brockton the first place in the state to install PV (Ribeiro, 2007).

Inspired by a meeting with the stakeholders of the Chicago Brightfield at the Brownfields 2000 National Conference, the city initiated a feasibility study and a community outreach program to explore the possibility of constructing a brightfield in Brockton. In February 2001, the city submitted a proposal requesting $30,000 from the US Department of Energy to perform a feasibility study. True to its nickname, Brockton was the first (together with Hanford, WA, and Atlantic City, NJ) to be selected nationwide to receive a Department of Energy (DOE) Brightfield Funds Award. The feasibility study executed by XENERGY (now KEMA) concluded that out of the 27 acres, only 10 acres were developable due to slope and wetland concerns and that a 1 MW PV array would be technically feasible. It was recommended, however, that a 500 kW installation be constructed to produce 600 MWh/year at an estimated cost of $3.6 million. Upon further analysis, it was decided that a mounting structure that would not penetrate the 18-inch cap put into place as part of the site's remediation process (completed in 2004) would be optimal. Also, it was determined that city ownership of the facility would be more economically feasible than private ownership, as the latter was unlikely to be profitable. XENERGY also made it clear that site aesthetics were essential for garnering community support.

The first public meeting regarding the project was held at the end of 2001, and the city presented the site plans to residents emphasizing that the project would be unobtrusive, non-polluting, and noise-free. The community was primarily concerned with aesthetic components of the solar array (i.e., glare from the panels, height of the installation, security issues). These were addressed at a second public meeting held in September 2002, where a more detailed landscape plan of the project was presented with information on project size and characteristics, such as vegetation and fencing designs.

Project Characteristics and Development

Once the idea received public support, it was time to consider the financing and legal implications of implementing a brightfield. To that end, the project was designed in a revenue-neutral way, meaning that project revenues would need to cover the debt service on city bonds issued to finance the project, as well as any operations and maintenance costs, which were projected at $3.6 million (Hersh, 2010). City Council issued Municipal Bonds (debt) worth $1.6 million and sought to raise the remainder from state and federal grants. The lack of funding programs was one of many hurdles that the city had to overcome during the five-year-long process of seeking financing. Available grants and funding (i.e., DOE Solar and Brightfield Fund) emphasized education, planning, and community engagement, but did not fund construction and installation.

After lengthy negotiations and the implementation of an educational component into the project, Brockton was able to secure $1 million from the Massachusetts Technology Collaborative (MTC) via an unsolicited proposal with the aid of Mayor Jack Yunits, MTC Director of the Renewable Energy Trust, and partners in Washington DC, including then Senators Kerry and Kennedy. The $1 million MTC grant was approved, however, under the condition that the amount did not exceed 28% of the total project budget. Subsequently, the grant was reduced to $840,600, and the available budget went from $3.6 million to $3,048,678, which would only allow the installation of a 425 kW PV system. Fortunately, third-party Bay State Gas Co. agreed to buy back the parcel that they had donated 30 years prior for $500,000 (virtually eliminating the city's site liability) and volunteered to provide the fencing and landscaping necessary to secure community support (Hersh, 2010). In the end, the brightfield contains 1,512 solar modules, with a generating capacity of 465 kilowatts (kW) that can produce enough energy to power 77 homes (see Figure 10.1). Given the importance of education, the city also constructed the Thomas A. Edison Solar Energy Learning Plaza in 2006 at the facility's entrance.

The US EPA's Office of Solid Waste and Emergency Response (OSWER) notes that "a number of green power aggregators and marketers expressed interest in purchasing renewable energy certificates/credits (RECs) from the solar Brightfield at a significant premium above and beyond what could be offered by the local market in return for compliance with the state's renewable energy target" (OSWER, 2011). Normally, RECs are issued on short-term (1–5 years) contracts, but the project team wanted a contract that would last the term of the brightfield's debt service of 20 years. The city of Brockton entered a 20-year agreement with Constellation New Energy to sell RECs at variable rates of $180 per MWh for years 1–5, $180 per MWh for years 6–15 (backed by a 'put option' agreement between the city and the Massachusetts Green Power Partnership assigned to Constellation New Energy guaranteeing that RECs could be sold at that set price), and market value for the remainder of the contract (Hersh, 2010). The Massachusetts Green Power Partnership was an innovative program

230 *Brightfields*

Figure 10.1 Brockton Brightfield, Massachusetts

designed to support the construction of renewable energy facilities and was the largest of its kind in Massachusetts. Under the Partnership, the Massachusetts Renewable Energy Trust agreed to purchase energy certificates from renewable generators and sell them to both residential and commercial electricity consumers to ensure long-term financing.

Benefits, Barriers, and Lessons Learned

The Brockton Brightfield produces 580Mwh annually, and the 460-kW system reduces annual emissions by approximately 677,000 lbs of carbon dioxide, 1,200 lbs of sulfur oxide, and 315 lbs of nitrogen oxide (Ribeiro, 2009). Furthermore, the Brockton Brightfield emits no noise, odor and creates no additional traffic (see project timeline, Table 10.1).

Since the 1,512 solar modules were manufactured locally in Billerica, MA, the brightfield project also added to the state economy. More extensive community benefits include the enhancement of local property values, educational opportunities for children and the public, and perhaps most important, a shift in the city's image away from a "dumping ground" back to an innovative city of firsts. Since education was a vital component in the procurement of capital, the city decided to create a Solar Energy Park featuring an educational display, which highlights the technology used as well as the economic development and benefits for Brockton. The city also organized scheduled tours of the site and community days and school trips.

A series of setbacks were responsible for delaying the Brightfield project, which took six years from conception to completion. One of the primary ones is common to many of the case studies analyzed thus far, which is the barriers to innovation imposed by a rigid regulatory framework, whether local, state, or federal. In this case, an interviewee noted that "first, it learned that Brockton, or any city or town in the Commonwealth, could not obtain a 20-year bond because, under the relevant sections of the state's enabling legislation addressing renewable energy projects, a city was limited to issuing a 10-year bond" (Hersh, 2010). This meant that the revenue-neutral design was jeopardized at least for the first ten years. Moreover, the city's legal counsel declared that the city did not have the authority to own a PV facility under the current state legislation. Faced with these added hurdles, the city drafted a revision of the state legislation that would issue them the proper authority to develop, finance, and own a solar-power-generating facility. The bill was approved by the state house and senate and signed into law by then-Governor Mitt Romney in February of 2005 (Hersh, 2010). The new law enabled the city to issue 20-year bonds and follow through with the original design of a revenue-neutral project.

The acquisition of funds, particularly for innovative projects whose outcomes fall outside of the neat jobs and development metrics preferred by most agencies, is another common barrier that affected the Brockton project. The project was financed, in large part, by the use of RECs and the so-called solar carve-out, which is a concept that requires utility companies to buy a certain proportion of their power from owners of qualified solar systems via special solar renewable energy credits (SRECs) (Hersh, 2010). The state of Massachusetts initiated a solar carve-out program in 2010 to support distributed solar energy facilities including residential, commercial, public, and non-profit projects, and to help the Commonwealth achieve the installation of 400 MW of solar PV across the state (Massachusetts Department of Energy Resources, 2013). An interviewee noted that "the credits have a price floor of $300 per MWh, nearly ten times the price of other renewable energy credits utilities must buy . . . If utilities are unable to comply with the requirements of the carve-out through SREC purchases, they are required to pay an alternative compliance payment (ACP) of $600 per MWh . . . In other words, the ACP price serves as a price ceiling for the Massachusetts SREC market" (Hersh, 2010). Early funding through the DOE seed funds was also essential to develop a more sustainable vision. Massachusetts' Renewable Energy Portfolio Standards began with an obligation of one percent in 2003 and then increased by one-half percent annually until it reached 4% in 2009 (Bolgen, 2009). It should be noted that the brightfields and solar market in Massachusetts hit a bump in 2016 when the state limited the amount of solar energy that public and private customers could sell back to the energy grid. While a compromise was reached to let many planned projects continue, including a proposed solar field on Brockton's former Thatcher Street landfill that opened in 2017, it did generate concerns about the market's future (Wickedlocal, 2016).

A third barrier suggested in the literature and by interviewees was the challenge associated with the decentralization of energy production in a system that is accustomed to and built for centralized production and distribution. Decentralized or distributed energy generation produces energy in closer proximity to consumers, compared to conventional, larger power plants, thus reducing transmission loss/costs, and includes PV, solar, small wind turbines, fuel cells, etc. In addition to the obstacle of creating new legal structures that allow for

Table 10.1 Timeline – Brockton Brightfields, Massachusetts (based on Ribeiro, 2006)

Year	Description
2000	Concept Development: Research, Support (Mayor, Council and Planning), Grants (DOE, MTC)
2001–2002	Feasibility Studies: Overall concept, technical, financial, community support, ownership options, engineering, project concept development plan
2003	Pre-development: Additional funding, partnership development, marketing, community relations, turnkey vendor RFP
2004	City Council Approvals: Grant acceptance, land transaction, enterprise fund, Home Rule petition to develop, finance, operate and maintain and Home Rule petition to convey land, debt financing, contracts
2005	State Legislation: Home rule petition to develop, finance, operate and maintain and Home Rule petition to convey land
2006	Design and Installation: Procurement, vendor selection, finalization grant agreements, finalize contracts, design, permitting construction, commissioning

local ownership and access to tax incentives, smaller energy facilities historically experience more significant challenges in securing enough capital.

As with many sustainability projects, Brockton overcame these barriers through the sheer perseverance of project champions from government and the citizenry, as well as intense community pressure for change and progress. By 2009, the Brockton Brightfield has been able to generate nearly $145,000 in annual revenue for the city, which went towards paying off the cost to build and maintain the brightfield. It was estimated that the loan would be paid off in full by 2026, and the city will begin to profit from the sale of RECs and electricity directly. The brightfield had a module warranty of 20 years, and with an expected system life of 30 to 50 years, the city should see profits for 10 to 30 years.

Holmes Road/Sunnyside Landfill, Houston, Texas

Site History

The 240-acre Holmes Road Landfill, also known as the Sunnyside Landfill, is situated ten minutes from downtown Houston, Texas, and was closed and later capped by the city sometime in the 1970s (US EPA, 2009) (see Figure 10.2). Adjacent to the site, to the northeast, lies the Sunnyside Community Center, Sunnyside Park, a police station, and a library. Closed landfill inventory reports from the Houston-Galveston Area Council (H-GAC) indicate that the Holmes Road Landfill was used "for disposal of brush, construction and demolition debris, household waste, industrial waste, tires and scrap" (SRA International, 2008, p. 7). The property was a principal city dumping ground and home to Houston's largest incinerator. Despite several proposals to redevelop the land, including one for a municipal golf course, the site remained unused until the mid-2000s, when the city began to explore the feasibility of the project summarized in this case study (US EPA, 2008). Native species of vegetation have reclaimed the vacant landfill owned by the city during the elapsed time (US EPA, 2009).

A mix of activities surrounds the Holmes Road brownfield, including several other landfills, Houston's basketball and football stadiums, an old Six Flags amusement park, industrial

Figure 10.2 Holmes Road/Sunnyside Landfill, Houston, Texas (Google Earth, n.d.)

lots, and residential neighborhoods. The residential community in closest proximity to the brownfield has a higher proportion of African Americans compared to other residential communities in the city. Indeed, the Holmes Road landfill and other landfills and incinerators in Houston feature prominently in Robert Bullard's seminal research on environmental justice (Bullard, 1994). Bullard points out that from the mid-1920s to the late 1970s, a form of de facto zoning resulted in all five (or 100 percent) city-owned municipal landfills being located in well-established African American neighborhoods. A riot in 1967 at Texas Southern University was precipitated by the death of an 11-year-old boy in a ditch on the fenceless Holmes Road Dump. Given this history, efforts to revitalize it would benefit from an approach that is socially, economically, and environmentally sustainable.

Project Vision

The city of Houston recognized that the size and location of the former Holmes Road Landfill presented several opportunities for redevelopment. An interviewee revealed that a preliminary plan (for 300 acres) was put forward to redevelop the former landfill into three sections, each with a separate land use: a 100-acre 10 megawatts (MW) solar farm; a 100-acre park that would connect to the existing municipal park (Sunnyside Park); and a 100-acre botanical garden. A $50,000 EPA Pilot grant was provided to the city to help finance the technical assistance required to determine the project's feasibility (US EPA, 2008).

Although Houston considers itself to be the energy capital of the country, the city wanted to diversify its energy portfolio to include more renewables as a hedge against the price volatility of conventional energy sources (SRA International, 2008). Interest in developing a solar farm was motivated by an internal dialogue between the city's seven divisions concerning issues of energy efficiency and renewable energy production. A confluence of favorable factors made the Holmes Road Landfill an ideal location for the solar farm that was being envisioned. The city owned the land, it was underutilized, was of substantial size, and, like the city in general, it received plenty of sunshine.

In addition to being an optimal location for a solar farm, the city was further motivated by the external benefits that redeveloping the land into a solar farm would produce. The city anticipated that the brownfield redevelopment would improve local and regional environmental quality and resident safety, promote the site's heritage, and highlight the city's sustainability efforts at a highly visible location. Developing a solar farm on the landfill would also support local economic development objectives by providing Houston with the opportunity to enter the emerging solar energy market (US EPA, 2008, 2009).

Project Characteristics and Development

The city presented its vision to redevelop the Holmes Road Landfill to the EPA and, in turn, secured technical assistance for the redevelopment through the EPA's Brownfields Sustainability Pilots program. The technical assistance offered by the EPA's provider, SRA, included an on-site photovoltaic project assessment; regulatory assessment; site engineering assessment; determination of PV system size, conceptual design elements, and specifications; development of installed cost estimates for the solar farm; and economic analysis of the proposed solar farm's characteristics (SRA International, 2008).

The analysis began with a site visit to the brownfield by both SRA and city of Houston staff in August 2008. The team noted that while the site was visible from the road, it was not accessible by car. Accessibility by foot was also limited due to the vegetation that had reclaimed the place. Despite the limited access, several important observations were made which prompted SRA to recommend the southern half of the landfill for solar farm development, including:

- the identification of a high capacity "distribution line, parallel to Reed Road, on the southern edge of the property"(SRA International, 2008, p. 4);
- given that solar panels need to be oriented southward and the absence of solar obstructions on the southern portion of the brownfield, it makes sense to locate them there;
- the solar panels will be highly visible to the public on the southern edge and provide an added public relations benefit;
- finally, siting the solar farm on the southern edge of the brownfield will eliminate the need to clear the "natural boundary of trees and overgrowth" in the northern portion (SRA International, 2008, p. 4).

The preliminary engineering report, prepared by SRA, considered the design, type, and weight of a photovoltaic system against the brownfield's history and physical characteristics. Two constraints were identified, including redeveloping the site without penetrating the soil cap into the waste area (SRA International, 2008, p. 12); and differential settlement, which refers to the uneven settling of waste material below the landfill cap affecting the weight load restrictions of surface development.

The preliminary engineering report maintained that preparing the landfill for redevelopment would require clearing, filling, grading, and compacting the site. The overgrown vegetation and trees would need to be cleared without disturbing the landfill cap or exposing the buried waste material. This is complicated by the fact that the soil cap is deeper in some places than others. The site would subsequently need to be graded and filled to achieve a uniform cap depth at a minimum of four feet (SRA International, 2008, p. 22). Finally, compacting the site would ensure a solid base for the solar infrastructure and mitigate potential settlement at the newly filled and graded site (SRA International, 2008, p. 12). SRA's preliminary engineering report "recommended that the site be developed with fixed tilt (30 degrees) mounting structures employing amorphous thin-film panels . . . This system type and design will have the least impact on the landfill site, and require the least amount of mitigation of the site during the project development" (SRA International, 2008, p. 14). SRA also calculated an approximate footprint for the solar farm based on the recommended technology and its technical requirements. The development of a 10 MW solar farm on the former landfill would require 150 acres, or 50 more acres than the amount initially envisioned by the city (SRA International, 2008, p. 15). With the aid of solar modeling software (PVWATTS), SRA estimated that the proposed 10 MW solar farm would generate approximately 12,526,260 kWh of electricity a year, which represents one percent of the city's yearly energy demand (SRA International, 2008, p. 17).

The regulatory analysis of the brownfield was subcontracted to Tetra Tech, who surveyed the applicable federal, state, regional, and local solid waste legislation and approval agencies pertaining to the project. Tetra Tech determined that since the proposed development is not an "enclosed structure," many of the legislative rules do not apply to the project or are applicable in certain situations only (SRA International, 2008, p. 8). Rule §330.953 of the TAC Chapter 330, Subchapter T, mandates soil testing based on the project's objectives. However, this rule appears to have been satisfied by the environmental assessment performed by Terracon in 2006. Tetra Tech's final recommendation to the city was to carefully consider the TAC Chapter 330 rules and that an authorization request to the TCEQ is necessary given that the landfill cap will be cleared, graded, filled, and compacted and, therefore, may be partially disturbed or penetrated during redevelopment (SRA International, 2008, p. 21).

The city of Houston planned to contract the design, construction, and maintenance of the solar farm to a third-party supplier and buy the renewable energy via a long-term power purchase agreement through its electricity provider, Reliant Energy (SRA International, 2008). As such, the technical report by SRA also analyzed the economic scenarios that would benefit the city under this arrangement, particularly how much money it would save. Three cost scenarios (low, medium, and high) provided by SRA indicated that while the city will be paying more for electricity generated by solar power than conventional sources, in the long run, the city can save money (SRA International, 2008, pp. 19, 20). Shortly after the technical report prepared by SRA International and funded by the EPA was submitted to the city of Houston highlighting the technical feasibility of the envisioned solar farm, the city put out a request for proposals (RFP). The cost to do this work was estimated to be about $7,000 per acre (Trevizo, 2019).

In September 2009, NRG Energy Inc. (NRG) was awarded the contract to design, build and maintain the solar farm, after which a long-term power purchase agreement between the city and NRG would be established (US EPA, 2009). As part of their RFP bid, NRG proposed an alternate location for the solar farm (on NRG-owned land), rather than the intended Holmes Road Landfill site, which accounted for a cost reduction in the bid (Bourg, 2009). The city effectually abandoned the plan to redevelop the landfill when the contract was awarded to NRG.

In 2016, the city proposed plans for combining the existing Sunnyside Multi-Service Center and Sunnyside Health Center into a single, new, $25 million, 60,000 square-foot facility to be constructed adjacent to the landfill (Trevizo, 2019). Citizens fought the idea, however, because they preferred the Center's existing location and for fear about the contamination. Even though the city maintained the site was environmentally safe, it scrapped the plan in 2018 (Harden, 2018).

In 2017, the Mayor of Houston joined C40 Reinventing Cities, a global competition for innovative carbon-free and resilient urban projects. In 2019, the Mayor announced that Sunnyside Energy (a partnership between EDF Renewables, MP2-Shell, and Wolfe Energy) won the competition with the idea of repurposing the former Holmes landfill into one of the largest urban solar farms in Texas and one of the largest brightfields in the country (Renewable Energy World, 2019). According to the project description, once the "methane leaking landfill" is remediated, the Sunnyside Energy Project will consist of the following four components. First, the Sunnyside Energy Solar Farm (200 acres) will be a large-scale, ballasted commercial solar array of approximately 70 MW (enough to supply 12,000 homes in Houston) complete with bioretention areas, integrated biking and walking path, an electric vehicle charging station, and battery backup for the nearby Sunnyside Community Center (Reinventing Cities, 2019). Houston Renewable Energy will provide solar installation training at Sunnyside Community Center, and graduates will have an advantage in securing a job constructing the solar farm. In addition to solar power, a bio-digester and battery storage will contribute to the energy performance, and the project aims to achieve carbon-positive status by year five. Second, a two-acre Agricultural Hub and Training Center will provide space for a community-driven aquaponic greenhouse, beekeeping, bio-remediation, and a training center. Third, Sunnyside Community Solar (12 acres) will allow city residents and non-profits to benefit from local solar energy for their homes and businesses and will provide discounts for low-income residents. Lastly, Sunnyside Energy Trust will consist of a local board of trustees to guide project decisions and manage funds raised in part through an annual allocation from the Solar Farm.

The next steps, as outlined by the city of Houston, will be to work with Wolfe Energy to complete the financial and environmental feasibility, finalize the design plan with community input, and negotiate contract lease terms for the site (city of Houston, 2019). The project is expected to begin in 2021, contingent on the lining up of investors.

It should be noted that increasing the use of solar power is a key component of Houston's Climate Action Plan, and it is estimated that about 92 percent of the electricity used by the city to operate its facilities comes from solar and wind sources, making it the largest municipal user of renewable energy in the nation. In April 2020, the Mayor announced that Houston has committed to purchasing 100% renewable energy to power all municipal operations (city of Houston, 2019).

Benefits, Barriers, and Lessons Learned

The motivation to redevelop the former Holmes Road Landfill into a solar farm was based on several projected benefits, including diversifying the city's energy portfolio, converting underutilized space into a sustainable land-use, local economic development, and community revitalization (see project timeline Table 10.2). While the first three benefits were touched upon in this case study, it was not evident in the initial proposal how the city planned to achieve the last one. Back in 2009, the EPA stated that "frequent communication between stakeholders . . . was essential to achieve positive results" (US EPA, 2009). The stakeholders identified in this case were the city of Houston, the state of Texas, the EPA, and the consultants. It is interesting to note that based on the projected benefits, the local community and surrounding residents were not considered to be stakeholders and were not included in the project's visioning or feasibility processes. To be a truly sustainable project the social impacts should have been considered alongside the economic and environmental ones. Public backlash leading to failed plans for building a new Sunnyside Multi-Service and Health Center and Sunnyside Health Center on the site also speaks to a lack of early consultation. It is hoped that the current solar farm proposal will achieve community buy-in, even though it is not clear the extent of community involvement in establishing the terms for the competition.

While there were few barriers identified as the brightfields project was being envisioned, constraints and challenges increased as the project progressed. The physical limitations presented by the landfill's uneven cap and differential settlement pattern, however, could be addressed by clearing, grading, filling, and compacting the site as well as in the design

Table 10.2 Timeline – Holmes Road/Sunnyside Landfill, Houston, Texas

Year	Description
September 1970	Holmes Road Landfill is closed according to the City of Houston records
Mid-1970s	Holmes Road Landfill is closed according to the State of Texas records
1970s to present	Vacant and unused
September 2006	City of Houston contracts an environmental site investigation to Terracon
August 2008	SRA International traveled to Houston; performs site visit
October 2008	Site visit and technical report recommending brightfield provided to City of Houston by SRA and EPA
September 2009	Plan to redevelop landfill abandoned in favor of alternate site
November 2009	Public private partnership between the City of Houston and NRG Energy Inc., suspended indefinitely
2016	City proposal to combine the existing Sunnyside Multi-Service Center and Sunnyside Health Center into a single facility on the site rejected by the community
2019	Mayor announces that Sunnyside Energy won a competition with the idea of repurposing the former landfill into an urban solar farm to commence in 2021

consideration of the solar PV infrastructure. Even so, economic factors initially appeared to have been more important than the projected benefits, resulting in the original plan being shelved. The initial effort, however, lit a path for the current project proposal, which seems to offer even more sustainability and community benefits.

References

Bourg, J. (2009). *Renewable energy on contaminated lands: Solar feasibility study for the Holmes Road landfill, Houston, TX (PPT Webinar)*. December 1, Presentation by Joe Bourg, SRA International for Vita Nuova Sustainability Series.

Bullard, R. D. (1994). The legacy of American apartheid and environmental racism. *Journal of Civil Rights and Economic Development*, 9(2), 445–474.

City of Houston. (2019). The city of Houston selects firm proposing solar energy farm at former Sunnyside landfill. Office of the Mayor, Green Houston. https://cityofhouston.news/the-city-of-houston-selects-firm-proposing-solar-energy-farm-at-former-sunnyside-landfill/

Google Earth. (n.d.). Holmes Road/Sunnyside Landfill. 29°39'58" N and 95°22'23" W. December 4, 2020.

Harden, J. D. (2018) Houston officials back off placing new Sunnyside center near former landfill. February 9, *Houston Chronicle*.

Hersh, R. (2010). *Promoting solar power on brownfields in Brockton, Massachusetts*. Center for Public Environmental Oversight.

Massachusetts Department of Energy Resources (2013) *Task 3a Report: Evaluation of the 400 MW solar carve-out program's success in meeting objectives*. September 30. Report prepared by Cadmus, Meister Consultants Group, and Sustainable Energy Advantage, LLC.

OSWER. (2011). Brockton brightfields: Innovative green power renewed life to a brownfield site, Innovation pilot results fact sheet. *ReFocus*, 47 (March/April).

Reinventing Cities. (2019). *Sunnyside landfill: Houston, United States*. July 3. Reinventing Cities.

Renewable Energy World. (2019). Solar array in revitalization plan. September 3. Renewable Energy World.

Ribeiro, L. (2006). *Does it have to be so complicated? Municipal renewable energy projects in Massachusetts* [Unpublished Master's thesis]. Massachusetts Institute of Technology, Dept. of Urban Studies and Planning.

Ribeiro, L. (2007). Waste to watts: A "brightfield" installation has the potential to bring renewed life to a brownfield site. *Refocus*, 8(2), 46–49.

SRA International. (2008). *Technical assistance: Solar power analysis and design specifications* (Report Contract No. EP-W-07-023). US EPA Brownfields Program.

Trevizo, P. (2019). Hopes rise that proposed solar farm will transform former Sunnyside landfill site. October 4, *Houston Chronicle*.

US EPA. (2008). *Brownfields sustainability pilot fact sheet, Houston solar project* (Report EPA-560-F-08-269). US EPA Office of Solid Waste and Emergency Response.

US EPA. (2009). *Brownfields sustainability pilots, solar power on closed landfill in Houston* (Report EPA-560-F-09-505). US EPA Office of Solid Waste and Emergency Response.

US EPA. (2019). RE-powering America's land initiative: Tracking completed projects on contaminated lands, landfills, and mine sites, October 2019. US EPA Office of Communications, Partnerships, and Analysis, Office of Land and Emergency Management.

Wickedlocal. (2016). Legislation paves way for more solar projects. April 9, *Wickedlocal*.

Interviews

Brockton Brightfield, Brockton, Massachusetts

- Bolgen, N. (2009). Program Director, Clean Energy, MA Technology Park Corp. Brockton, Massachusetts.
- Gurley, P. (2009). Administrative Assistant to the Planning Board and Conservation Commission, city of Brockton, MA.

- Harrington, J. (2009). Mayor, city of Brockton, MA.
- Landerholm, C. (2009). President, Landerholm Electric Company, city of Brockton, MA.
- Moskal, J. (2009). US Environmental Protection Agency, Region 1, New England, Energy and Climate Unit.
- Ribeiro, L. (2009) Brightfields Project Director, Blue Wave Strategies, Boston, MA.

Holmes Road/Sunnyside Landfill, Houston, Texas

- Dadoush, I. (2009). Director of General Services Department, city of Houston, TX.

11 Project Characteristics and Lessons Learned

This chapter provides a brief synthesis of all of the case studies examined in the previous chapters in relation to project procedures, characteristics, sustainability features planned/implemented, obstacles, benefits, and lessons learned. The Cleveland Resource Recovery pilot, which was more of a research project on decommissioning residential structures, and the Community Center Rooftop Garden in Oklahoma, which was terminated quickly due to technical factors, have also been included where appropriate for a total of 16 Pilots and 10 BMPs. The analysis takes into consideration the results from interviews conducted with project coordinators at the outset of the research project and the updates made since. The discussion below is organized according to the development process to make it easier to follow.

Motivation, Visioning, and Leadership

A significant contributor to the shift in brownfields' perception as sites of risk and liability to spaces of redevelopment opportunity was visioning and leadership from government officials along with concerned stakeholders and community residents. So, it comes as no surprise that public sector agencies at the local level took the lead in over half of the sustainable brownfield development cases examined (14), followed by non-profits (8), and the private sector (4). The EPA's Sustainable Brownfields Pilots are led mainly by the public (9) or non-profit (5) sectors (only 2 private-sector), while BMPs are a tad more balanced (public 5, non-profit 3, private-sector 2).

When asked back in 2009 and 2010 why these sites were selected for redevelopment, project coordinators' most common justifications were rather conventional for brownfields, including a desire to stimulate local development activity and repurpose blighted, underutilized, or vacant property. Less than a fifth mentioned the creation of green space, and only a couple highlighted a desire to improve public health or address environmental justice concerns. Other common responses focused on an array of standard real estate issues, such as the location's marketability, land supply and demand, and the project's ties to larger development initiatives. Indeed, the vision for many of these projects began to materialize long before activity commenced in the late 2000s, with eight originating in the 2000s, nine in the 1990s, and planning efforts in Boston's Jackson Square and Portland's South Waterfront reaching back to the late 1970s. Project coordinators noted that pre-existing neighborhood plans informed the visions for about a third of the cases (e.g., the Granary District in Salt Lake

City, Portland Central City Plan). Concepts for almost half of the projects were informed by the general public, as well as by private and non-profit sector proponents and other groups (e.g., coalitions of community groups, business groups, consultants), by way of meetings and the development of preliminary design guidelines, guiding principles, charrettes, or citizen surveys.

Interest in incorporating sustainable and green elements also typically originated from the public sector for over half of the projects. It was either put forth as an essential project objective or mandated as part of a public-private partnership. While the EPA had a direct hand in seeding sustainability for the Pilots, research revealed that it also encouraged several BMPs to incorporate sustainability by incentivizing it, as in the Menomonee Valley, or requiring it, as in Atlantic Station. Strong mayoral support for innovative development was also crucial in some cases, as seen in Chicago with Mayor Daley's push for green building, Milwaukee Mayor Norquist's interest in New Urbanism, and New York Mayor Bloomberg's interest in parks. Unfortunately, very few of the cases are led by private-sector developers keen on design innovation from the outset, like at Montgomery Park, which worryingly speaks to tepid interest from most in the development community along with the consumers they serve. Interestingly, while attitudes toward greening are typically favorable, many of the brownfield to park developments examined in this book also emerged due to an adverse reaction from the community to alternative proposals. Hence, cities in those cases become reactionary proponents.

The push to advance a sustainable brownfield project vision was, for a third of the projects, in reaction to a site-specific issue, opportunity, or dilemma (e.g., Oregon Health and Science University considering relocation or expansion in South Waterfront). A quarter of them responded to community pressure (i.e., lack of park space, adversity to another proposal, encroachment of other activities). Only a fifth emerged of a proponent's own volition. Additional motivations for sustainability expressed by coordinators included abiding with regulatory requirements, the availability of public funding support, and the opportunity to reduce capital and operating costs. Interestingly, when asked if there was any opposition to the project visions initially, over two-thirds of coordinators noted concern over public costs, pollution, the proposed end-use, sustainability requirements, and potential traffic, particularly those involved in Pilots. While all stakeholders expressed these concerns, private-sector partners were particularly worried about the extra cost associated with sustainable design (e.g., green building, landscaping, infrastructure) and the potential loss of opportunity from sustainable reuse options (e.g., green vs developable space, affordable vs market-rate housing, for-profit vs non-profit use).

Lesson: *Key project drivers continue to focus on stimulating local development and making brownfield sites more attractive through blight removal, new construction, adaptive reuse, and greening (sustainability, green building, and environmental justice considerations are not primary motivators).*

Lesson: *Public leadership is essential for advancing sustainability in brownfield redevelopment. In most BMPs led by public and private partners, sustainability was a response to a government objective (e.g., Chicago Center for Green Tech, Brockton Brightfield) or requirement*

(South Waterfront, Atlantic Station), while for some BMPs and most Pilots, sustainability ideas were seeded early on by government incentives (e.g., EPA funds to the Pilots, Menomonee Valley).

Lesson: Sustainability is facilitated when early visioning activities address the objectives of multiple stakeholders and community members, which also helps form a coalition of supporters.

Lesson: Most projects faced concerns and barriers typically associated with brownfield projects, with private sector partners expressing some concern regarding extra costs and the perceived loss of opportunity associated with sustainability measures.

Location, Market, and Reuse

The majority of the brownfields slated for redevelopment were originally industrial parcels (17) or commercial/retail sites (8), followed by a few landfills, offices, and residential spaces. About a third of them were mixed-use, with BMPs more likely to be industrial or industrial/mixed and Pilots industrial/mixed or commercial/retail. Interestingly, many of these sites are not located in the downtown core, but just near it, in mid-town locations, or outside the central city. Thus, their blight and opportunity are visible, but they often need public support to be viable, with sustainability tied to that support. The downside of the locations is that most projects are automobile-oriented despite efforts to encourage alternative transportation.

In terms of the proposed new land-uses, 18 of the projects involved developing a publicly accessible park, open space, or trail (five as the sole use and the remainder as a component of the project). Half involved commercial (retail/office) development and slightly less than half residential (9), typically in combination as 11 were mixed-use. Institutional uses, including some form of community center or space, were a component of about a third of the projects. Some of this space is managed by a non-profit (e.g., Commercial Street, Delta House) and some community spaces or acivities were lost with a change of use or cut in funding (e.g., CCGT, Jackson Square, Tabor Commons, Moran Plant). Two projects focus mainly on solar power generation. Despite being the most common previous use, manufacturing remains core to only the Menomonee Valley. Most Pilots incorporate some public open space or trail (11), and those that don't often contain green space for site users that can be informally accessed (e.g., Tabor Common and Delta House) or were on main streets that had park space (e.g., Focus Hope, Commercial Street). Pilots were similar in terms of commercial, residential, and community uses, while most of the BMPs became offices and provide public open space (7) and some residential use (3).

Lesson: Understanding the local market is essential, particularly in secondary markets near and outside the downtown core. Projects in these markets may have more difficulty attracting tenants/development, leading some to be delayed and others to change use.

Lesson: Redevelopment projects must be mindful of the market viability of planned new uses. Unless the proposed use is public, the government should target their support to private and non-profit projects that are economically and operationally viable in order to realize both brownfields and sustainability objectives.

Lesson: Reindustrialization is a challenge, and most redevelopment will focus on office, retail, or residential use, or public services associated with green space or community facilities.

Lesson: Greening is and can be an aspect of virtually all brownfield projects, regardless of end-use.

Land Acquisition and Assembly

These projects' total land area is just over 4000 acres with an average size of 182 acres and a median of 23.5 acres. BMPs are typically larger properties and mixed-use (e.g., Freshkills 2200 acres, Menomonee Valley 1200 acres, Atlantic Station 138 acres), while many Pilots are smaller (e.g., Delta House 0.4 acres, Tabor Commons 0.3 acres). Most of the brownfields were owned by private entities (20), with a few primarily under public ownership (4). While many of the brownfields were acquired via a willing sale (15), just under half involved government intervention supporting acquisition through eminent domain (3) or other arrangements (7) (e.g., US Marshalls, Public Trust Doctrine, a land donation to city, donation of public streets). As mentioned, local governments also acquired some of the park projects after an adverse public reaction to an alternative proposal.

Lesson: Government, particularly at the local level, plays an important role in land acquisition and assembly of privately owned parcels, as well as the inclusion of publicly owned ones, which provides leverage for encouraging sustainable reuse.

Planning

Preliminary planning and design activities that laid the foundation for many of these projects took place over a one- to three-year period starting in the late 1990s and early 2000s running into the mid/late 2000s. While this was similar for both Pilots and BMPs, plans for several of the latter focused on the first phase of a multi-phase redevelopment process. At this stage, most engaged in consultation to inform planning and design with citizen advisory committees or other groups (16), which was expected as part of the EPA's Pilot funding. Most BMPs incorporated public consultation (7) along with participation from private-sector groups (6) and non-profits (5). Large-scale consulting and development firms played a role in planning and advancing many of the projects. Indeed, the core objective of the EPA's Pilot funding was for large national/international technology and engineering consulting firms such as SRA International and Tetra Tech to provide technical assistance to inform planning, design, deconstruction, and other activities. As mentioned, the EPA also played a role in supporting and shaping sustainability in the planning and design of BMPs such as Atlantic Station and Menomonee Valley. An interesting observation is the role of local architecture and planning schools and some student research in advancing sustainable redevelopment at some of the BMPs and Pilots (e.g., Menomonee Valley, Tabor, Delta House, Atlantic Station), as well as professional Architectural associations (CCGT) and keen professionals interested in trying out something new and innovative (e.g., Heifer International, Delta House).

Lesson: *Advancing sustainable innovation can benefit from the support and technical expertise of the federal government, national/international consulting service firms, universities, and professional associations.*

Lesson: *Sustainable brownfield development benefits from being accompanied by planning and design actions that establish a comprehensive vision and plan for the initiative, a detailed roadmap for undertaking it, and, if broad in scope, a viable catalytic project to start it off.*

Lesson: *Visions and plans work best when they incorporate community input, tie into an area-wide vision and plan for the neighborhood, and contribute to achieving multiple stakeholder and community objectives. As such, sustainable brownfield development benefits from public and stakeholder buy-in, public-private partnership, and intergovernmental cooperation.*

Site Preparation (Remediation, Building Rehab, Infrastructure)

All projects involving assessment and remediation activities went through the appropriate state voluntary cleanup programs. The public sector played a central role in overseeing, supporting, and funding cleanup. The sites were most commonly affected by petroleum hydrocarbons and metals, followed by asbestos, metalloids (arsenic), and non-hazardous waste materials like construction debris and litter, or a combination of these. The management of contamination was relatively conventional, with many projects involving material and soil removal (11), caps (7), demolition (6), material recycling (4), UST removal (4), groundwater treatment (1) (other at 5). Many BMPs involved soil removal (8) and over half also involved a mix of other techniques. In large projects, governments were involved in the remediation of public property while also supporting the cleanup of individual parcels as they were redeveloped. They also built public infrastructure to make projects accessible, focusing on roads and bridges for automobile and truck access and transit, bicycle, and pedestrian infrastructure. Green infrastructure is also a key focus of many BMPs and Pilots, bringing together stormwater management, ecological enhancement, aesthetic improvement, and public access and use.

Half of the projects involve building restoration and adaptive reuse (two-thirds of Pilots, one-third of BMPs). While heritage value and aesthetics matter for some projects (e.g., Montgomery Park, Langdale Mills), many of the reused buildings were not architecturally spectacular and included former gas stations, office buildings, and power facilities. That said, the high cost to make structures safe for reuse and the high cost/low resale value of deconstruction often makes demolition the only viable option, even for buildings with perceived cultural value.

Lesson: *While states are primarily responsible for regulating cleanup, many government agencies at various government levels are involved in funding the remediation of public and private spaces.*

Lesson: *While some more sustainable/green remediation techniques such as capping, material recovery, and institutional controls were used to reduce waste and address pollution, the application of sustainable remediation practices, including more innovative techniques (e.g., phytoremediation and bioremediation), were not highly demanded by developers, stakeholders, or the general public.*

Lesson: *Adaptive reuse is an option for many older buildings, not just those with heritage value, but the decision to reuse, deconstruct, or demolish must still be based on sound fiscal principles.*

Funding and Financing

Regardless of whether the projects are small or large, the role of the public sector in providing financial support was vital for most aspects and phases of the sustainable brownfield projects examined. This is particularly evident when a project lies in a more peripheral or secondary market location where it is hoped that it will cleanup past blight, add new infrastructure, and spark change. Despite making best efforts to track project funding, it is always a challenge given the multiple levels of government and stakeholders involved, the array of funding methods (i.e., grants, loans, in-kind donations, infrastructure, capital, operations, etc.), project duration, the number of parcels/sub-development at more extensive projects, and issues of transparency. Larger projects such as Portland's South Waterfront in the North Macadam Urban Renewal Area and the Menomonee Valley pursued and creatively assembled funding from numerous sources. TIF represented about a quarter of the estimated $200 million in public funds invested in the Menomonee Valley, slightly over half of the public funding invested in South Waterfront, and virtually all for Atlantic Station. Large singular developments like Montgomery Park also pieced together funds from an array of public and private sources, with 45% coming from the private sector, 15% from public sector loans, and the remainder from an assortment of public grants and tax credits. Needless to say, public projects require public funding for the entire project, but here too, funds are sometimes derived from municipal and other public sources. Interestingly, Heifer International stands out for receiving very little financial support from the public for its new headquarters building, which was supported by a capital campaign expressly set up for building construction, along with low-interest loans.

The financial stories for the Pilots are much more difficult to untangle, given their variability. Both Delta House and Tabor Commons in Portland, for instance, received substantial funds from an array of public sources, private donors, and volunteer support. Whether they are public use projects like the Moran Plant and Haynes Recreation Center, or aim to address barriers and provide public infrastructure to leverage private development like Anvil Mountain, Langdale, and The Waterfront, cities assumed considerable financial risk and investment to advance these projects, sometimes with support from other levels of government. Pilots targeting weaker market and lower-income areas to address environmental and social justice issues have been incredibly creative at piecing together funds and incrementally working through projects. Boston's Jackson Square provides a hopeful case of what can happen when established non-profits, private developers, and government units come together with robust funding programs and sustainability policies to support affordability, justice, and green building goals.

While it is clear that sustainability visions and elements benefit from public support, it is essential that the projects themselves are economically viable and supported, otherwise the whole thing is a no go. Other than green space elements, sustainability features and efforts touted early on sometimes fell by the wayside when projects found themselves struggling to move forward, especially private and publicly led ones. Many Pilots have been delayed and or lowered their original sustainability expectations due to financial issues and the fear that high development expectations might scare away private partners (e.g., Green Avenue, Commercial Street, Allen Morrison, The Waterfront, Langdale and Riverdale Mills, Anvil Mountain, Samoa Peninsula, Moran Plant, Houston Solar). At BMPs too, public investment combined with planning requirements, stakeholder and community involvement, and continued political support is often essential for keeping sustainability priorities alive over the long term despite the ongoing pushback (e.g., CCGT, Menomonee Valley, South Waterfront, and Atlantic Station).

Lesson: *Public funding must be pursued and creatively assembled from numerous sources to address the many cost barriers that impede brownfield redevelopment and sustainability elements related to green development, affordable housing, and other community programs and activities.*

Lesson: *Cities will likely need to assume considerable financial risk to advance brownfield projects in weaker markets but can use this to leverage environmental and social benefits.*

Lesson: *Besides greening, sustainable visions and sustainable elements are most often seeded, mandated, or core to the mission of the public/non-profit proponent, as opposed to being in high demand by the marketplace.*

Lesson: *Projects should not be given sustainability funding in the hopes of becoming financially viable. Instead, financially viable projects should be given sustainability funding in the hopes of becoming developed.*

Construction

A significant difference between the BMPs and the Pilots is that all BMPs have been constructed, meeting and exceeding their redevelopment expectations, with several moving on to subsequent phases. However, half of the proposed Pilots have been scaled down and delayed due to weak market demand affecting their financial viability and sustainability, something that a shorter-term review of the case studies would have missed. This speaks to the ongoing importance of assessing a project's economic viability as part of the decision to support sustainability features, despite some of the inherent contradictions this may pose in relation to socioeconomic and environmental objectives.

Green Features

Of the 26 case studies, most planned for the development of green space or habitat elements (21) and green infrastructure (i.e., stormwater management) (19). More than half include green building design elements (16), energy efficiency, conservation, or generation features (16), and alternative transportation infrastructure for public transit, walking, and cycling (15). Other customary green practices include resource/waste recovery and reuse (10), innovative cleanup/technology (10), green roof technology (8), and urban agriculture (6).

BMPs tended to have more green components per project, mainly green infrastructure (9), energy efficiency, conservation and generation (9), alternative transportation infrastructure (8), green building design (8), and public green space or habitat elements (7) (innovative cleanup, resource recovery, green roofs 5 each and agriculture at 3). Pilots typically had fewer features, focusing on green space or habitat (14), green infrastructure (10), green building (8), alternative transportation infrastructure (7), and energy efficiency, conservation or generation (7) (innovative cleanup and resource recovery at 5 each and agriculture and green roofs at 3 each). All seven of the BMPs that involved the construction or reuse of buildings followed sustainable design guidelines such as LEED and Green Globes, although only five formally registered. While seven of the Pilots proposed to pursue LEED, most have yet to officially register due to high registration costs, changes to the original development plan, delayed completion, or the scaling down of green building features. While Jackson Square is registered as LEED ND and a few buildings have officially registered (e.g., Jackson Square), most buildings are unregistered and considered LEED "certifiable" because they follow Boston's Article 37 green building rules.

In terms of what motivated the selection of green design features, common reasons outlined by coordinators included site-specific circumstances related to dealing with a physical site opportunity or constraint, appeasing project partners, reasonable green technology costs, reducing environmental impact, the availability of green programs providing financial and political support, and public involvement. Pilot coordinators were more inclined to highlight a program such as the Sustainable Brownfields Pilot, while BMPs highlighted site-specific factors.

When asked about what green elements failed, coordinators focused more on what caused failure vs what technologies failed. The most common response from a quarter of the group focused on the complexity/incompatibility of planning policies and regulations (6), which forced the need to stall plans and scrap green elements (6). Many also pointed to the high cost of sustainable technology (5), difficulties associated with incorporating green components into building design (4), and the complexity of non-planning factors such as procurement rules, jurisdictional issues, and financing (4). Pilots were most likely to stall or scrap green elements (6) due to complexities faced with planning policy or regulation (5) or challenges related to incorporating green components into building design (4). BMPs pointed to high sustainable technology costs (3), problems with reconciling green objectives such as managing stormwater on a capped brownfield (2), and the complexity of non-planning policy or regulation (2).

Overall, BMPs and Pilots employed green space, infrastructure, building, and other sustainable elements to help erase the memory of past blight and to draw people and businesses back to areas that had been forgotten or bypassed for a long time. Most of the BMPs achieved the green objectives that they put forward early on in the visioning process, although some, like Chicago's Center for Green Technology, had to terminate their green building education programming over time due to funding cuts. Many have also seen the green design and building activities implemented in the early phases of the project continue into subsequent stages. Pilots have had a bit more trouble over time. A few have been able to implement many of their ambitious green goals, but not all, like the Living Building ones put forward for June Key Delta House in Portland or the green roofs at Jackson Square that were replaced with white roofs and solar panels. Others have seen their ambitions green objectives narrow considerably (e.g., Burlington's Moran Plant) or shift (e.g., from green workforce housing to a green space in Greenville). Some organizations achieved development objectives and momentum but did not fully realize their green objectives (e.g., green building in Commercial Street, Focus Hope's green street). It is still too early to tell at several Pilots because they are delayed and will likely continue to be due to the COVID pandemic (e.g., green building at The Waterfront, energy conservation design at Anvil Mountain, brightfields in Houston, resource recovery, green space, and other green elements at Allen Morrison and Langdale and Riverdale Mills).

Lesson: Green Space and infrastructure are the most popular green elements because they provide a green aesthetic to erase past blight and attract users while also performing ecological and environmental functions. Energy efficiency, building design, and alternative transportation infrastructure are also popular to alleviate costs and improve access.

Lesson: Sustainable and green design guidelines like LEED provide very useful direction, although certification costs present a barrier.

Lesson: Governments can play an important role in promoting and supporting the consideration and implementation of green elements and practices in site reuse and redevelopment. But they also need to make sure that their regulations don't inhibit innovation and application and that they provide technical assistance and funding to "sustain" sustainable efforts to completion.

Community and Quality of Life Features

Virtually all projects put emphasis on improving quality of life (23) and aesthetics issues (19), according to interviews and the review of project documentation. About half, mainly Pilots, led by public and non-profits, also emphasized cultural goals related to celebrating neighborhood history and increasing opportunities for social interaction and exchange (12). Pilots also engaged in more citizen outreach, support, and even control, while BMPs involved support and outreach. When asked what sustainable community and quality-of-life components were planned, most highlighted efforts to remove blight (22) and enhance neighborhood appeal (22), and to improve the availability and access to amenities (e.g., parks, trails, paths) (17). Other common features included the provision of community-oriented facilities and activities (e.g., community center, educational workshops) (13), affordable housing (8), historical preservation (7), and public health improvement (6). Pilots and BMPs were similar in their components. When asked early on what failed, most did not respond, while a few noted a desire for more community involvement and physical infrastructure that continues to inhibit community access to the properties.

Over time, most BMPs and Pilots have successfully removed blight, enhanced property and community appeal, and improved public health through remediation and the provision of amenities. The promise to incorporate affordable housing has also remained relatively resilient despite challenges from the development community (e.g., South Waterfront) and, in some cases, remains at the forefront of the project (e.g., Samoa Peninsula, Anvil Mountain, Jackson Square). While there have been a few disappointments related to community education (CCGT) and ownership (Tabor Commons), these projects still host users with green and community-oriented missions. Historical preservation also continues to be imperative, although the degree of preservation is dependent on cost.

Lesson: Community and quality-of-life interventions are generated with community involvement and tend to focus on improving aesthetics and providing community spaces and activities.

Lesson: Non-profits seem to be particularly effective at tackling complex social and environmental justice issues related to demographics (i.e., race, income, crime), housing, and health.

Economic Features

The economic objectives and features emphasized for most projects mainly focused on building activities onsite, with some also stressing potential spin-off benefits off-site. Only a few coordinators noted the role of sustainability in improving a project's financial performance or being part of its long-term economic goals. In terms of the sustainable economic components planned, about two-thirds stressed the investment in an economically depressed area (16) and the creation of employment (14), while about a third also noted using redevelopment to raise land values (9), increase the local tax base (7), and job training opportunities (6). Those representing Pilots and BMPs mentioned similar motivations at similar frequencies. Large BMPs (e.g., MVP and South Waterfront) emphasized multiple tax and employment generation motivations to justify public investments. Many the BMPs aimed to create or stop a potential loss of employment (e.g., South Waterfront and Menomonee Valley) and link jobs to local residents by improving access (e.g., transit, auto, bridge infrastructure) and through workforce development. Interestingly, a few also aimed to provide training for brownfields, restoration, development, landscaping, and other green employment options (CCGT, Tabor Commons).

While many did not provide an economic rationale, a fifth of coordinators noted favorable market conditions or the opportunity to reduce cost or acquire property at a fair price. A few indicated that economic interventions were a condition of public investment or core to the mission of the non-profit or lead proponent (e.g., "family-supporting jobs" in the Menomonee Valley, green jobs at CCGT). Stakeholders were also involved in over half of these projects, mainly via consultation and partnership, to help achieve economic objectives. In terms of barriers leading to the failure to achieve economic goals, over a third noted the limited availability of funds to move initiatives forward efficiently, a quarter reported regulatory hurdles affecting access to funds, and a few noted high contamination costs and low buyer demand as economic barriers. As mentioned above, many of the Pilots, in particular, have faced financial challenges that have resulted in delays and cuts in the sustainability features they hoped to offer.

Lesson: *The value of sustainable brownfield development is still largely tied to conventional economic objectives associated with property development, tax revenues, and employment, which is typically needed to justify public investment. While there seems to be an assumption that addressing these objectives will also address the more complex economic and employment problems affecting many of these communities, more projects would benefit from making sustainable economic goals and requirements more explicit (e.g., minimum wage levels, local employment and ownership objectives, provision of health insurance, employment density, and workforce development).*

Lesson: *Using redevelopment projects to create jobs for neighborhood residents requires improving connectivity and workforce development.*

Roles and Responsibilities

Many stakeholders have been actively involved in advancing both sustainability and brownfield development aspects of the projects examined. The US EPA has engaged in all of the Pilots and most of the BMPs, providing funding and technical support to advance sustainability elements and funding brownfields assessment and cleanup in a few cases. Other critical federal agencies and initiatives include support from HUD for housing and employment, along with tax credit programs supporting investment in lower-income communities, heritage preservation, federal funds earmarked for infrastructure or restoration work, and transportation funding for road, trail, and other forms of mobility infrastructure. States have also been involved via their voluntary cleanup programs and, in a few cases, have provided funding or loans for assessment and cleanup. State economic development and finance departments are also involved in supporting employment and transportation infrastructure, including trails.

The role of local government has been integral to all of the projects examined, whether it takes the direct lead (12 projects) or is a crucial funder (6), partner (4), or supporter (2). Specific departments often include economic development, planning, parks, and economic/urban development agencies, but usually it is a team effort led by one. For the BMPs, for instance, local government entities acted as the proponent for four projects (CCGT, Brockton, Elmhurst & Freshkills Parks), lead partner for two (South Waterfront, Menomonee Valley), a major supporting partner for Atlantic Station and Heifer International (e.g., land assembly, donation land and infrastructure, tipping fees), and supporter for Artscape. For the Pilots, local governments are proponents for half, key funders for four, lead partners at Anvil Mountain, and supporters of the others.

As for the private sector, it was not involved in many cases. It only led the way in four of the 26 cases examined (Montgomery Park, Atlantic Station, the Waterfront, and Samoa), with the public sector acting as strong supporters and funders. It was a major development partner for seven, contingent on the public sector getting the land ready for redevelopment (e.g., Menomonee Valley, South Waterfront, Anvil Mountain, Tabor Commons). This is somewhat problematic given that the private market drives most brownfield redevelopment, and the share of publicly supported brownfield projects going through VCPs is often low. Therefore, unless green building, affordability, and other sustainability elements are required by local regulations or building codes, as they are in places like Boston and Portland, sustainable brownfield development is unlikely to happen on a grand scale.

Non-profit organizations played a leading role as proponent for six projects, including those with defined missions that operate at a national or regional level (e.g., Heifer, Artspace, Delta) and those that are neighborhood-based (e.g., Tabor, Focus Hope, Jackson Square). At a few large BMPs, non-profits were also established (e.g., Menomonee Valley Partners, South Waterfront Community Relations, Freshkills) to help guide development, planning, marketing, consultation, community-building, and to ensure long-term commitment to sustainability. It is also important to note that virtually all of the Pilots and BMPs administered by non-profits have been completed or had initial phases completed with future phases ongoing. Even the non-profit that used Pilot funds to examine a rooftop garden's viability on an old school building in Oklahoma quickly pulled the plug on the project once they learned of the structural challenges and exorbitant costs associated with the project. This points to the fiscal rationality of the non-profit sector in delivering their sustainability-oriented missions and the future potential of using this sector to advance sustainable brownfields development for an array of affordable housing, community, parks, and other projects.

Public participation was also an important feature in most of the case studies examined, although the degree of involvement varied considerably. Participation was most active in projects where communities reacted to a problematic site like Tabor Commons or alternate proposal like Elmhurst Park and took a lead in redevelopment through neighborhood associations. Most projects led by non-profits, public agencies and even the private sector also incorporated public participation to allow affected communities to provide input throughout the process. Some have been exemplary, like Burlington's efforts for the Moran Plant, while others like the original Houston Solar project were criticized by the community for being tokenistic and ineffectual.

Robust and well-coordinated stakeholder participation that includes public, private, and non-profit representatives from multiple organizations and agencies, as well as associations representing affected communities, has been vital for most of these projects. These have been essential for defining the vision and moving projects through to development and implementation.

Lesson: *Strong inter- and intra-governmental cooperation, public-private partnerships, and public-non-profit partnerships are vital for sustainable brownfield redevelopment efforts to succeed.*

Lesson: *Robust stakeholder participation, which includes representation from affected communities, is an essential element in all of these projects, along with opportunities for public consultation in general.*

Project Impacts and Lessons Learned

Coordinators were asked early on to reflect on their projects' impacts and lessons. Concerning the obstacles to incorporating sustainability into the brownfield projects, BMPs and Pilots faced similar challenges concerning obtaining funds to pursue it (10), incompatible policy, zoning, and permit procedures (9), design challenges (7), unfavorable market conditions (sale or purchase) (5), the limited capacity of local firms to implement sustainability (4), stakeholder concerns about affordability and effectiveness (4), negotiating concessions with landowners and developers (3), liability and insurance (3), and contamination issues (2). In terms of the benefits resulting from developing brownfields, coordinators pointed to improvements to the local community (17), furthering organizational goals and community visions (10), sparking more brownfield initiatives (8), creating a new revenue stream (2), securing alternative sources of energy (1), and reducing demolition costs (1). As for incorporating sustainability into brownfield development, coordinators felt it would promote further sustainable development in the community (11), improve the character of re-urbanization (10) and long-term preservation (8), prove the viability of sustainable development as a model (3), and empower the community. Those engaged in Pilots focused more on furthering sustainable development and long-term preservation benefits, while BMP representatives focused more on the character of re-urbanization.

When asked what factors helped move the projects and the sustainability components forward, coordinators working on both Pilots and BMPs highlighted proponent capacity, multi-stakeholder involvement, favorable regulations and incentives, and financing. As for mechanisms or suggestions for promoting and facilitating sustainability in future brownfield projects, coordinators most commonly noted technical assistance and information to improve capacity, financial incentives, support for sustainable visions, and supportive policies and frameworks. Other suggestions included engaging professional engineers, architects, and planners with knowledge in the field, demonstrating sustainable design's economic value, cohesive green policies that emphasize brownfields, process streamlining, and dedicated technical support staff.

When reviewed over time it is clear that the mechanisms outlined above are needed for sustainable brownfield development to be successful, along with favorable market conditions to support development and political conditions to help projects move forward and stay true to their sustainability objectives.

Overall, non-profits involved in both BMPs and Pilots have been very successful at getting their sustainable brownfield projects developed. Their tenacious spirit, ability to bring together affected communities, stakeholders, and funding, and to stay true to sustainability objectives is inspiring. Non-profits have also been able to adjust, compromise, and modify to keep projects moving along in a sustainable direction. Whether it's shifting from green to white/solar roofs in Jackson Square, putting the green street on hold while working on other green community initiatives in Detroit, or leasing space to a community-supporting organization when the community-run café didn't work out at Tabor Commons, non-profits seem able to pivot and keep things moving in a direction that stays true to their mission and values. Their ability to deliver sustainable brownfield development reinforces the need to further invest in the programs, policies, and funding mechanisms that allow them to operate. It also speaks to the need to aid in the establishment and growth of community-based non-profits interested in brownfields and sustainability, while also improving the capacity of national and reputable non-profits to support their work and that of community-based partners.

Government entities at the local level have had relatively good success. Some civic and park developments have been successful (e.g., Elmhurst Park, Freshkills, CCGT, Brockton Brightfield), while others have slowed down (Allen Morrison, Moran Plant, Houston Solar). Some public-private partnerships have also been very successful (Menomonee Valley, South Waterfront), while others face delays (Langdale and Riverdale Mills, The Waterfront, Anvil Mountain). It seems that the size of the community does play a role in terms of the strength of its market and the capacity of staff to navigate the complexity of the sustainable brownfields development process, including the partnerships needed to make it happen. While technical support from the EPA and other forms of funding have benefitted smaller communities, more needs to be done to ensure that sustainable brownfield development projects can be sustained over time.

Private sector entities have also had mixed success. Montgomery Park and Atlantic Station are both early best practice projects by respected developers that positively influenced the character of development activities in their respective markets, even though they are still working toward realizing their full potential. The Waterfront and Samoa Peninsula are also large projects in smaller markets that seem to be plodding along, but one worries whether they will shed their sustainability elements with time. Given that most brownfield development follows a developer-centered approach, the predicament associated with desiring or requiring sustainability from those coming voluntarily to brownfields is as challenging today as it was when Eisen noted it over a decade ago (Eisen, 2009). While some seem agreeable to investing, removing blight, green space, green infrastructure, and some green building elements, there is still a hesitation in imposing a broader package of environment, social, and economic sustainability objectives. The beneficial outcomes realized by the sustainable brownfield development projects examined here do provide inspiring examples for developers keen on pursuing similar projects, but much more research measuring the value of sustainability interventions is still needed if we want the development sector and consumers to embrace sustainability voluntarily. This information is also important for maintaining public sector incentives for sustainable development efforts, given that only a few strong-market cities seem willing to mandate aspects of it (e.g., green development in Boston).

In all, the sustainable brownfield projects examined here and the people involved in their planning and development provide inspiration for those seeking to take these icons of a polluted past and turn them into beacons of a more sustainable future. While challenges to realizing sustainable brownfield development remain, it is hoped that sharing these projects and the benefits that they have brought to their respective communities will help sustain those pursuing ongoing efforts and motivate others to take on the challenge.

Reference

Eisen, J. B. (2009). Brownfields development: From individual sites to smart growth. In J. C. Dernbach (Ed.), *Agenda for a sustainable America* (pp. 57-70). Environmental Law Institute.

Index

Adams, D. 25
adaptive reuse 33, 60, 216, 218, 241, 244-245
African American 138, 144, 157, 212, 233
agriculture 3, 5, 23-24, 71, 76, 217, 247
Alabama 190, 214-216, 218-219
Alberini, A. 23-24
Allentown, Pennsylvania 28, 190, 219-222
American Institute of Architects (AIA) 35, 42, 82, 144
apartment: building 96, 170, 201; complex 87; units 69, 180, 182, 194
aquaponics 76, 82, 236
Arkansas 60, 70-75, 77, 81-82
Army Corps of Engineers 126, 128, 130
artist studios 87, 89-90
asbestos 50, 65-66, 70, 104-105, 107, 142, 145, 147, 159, 166-167, 184, 216-217, 244
assessment *see* environmental site assessment
ASTM International 8-9, 26
Atlanta, Georgia 28, 190-201
attenuation 10, 46, 140, 159

Baltimore, Maryland 23, 28, 60-62, 65, 67-70
Bartke, S. 25
Bartsch, C. 3
benchmark 22, 27, 48-49, 52, 114
benzene, toluene, ethylbenzene and xylene (BTEX) 159, 228
Berman, L. 25
bicycle 47, 106, 151, 205, 210, 244
biodegradation 46
bioremediation 9, 245

bioretention 62, 127, 221, 236
bioswale 38, 75, 127, 151, 158-160
Bleicher, A. 26
Bloomberg, Mayor M. 112, 123, 241
Boston, Massachusetts 165, 175-182, 227, 240, 245, 247, 251, 253
breweries 42, 53, 69, 148
brightfield 28, 42, 227-237, 241, 248, 253
Brockton, Massachusetts 28, 227-232, 241, 250, 253
Brownfields Action Agenda 7, 19, 26
Brownfields Utilization, Investment and Local Development (BUILD) Act 8
Bullard, R. 24, 233
Burlington, Vermont 28, 101-109, 134, 248, 251
Business Improvement District (BID) 44, 56, 146, 148, 236

California 24, 165, 170-175, 197
canoeing 56, 127
canopy 36, 52, 132, 151
cap 10, 39, 50, 112, 116, 124, 192, 194, 228, 235, 237, 244
carbon dioxide 64, 230
Carroll, A. 24
casino 43, 53, 56
Center for Disease Control (CDC) 212
Chacon Creek 101, 125-130, 134
charging station 80, 236
charrette 36, 45, 49, 53-54, 56-57, 92, 116, 120, 148, 193, 215, 219, 241
Chattahoochee river 214-215, 217-218
Chicago, Illinois 5, 28, 33-42, 248

256 Index

Chicago Center for Green Technology (CCGT) 33-42, 242, 244, 246, 249-250, 253
cistern 38, 63, 65, 75, 141, 221
Clean Air Act 20, 120, 192, 195
Clean Water Act 20, 129
cleanup: methods 9; standards 73, 140; innovative cleanup 247
Cleveland, Ohio 28, 240
climate: action 17, 236; change 3, 121; control 89, 214
Clinton, President B. 70-71, 73, 77, 79, 81
Colorado 22, 24, 85, 93-95, 97-98
commercial: building 85, 148, 165, 171, 182, 198; development 86, 111, 127; property 3, 150, 157, 171
Community Development Corporation (CDC) 88, 169-170, 182, 212
community involvement 7, 21, 181, 237, 246, 249
compost 132, 160
Comprehensive Environmental Response, Compensation, and Liability Act (CERCLA) 1, 4, 6-8, 21-22
concrete 39, 50, 57, 65, 75, 90, 104, 127, 133, 154, 194, 216
condominium 206, 211
congestion 68, 118, 192, 196, 198-200
contamination: groundwater 43, 46, 88, 105; soil 46, 50, 66, 68, 93, 98, 105
COVID 67, 96, 222, 248
creek 101, 115, 119, 124-131, 134
creosote 73
crime 86, 126-127, 158, 228, 249
cycling 63, 68, 116, 203, 247

Daley, Mayor R. 35, 40-41, 241
daylighting 47, 52, 74-75, 142, 184
Deason, J. 24
debris: building 50; construction 42, 194, 244; demolition 34, 50, 228, 232
deconstruction 107, 109, 133-134, 201, 216-217, 243-244
Deitrick, S. 5
demonstration project 122, 140, 146
Department of Energy (DOE) 24, 42, 72, 77-78, 95, 228
Department of Transportation (DOT) 22, 47

Department of Housing and Urban Development (HUD) 22, 25, 34, 39, 67, 106, 161, 167-168, 185, 250
design guidelines: green 248; sustainable 47-48, 52, 56, 247
Detroit, Michigan 28, 165-170, 252
Dewar, M. 5
disabilities 87, 175
Dixon, T. 25-26
dump 9, 115, 194, 199, 233

ecological function 38, 41, 113, 117
economic development: impact 26; strategy 106, 121; local 215, 221, 234, 237; sustainable 106
economy: green 143; local 68, 96, 156, 161; regional 183
ecosystem 19, 24-25, 114-116, 118-122, 126, 128-130, 173
education: center 35, 72-73, 75-76, 79, 82; environmental 35, 50, 56, 126, 151, 156; public 35, 41, 106, 122
Eisen, J. B. 18, 21, 253
eminent domain 10, 49, 132, 243
emissions 17, 52, 65, 94, 97, 120, 195, 197, 230
employment: creation of 249; density 250; growth 40; opportunities 17, 38, 40, 81, 171, 175, 206; green 249; local 250; loss of 249
empowerment zone 34, 61-62, 67-68
energy: alternative 47, 95, 176; clean 17, 228; conservation 35-36, 95-96, 104, 160, 248; facilities 24, 227, 230-232; generation 176, 231
environmental: assessment 11, 56, 66, 94, 147, 158-162, 204, 222, 235; cleanup 12, 39, 127, 151; conservation 105, 111-112, 114, 119; contamination 3, 7, 116; justice 4, 19, 21, 23-24, 54, 126, 178, 228, 233, 240-241, 249; quality 25, 27, 36, 47, 234; regulation 5; site assessment 8-9, 13, 39, 45, 73, 98, 105, 133, 151, 166, 178, 184, 216, 220; standards 13
excavation 39, 66, 105, 133, 140, 180
exposure 3, 8-10, 39, 97, 221

factory 62, 170, 175-176
farm see urban farm

financing: bond financing 197; project 39, 67, 77, 88, 97, 106, 143, 153, 160, 196, 208; Tax Increment Financing 12-13, 40, 196, 208
fishing 56, 127, 217
fitness 65, 105, 127
flood 43, 50, 126, 128-130, 134, 221
flooring 64, 90, 217
food 18, 76, 82, 86, 169, 180
foreclosure 10, 39
forest 53, 166, 202-203
foundry 74, 228
FRAME 74, 107-109
Freshkills 101, 115-122, 124, 243, 250-251, 253
funding: private 169; project 20-21, 55, 98, 108, 245; public 53, 241, 245-246; seed 55
fundraising 141, 143-145, 149

garage 34, 62, 159, 167, 179, 222
garbage 73, 154, 217
garden: community 38, 50, 90, 127, 149, 159-160, 169, 212, 216, 218; educational 76; urban 142
Gas: station 2, 4, 62, 138-162, 171-172, 176, 186, 212, 244; tank 110-112, 123
generation: energy 176, 231; power 242
gentrification 18, 24, 89, 176, 181, 211
Georgia 190, 192-197, 201, 214, 218
geotechnical 49, 52, 104, 147
geothermal 36, 92, 95, 142, 198
glass 50, 62-63, 75, 81, 143, 145
golf 119, 232
green: code 173; design 21, 36, 41, 78-80, 87, 89, 127, 140, 145, 151, 173, 184, 186, 198, 247-248; features 27, 127, 153, 247; infrastructure 23, 69, 129, 186, 244, 247, 253; jobs 157, 249; power 229; roofs 63, 132, 153, 173, 176, 214, 221, 247-248; street 149, 165-166, 170, 248, 252; technology 69, 77, 97, 247; workforce 248
green building: design 85, 166, 174, 247; elements 48, 105, 153, 253; features 52, 62, 68-69, 92, 106, 143, 247; rating 36, 80; techniques 25, 143, 198, 203
Green Globes 73, 80, 247
green job training 150, 153
green space 2, 24, 27-28, 43-44, 50, 70, 94, 96, 126, 129-130, 132, 134, 158, 160-161, 167, 198, 201, 217, 240, 242-243, 247-248, 253

greenbelt 70-71
Greenberg, M. 24
Greencorps Chicago 35, 38, 40-41
greenhouse 17, 76, 131-132, 236
greenway 43, 46, 119, 125, 169, 203, 205, 207-209, 212, 214
greywater 62-63, 65, 75, 184
Gross, M. 26
growth: economic 17, 106, 121, 199; urban 20, 209
Gurda, J. 42-43

habitat: conservation 126, 129-130; elements 247
Hank Aaron State Trail 46, 49-50, 52-53, 55-57
harvesting 141, 207
HATponics 76, 82
hazardous material 4-5, 132-133, 217
health: center 44-45, 47-49, 52, 236-237; risk 10, 95
Heberle, L. 25
Heifer International 60, 70-79, 81-82, 244-245, 250
heritage preservation 60, 95, 98, 250
Hersh, B. 24
Hersh, R. 228-229, 231
hike 126-130
historic: buildings 69, 175; district 53, 165, 183, 185-186, 199; elements 67, 183, 186; preservation 67, 108, 168, 171, 173, 184, 186; structures 86, 132, 171, 173
Hollander, J. 25
homeless 167
homeowners 95-96, 173, 196
homeownership 206, 212
housing: affordable 5, 85-86, 89, 93-95, 97-98, 138, 156-157, 165, 169, 174-175, 178-182, 185, 190, 203-204, 206-207, 209, 211-213, 246, 248-249, 251; energy-efficient 85; low-income 13
Houston, Texas 28, 232-237, 246, 248, 251, 253
Hula, R. C. 23
Humboldt County, California 148, 165, 170-175
hydrocarbons 66, 88, 140, 178, 244

Illinois 27, 34, 37, 39, 42
impermeable 116, 120, 124
incinerator 232-233
inclusion 62, 68, 128, 156, 243
inclusionary zoning 207
inclusive 17, 23, 186, 204
income: household 96, 227; low 5, 13, 23-24, 76, 81, 88-89, 126, 150, 170, 173, 176, 180, 212, 236; median 89, 96
incubator 40, 156, 181, 207
indicator 17-18, 23-25, 27, 48-49, 52, 208
indigenous communities 8, 202
industrial: decline 33, 202, 209, 213; development 20, 49, 124, 202, 213; land 61, 70, 112, 121, 131, 176, 201; use 39, 42, 71, 76, 86, 101, 122, 131-132, 172, 191
industrialization 40, 42, 53, 190, 209
infill 11, 17-18, 195, 197-198, 200, 210
infiltration 62, 120, 128, 141, 159
infrastructure: cycling 68; green 23, 69, 129, 186, 244, 247, 253; grey 129; public 50, 86, 244-245; transit 89
institutional controls 4, 9-12, 39, 178, 245
insulation 63, 74, 90, 95, 173, 184
insurance 12-13, 48, 62, 134, 148, 150-151, 153-155, 250, 252
intensification 17, 122, 155, 176
International City/County Management Association (ICMA) 25
inventory 1, 4, 8, 13, 19, 127, 133, 216-217
irrigation 62, 76, 78, 141

Jamaica Plain, Massachusetts 175-176, 180-182
jobs: family-supporting 45, 55, 249; green 157, 249; creation 4, 35, 55, 161, 211, 218
June Key Delta House 141, 248

kayaking 56, 118
Kotval-K, Z. 23

labor 19, 43, 154, 213, 217
land: acquisition 55, 185, 222, 243; assembly 11, 250; banking 97
landfilling 43, 115, 119
landfills 4, 120, 194, 227, 232-233, 242
landscape: architecture 40, 69, 113, 116, 124; design 39, 114, 117-118, 120, 122; features 19, 151, 154, 158-159; plan 147, 229

landscaping *see* native landscaping 75, 159-160, 166
Lange, D. 23
Laredo 28, 101, 125-128, 130, 134
leachate 116, 120, 205, 221
lead: contamination 175; paint 66-67, 70, 105, 107
LEED (Leadership in Energy and Environmental Design): certifiable 179-180; Certified 27; Gold 60, 62, 65, 68, 85, 87, 89, 92, 106, 151, 180, 210; Platinum 36, 40, 42, 60, 70, 72, 79, 169, 213-214; rating 33, 47, 72, 79-80, 82, 178; Silver 79
legal 6, 9-10, 12, 20, 42, 154, 200, 229, 231
liability: limited 203; protection 8, 73
Living Building Challenge 141-144, 147-149, 248
local business 43, 74, 80, 150, 152, 154, 182
local government 4, 6-7, 10, 13, 20-21, 24, 55, 104, 151, 156, 165, 195, 227, 243, 250
loft 43, 86, 183
Love Canal 1-2, 6
Lynchburg, Virginia 28, 101, 130-134

marina 102, 119
market conditions 34, 43, 68, 161, 211, 249, 252
Maryland 23, 60-67, 69-70
Massachusetts 165, 175-180, 182, 227-232
McCarthy, L. 24
memorial 111, 114, 124, 144, 149, 161-162
Menino, Mayor T. 176, 182
Menomonee Valley Benchmarking Initiative (MVBI) 48-49, 51
Menomonee Valley Partners (MVP) 44-45, 47-48, 50, 52-56, 249
mercury 64, 166
metals 9, 64, 178, 221, 244
methane 50, 52, 110, 212, 236
Meyer, P. B. 7
Michigan 165, 167-168, 170
microbrewery 184, 186
microclimate 24
Milwaukee, Wisconsin 5, 11, 27-28, 33, 41-57, 241
mine 22, 227
minority: contractor 143, 147; workers 148
Misky, D. 50
Mississippi 74

Missouri 165, 183, 185-186
mixed use 18, 183, 192
multifamily 169, 173, 191
music 82, 86, 153, 157, 183

naphthalene 159, 178
National Association of Homebuilders (NAHB) 22
National Association of Local Government Environmental Professionals (NALGEP) 24, 227
National Environmental Policy Act (NEPA) 18
native landscaping 75, 159-160, 166
natural: attenuation 10, 46, 140, 159; environment 1, 72; gas 110, 123; light 65, 80, 89-90; resources 18, 22, 41, 44-47, 57, 115, 207, 218
naturalization 46
nature preserves 24
negotiation 11, 93, 111, 150, 154, 229
neighborhood: association 46, 148, 150, 155, 158, 160-162, 251; coalition 148, 153, 155; development 27, 134, 173, 176, 178-179, 181-182, 210; park 114, 167, 205, 213; planning 109, 192; revitalization 4, 166, 178, 182
netzero 148
New Market Tax Credit (NMTC) 13, 50, 85, 88, 92, 107, 180, 185
New York City, New York 64, 101, 110, 115, 118, 121-122, 124
nitrogen 75, 197, 230
Norquist, Mayor J. 43, 241

odor 4, 116, 230
office: building 52, 60-61, 65, 74, 78, 159, 194, 198, 211-212, 219, 222, 244; redevelopment 60-82; space 35, 52-53, 60, 65, 68-69, 71, 77, 167, 177, 180, 182, 194, 198-199, 216, 221-222; Use 43
oil 62, 64, 66, 70, 104, 159
Oklahoma 28, 240, 251
open space 11, 45, 49, 86, 102-103, 116, 121, 124, 138, 142, 176, 178, 190, 203-204, 208-210, 242
Opportunity Zone 13
Oregon 22, 138-140, 142-145, 148-155, 190, 201-207, 213-214, 241
outreach: community 139, 148, 212, 228; public 43, 200

PAHs (Polycyclic aromatic hydrocarbons) 88, 105
paint *see* lead paint
parking: green 129; public 185-186; structure 90, 129, 222; surface 61-62, 68, 90
participation: public 7, 103, 108, 110, 120, 200, 251; stakeholder 43, 251
passive park 112, 158-160
path: bike 87, 89, 181; walking 222, 236
Paull, E. 13, 60-61, 67
pavement 47, 74, 151, 159, 221
pedestrian: alleyway 185-186; area 36, 192; bridge 205, 214; environment 156, 208; infrastructure 244
Pennsylvania 190, 194, 196, 200, 219-220, 222
performance measure 26
permits 145, 205, 207, 218
pervious 154, 159, 173, 221
pesticides 3
Peterangelo, J. 50, 53
petroleum: contamination 178-179; hydrocarbons 88, 140, 178, 244; storage 73, 102
Phoenix Award 21, 42, 57, 70, 82, 198, 201, 212
photovoltaic 35-36, 227-228, 234-235
phytoremediation 9, 245
picnic 160, 167
placemaking 169
planning: master 116, 133, 200, 216; urban 18, 45, 150, 203, 211
playground 108, 112-113, 119, 169
plaza 81, 132, 159, 181, 229
plumbing 37, 64-65, 71, 90, 154, 179
pollutants 6, 38, 120, 138, 192
polychlorinated biphenyls (PCBs) 66-67, 88, 107, 166
pond 38, 50, 62, 74, 158, 194, 198
population: decline 218; density 18; growth 122, 191, 195, 218
porous 62, 68-69, 127, 151, 161, 221
Portland, Oregon 28, 138-140, 142-157, 190, 201-214, 240-241, 245, 248, 251
poverty 13, 17, 60, 70-73, 76, 80, 157, 165, 167
preservation *see* historic preservation
pro forma 11-13, 200
public art 56, 112, 118, 185
public consultation 103, 124, 171, 243, 251
public engagement 38, 109, 120-121, 160

public-private partnership 10, 35, 44, 54, 196, 200, 208, 210, 223, 237, 241, 244, 251, 253
public transit 36, 68-69, 89, 106, 173, 203, 205, 208, 214, 247

Queens, New York 110, 114, 123-124

racism 165
rail: corridor 85, 131, 169, 199; stop 89, 212; trail 222; yard 34, 71, 81, 212
rainwater 38, 62, 75, 141
reclamation 73, 101, 116-118, 121-122, 217
reconstruction 44, 47, 69, 174, 196
recreation: active 116, 129, 132; center 101, 103, 125-130, 181, 245; space 172; use 102-103
recreational use 102-103, 118, 132, 218
recycling: land 101, 222; material 56, 244; waste 166
reforestation 128
refurbish 167
regeneration 18, 25-27, 77, 79, 169
reindustrialization 54, 243
renewable energy: credits 231; facilities 24, 227, 230; technology 36, 41, 122, 198
rental: apartment 96, 98, 180-182; housing 179; units 177, 179
residential: apartment 181-182, 201, 217; development 24, 94, 111-112, 157, 172, 199; neighborhood 23, 71, 131, 149, 191, 200, 233; structure 128, 172, 240; units 89-90, 158, 173, 194, 197, 206-207
resilience 18, 23
resistance 130, 152, 200
Resource Conservation and Recovery Act (RCRA) 5, 20
resources: building 39, 41; employment 55; financial 41, 108, 118; historic 19; natural 18, 22, 41, 44-47, 57, 115, 207, 218
restoration: building 173, 244; ecosystem 126, 128-130; habitat 45; riverbank 56, 211; wetland 128
restriction 50, 96-97, 133, 235
retrofits 80
rezone 13, 191, 194, 220-221
Ribeiro, L. 24, 227-228, 230, 232
Ridsdale, D. R. 25
riparian 128, 202

riverbank 56, 204, 210-211, 221
riverfront 50, 74, 128, 205, 209, 215, 217, 220-221
riverwalk 53, 221
roadway 44, 50, 116, 119, 222
roof: green 28, 36, 38, 63, 67-69, 106, 127, 151, 178-179, 247; white 179, 248
roofing 95, 108, 146
Roxbury, Massachusetts 175, 182
runoff see stormwater runoff

Salt Lake City, Utah 28, 85-87, 91-93, 240
salvage 133, 217
Samoa Peninsula, California 165, 170-175, 246, 249-250, 253
sampling 9, 45-46, 66, 70, 120, 159, 162
Sarni, W. 25
Schenkel Farm 131-132
Schilling, J. 24
school: elementary 150, 156, 169; high 140, 152-153
scrap 86-87, 90, 92-93, 133, 216, 232, 247
seawall 69
sediment 159, 221
segregated 192
sequestration 67
sewage 172
shoreline 101, 116, 205
sidewalk 74, 113, 161, 208
signage 49, 96, 149, 161, 185
silos 85
Silverton, Colorado 28, 85, 93-96, 98
Simons, R. 4, 8, 27
simulation 57, 98
Sixteenth Street Community Health Center (SSCHC) 44-45, 48-49, 52, 56
skate park 96, 105, 132
skating rink 181
slag 93, 194, 220-221
smart growth: interventions 193; practices 203; principles 22, 192, 210; project 195
smelter 93-94
social: capital 134, 218; indicators 48; justice 24, 245; services 38, 69, 183, 186; sustainability 40, 114, 120, 156, 209
soil: cap 235; contamination 46, 50, 66, 68, 93, 98, 105; sample 66, 70; testing 77, 147, 235

solar: array 148, 229, 236; energy 36, 95, 142, 228-231, 234, 236; farms 236; panels 36, 90, 142, 149, 153, 159-160, 169, 179-180, 186, 234, 248
species 3, 48, 128, 161, 212, 232
sports 116, 118, 127, 129
sprawl 1, 17-18, 192, 198
Springfield, Missouri 28, 165, 183, 185-186
SRA International 147, 232, 234-237, 243
stadium 42-43, 46, 53, 103, 131-132, 232
Staten Island, New York 115, 117, 120
stockyards 42, 52, 57
storage tank *see* underground storage tank
stormwater: infrastructure 158, 178; runoff 62-63, 72, 75, 114, 154, 159, 205, 211; treatment 52, 105
stream 62, 66, 126, 252
streetcar 74, 175, 205, 209-210
streetscape 161, 165-166, 169, 186, 197
studios 87, 89-90
subdivision 96-97, 193
subsidy 13, 107, 195, 213
suburban 24, 50, 157, 190-192, 199
Superfund *see* Comprehensive Environmental Response, Compensation, and Liability Act (CERCLA)
Superfund Amendments and Reauthorization Act (SARA) 6
swale 154

Tabor Commons 138, 149, 151, 153-156, 242-243, 245, 249, 251-252
tannery 42-43
Tax Credit: Historic 106, 180; Low Income Housing 167; New Market 12, 50, 85, 88, 92, 107, 180, 185
tax increment financing (TIF) 12-13, 40, 50, 52-53, 106-107, 184-186, 196, 208, 245
testing 3, 8, 65, 77, 112, 145, 147, 159, 235
Tetra Tech 128, 158-161, 235, 243
Texas 64, 101, 125, 128, 130, 232-233, 236-237
textile 63, 157, 214-215, 218
timber 66, 170, 175, 198, 202
tire 90, 127-130, 228, 232
tourism 76, 96, 103, 126, 217-218
tours 39, 41, 55-56, 72, 230
tradeswoman 143, 148, 150, 153

trail: bike 76, 126-130; walking 119, 132
tram 203, 205, 210
Transit Oriented Development (TOD) 28, 190-191, 199
transportation: modes 76; options 55, 203, 210; routes 205, 211
tree canopy 36, 52, 132
tribal 7-8, 23
trichloroethylene (TCE) 105

underground storage tanks (UST) 66, 112, 114, 133, 140, 151, 159-160, 162, 167, 178
unemployment 33, 42, 157, 209, 228
urban agriculture 23-24, 247
urban farm 76, 82, 132
urban form 17, 207
urban planning 18, 45, 150, 203, 211
urban sprawl 17-18
urbanism 22, 171, 190, 193, 241
US Conference of Mayors 4, 13, 27
US Green Building Council (USGBC) 36, 182
Utah 22, 85-88, 90-93
utilities 45, 50, 64, 94-95, 108, 113, 153, 173-174, 196, 222, 231

vacant: building 39, 74; land 24, 93; lot 34, 158, 176, 213; property 111, 240
vandalism 149, 175
vapor 9, 167
vegetation 114, 126, 129, 221, 229, 232, 234-235
vehicle: charging 119, 236; miles 190, 195, 197, 199
ventilation 37, 63, 75, 173
Vermont 101-105, 108-109
veterans 114, 124
viaduct 46-47, 57
Virginia 101, 130-131, 133-134
Vita Nuova 106, 141, 147, 171, 173, 178-179, 184
volatile organic compounds (VOCs) 37, 65-66, 142, 178, 228
voluntary cleanup program (VCP) 7-8, 23, 66, 69-70, 87, 92-93, 204, 244, 250
volunteers 41, 132, 144, 153-154, 156, 169, 175

wage 47-48, 52-53, 106, 206, 250
walkability 11, 159, 166
walkway 46, 52, 105, 185

waste: disposal 3, 115; diversion 65; heat 63; management 4-5, 119; material 34-35, 39, 235, 244; recovery 247
wastewater 167, 173, 207, 228
waterfront; access 108, 110, 202-203, 214-215; development 221; greenway 205, 208, 214; redevelopment 202-204, 209-213; revitalization 102, 106, 109
waterways 190
weatherization 38, 153
Wedding, G.C. 25
Wernstedt, K. 24
wetland 38, 70, 72, 74-75, 78, 104-106, 115, 119, 126-129, 173, 228
wildlife 38, 70, 74-75, 78, 117, 119, 128, 166

wind 24, 227, 231, 237
Wisconsin 27, 44-48, 50-52, 56-57
wood 64-66, 93, 133, 173, 217
workforce: development 22, 169, 249-250; housing 96, 158-160, 172, 180, 248; training 152
workshops 38, 41, 43, 76, 118, 120, 124, 138, 152-153, 248
workspace 63-64, 81, 86

youth 120, 167, 176-177, 180-182

Zetts, C. 52
zoning 11, 41, 44, 74, 114, 130, 143, 178, 191-192, 194-195, 207-208, 218, 220, 227, 233, 252

For Product Safety Concerns and Information please contact our EU representative GPSR@taylorandfrancis.com
Taylor & Francis Verlag GmbH, Kaufingerstraße 24, 80331 München, Germany

www.ingramcontent.com/pod-product-compliance
Lightning Source LLC
Chambersburg PA
CBHW081546300426
44116CB00015B/2775